SAMUDRA
MANTHAN

C. RAJA MOHAN

SAMUDRA
MANTHAN

Sino-Indian Rivalry in the Indo-Pacific

CARNEGIE ENDOWMENT
FOR INTERNATIONAL PEACE

WASHINGTON DC ▪ MOSCOW ▪ BEIJING ▪ BEIRUT ▪ BRUSSELS

Carnegie Endowment for International Peace
1779 Massachusetts Avenue, N.W.
Washington, D.C. 20036
202-483-7600, Fax 202-483-1840
www.ceip.org

To order, contact:
Hopkins Fulfillment Service
P.O. Box 50370, Baltimore, MD 21211-4370
1-800-537-5487 or 1-410-516-6956
Fax 1-410-516-6998

Cover design by Jocelyn Soly
Composition by Oakland Street Publishing
Printed by United Book Press

Library of Congress Cataloging-in-Publication Data
Mohan, C. Raja
Samudra Manthan: Sino-Indian rivalry in the Indo-Pacific / C. Raja Mohan.
    p. cm.
Includes bibliographical references and index.
ISBN 978-0-87003-271-4 (pbk. : alk. paper) -- ISBN 978-0-87003-272-1 (cloth : alk. paper) 1. China--Foreign relations--India. 2. India--Foreign relations--China. 3. Indo-Pacific Region--Foreign relations. 4. Strategic rivalries (World politics) I. Title.

JZ1734.A57I4 2012a
359'.03091823--dc23

                                2012024786

17 16 15 14 13 12   1 2 3 4 5   1st Printing 2012

In the Hindu fable of Samudra Manthan, *angels and demons churn the ocean in search of an elixir that will give them immortality. Lord Vishnu intervenes at every stage to tilt the long quest in favor of the angels and ensure they emerge victorious in the end. The legend of* Samudra Manthan *lives again as the United States shapes and is shaped by the rivalry between China and India in the waters of Asia.*

Contents

Acknowledgments

I would like to thank Ambassador Gopinath Pillai, chairman of the Institute of South Asian Studies, Singapore, for encouraging me to take up this project on Sino-Indian relations. The director of ISAS, Professor Tan Tai Yong, and his colleagues were very generous in their support. Special thanks are due to Dean Barry Desker of the S. Rajaratnam School of International Studies at Nanyang Technological University, where I did the initial research for this volume. Chong Yee Ming, the librarian at the RSIS, was of great help. Ajaya Das at the RSIS South Asia program gave me enthusiastic research assistance.

This volume could not have been completed without the access I enjoyed to the extraordinary wealth of the U.S. Library of Congress in Washington, D.C., as the Henry A. Kissinger Chair in Foreign Policy and International Relations at the John W. Kluge Center during 2009–2010. My two-month stint at the Center for Strategic Studies, as the Kippenberger Fellow at the Victoria University of Wellington in New Zealand during February–March 2011, provided a very congenial setting to revise the volume. It was only fitting that I finalized the manuscript at the ISAS in Singapore in January–February 2012.

I owe a special debt of gratitude to Michael Green, Gurpreet Khurana, Shyam Saran, Ashley J. Tellis, and others who would like to remain anonymous who went through the initial drafts of the manuscript and offered thoughtful comments. I am grateful to the anonymous reviewers at the Oxford University Press, New Delhi, and the Carnegie Endowment for International Peace in Washington, D.C., for their valuable suggestions for the revision of the manuscript. I alone, however, am responsible for any shortcomings of the work.

This book is dedicated to my wife, Nirmala, whose sustained encouragement gave me the strength to stay the course.

–C. Raja Mohan
New Delhi, June 2012

Foreword

Raja Mohan is one of India's most talented and estimable strategic analysts. In *Samudra Manthan*, Mohan turns his attention to one of the most important relationships shaping the twenty-first century, that of India and China.

This relationship is rivalrous but not yet hypermilitarized and proper but not warm or encouraging. It manifests the concept of a "security dilemma": Each state perceives itself to be acting defensively to protect its national security, but these actions are perceived as threatening by the other. Each then reacts by increasing its defensive preparations, which the other in turn interprets as offensive, escalating the cycle of insecurity.

Security dilemmas can exist and grow unendingly. They can erupt into war. They can also become alarming enough to motivate leaders and policy shapers to negotiate confidence-building mechanisms that clarify intentions and structure capabilities in ways that relieve insecurities.

Since their modern incarnations in 1947 and 1949, respectively, India and China have managed their rivalry moderately well. They fought a war in 1962, but it was a relatively restrained conflict that was quickly ended. Their land borders remain disputed or unresolved and there is little belief on either side that they will be settled soon, but leaders in both states clearly understand that war would divert them disastrously away from internal development, which must be their overwhelming national imperative.

India is extending the reach of its ballistic missile program with China in mind, and Chinese experts wonder how Indian ballistic missile defense cooperation with Israel and the United States could undermine China's deterrent. But, as nuclear rivalries go, this one is mild-mannered. Sino-Indian trade grows rapidly, and with it tensions over imbalances favoring China. But Indians know that their main economic impediments are internal.

The oceans may be different, though. The growing power, wealth, and ambition of China and India are pushing them out to sea as never before. As they build capacity to project power and secure their lines of communication in increasingly distant waters, China will seem to encroach on India's sphere of influence in the Bay of Bengal and Indian Ocean, while India will seem misplaced in the South China Sea and the Strait of Malacca.

It is this projection of the swelling Sino-Indian security dilemma into the Indian and Pacific oceans that Raja Mohan describes and analyzes in this volume with verve.

As the two Asian colossi extend their reaches and brush and bump against each other in the Indo-Pacific littoral, the world will have to take notice. The United States will be especially entangled, for it has been the dominant power in both oceans for decades. It may welcome India's growing capabilities as a potential comrade in arms, but this can in turn alarm and agitate China to varying effects. India may not share Washington's judgments on when, where, and how to exercise naval power, reverberating shocks of disappointment. The possibilities are nearly endless, which is all the more reason to join Raja Mohan in tracing them.

The Carnegie Endowment prides itself on the quality of its research and publications. With offices in the United States, Asia, Russia, the Middle East, and Europe and scholars from around the world, we demand publications that represent the best of what a given country or region can offer. Sometimes these publications are closely detailed "in the weeds" treatments of a given country, region, or problem. Other times, the altitude is much higher for a bigger picture view.

Samudra Manthan is a big picture book, written from a satellite-wide perspective of the Indo-Pacific region, while informed by close on-the-ground knowledge of the strategists who are shaping policies in India, China, and the United States. It is an early word, certainly not the last word, in a story that will be written and told over the next several decades. As such, we are honored to publish it.

–George Perkovich
Vice President for Studies
Carnegie Endowment for International Peace

Chapter One

INTRODUCTION

The "churning of the oceans," or *Samudra Manthan*, is one of the more enchanting episodes of Indian mythology. It traveled across maritime Asia, took root in Khmer cosmology, and was immortalized in the extravagant riches of Angkor Wat.[1] What relevance does the image of angels and demons churning the oceans by putting a mountain on top of a tortoise and spinning it around with a gigantic reptile have for this study of Sino-Indian relations? Plenty. First and foremost is the fact that a rising China and an emerging India are turning to the sea in ways that they did not before. This fact alone has the potential to radically alter the world's maritime environment. The early years of the twenty-first century have already generated an outpouring of popular and academic literature on the meaning of the rise of China and India. The metaphor of the dragon and the elephant turning the world inside out is now quite commonplace. Whether it is the mitigation of global warming, managing the world's energy markets, refashioning the international economic order, sustaining food security, or the construction of a stable balance of power in Asia, China and India have become central to the debate.[2] The dynamic interaction between the two and their impact on the international relations of Asia, Africa, and the Middle East have all begun to draw renewed attention from scholars and policymakers

1

around the world. This volume focuses on the consequences of the rise of China and India for the world's maritime spaces, especially the Indian and Pacific Oceans.

Second, the unfolding maritime orientation of China and India is historic; it marks a fundamental shift in both countries away from the traditional obsession with controlling land frontiers. If Beijing built a great wall to stop the marauding tribes from the north and west, the empires in India, too, were focused on just one unending external threat—the invasion of the subcontinent through its northwestern frontier. To be sure, as two old civilizational states with long coastlines, China and India have always been interested in the waters around them. At different periods of time, the two civilizations did reach out to nearby lands through the seas. But navies and maritime power never acquired sustained attention and resources from either of the two old civilizations. In recent centuries, as China and India entered a prolonged period of rapid relative economic decline, the seas seemed to matter even less to statecraft in Beijing and New Delhi. Reemerging as modern states in the middle of the twentieth century, China and India began to appreciate the importance of sea power. National enthusiasts of sea power argued that both nations were defeated by invaders from the sea and not from the traditional land routes that the empires in both countries had done so much to guard themselves against. These exhortations, however, did not have an immediate impact, as China and India deliberately de-globalized and turned inward. In the mid-1950s, both nations unveiled disastrous experiments in finding a possible "third way" between the political and economic models of the East and the West. When they returned to reconnect with the world—China in 1978 and India in 1991—the maritime universe began to loom large in both Beijing and New Delhi. The new and enduring interest in the seas was an inevitable consequence of the enormously successful globalization of the Chinese and Indian economies in recent decades.

Third, as their economies boomed and commerce became the principal interface between the two Asian giants and the rest of the world, the trade volumes of China and India began to soar. China's two-way trade stood at around $3.5 trillion (2011 estimate). The combined value of India's merchandise exports and imports was around $750 billion in 2011. Most of this trade is seaborne. The protection of the sea lines of communication became an important commercial concern as well as the principal justification of naval bureaucracies in both China and India. That both countries chose to embark on ambitious and costly naval expansion programs marked a fundamental shift in the worldview of the political leadership in Beijing and New Delhi. Historically, the national security establishment in Beijing and New Delhi have tended to treat the navies as stepchildren. In the past two decades, Chinese and Indian political leaders have become strong supporters of maritime power and were ready to devote an ever-larger share of the defense budget to naval modernization. Outside observers have seen the influence of the great American naval thinker Alfred Thayer Mahan in the evolution of naval strategy in China and India.[3] In India, Mahan inspired early navalists such as K. M. Panikkar, who contributed significantly to modern India's strategic thinking.[4] The quest for maritime power was no abstract ambition in young India. It was reflected in India's decision in the mid-1950s to acquire an aircraft carrier.[5] At the same time it was quite clear that the Indian state was in no position to consider an ambitious naval strategy. The same was true of China.[6] By the end of the first decade of the twenty-first century, Delhi and Beijing had unveiled plans for the construction of more than one aircraft carrier each and signaled their political commitment to build blue-water capabilities.[7] If Mahan articulated the case for the United States turning to the seas at the end of the nineteenth century, his sensibility about the geopolitical relationship between rising powers and the maritime imperative offers an important insight into current naval thinking in China and India.

Fourth, the new emphasis on aircraft carriers in the naval headquarters in New Delhi and Beijing underlines an incipient interest in both capitals in power projection. Although China and India deny great-power ambitions or insist that their rise will be peaceful, there is no doubt that their strategic vision and geopolitical aspirations have begun to expand in the twenty-first century. Beijing and Delhi are beginning to appreciate that rapid economic growth and rising levels of prosperity in their large nations cannot be sustained without secure access to raw materials—minerals as well as energy resources such as hydrocarbons—in other countries. The Chinese and Indian maritime interests, then, are not limited to safe transportation of vital resources from far-flung territories but also include ensuring reliable access to them in, say, Africa and the Middle East, through special relationships and active local engagement. Both China and India insist in public that their commitment not to intervene in the affairs of other countries is indeed absolute. Yet, given the stakes involved—the prosperity of more than a billion people each in China and India—it would not be unreasonable to assume that Beijing and New Delhi would begin to consider the development of military capabilities necessary for protecting their economic interests far from their shores and a growing number of citizens working in distant lands. The first signs have emerged of a debate in both China and India on the conditions under which they might deploy military forces beyond their borders.[8] As they begin to develop expeditionary capabilities, the navy will naturally be the principal instrument for delivering Chinese and Indian forces to distant lands. From the end of 2008, China and India deployed their navies to the Gulf of Aden to protect international shipping from Somali pirates.[9] Both countries sent their warships to assist in the evacuation of their citizens from Libya during the popular rebellion and the crackdown by Muammar al-Qaddafi in early 2011.

Fifth, as the Chinese and Indian navies begin to operate far from their immediate waters, they are likely to step on each other's toes and those of the Americans, the world's dominant maritime power. As their maritime interests and strategic horizons widen, China and India are looking beyond their traditional ocean spaces. Until recently the principal concern for India has been the Indian Ocean. For decades, New Delhi had proclaimed that its strategic interests stretched from Aden to Malacca—the two choke points that guide the entrance into the Indian Ocean. Yet in recent years, India has begun to make regular naval forays into the Pacific Ocean. After an initial thrust into the South China Sea in 2000 for joint naval exercises, India sent its aircraft carrier into the region in 2005 and has conducted major naval expeditions up the Pacific since 2007. Since then India has participated in frequent naval exercises in the western Pacific with the United States, Japan, and the regional powers. Some analysts have seen these naval excursions as part of a larger strategy to expand India's influence beyond the Indian Ocean into the western Pacific Ocean.[10] China, meanwhile, has steadily raised its naval profile in the Indian Ocean. Initially, China's strategic focus was aimed at Burma (Myanmar), where Beijing had sought a range of security cooperation. Since then, its interests in the South Asian waters came to light, as it moved into the development of maritime infrastructure in Gwadar (Pakistan) and Hambantota (Sri Lanka). China has begun to look beyond South Asia in recent years toward the key island states in the western Indian Ocean—Seychelles and Mauritius.[11] As China and India reach out to waters beyond their traditional maritime domains, the notion of a rivalry between the two is beginning to gain ground. If China has aspired to dominance over the South China Sea, India has nursed similar ambitions in the Indian Ocean. While neither has a dominant role at the moment, each views with great suspicion the expanding naval profile of the other into waters close to its own territory. Before the rising naval powers crash into each other, they will run into the United States, which for now and the foreseeable future will remain the dominant force in both the Indian and Pacific Oceans. As Robert Kaplan argues, a triangular maritime dynamic now appears inevitable. "Precisely because India and China are emphasizing their sea power, the job of managing their peaceful rise will fall on the U.S. Navy to a significant extent. There will surely be tensions between the three navies, especially as the gaps in their relative strength begin to close."[12] The historic Western and the more recent American dominance of the Indian and Pacific Oceans is likely to be tested by the rise of Chinese and Indian maritime power in the coming decades. For the foreseeable future, the gap between the Indian and Chinese capabilities on the one hand and those of the United States on the other will be tilted in favor of the latter. Neither of these rising powers can hope to supplant the United States as the dominant naval power and principal security provider in the Indian and Pacific Oceans at this time.

Finally, the rising profile of China and India and the unpredictability of their bilateral relations as well as the trilateral one with the United States will have the greatest impact on the region stretching between the eastern coast of Africa and the East Asian littoral. The reference to the "Indo-Pacific" in the subtitle of this volume is aimed at capturing the increasing integration of the regional theaters in the Eastern Hemisphere. Yet many in Asia and North America find it hard to accept "Indo-Pacific" as a new geopolitical frame of reference. They would prefer to treat the Pacific and Indian Oceans as two different realms. That the major powers of East Asia, especially Japan, China, and South Korea, are increasingly dependent on the energy and mineral resources of the Indian Ocean has been known for quite some time. In recent years, this dependence has begun to make an impact on the strategic thinking in East Asia.[13] Securing the seaborne trade through the Indian Ocean and its entry into the western Pacific through narrow choke points in Southeast Asia has also become a major strategic concern for both Japan and China.[14] It is not a surprise that the Sino-Indian maritime rivalry finds its sharpest expression in the Bay of Bengal, the South China Sea, and the Strait of Malacca that connect the two oceans. The term "Indo-Pacific" has wide acceptance among the oceanographers as representing a "bio-geographic" region comprising the warm tropical waters of the Indian Ocean and the western and central Pacific Ocean. As the strategic community worldwide begins to focus on China and India, the usage of the term "Indo-Pacific" and the conception of a single underlying geopolitical theater have gained some ground.[15] Other scholars have been demanding an end to the traditional separation between the Indian Ocean and the Pacific Ocean and think in terms of a maritime Asia.[16] Some political leaders in East Asia have articulated the significance of the "confluence of the two seas," the Indian and Pacific Oceans, amid the rise of China and the emergence of India. In a speech to the Indian Parliament in August 2007, Shinzo Abe, the prime minister of Japan at the time, argued that "the Pacific and the Indian Oceans are now bringing about a dynamic coupling as seas of freedom and of prosperity. A 'broader Asia' that broke away geographical boundaries is now beginning to take on a distinct form."[17] The phrase "Indo-Pacific" acquired some currency under the Obama administration as Washington proclaimed a "pivot" to Asia in 2011 after a prolonged preoccupation with the Middle East.[18] That the Indian foreign policy establishment, traditionally conservative, has begun to adopt the phrase highlights India's new interest in the Indo-Pacific geopolitical framework.[19]

The book uses a thematic framework to organize the discussion on the impact of a rising China and emerging India on the Indo-Pacific region. Chapter 2, which follows this introduction, focuses on the essential structure of Sino-Indian relations. Despite the significant improvement in Sino-Indian relations in recent years, the notion of rivalry between them has been an enduring one. This chapter reviews the competitive dynamic between the two Asian giants in a variety of spheres to set the stage for consideration of their relationship in the Indo-Pacific. Chapter 3 lays out the sources of the emerging maritime orientation of China and India. It offers an assessment of the extraordinary consequences of globalization for the national security thinking in Beijing and New Delhi, two great cities that were dominated by landlubbers for so many centuries. Looking at their growing dependence on imported natural resources and external markets for their manufactured goods, the chapter attempts to capture the meaning of more than two billion people turning to the seas. Chapter 4 examines the changing missions of the Chinese and Indian navies. It traces their evolution from coastal defense and sea denial toward blue-water missions and the ability to operate far from their home territories.

As China and India exert gravitational pull on the ocean space around them, it is also important to look at the implications of their nuclear arsenals on their maritime strategies. Chapter 5 looks at the pressures on China and India to deploy their nuclear weapons at sea and what this might mean for the Indo-Pacific region as a whole. Examination of the nuclear doctrines of China and India will also take us into a survey of their linked policies on military uses of outer space and their emerging interest in missile defense. Chapter 6 looks at India's new strategic thrust into the Pacific Ocean. For the past six decades, India's maritime policies have been examined from the perspective of the Indian Ocean. After a brief review of the debate about India's Indian Ocean strategy, the chapter turns to an analysis of India's strategic aspirations in the Pacific Ocean. Chapter 7 in turn focuses on the importance of the Indian Ocean to China. Beijing's maritime outlook was traditionally shaped by the cross-straits relations with Taiwan, its historic claims in the South China Sea, and more broadly the dominant American presence in the western Pacific. There is a growing recognition, however, of the long-term importance of the Indian Ocean in Beijing's strategic calculus. The chapter analyzes the rising profile of the Chinese navy in the Indian Ocean and the factors driving it. Together chapters 6 and 7 provide the basis for thinking about the Indian and Pacific Oceans within the single frame of the Indo-Pacific.

Chapters 8 and 9 look at the deepening "security dilemma" between China and India in the Indian and Pacific Oceans. Chapter 8 looks at the expression of the security dilemma in the small island states of the Indian Ocean. Control of the strategically located islands has always been central to the maritime strategies of the great powers. As China seeks to build long-term access arrangements with them, India has reacted by trying to limit Beijing's influence in the Indian Ocean islands and stepping up its own efforts to consolidate long-standing economic and security cooperation with Mauritius, Seychelles, Maldives, and Sri Lanka. Chapter 9 extends the investigation of the Sino-Indian security dilemma to the littoral of the Indian and Pacific Oceans. While a competitive logic is driving China and India in the Indo-Pacific, its expression varies from one subregion to another. We look at the Sino-Indian rivalry in the Arabian Sea, the Bay of Bengal, and the South China Sea.

Chapter 10 focuses on three potential ways in which the Sino-Indian rivalry could be mitigated. It explores the record of Sino-Indian confidence building and the many problems with it. The chapter explores the prospects for a bilateral maritime security dialogue that allows an open discussion of each other's apprehension and finds ways to harmonize or limit the conflict between their interests in the Indian and Pacific Oceans. Chapter 11 focuses on the consequences of Sino-Indian rivalry for the geopolitics of the Indo-Pacific and explores different possible outcomes in the Indo-Pacific regional order. The concluding chapter 12 offers an assessment of the emerging and consequential triangular dynamic between China and India, the rising powers in the Indo-Pacific, and the United States, which has been the dominant power in the two oceans for decades.

A word about sources and assumptions is appropriate at this stage. Not being proficient in Mandarin, the author relies largely on secondary sources and a few primary sources available in English to outline the logic and elements of China's naval modernization. This volume does not seek to delve deeply into the domestic debates over maritime strategy in either China or India. The objective is to paint a picture, with the strokes of a broad brush, of the emerging naval capabilities and changing maritime orientation of China and India. A growing body of literature, including book-length volumes, examines in detail the history and the more recent evolution of the Chinese and Indian navies as well as the related political and policy debates in Beijing and New Delhi. The objective here is to assess the geopolitical consequences of China and India turning to the seas. The special emphasis of this volume is on the interactive dynamic between the emerging naval strategies of Beijing and New Delhi and their intersection with the maritime interests of Washington, which remains the preeminent power in the waters of both China and India.

in a very different direction. The construction of a strong Indo-U.S. military alliance would surely be seen in Beijing as provocative and result in Chinese countermeasures. As the distribution of power in Asia changes, great strategic uncertainty is prevalent in the region. Subjective failures of policymakers and an objective mismatch between the unfolding power shift and inadequate mechanisms for strategic communication, consultation, and cooperation increase the possibility of great-power conflict in the Indo-Pacific. Understanding that danger is the first important step in the effort to mitigate it. Underestimation of that potential would only invite danger.

Chapter Two

THE STRUCTURE OF THE RIVALRY

The evolution of Sino-Indian relations in the twentieth century and after points to a paradox—repeated attempts by the two nations to develop good neighborly relations and their relentless drift toward political rivalry. This chapter delineates the broad structure of the Sino-Indian relationship, which has been caught between the aspirations for cooperation and the imperatives of competition. Many American Sinologists point to the formal arguments in Beijing that it sees no threat from India and argue that the notion of "relentless rivalry" is more in New Delhi's strategic imagination. To be sure, the suggestion that Sino-Indian rivalry is one-sided is not without a basis. After all, India is the weaker of the two Asian giants, and the gap in capabilities between them is growing in favor of China. Yet, the history of Sino-Indian relations records Beijing's acute concerns about New Delhi's role in undermining Chinese territoriality in Tibet and India's attempts to impede China's natural role in the subcontinent. New Delhi's de facto alliance with the Soviet Union and its presumed Asian proxies did bother Beijing during the Cold War. India's search for a strong strategic partnership with the United States and its Asian allies in the first decade of the twenty-first century has drawn considerable military attention in China. India is unlikely to match the growing Chinese power, measure for measure, in the coming years. Nevertheless, as India expands its defense capabilities and deepens its engagement with China's potential adversaries, Beijing has begun to factor New Delhi into its strategic calculus. China is considering the possibilities for both countering the potential threat from a rising India and at the same time deepening political cooperation with New Delhi.

This chapter begins with a brief review of the engagement between the two counties since the early decades of the twentieth century, when continual efforts to build a partnership could not prevail over the logic of conflict. It then analyzes the unresolved territorial issues between China and India at the core of their unsettled relationship and assesses the central role of Pakistan and other powers in defining the balance of power between the two nations. It then outlines the Sino-Indian regional rivalry and moves to explore the emerging global dimensions of the two nations' competition. This geopolitical overview sets the stage for the more detailed examination of their emerging contestation into the maritime domain in subsequent chapters.

THE PARADOX OF SINO-INDIAN RELATIONS

Well before India and China established diplomatic relations in 1950, the leaders of the two national movements reached out to each other and explored the bases for future cooperation. Representing two great civilizations emerging out of prolonged decline at the turn of the twentieth century, the Chinese and Indian nationalists believed that together they were destined to reshape Asia and the world.[1] Yet as the Second World War engulfed them, they found it impossible to cooperate. As the Indian national movement began to develop a perspective on global affairs in the interwar years, the expression of solidarity with the Chinese people in their resistance to Japanese imperialist occupation became a major act in India's nascent internationalism in the interwar period.[2] Nehru's interaction with the Chinese delegates at the anti-imperialist congress in Brussels in 1927 produced a joint manifesto for cooperation against imperialism.[3] Nevertheless, the fact that India and China faced different imperial powers stymied political cooperation between the two national movements when it mattered most. The British got Chiang Kai-shek to travel to India in February 1942 to try to persuade the Indian National Congress to cooperate with London in the war effort against Tokyo. The Indian nationalist leaders, including Gandhi, focused as they were on ousting Britain from India, would not agree.[4]

At the intellectual level, too, the big ideas that moved China and India did not always connect. Despite their common struggle against the domination of the West, they did not see eye to eye on critical political and philosophical assumptions. The main lines of Chinese and Indian national movements differed deeply on the notion of what constituted "the East," the strategies of economic and political modernization, and the relationship between tradition and modernity.[5] In the early years after claiming their independent nationhood, India and China once again embarked on a new effort to build political cooperation. Their romanticism was marked by the slogan of "Hindi-Chini bhai-bhai" in the 1950s. Yet by the late 1950s, the relationship began to sour over the turbulence in Tibet and their unresolved boundary dispute. It culminated in a brief military conflict at the end of 1962 that destroyed Nehru's ambitious project to build a solid partnership with China. Ironically, nearly four and a half decades after his death and his ardent championing of India's building good relations with China, Nehru remains, for Beijing, the symbol of "Indian hegemonism."[6] Nehru's "forward policy" on the Indo-Tibetan frontier and his perceived interference in the internal affairs of Tibet were seen in Beijing as the continuation of the imperial policy of Lord Curzon, the British Viceroy who ordered the opening up of Tibet at the turn of the twentieth century.[7] The 1962 border war was followed by a prolonged chill until the 1980s, when an effort was made to normalize bilateral relations. While the boundary dispute dominated the relationship, China and India found their worldviews were divergent and their interests at odds in Southeast Asia and South Asia. Sino-Indian differences on the future of the security order in Asia and the Indian Ocean were strong, and when the Cold War came to a conclusion in the late 1980s they found themselves on opposite sides.

At the turn of the twenty-first century, Sino-Indian relations seemed to enter one of their better phases. The normalization efforts begun in the final years of the twentieth century seemed to bear fruit as two-way trade between the two countries galloped from about $1 billion in 1998 to nearly $74 billion in 2011. Sustained high-level exchanges and broadening people-to-people contacts were supplemented by important efforts at military confidence building and a political effort at resolving the all-important boundary dispute. Yet, by the end of the first decade of the twenty-first century, Sino-Indian relations seemed to revert to the mode of conflict and rivalry amid renewed border tensions, differences over Tibet, nuclear politics, and a range of other issues that divided them in the twentieth century.[8] Some have seen this renewed rivalry as rooted in the relentless logic of geography.[9] Since they shared the same space in Asia and both nations sought to expand their influence on the nations across their borders, a contestation for influence in Central Asia, South Asia, and Southeast Asia became inevitable. The competition was not limited to land spaces but extended to the Indian Ocean and the western Pacific Ocean, as China and India, with their new focus on trade, sought to protect their now-vital sea lines of communication. Nor was the rivalry limited to their immediate environs. It expressed itself in far-flung places from Siberia in the Russian Far East to Colombia in Latin America and from Africa to the South Pacific, thanks to their growing dependence on resources—both energy and mineral—far from their shores.

In their enhanced bilateral engagement at the turn of the twenty-first century, both China and India have sought to downplay the prospects for rivalry. They continually declared that they were not a threat to each other. They also insisted that there was enough space in the world for the peaceful rise of both China and India and that cooperation between them would be critical for the emergence of the Asian century.[10] Despite the repeated formal declaration of the commitment to political cooperation and the rapidly expanding bilateral economic engagement, China and India constantly sought to limit each other's influence. At one end were those who wanted to reinvent the old notions of "Hindi-Chini bhai-bhai" and talked about building "Chindia"—or a real strategic partnership—in the twenty-first century.[11] At the other end were those arguing that the contradictions between the Indian and Chinese pursuit of greatness may be irreconcilable.[12] Beijing and New Delhi are aware that their bilateral relationship remains sensitive to their relationships with other powers—both global and regional. New Delhi and Beijing have used their relationships with the United States, Japan, and Russia to try to gain advantage over the other. As a consequence, the fear of encirclement by the other has gained ground in both capitals and laid the basis for what could be a deepening security dilemma between the two countries. What one nation sees as a necessary step in protecting its own interests is seen by the other as an aggressive move to undercut its positions. As noted above, the notion of a Sino-Indian rivalry is not new. What makes it different in the early twenty-first century are a number of factors. Rising China and emerging India are more powerful nations today on the cusp of great-power status. Their interests are wide-ranging, driven by strong nationalist impulses. They have staked their domestic political legitimacy on their ability to sustain high rates of growth that in turn depend on their realization of key external objectives in an increasingly interconnected world. And they have often found themselves at odds in reshaping international institutions, including the global nuclear order, the United Nations Security Council, and the building of regional communities in Asia.

CONTESTED TERRITORIALITY

Despite two major political efforts after the 1962 border war, one in the closing years of the twentieth century and another in the first decade of the new century, India and China are as far as they have ever been from a settlement of their dispute over a boundary that runs a little longer than 4,000 kilometers (2,485 miles) along the Himalayas.[13] The first effort was initiated by Indian Prime Minister Rajiv Gandhi in 1988. In traveling to China, the first prime minister to do so in three decades, Rajiv Gandhi ended the prolonged chill in bilateral relations after the 1962 war by de-linking the normalization of bilateral relations from a resolution of the boundary dispute and seeking to pursue both with some vigor. This new approach certainly led to an expansion of the bilateral relationship, but no breakthrough was forthcoming in the negotiations on the boundary. The emphasis shifted slowly to the maintenance of peace and tranquility on the border rather than finding a final settlement to the dispute.[14] This was in tune with China's own efforts to stabilize its many disputed frontiers as it sought to create a peaceful environment for its economic reforms and national reconstruction.[15] The second effort, initiated by Indian Prime Minister Atal Bihari Vajpayee, was more ambitious, predicated on a "political" resolution of the dispute rather than negotiating the border from the perspective of historical and legal claims. During Vajpayee's visit to Beijing in June 2003, the two sides agreed to elevate the negotiation to the level of empowered special representatives and pursue purposefully the resolution of the boundary dispute.[16] This did produce a framework of broad principles that would form the basis for resolving the boundary dispute.[17] This framework was significant in the sense that it was the first-ever formulation of the guidelines for a settlement, and there was considerable optimism in New Delhi that the new approach would produce a solution. The two sides seemed willing to make a few important compromises that would make a settlement conceivable. The agreement on the guidelines was to be the first of three phases in the resolution of the boundary dispute. In the second phase, the two sides hoped to arrive at mutually acceptable territorial concessions, to be followed by a final phase in which the boundary would be demarcated.[18] Despite many rounds of negotiations from 2003 to 2012, however, the two sides could not come up with a framework of mutual territorial concessions. Instead, both sides began to argue about the interpretation of the agreed principles. This put to rest the prospects for the only basis on which a settlement could have been produced: the legitimization of the current status quo on the border, with India giving up its claims for additional territory in the west and China in the east. China, which seemed to offer such a settlement in 1960 and 1980, now demanded significant territorial adjustments in the east, especially in the Tawang sector, which China considers an extension of Tibet. India, which believes it was the victim of Chinese aggression in 1962, had no political room or inclination to make additional territorial concessions.[19] Some analysts have argued that China's position in the negotiations since 2003 might reflect a strategic decision to keep the boundary dispute open and to leverage it to keep India off balance.[20] It is reasonable to presume that India's deepening defense and security cooperation with the United States in the second term of the Bush Administration (2005–2009) and the civil nuclear initiative of July 2005 strengthened Beijing's logic to delay the resolution of the boundary dispute.

The frequent and intense rounds of boundary talks during 2003–2012 revealed one of the central difficulties of the negotiation. It was as much a territorial dispute as it was about irresolvable conceptions about territoriality. Beijing's dispute with New Delhi is in essence about the Indo-Tibetan border. Beijing says it cannot accept any settlement that does not involve substantive Indian concessions on territory it says historically belonged to Tibet. India, meanwhile, cannot give away large chunks of a territory that is now a province of India and sends elected representatives to the parliament. This central difficulty is in turn made more complex by the perception of a changing balance of power between the two. China's seeming "concessions" were offered when Beijing was weak and on the defensive in Tibet. India was not prepared to respond to the Chinese proposals during the period of 1959–1960 and the early 1980s, given its own internal political compulsions. When it was ready to test China's flexibility in the first decade of the twenty-first century, Beijing's demands were far more onerous than New Delhi had expected.[21]

Finally, the Sino-Indian border dispute is deeply intertwined with China's insecurities in Tibet, its anxieties about India's enduring special cultural and historic bonds with Tibet, and New Delhi's support of the Dalai Lama, who has run a government in exile in India along with his followers. When Tibet is relatively quiescent, it is possible for India and China to keep their fundamental disagreements on the back burner and move forward with the normalization of bilateral relations.[22] When Tibet is restive, as it was during 2008 and since, it comes back to cast a big shadow on Sino-Indian relations. India is among the few countries that refuse to accept Beijing's formulation that Tibet is an "inalienable and integral" part of China. While accepting that the current Tibet Autonomous Region is part of the People's Republic of China, India continues to back the Dalai Lama's formulation that historically Tibet was not always part of China. India also insists on the rights of Tibetans to cultural and political autonomy in China. Tibet's central role in the Sino-Indian disputes is unlikely to go away with the passing of the Dalai Lama, which is bound to happen in the next two decades, as many in China hope for.[23] In fact, it could make matters worse, as the battle for the Dalai Lama's succession begins between the Dalai Lama's followers in India and Beijing. The identification of two different successors—coupled with the fact that the Karmapa, whose legitimacy is accepted by both Beijing and the Tibetan exiles, lives in India—is bound to increase tensions between Beijing and New Delhi. The death of the current Dalai Lama is likely to remove any impulses for moderation within the Tibetan community and deepen India's current ambiguities on Tibet. Meanwhile, China's vulnerabilities in Tibet came into public view in 2008. Notwithstanding the real and positive economic changes in Tibet since the launching of reforms by Deng Xiaoping, the protests since 2008 have shown that the region's integration into China remains fragile. Despite the rather small population of Tibetans dispersed over a large area, they have demonstrated extraordinary ability to probe the fundamental weaknesses in modern China's territorial nationalism.[24] In an ideal world, Tibet could find its historic role as the bridge between the Chinese and Indian civilizations. In the real world, though, Tibet is likely to be at the very core of an unending tension between China and India in the coming years. This is reflected in Beijing's new offensive against the Dalai Lama since 2008 and its objections to Indian leaders visiting Arunachal Pradesh, a state on the disputed border with China. Beijing has begun to call the province "Southern Tibet" and has long claimed it to be an integral part of Tibet and therefore of China.

If India remains a complicating factor in China's effort to consolidate its territoriality, so does Beijing in New Delhi's. China's occupation of a considerable swath of the state of Jammu and Kashmir and Beijing's support of Islamabad in its enduring rivalry with India make the consolidation of India's own territorial nationalism vulnerable to Chinese policies. Indian public discourse rarely thinks of China when it debates its disputes with Pakistan over Kashmir. If Tibet is China's Achilles' heel, Kashmir has been India's, and Beijing has always seen itself as an important factor in the final disposition of the status of J&K.[25] Beijing began to remind New Delhi in 2008 of its ability to worsen India's problems in Kashmir by issuing visas on separate pages to Indian citizens from the disputed state. This in turn drew official Indian protests.[26] India also made the question of China's policy on Kashmir visas one of the central issues in the discussion with the Chinese Premier Wen Jiabao during his visit to New Delhi in December 2010. Beyond its own territorial disputes with India in Kashmir, Beijing modulated its position on Indo-Pak conflicts over Kashmir in sync with the state of its ties with India. During the 1960s and 1970s, China supported the extremist factions of the communist movement that sought a violent overthrow of the Indian government. It also backed the various separatist movements in India's turbulent northeastern region. Amid increasing tensions in the bilateral relationship since 2008, there has been some concern in New Delhi that China might be reviving its contact with

of geography is unrelenting in Asia where Indian and Chinese interests intersect.[42] Related to this logic of geography might well be the burden of history and the indelible memory of threats to the survival of the state and empire in China and India from the peripheral regions. The rise and fall of the empires in the two civilization areas and the waxing and waning of their territorial size were profoundly dependent upon the ability of the heartland to control its peripheral regions. The modern states in China and India have been acutely conscious of their vulnerability in the outlying frontiers of the state—Beijing in Inner Mongolia, Xinjiang, Tibet, and Yunnan and New Delhi in Kashmir, Punjab, and the northeastern provinces. Given the geographic proximity and the enduring historic links between the peripheries of one state and those of the other, both have been intensely wary of the potential intervention by the other in their own internal affairs. Beyond their mutual distrust, both China and India have been deeply suspicious of the spoiling role of other powers in their respective peripheries and have been determined to keep the Western powers, especially the Americans, out of their own frontier regions as much as possible. India's cooperation with the United States in supporting Tibetan rebels during the late 1950s and early 1960s was a major provocation from the Chinese perspective.[43] Even the slightest hint of Indian consultation or cooperation with the United States on Tibet brings forth strong responses from Beijing and complicates India's China policy, as was seen when New Delhi let Nancy Pelosi, then the speaker of the U.S. House of Representatives, visit Dharamashala and meet with the Dalai Lama during the Tibetan protests in the spring of 2008.[44]

The sense of internal vulnerability has not disappeared despite the relative improvement of the Chinese and Indian positions in the international system, and it is bound to play itself out in the next two decades. Given their improved capabilities, their rivalry in the periphery is likely to be rather consequential. Amidst the growing consciousness of the peripheral communities in both states and their deepening network of international contacts, Beijing or New Delhi find it difficult to cut off these regions from the rest of the world or insulate them from each other. At the same time, their newly powerful international economic standing, to be sure, has made it more costly for Western nations to interfere in issues of territorial concern for Beijing and New Delhi, as seen in the Western reluctance to push China on Tibet and India on Kashmir. This logic, however, does not apply to the deepening mutual suspicion between Beijing and New Delhi. Because the mistrust is driven by a security dilemma and shaped by concerns of territorial integrity, China and India might be condemned to step on each other's toes in their peripheral regions.

Further, their very attempt to overcome the vulnerability in the frontier regions intensifies the mutual distrust and sense of the security dilemma. China's effort to develop its far-flung territories, including its western and southwestern regions bordering India, is sensible from Beijing's point of view, but its consequences, as in Tibet and Yunnan, which border the subcontinent, are often seen as threatening in New Delhi.[45] China's development of water resources, for example, in Tibet could have a huge impact on the many rivers that flow into the subcontinent from the plateau. Water-related issues are emerging as a major new element in the Sino-Indian conflict.[46] China's determination to improve the connectivity of Tibet and Xinjiang through the construction of modern rail and road transport corridors has also made New Delhi apprehensive. India in turn has announced plans for a massive developmental strategy in the provinces bordering China.[47] These seemingly economic approaches have the potential to improve the military capabilities of both countries in their border regions and even alter the conventional balance of power and its deployability in sensitive areas. There is no doubt that Beijing and New Delhi are interested in a lot more than economic development of their frontier regions and improved connectivities to the heartland as well as to external markets. Both Beijing and New Delhi have always been conscious of the need to maximize their influence in the states and regions lying across their borders in order to minimize the vulnerability of their own frontier regions.[48] This in turn deepens the mutual distrust and compels both of them to respond to what they see as hostile strategies of the other. Above all, it has set up the template for an expanding rivalry in the Asian neighborhoods that the two countries share—Central, South, and Southeast Asia.

THE CENTRALITY OF PERIPHERY

Although such rivalry is not new, it is certain to acquire a more virulent form in the next twenty years, as Beijing and New Delhi intensify their search for stronger regional influence in Asia. The manner in which this might manifest itself over the next two decades in different subregions of Asia, which form the shared periphery of China and India, is bound to vary. It will be shaped by the geopolitical specificity of each region, the local dynamic of great-power relations, and the particular histories of Indian and Chinese engagement with them. Three regions—Central Asia, South Asia, and Southeast Asia—are part of the overlapping peripheries of China and India.

In Central Asia, both China and India have made a determined bid to raise their profile since the end of the Cold War and the collapse of the Soviet Union. Their interests in Central Asia are articulated in terms of access to the rich energy and mineral resources, the region's historical links to empires in China and India, the vulnerability of regimes in the region to religious extremism and terrorism and their wider regional consequences, and the potential threat from other powers that could influence the evolution of the region to the disadvantage of either China or India. This core framing of the Chinese and Indian interests in Central Asia is likely to endure over the next two decades. How China and India pursue these interests, however, will vary given their different circumstances. Beijing inherits the advantages and burdens of a long border with Central Asia. Long borders have meant China can easily harness the energy and mineral resources of landlocked Central Asia but must ensure that destabilizing forces do not spill over into China, especially into the restive Xinjiang province. To that extent, there is a measure of defensiveness in China's strategy toward Central Asia.[49] India, in contrast, is constrained by the absence of direct physical access to Central Asia but is also therefore partly insulated from the internal turbulence and great-power intervention in Central Asia to a certain extent. The sense of a historical connection, the presence of large energy resources, and the aspiration to expand its regional influence make Central Asia an important one in the list of India's foreign policy priorities.[50]

The Chinese and Indian concerns about great-power presence in Central Asia are pointed in different directions. Beijing's main apprehensions are about the U.S. presence in Central Asia, which is seen to affect China's national security in many ways.[51] A significant U.S. military presence on its western borders in Central Asia would clearly seem to complete the circle of containment against China. The military balance of power considerations, however, are perhaps less important for Beijing than the consequences from the American agenda of democracy promotion in Central Asia. The Chinese fear of "color revolutions" supported by the Bush administration in the first decade of the twenty-first century is rooted in Beijing's perceived threats from political pluralism and democracy on its periphery. If limiting American influence in Central Asia will remain a principal aim of Beijing, New Delhi has no direct quarrel with Washington in Central Asia. India, in fact, sees the U.S. presence as a useful counter to the prospect of a long-term expansion of Chinese influence in the region. It is no surprise that India has been lukewarm about the utility of the Shanghai Cooperation Organization, a major strategic initiative of China, despite being an observer in the organization and seeking full membership.[52] India, as it might have during the Cold War, has also not called for the withdrawal of the American military presence in Central Asia. It was deeply disappointed when Washington announced plans in 2009 to end the U.S. combat role in Afghanistan by 2014. India has welcomed the Obama administration's initiative to promote a New Silk Road that would connect Afghanistan with South Asia and Central Asia.[53] China has been lukewarm; so has Russia.

For different reasons, Beijing and New Delhi find it both necessary and convenient to work with Moscow in expanding their own influence in Central Asia. Although the dominance of the United States has brought Russia closer to China, the contradictions between Moscow and Beijing are likely to manifest themselves in the next two decades. New Delhi, in contrast, has no reason to contest Russian influence in the region. From the Indian perspective, a cooperative relationship between Moscow and Washington would best serve its interests in Central Asia by limiting the expansion of a Chinese role in the region. Russo-American tensions, meanwhile, would turn Western ire against Moscow, improve China's leverage with Russia, and create more space for Beijing in different subregions of Asia.

The rapidly changing Chinese and Indian attitudes toward American power are also reflected in South Asia.[54] India is not unaware that it needs the full power of the United States to address the real source of turbulence in Central Asia and South Asia—the incubating radical Islam in the border regions of Pakistan and Afghanistan. India has historically insulated itself from other great powers by maintaining a buffer zone between the Indus River and the Hindu Kush mountains—precisely the region that Americans now call "Af-Pak." Pacification of the Af-Pak region, with the possible help of the United States, holds the key to the realization of India's strategic aspirations in Central Asia and reclaiming its centrality in the South Asian subcontinent. India needs a measure of tranquility in its northwestern frontiers and normal relations with Pakistan in order to access the Central Asian region and its natural resources as well as end the unresolved post-partition conflicts in the subcontinent. This core project of India's grand strategy will become all the more challenging in the next two decades as American attempts at nation building in Afghanistan falter and extremist forces steadily expand their influence in neighboring Pakistan.

Although China and India have similar concerns about religious extremism and terrorism, Beijing is unlikely to acknowledge and oppose the central role of the Pakistan army and its intelligence agencies in fomenting the forces of destabilization in the region. Beijing remains confident that its long-standing alliance with the Pakistan army provides insurance against such threats and finds no reason to end its rather successful policy of using Islamabad to balance New Delhi on the subcontinent.[55] India's improving political relationship and deepening security cooperation with the United States are likely to tighten the bonds between China and Pakistan. This line of reasoning in Beijing could change if the Pakistan army becomes ineffective in dealing with the threats to Chinese security, for example in Xinjiang, emanating from Pakistani soil. Deepening instability in Pakistan and Afghanistan and the dangers of its spillover into western China have also begun to prompt Beijing to support Pakistan's normalization of relations with India.

Meanwhile, the triangular relationship among the United States, India, and Pakistan, too, is evolving and its direction remains uncertain. On the face of it, New Delhi and Washington have similar goals in the Af-Pak region—stabilizing the tribal lands straddling the border between Afghanistan and Pakistan, redefining the civil-military relations in Pakistan, ending the extended dalliance between the Pakistan army and the forces of extremism, and reducing the salience of Pakistan's nuclear weapons.[56] In practice, though, the U.S. dependence on the Pakistan army to pursue its objectives in Afghanistan has tended to limit the range of Indian-U.S. partnership in

Afghanistan. A dramatic rupture in U.S.-Pakistani relations amid the U.S. withdrawal from Afghanistan could alter the historic Indian resentment against the U.S. partnership with Pakistan. As India watched the steady deterioration of U.S.-Pakistani relations after the raid and execution of Osama bin Laden carried out by American Special Forces in May 2011, New Delhi had to consider the prospect of Beijing's emerging as the Pakistan army's principal external supporter.[57] In an irony, the downslide in U.S.-Pakistani relations has been accompanied by a slow thaw in the relations between New Delhi and Islamabad during 2011–2012. The civilian government led by President Asif Ali Zardari has made bold moves to open up trade relations with India and deepen political engagement with New Delhi.

A new triangular dynamic in the region, involving New Delhi, Beijing, and Washington, is also reflected in the rest of the subcontinent. The single most important geopolitical development in South Asia in the first decade of the twenty-first century has been the emergence of China as a powerful external player in the region. To be sure, Beijing has always refused to recognize India's claims of an exclusive sphere of influence in South Asia, insisted on the right to full and unhindered cooperation with New Delhi's neighbors, aligned with forces that were seen as inimical to New Delhi, and pursued a relentless policy of trying to keep India off balance in its own neighborhood. What has changed since the turn of the century are powerful new instrumentalities in Beijing's hand—as a trade partner, supplier of arms, major provider of economic assistance, and exporter of infrastructure projects. This leverage is bound to get stronger in the next two decades and compel India to come up with a more vigorous strategic response. As part of the effort to regain its primacy in the region, New Delhi has ended its decades-long suspicion of the U.S. role in South Asia, begun a regional security dialogue with Washington, focused on unilateral economic concessions to its neighbors, and reinvigorated the regional institutions. Both the Bush and Obama administrations have extended support to India's attempts to improve its relations with the smaller neighbors. There is no doubt that geography is in India's favor on the subcontinent. New Delhi's efforts in the coming years will focus on developing a security strategy that leverages its advantages, resolves the political differences with its neighbors, encourages them to see their long-term stake in a deeper relationship with India, and makes itself an attractive partner for the smaller nations of South Asia.

If Sino-Indian rivalry in South Asia is about Beijing's reluctance to concede New Delhi's primacy in the subcontinent, New Delhi is trying to raise its profile in parts of Southeast Asia that have experienced greater economic integration with China. The region has long been subject to both Chinese and Indian cultural influences, and many parts of the region have evolved through history as links between the two great civilizations.[58] Since the emergence of modern independent states in China and India during the middle of the last century, however, the dynamic between the two nations in Southeast Asia has been a competitive one.[59] As a result of India's relative marginalization from the region in the 1970s and 1980s, coupled with China's rapprochement with the United States and Japan in the same period, New Delhi steadily fell behind Beijing in Southeast Asia. Since the proclamation of a "Look East" policy in the early 1990s, India has made a determined bid to re-inject itself into the region. Although India's relative weight in this region has increased during recent years, it continues to remain well behind China's.[60] This, however, has not stopped India from competing with China for influence in Burma, expanding its military and political cooperation with various Southeast Asian nations, and deepening its ties with the United States and Japan in order to balance the rising power of China. This imperative is likely to get stronger in the next two decades. At this stage it might be reasonable to project that in its immediate border regions—from northern Burma and northern Thailand to Indochina—Beijing's influence is likely to grow rapidly. This in turn is likely to encourage maritime Southeast Asia and India to work together to sustain a regional balance of power. That Singapore and Indonesia (along with Japan) were critical in ensuring Indian membership in the East Asia Summit against the opposition of China underscores this reality. An India that steadily increases its economic and military capabilities over the next two decades could help generate options for maritime Southeast Asian nations that have not previously existed.[61] India, on its own, is in no position to become a counterweight to China in Southeast Asia. Acting in concert with the United States and Japan and through deeper engagement with the region, India can contribute to a more stable balance of power in Southeast Asia.

BEYOND THE SHARED PERIPHERY

As the contest between China and India in their shared periphery intensifies, both Beijing and New Delhi insist that they are interested in a cooperative relationship with the other and are committed to managing their differences in an amicable manner. They point to the rapidly expanding economic cooperation and political consultations between the two nations. Leaders in both countries emphasize their recognition of the dangers of a potential conflict. As the weaker of the two parties, India has much to lose from a confrontation with China. Beijing is aware of the dangers of pushing India into a closer alignment with the United States. In early 2012, after nearly three years of standoff on a number of political and military issues, top officials from the two countries, in an orchestrated effort, signaled their determination to build a productive and peaceful relationship. In a speech at the Chinese Embassy in New Delhi, India's national security adviser, Shivshankar Menon, rejected the notion that "India and China are bound to be strategic adversaries." Menon insisted that such "determinism" is misplaced and argued:

> The issue is whether we can continue to manage the elements of competition within an agreed strategic framework which permits both of us to pursue our core interests. I see no reason why that should not be so. Indeed I would go further and say that the rapid changes in the international situation today also create an opportunity for India and China to work with others to shape benign international outcomes.[62]

His counterpart, Dai Bingguo, China's top diplomat, reciprocated the sentiment a few days later in a signed article published in an Indian newspaper. Dai declared that New Delhi should have "confidence in China's tremendous sentiment of friendship towards India." Reassuring that China is not a threat, Dai argued that "there does not exist such a thing as China's attempt to 'attack India' or 'suppress India's development.'" Predicting a "golden period" ahead in Sino-Indian relations, Dai said, "We need to view each other's development in a positive light and regard each other as major partners and friends, not rivals. We always need to be each other's good neighbor, good friend and good partner."[63] Skeptics would say that such shared sentiment, expressed after fourteen rounds of inconclusive talks on the boundary dispute during 2003–2011, is merely the triumph of hope over experience. Political realists would say that the latest effort to mitigate the security dilemma between the two countries would fall into the familiar paradox of Sino-Indian relations we identified at the beginning of this chapter.

Few will, however, disagree that the consequences of yet another failure will be much larger for China, India, and the world. In the last two decades, the global interests of China and India have expanded and with them the potential for the extension of Sino-Indian rivalry to regions beyond their shared periphery in Africa, the Middle East, and the Western Pacific. Globalization of the Chinese and Indian economies has made the two countries dependent on the rest of the world for resources as well as markets for their goods. Managing this interdependence has become a "vital interest" for their leadership, who must provider higher living standards for populations above a billion each in China and India. Ideally, this challenge must be met by greater cooperation between Beijing and New Delhi and between them and other great powers. In the real world, though, both countries have been drawn to national policies that emphasize energy security, cultivation of special bilateral arrangements with producers of energy and mineral resources, and the building of large and modern navies to ensure access to and safe transportation of natural resources.

Both Chinese and Indian leaders have increasingly talked about a "manifest destiny" for their navies. Both have begun to emphasize the importance of naval power as a necessary complement to their rise in the international system. Their simultaneous advances on the maritime front are setting the stage for a new arena of rivalry between China and India in the Indian Ocean. As its dependence on Indian Ocean sea lanes is increasing, Beijing has begun to agonize over what is now called the "Malacca dilemma."[64] Given the fact that most of China's seaborne trade with Africa and the Middle East passes through the Strait of Malacca, China has a natural interest in ensuring there are no threats to its energy and resource lifeline. As Beijing's maritime profile rises in the Indian Ocean, New Delhi would like to hedge against China's potential acquisition of military bases and naval facilities and prevent Beijing's maritime encirclement of India. Meanwhile, India's trade and other interests in the western Pacific are growing and New Delhi has launched naval engagement with China's neighbors that is of some concern to Beijing. The notion of a security dilemma that has defined Sino-Indian relations in so many other spheres is now expanding to the maritime domain and will acquire a sharper edge in the coming decades. In chapter 3 that follows, we begin to explore the emerging maritime contestation in the Indian and Pacific Oceans, the prospects for its mitigation, and its intersection with the interests and policies of the United States.

Chapter Three

IN SEARCH OF SEA POWER

Nationalists in modern China and India have often invoked a "glorious" maritime past to justify the contemporary need for a vigorous maritime strategy and a powerful navy. In India, K. M. Panikkar, the amateur historian, administrator, and diplomat, writing on the eve of independence in the middle of the twentieth century, made the case for a strong maritime orientation for India. He asserted that India has had a powerful naval tradition and had enjoyed the command of the seas around it until the beginning of the sixteenth century. He also insisted that the neglect of sea power was at the root of India's loss of independence, relative decline, and global marginalization in the centuries since then.[1] In China, at the turn of the twenty-first century, the state is leading a massive effort to remember and celebrate its past maritime traditions. As they seek to build a powerful modern navy, China's communist leaders have found great value in marking the six-hundredth anniversary of the first of seven epic voyages by the great Chinese admiral Zheng He to the south and west into the Indian Ocean in 2005.[2] These celebrations became an important part of promoting maritime consciousness at home and signaling to the rest of the world that China's rise would be peaceful and nonviolent.[3] The Chinese government has also sought to promote the worldwide popularization of

Chinese maritime tradition and how it predated the rise of European maritime dominance.[4] While some might argue that New Delhi does not have a similar "usable maritime past," India's navalists insist that a grand maritime narrative is indeed part of India's historic memory.[5] There is wide agreement within the scholarship of Asia and its history that neither of these great Asian civilizations had emphasized sea power on a *consistent* basis in the past. The respected historian of China, Wang Gungwu, for example, argues that despite building an impressive navy by the fifteenth century, imperial China never abandoned the primacy of its continental commitment. "The simple fact was that its really dangerous enemies had always come overland (from the north and the west) and certainly never by the sea. As a result, the interplay of overland and maritime concerns has always been unbalanced and most Chinese rulers never took naval power seriously."[6]

THE CURSE OF CONTINENTALISM

If China's quest for sea power was always constrained by its continental security imperatives,[7] the situation was no different in India. To be sure, India has had a long maritime tradition in different parts of its coastline from Gujarat in the west to Kalinga in the east. Peninsular India's maritime contacts through the precolonial ages with the Mediterranean, Africa, the Gulf, Southeast Asia, and the Pacific have been recorded by modern scholarship.[8] Yet it would be right to say that India's security paradigm was defined in most part by its northwest frontiers. Just as China built a great wall to stop the invaders from the north and west, India's major empires had to devote much of their defense planning to cope with security threats from the northwestern frontier. Ever since Alexander the Great showed up at India's northwestern gates in fourth century BC and up until the Europeans arrived by sea at the end of the fifteenth century, the region between the Indus and the Hindu Kush has remained the main corridor of invasion into the subcontinent. At the same time, the trans-Indus territories tended to be volatile and were not easily brought under the control of the centralizing states in the heartland of the Gangetic Plain. The Moguls, who came from Central Asia and built a base in Afghanistan before taking charge of India, had to constantly ward off interlopers from the northwest as well as put down the rebellious tribesmen between the Indus and the Hindu Kush.

Although the Moguls did have widespread maritime contacts, sea power was not their priority and their dynasty was ultimately overwhelmed by the European colonizers who came from the sea. The roots of the Mogul state's indifference to maritime power is traced by historians Kulke and Rothermund to the principal source of its finances—land revenue.[9] Unlike many other states with a maritime orientation, taxing external trade was not of great attraction for the empires in New Delhi.

This takes us to a related point that historian John Perry makes about maritime orientation. "Coastal states, even islands, are not necessarily oriented toward seagoing endeavors. They may be landbound. This is a matter not of location but of choice. Landbound societies are indifferent to the ocean; seagoing societies embrace it. . . . Those societies on the sea that transcend the landbound and become seagoing do so as a result of a complex series of cultural decisions and attitudes."[10] In India, the religious prohibition on overseas travel by upper-caste Hindus through the medieval ages must have had a powerful impact on the Indian society's becoming one of landlubbers. The historian Jadunath Sarkar points to a more fundamental cultural reason—the defeat and absorption of Buddhism into Hinduism and the consequent dissipation of external contact. "The intimate contact between India and the outer Asiatic world which had been established in the early Buddhist age was lost when the new Hindu society was reorganized and set in rigidity like a concrete structure about the eighth century AD, with the result that India again became self-centered and isolated from the moving world beyond her natural barriers."[11] The British, who came to India from the sea, became obsessed, eventually, with securing the land frontiers of India in the northwestern subcontinent. That the British were largely modeling their own empire on the Mogul concept and the continuity between the two empires in organization and management is well known.[12] Although the British in many ways brought unprecedented internal coherence to India and clearly articulated its geopolitical concerns in a manner that few earlier regimes had done, they, too, were tied down by continentalism.

In the first half of the twentieth century, the nationalist leaders in China and India bemoaned the neglect of the sea by the old regimes in Beijing and New Delhi and highlighted the fact that they were occupied and colonized from the sea by the Europeans. Yet when they took charge of their new nations, neither the Chinese and nor the Indian leadership could apply decisive corrective action. In China during the civil war, "naval capabilities had no role in determining the decisive victory of the Communist Party in 1949."[13] China did face maritime threats from the U.S. Navy in the 1950s, and in response Beijing developed a defensive maritime capability. The Maoist rhetoric on people's war, which led to a reduced interest in the navy, which in its essence is a technology-oriented force, and the territorial conflicts with India and Russia tended to reinforce the continental dimension of China's national security strategy.[14] Territorial defense vis-à-vis its neighbors was only one element of the national security challenge that Mao's China had to confront. It also had to devote much energy to putting down internal revolts and consolidating its sovereignty over one of the largest territorial expanses that Beijing had ever claimed. This emphasis on China's territoriality inevitably reduced the salience of sea power in the early decades of the People's Republic.

India's own dilemma was similar. Despite the exhortations on sea power by Panikkar and others, India was compelled to secure its new land borders after the great partition of the subcontinent that created Pakistan. Worse still, India found itself facing Communist China on its borders with Tibet. India's series of wars with Pakistan (1948–1949, 1965, and 1971) and a humiliating military confrontation with China (1962) pushed India's strategic vision to the farthest distance possible from oceans—to its inner Asian frontiers in the great Himalayas.[15] India, too, had internal conflicts of its own, especially in the northeast, in Jammu and Kashmir, and in the south. The fears of disintegration were acute in postindependence India. So were the challenges of overcoming the ravages of partition, the integration of the princely states, the multitude of political and administrative structures inherited from the British, and the clarification of its far-flung but undefined territorial boundaries.[16] As in China, the navy in India was not the priority for the political leadership. As the current Indian naval leadership argues, "Despite the permanence of 'territorial defence' in the national mindset, the Indian navy refused to lose hope and believed that a country as large and diverse as India would one day realize that it has substantial maritime interests."[17]

The many similar concerns in China and India that reduced the urgency of making the long-term commitment to building a credible naval capability were reinforced by their respective national economic strategies. From the mid-1950s, both began to disconnect themselves from the global economy, China in the name of communism and India in the name of socialism. Although the two countries had significant differences in their economic strategies, both began to turn inward, emphasizing political autarchy and economic self-reliance. As a result, China and India down-played the importance of engaging the global economy, minimized the necessity of imports, and rejected the logic of export-led economic growth that others in Asia were about to successfully embark upon. A deliberate de-globalization and a de-emphasis on trade meant there was little scope for a maritime vision. It was only when China and India were less obsessed with territorial defense and embarked on a globalization policy that they would rediscover an expansive approach to maritime strategy.

Deng Xiaoping's reintegration of China into the world economy, his emphasis on good relations with the major powers, and the pursuit of a peaceful environment created the basis from the early 1980s for a reduc-tion of the tensions on its borders. As China began to resolve its disputes on land borders and improved the internal security conditions, it had greater room for a productive consideration of the maritime imperatives. Reinforcing the move away from territorial defense was the new empha-sis on economic globalization. The dramatic and sustained high growth rates since the early 1980s brought into play one of the key elements of maritime power-growing seaborne trade. The situation was similar in In-dia after the launch of its economic reforms in 1991. Although territorial troubles and internal security difficulties have persisted in recent decades, India's own naval expansion coincided with an outward-looking strategy from the mid-1980s, launched tentatively by the young prime minister Rajiv Gandhi. India's more purposeful globalization from the early 1990s generated high growth rates and a sustainable basis for a solid maritime strategy. In a matter of two decades, the landlubbers in Beijing and New Delhi would become enthusiasts for expansive national maritime power.

GLOBALIZATION AND SEA POWER

Many Western observers see heavy influence of Alfred Thayer Mahan, the American evangelist of sea power,[18] on the current ambitious plans of

Beijing and New Delhi to build powerful navies. Mahan "is now hugely admired in Asia's two most populous powers. For China's strategic planners, securing sea lanes against hostile powers has become perhaps the chief preoccupation. For India's, it is the growth of China's presence in its backyard, in and around the Indian Ocean. In both countries Mahan is pressed into service in one planning paper after the next."[19] Some scholars, too, have gone to great length to suggest that modern Chinese and Indian naval leadership has turned to Mahan to justify naval modernization.[20] Mahan's influence on the navalists in Beijing and New Delhi could easily be overstated. The relevance of Mahan on Chinese and Indian thinking is less about his doctrine on decisive naval battles on high seas and more about the relationship between a rising power with global interests and its maritime strategy.

Mahan's exhortations to the Americans to look outward and turn to the seas came at the end of a prolonged territorial expansion of the United States in the nineteenth century. His big ideas on the importance of seaborne commerce and the control of it through naval power emerged as the United States became the largest industrial nation in the world but, remarkably, did not have either a global or maritime orientation. Mahan was also urging the United States to shed its isolationism of the nineteenth century and the traditional reluctance to get involved in the power politics of the old world. As America's economic sinews grew rapidly in the nineteenth century, Mahan was peering at a larger global role for the United States and saw no reason for America to limit itself to a regional role in the Western Hemisphere. Put simply, Mahan's grand strategic formulations on sea power were very much part of an inevitable reconstruction of the worldview of a rapidly rising power. Mahan's emphasis on relating America's expansion of its internal industrial capabilities with the vision of a global role fits in quite naturally with the economic transformation that is taking place today in China and India. The changed internal economic orientation of China and India and their rapid globalization since the end of the twentieth century must be seen as the principal source of the new navalism in Beijing and New Delhi. As a Chinese writer put it, "When a nation embarks upon a process of shifting from an 'inward-leaning economy' to an 'outward-leaning economy,' the arena of national security concerns begins to move to the oceans. Consequently, people start paying attention to sea power. This is a phenomenon of history that occurs so frequently that it has almost become a rule rather than an exception. Therefore, it is inevitable that such a shift is taking place in today's China."[21]

The globalization of the Chinese and Indian economies in the last quarter of the twentieth century has resulted in a dramatic expansion of their external trade. Once they ended their deliberately chosen economic isolation, China in 1978 and India in 1991, the weight and scope of their integration with the world economy increased rapidly. From deliberately discouraging foreign trade and encouraging import substitution, China and India have made exports a key element of their growth strategy and eased the many restrictions on imports. As a consequence, trade growth in both countries has been explosive. China's two-way trade in merchandise soared from $115 billion in 1990 to $2.9 trillion in 2010. In the same period, India's merchandise trade leapt from $44 billion to nearly $550 billion. More important than the absolute figures of trade is the critical role that external commerce has acquired in the two countries. In 1990 merchandise trade was about 32 per cent of China's GDP and 13 per cent of India's. That figure for China peaked in 2007 at 62 per cent. In India it topped 42 per cent in 2008.[22] The numbers have come down in the aftermath of the global financial crisis, but the external dependence of the Chinese and Indian economies is now profound. Much of world trade today, as in the age of Mahan, continues to be carried by sea. The seaborne trade in China and India now hovers above the range of 90 percent of total trade in both countries. Given the size of their economies, their rapid pace of growth, and the expanding international component of their economic activity, protecting seaborne trade has become an important justification for China's and India's investments in naval modernization. New Delhi, for example, states that "India's economic resurgence is directly linked to her overseas trade and energy needs, most of which are transported by sea." India's *Maritime Military Strategy* draws a clear linkage between "our economic prosperity and our naval capability, which will protect the nation's vast and varied maritime interests."[23] In China, too, the political leadership has become acutely aware of the profound relationship between national economic development in the era of globalization and sea power, and it has constantly affirmed the determination to build a strong and modern navy.[24] Before globalization became a major imperative for naval modernization of the Chinese and Indian navies, other factors were at play. The U.S. decision to send aircraft carriers into the Taiwan Strait to counter Beijing's intimidation of Taiwan in 1996 might have acted as a major political spur to the Chinese leadership in developing the capabilities to limit future American interventions and consider a significant reorientation of its maritime strategy.[25] Wide-ranging maritime territorial disputes with its Asian neighbors were another factor encouraging the modernization of the Chinese navy. While India has less intensive maritime territorial disputes, its need to protect a large, exclusive economic zone and its far-flung island territories has been an important motivation behind New Delhi's naval expansion. The American dispatch of the aircraft carrier USS *Enterprise* during India's war with Pakistan in 1971 is often cited in New Delhi as a landmark event that underlined India's need for a powerful navy.[26]

If the relationship between seaborne commerce and naval power has been a consistent pattern in the history of international relations, China and India today face a very special imperative that has given an extraordinary edge to their thinking on maritime security. Put simply, this imperative can be termed "resource security." It involves the massive dependence of China and India on imported resources to feed domestic economic growth and national well-being. A vast body of literature dissecting every aspect of energy security in China and India has come out in recent years and examines not only the domestic but also external aspects of the rapid expansion of energy consumption in China and India. Our interest here is limited to the question of how the two Asian giants can gain access to energy and mineral resources at reasonable prices and ensure their transportation to the consumption centers at home. Since 1993, China has become an importer of hydrocarbons. India has been less fortunate than China in the natural endowment of petroleum resources and has always been an importer of oil. This problem is no longer limited to energy resources but applies to the full range of mineral resources. As the levels of prosperity increase in China and India, food imports, too, will be on top of the list of critical imports. Resource security, then, will be the greatest challenge confronting China and India as they continue to develop at a rapid pace. What we have, then, are a few simple propositions. Even at relatively modest levels of per capita incomes, China and India would put substantial pressure on the availability and price of natural resources around the world. The two Asian giants will be unable to sustain reasonable growth rates and maintain domestic tranquility without a significant import of natural resources from outside their borders.[27]

The massive dependence on imported natural resources is increasingly seen as a major strategic vulnerability in both China and India, and addressing it has become a major national security priority in Beijing and New Delhi. Corporations in both countries have received considerable support from their governments in exploring and acquiring resource assets around the world. Chinese and Indian equity investments in oil and mineral resources have increased rapidly since the late 1990s.[28] Acquiring assets abroad is only one part of the challenge of resource security. China and India are increasingly focused on ensuring the reliable transportation of these assets to the home markets. The sense of vulnerability to potential disruptions in the supply of natural resources has become an important strategic question. This in turn has led to a new emphasis on naval power to protect the sea lines of communication. The study of how China and India view the intersection of resource security and naval power has emerged as an important field of inquiry in recent years.[29]

That the active participation of hundreds of millions of new consumers from China and India in the international market would lead to extraordinary pressures on the supply of natural resources and might even lead to conflicts has not been a difficult proposition to grasp.[30] This in turn has led to China and India chasing each other's tail in the quest for control of hydrocarbons and other mineral resources in every corner of the world. Many in the West and Japan tend to see Chinese and Indian obsession with oil and mineral assets around the world as ill-conceived. They argue that Beijing and New Delhi may be better positioned to use market mechanisms for ensuring their access to natural resources rather than gaining direct control over them. These arguments, however, do not appreciate the profound political concerns in Beijing and New Delhi about their new dependence on external natural resources for sustaining internal economic growth. These concerns are likely to deepen in the next two decades, given one simple reality: The prosperity of two billion people is tied to reliable access and supply of energy and mineral resources from abroad. Neither the Chinese state nor the Indian one can afford to get off the high-growth path and risk severe internal political turbulence. To the Western critics who recommend market-based solutions to resource security, Beijing and New Delhi would point to "the non-market special relationship" between Washington and the House of Saud. Given the scale of the stakes involved in resource security, Beijing and New Delhi will not only find it hard to abide by the market mechanism but also to rely on U.S. power to manage their external vulnerabilities. At the same time, China and India may find it increasingly hard to avoid a growing competition between themselves in their search for resource security.[31]

The Chinese and Indian emphasis on non-market mechanisms for ensuring resource security would inevitably mean fundamental changes in many aspects of their foreign policy. As their dependence on external resources becomes "vital" and "strategic," it would be entirely reasonable to assess that the external orientation of China and India in the next two decades would discard much of the traditional "third worldism" and reflect more and more great-power approaches to international affairs. The need for resources from other countries is likely to push them toward cultivating special relationships with the regimes that control the resources in different parts of the developing world through a variety of well-known instruments—economic assistance and arms transfers on liberal terms, the training of security forces and the offer of political protection to governments, and the threat of regime change. While some have seen the rising profile of China and India in Africa as an opportunity to accelerate the development of the vast continent, others have begun to attack the policies of Beijing and New Delhi as the early signs of their inevitable role as neo-imperialist powers.[32] China's and India's political ties with various regimes considered "rogue" in the West have come in for widespread criticism. What is important to note, however, is not the merit of this critique but the likely contours of Chinese and Indian foreign policy in the coming decades.

Both Beijing and New Delhi are acutely concerned about the vulnerability of energy and mineral resource supplies. They are concerned that the policies of other powers could put pressure on their supplies. With its dependence on the Indian Ocean sea lanes increasing, Beijing has begun to agonize over what is now called the "Malacca Dilemma."[33] Given the fact that most of China's seaborne trade with the Indian Ocean littoral and Europe passes through the Strait of Malacca, China has a natural interest in ensuring there are no threats to its energy and resource lifeline. As argued by a Chinese analyst, "If one day, another nation(s) finds an excuse to embargo China, what can China do? Any substantial blockage of its foreign trade-dependent economy and/or its energy supply could gravely imperil China." He adds the larger argument that "the history of capitalism and its spread globally have shown that it is often accompanied by cruel competition between nation-states. Those countries that lose out are not necessarily economically or technologically underdeveloped or those with a low level of culture. Rather, they are most often those nations who forgo the need to apply their national strength to national defense and therefore do not possess sufficient strategic capability."[34] Most Indian security analysts are likely to agree with Zhang's proposition on the centrality of national means for securing national interests. They have added the notion of a "Hormuz Dilemma" that affects the energy security of both New Delhi and Beijing in the Persian Gulf.[35]

The Indian establishment would have little quarrel with Zhang's other propositions: the importance of offshore defense in protecting global interests of a rising power. Zhang argues that "independent of wealth, a guarantee of access to global trade and resources necessarily requires sufficient power to defend one's interest in the trade and resource transportation sea routes. Economic globalization entails globalization of the military means for self-defense, because the national defense must go where a nation's economic interests lie." Zhang goes on to say, "China's national security was largely confined to border security because it did not have many global interests. Rather, China's core concern was one of survival. . . . Today, China's core national security not only narrowly centers on survival but includes a broader development goal which extends beyond the nation's territory."[36] Indian leaders, too, have begun a more comprehensive definition of security interests beyond territorial defense. As Prime Minister Manmohan Singh argued in 2006, "India's transformation over the last few years has also meant that our stakes in the world and our interdependence with the world [have] increased exponentially. Our lines of communication which need to be protected are today not just the maritime links that carry our foreign trade and vital imports, but include our other forms of connectivity with the world."[37] This broader definition of national security interests by China and India takes us to the question of forward naval presence so critical to secure their sea lines of communication.

FORWARD PRESENCE

Forward military presence and foreign military bases have been anathema to the modern Chinese and Indian worldview. For Mahan, the relationship between the home country and its commerce with the colonies in a world of expanding industrial production and global trade was critical. Protecting one's own lines of communication and developing the capacity to disrupt those of the adversaries was an integral element of Mahan's conception of sea power. It was logical for Mahan then to underline the significance of acquiring bases all along the sea lines of communication between the two entities. The worldview of the Chinese and Indian leaders as they led their nations for a renewed engagement with the world could not have been more different from that of Mahan. Emerging from alien domination, the leaders of the two countries saw foreign bases as the very symbols of imperialism and neocolonialism. Given their seemingly absolute commitment to anti-imperialism and the empathy with the anti-colonial struggles of their fellow developing countries, Beijing and New Delhi naturally opposed the forward military presence of great powers, which expanded significantly at the intensification and globalization of Soviet–American rivalry during the Cold War.[38] As the largest developing nations, China and India became the most vocal opponents of foreign bases as a matter of high ideological principle as well as direct national security concerns about great-power meddling in their neighborhood.

New Delhi, which founded the Non-Aligned Movement, also helped develop the criteria for its membership. These included non-participation in military alliances and no hosting of foreign bases.[39] Beijing has long called for the withdrawal of foreign military forces from Asia. India has supported similar demands against the so-called "extra-regional" powers in the Indian Ocean. As they campaigned against foreign military presence in Asia and the Indian Ocean, Beijing and New Delhi declared that they had no intention of seeking bases on the territories of other nations. These principles, in some sense, seemed absolutely immutable in the Chinese and Indian worldviews. Yet before the opposition to foreign military presence congealed into a political axiom, the early maritime thinkers of modern India had no problem articulating the importance of bases as an integral part of the nation's long-term naval strategy.[40] But the early talk of forward bases for the Indian navy was entirely academic, as the conditions for outward-looking maritime policy were nonexistent. China, too, maintained the rhetoric against the U.S. military bases in Asia but largely chose to live with it once its primary threat perceptions began to focus on the Soviet Union.

The context, however, has changed fundamentally in the early years of the twenty-first century. As they underline the importance of maritime commerce, pursue resource security, seek to protect their nation's economic lifelines at sea, and recognize their larger global political responsibilities, both China and India are signaling the political will to deploy their navies far from the national shores.[41] This in turn is bound to result in a more intensive consideration of forward military presence and military bases abroad. Although Beijing denies it has any intentions of acquiring foreign bases, its alleged interest in acquiring various military facilities in Burma has been an interesting field of academic inquiry.[42] If the Chinese interest in a forward presence in Burma was seen as somewhat unusual, Beijing's attempts to acquire naval facilities across the Indian Ocean have become a more widely circulated thesis in recent years. Many analysts indeed question the notion of China's quest for a "string of pearls" in the Indian Ocean, and it may be somewhat premature to describe China's construction of maritime infrastructural facilities in South Asia and elsewhere as motivated by military considerations.[43] We will take up a more comprehensive review of the issues relating to China's interest in bases and naval facilities in the Indian Ocean in chapter 7. For now it is enough to note the emerging debate on the prospects of a Chinese forward military presence. The same holds true for India. All indications are that India, too, might be exploring opportunities for acquiring facilities that would boost its ability to operate far from its national shores.[44]

Whether or not China and India will eventually acquire military bases, it is quite obvious that the new outward maritime orientation is a structural shift in their worldviews. Some in Beijing see a "symbiosis" between becoming a great power and developing a strong naval capability.[45] The Indian strategic community also has begun to recognize a similar maritime imperative. New Delhi would agree with Ni's thesis that "while our nation's economic structure is completing the epic shift from an inward-leaning to an outward-leaning one, the choice of a sea power strategy has become an urgent task"[46] Once this logic is accepted, it will not be difficult to understand the current high priority in China and India on imports of natural resources, the focus on a strategy to acquire natural resources, the protection of their nations' economic lifelines on the sea, and the prospective search for a forward military presence. As China and India rise in the international system, their strategic behavior might look a lot like that of traditional great powers. Beijing and New Delhi have already begun to define their national interests in an expansive way and to develop military capabilities to pursue them around the world. As a consequence, the navies of China and India are being transformed—from forces conceived for coastal defense and denying their neighboring waters to hostile powers to instruments that can project force far beyond their shores. That large theme can only be treated in detail, separately and in its own right, in the next chapter.

new range of foreign policy instruments to ensure resource security. It is not difficult to speculate on where the new approach might be headed. "In addition to economic aid, Beijing could provide assistance in training and equipping the militaries and security forces of friendly governments, perhaps offering to share China's expertise in monitoring modern means of telecommunication, breaking up incipient protest movements, and controlling demonstrations. The Chinese intelligence services may become involved in mounting covert operations to defend (or overthrow) local governments, as well as gathering information."[5] Conventional thinking in Beijing might reject any intention to adopt these instruments. But these stratagems, after all, have been used by all other great powers, including the liberal ones like the United States. Even more important is the fact that as China becomes a large economy and its interests become global, it will be compelled to find ways to defend these interests. And this in turn is bound to include the threat and use of force around the world. A review of the recent Chinese debate on use of force abroad argues that "Chinese leaders accept that their country's expanding global interests will eventually come into conflict with those of other nations, and that the PLA [People's Liberation Army] must be prepared to defend these expanding national interests. To accomplish this objective, they believe that China's military force must be commensurate with its rising international status, and the PLA's mission will naturally follow China's interests, wherever they lead."[6] If China's far-flung national security interests must be defended, it was inevitable that Beijing would strengthen the most appropriate instrument for such a strategy, the navy. It is now formally acknowledged by Beijing that its naval forces must have the ability to operate far from its shores. As the government's white paper on defense declared in early 2009, "Since the beginning of the new century . . . the Navy has been striving to improve in an all-round way its capabilities of integrated offshore operations, strategic deterrence and strategic counterattacks, and to gradually develop its capabilities of conducting cooperation in distant waters."[7]

If the Chinese navy is coming out of the closet, so is its Indian counterpart. The style of debate, the manner of official articulation of change in policy, and the historical and institutional context are clearly different in Beijing and New Delhi. But the logic and direction of the two national debates on use of force abroad and the importance of naval forces in achieving the nation's interests far from one's own borders have been very similar. Unlike China, India has been an active participant of international peacekeeping operations under UN auspices from the 1950s. As an exponent of nonalignment, India was cautious on international use of force, especially after the controversies surrounding the UN intervention in the Korean Peninsula. After that it chose to join only those international coalition operations that were explicitly authorized by the UN Security Council. This helped prevent the Indian military forays from supporting either of the superpowers in the Cold War.[8] India, before partitioning in 1947, had a more consequential tradition of sending expeditionary troops all along the Indian Ocean littoral as part of the British assertion of its imperial authority.[9] India also contributed more than a million soldiers to the British participation in each of the world wars.[10] If the nationalist movement opposed the use of Indian troops on imperial missions, independent India limited their involvement to UN-mandated operations. After the turn of the century, as UN operations evolved into a more complex form that often looked beyond peacekeeping toward peace building and peace enforcement, India's own policy had to confront new challenges. One set of these challenges was limited to international peacekeeping under the United Nations. Another related to participation in coalition operations outside the UN framework.

In 2003, India gave careful consideration to the U.S. request to join the stabilization operations in Iraq but ultimately decided not to participate amid growing domestic political anxieties about that mission. In late 2004, in an important shift, India ordered its navy to coordinate its tsunami relief operations in the Indian Ocean with those of the United States, Japan, and Australia.[11] In June 2005, India and the United States signed a defense framework that opened the door for military cooperation outside the UN framework.[12] The idea that India must deploy its forces abroad in pursuit of national security and foreign policy objectives remains a controversial one, albeit one that is being raised more openly than in the past. But the political resistance, too, is real. As India's power increases, it will inevitably confront the questions of when and where to use force.[13] Although the public debate remains muted, the Indian navy has been quite explicit that the new missions that confront it include operations far beyond India's borders. Like its Chinese counterpart, the Indian navy has no problem seeing the link between maritime policy, naval deployments, and foreign policy objectives. The Indian navy's identification of its objectives could not have been put more clearly:

> The Maritime Military Strategy recognizes that the major task of [the] Indian Navy during the 21st century will be to use warships to support national foreign policy. During the long years of peace, we need to project power and show [a] presence; catalyze partnerships through our maritime capability; build trust and create interoperability through joint/combined operations and international maritime assistance. The strategy also highlights the Indian Navy's role in helping to maintain peace and tranquillity in the Indian Ocean Region and in meeting the expectations of our friends when needed.[14]

Clearly, the navies of China and India are raring to go out in defense of larger national interests, and the political leadership seems ready to support them. But between the new ambition and current reality is a shadow that raises a number of questions. What kind of naval force structure would China and India need to meet their expansive maritime ambitions? Do Beijing and New Delhi have the human and institutional resources to develop and sustain a forward naval presence? Are their political elites ready for a larger national security role beyond their borders? Although no clear-cut answers to these questions exist in either Beijing or New Delhi, leaders in both countries are well down the road of naval modernization and developing the capabilities for projecting force beyond their borders.

NAVAL MODERNIZATION

The military modernization efforts of China and India over the past two decades have enjoyed significant political and financial support and are beginning to move their armed forces into the top ranks of the global military hierarchy. On the naval front, the modernization efforts have covered the full spectrum from platforms to weapons systems and from infrastructure to the software that runs the two fighting forces. In this section we will review very briefly the broad elements of the modernization effort.[15] The traditional assumption has been that the principal motive for Chinese naval modernization is the creation of credible military options in relation to the unification of Taiwan. But a range of other ambitions is also beginning to define the process. These ambitions include securing China's many disputed maritime territorial claims all along its eastern seaboard, legitimizing its interpretation of international law on the freedom of navigation, protecting China's sea lines of communication to the Indian Ocean on which the nation's economy depends, underwriting China's emerging role as a great power, and promoting Beijing's influence in the Indo-Pacific and beyond.[16] Thanks to the resources available to military modernization in a rapidly growing economy and the political leadership's recognition of the importance of maritime power, budgetary support for upgrading naval capabilities in China has been significant.

The most impressive element of the unfolding naval transformation in China is the rapid expansion of the submarine fleet. China hopes that its emerging, powerful fleet of submarines will simultaneously provide a deterrent that is cost-effective and be able to take on the far more powerful surface fleets of the United States and Japan. Given the centrality of Beijing's mission to integrate Taiwan and the need to limit American capacity to intervene in such a conflict, it is not surprising that China has devoted significant energies to building submarines. Since the mid-1990s, China has acquired twelve Russian-made *Kilo* class conventional attack submarines. China is also building its own *Song* and *Yuan* class submarines. Reports indicate that China is interested in incorporating the revolutionary AIP (air-independent propulsion) technology that allows diesel submarines to operate underwater for far longer periods without surfacing. Excluding the twelve Kilos purchased from Russia, the total number of domestically produced conventional submarines placed into service between 1995 and 2007 is 23, a remarkable number. The pace of their construction, quality, and armaments has begun to impress observers, and the expectation is that sooner rather than later, China might have more submarines than the United States, the world's foremost naval power.[17] Although the American submarines are technologically far superior, their declining numbers vis-à-vis the People's Liberation Army Navy (PLAN) are a source of concern for many in the United States and Asia.

While the submarine force is critical in the active defense naval strategy of China, it cannot help secure China's sea lines of communication. Submarines are fundamentally a force for interdiction, not of power projection. To acquire a true blue-water capability, China has emphasized the importance of building capable surface combatants that have the range and endurance to operate at longer distances from China's coastline for extended periods of time. In the past few years, China has bought and built a new array of destroyers and frigates. These include four *Sovremenny* class destroyers purchased from Russia, five new classes of indigenously built destroyers, and four new classes of frigates. These new ships incorporate many advanced design concepts such as stealthy superstructures, vertical-launch air defense systems, long-range anti-ship missiles, phased array radars, and sophisticated search and guidance systems for the weapons. All these improvements have given the ships a respectable air-defense capability that is crucial for operation at long distances from home shores.[18]

China has devoted some substantive attention to amphibious warfare. Of special importance has been the building of large amphibious ships that incorporate many modern Western designs that allow dispatch of troops and support equipment. Although China's current and planned amphibious ships have some value for conducting offensive actions against Taiwan, some analysts believe that China is looking at operating them for a variety of interventionary actions far from its shores. These operations could include anti-piracy, evacuation, humanitarian relief, and naval diplomacy. Key to blue-water operations are supply and replenishment ships that let naval contingents operate for extended periods of time at sea. Determined to overcome one of its traditional weakness, China is now building supply ships, some of which have been deployed in its recent anti-piracy operations off the Somali coast. China is also aware that any blue-water aspirations for its navy must include critical aerospace capabilities, integration of air and space platforms into naval operations, and deployment of credible C4ISR (command, control, communications, computers, intelligence, surveillance, and reconnaissance) capabilities. Despite major imbalances in this area, China has devoted enough resources to achieve comprehensive aerospace capabilities. China has made significant advances in building and deploying micro-satellites, moving toward self-reliance in satellite navigation by launching its own Beidou geostationary satellite system. Meanwhile China's medium- and intermediate-range missile force is one of the most impressive in the world, and Beijing has been producing these missiles at a rate few countries can conceive of. Besides the large production of missiles, China is coming up with innovative uses for them. This includes the modification of its DF-21 missile with its 500 kg warhead to target American aircraft carriers. China is reportedly equipping its missiles with maneuverable reentry vehicles, or MaRVs. If the PLA can integrate these missiles with effective real-time information, the United States might find it hard to cope with the Chinese anti-ship ballistic missiles.[19]

In overall terms, the navy has emerged as the fastest-growing force in the Chinese military. By 2020 the PLAN is expected to have 73 principal combatants; 78 submarines, including 12 nuclear; 80 medium and heavily amphibious lift ships; and 94 guided missile boats. Chinese analysts see the period up to 2020 as one of transition to a blue-water force.[20] Besides the Taiwan contingencies, Beijing is emphasizing the creation of capabilities for sustainable blue-water operations beyond the so-called first island chain. China's maritime geography is defined in terms of island chains running parallel to its coastline. The first island chain runs along the Kuril Islands, Japan, the Ryukyu Islands, Taiwan, the Philippines, and Indonesia. The second island chain runs from a north-south line from the Kurils through Japan, the Bonins, the Marianas, the Carolines, and Indonesia. Together, they encompass maritime areas out to approximately 1,800 nautical miles from China's coast, including most of the East China Sea and East Asian Sea lines of communication, as shown in figure 1. The U.S. Navy has dominated the two island chains since the Second World War. Breaking free from this domination is one of the central objectives of China's blue-water ambitions.

In April 2010, China for the first time conducted naval exercises passing through the first island chain.[21] A flotilla of ten ships from the East Sea Fleet, including two destroyers, three frigates, and two submarines, transited the Miyako Strait between Okinawa's main island and Miyako Island on its way to the Pacific Ocean. As the Chinese navy stepped up its activity all across the waters of the first island chain and emerged into the open oceans, there was inevitable concern in the region and the United States.[22] But a rising China and its increasingly powerful navy were not going to remain subdued in the waters along the country's long coastline forever.

In contrast to China, whose maritime access is constrained, India enjoys free access to the open seas. Placed at the very heart of the Indian Ocean, India is in the happy geographic situation of sitting on top of the sea lines

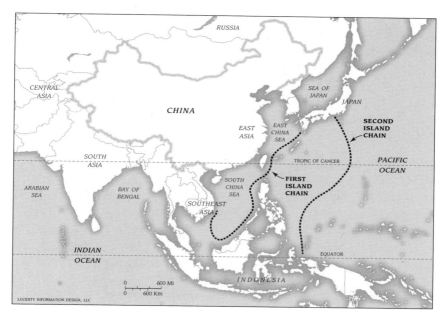

Figure 1. China's Pacific Island Chains

of communication in the ocean and with easy access to all the choke points that control entry into it, as shown in figure 2. As in the western Pacific, it is the U.S. Navy that dominates the Indian Ocean today.

India, however, is some distance away from reinforcing its natural geographic advantage through the construction of a powerful naval force. Compared with China's rapid naval modernization, India's effort is far less impressive. But there is no question, in absolute terms, that India is following an ambitious strategy of its own naval modernization with a view to project power. The absence of large maritime threats meant that India could focus on the development of a balanced navy with blue-water capabilities. Since the late 1990s, India has embarked on a program aimed at making its navy a consequential force in the Indian Ocean region.[23] Critical to this has been the political leadership's recognition of the importance of maritime power. Treated as a "Cinderella service" for a long time, the navy could no longer be ignored as India came out of the 1990s. In the first decades of independence, the share of the Indian navy in the defense budget varied from 5 to 10 percent. During the years of military expansion (1984–1989) under Rajiv Ghandi, it rose to around 12 percent. An

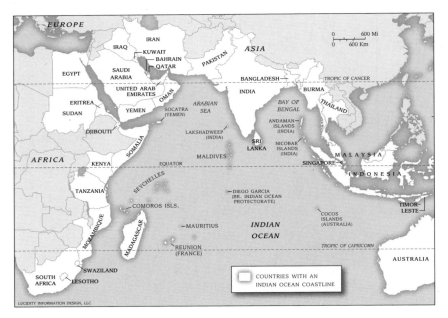

Figure 2. India and the Indian Ocean Area

ambitious twenty-five-year naval modernization plan was announced in 1990, but the program ran out of steam pretty quickly amid the resource crisis at home and the collapse of the Soviet Union abroad.[24] The Kargil War of 1999, however, changed the context in which India's naval modernization effort had languished. The war forced the government to end the long-standing neglect of defense spending in the period of belt-tightening that was inevitable when India had begun the structural adjustment of its economy and initiated reforms. Even without the war, the nationalist Bharatiya Janata Party, or BJP, which was elected to power in 1998, had promised a strong national security program. Its two leading strategic thinkers, Foreign Minister Jaswant Singh and National Security Adviser Brajesh Mishra, as well as Defense Minister George Fernandes were strong supporters of expanding India's maritime profile and fully backed modernization of the navy. As India's economic reforms began to pay off at the turn of the millennium and the nation embarked on high growth rates, more money was available for defense modernization in general. In the context of general expansion of the defense budget, allocations to the navy also went up, from 14 percent during 1999–2000 to 18.5 percent in 2008–2009.

Both in relative and absolute terms, then, the navy was now the beneficiary of budget increases. Visionary leadership of the navy made full use of the new opportunities to lay down ambitious goals that were outlined in the Maritime Doctrine of 2004 and the Maritime Strategy of 2007. The navy also spent a relatively larger portion of its budget on capital expenditures.

The navy's new ambitions were reflected in the force structure plans announced in the late 2000s that called for increasing the fleet to around 160 ships by 2022. This number would include three aircraft carriers and 60 major combatants; together with 400 aircraft, that puts India's navy in the league of the world's five largest. In the interim, the number of ships would actually shrink, thanks to the much-delayed modernization efforts. But there is no denying the rapid improvement in the quality and effectiveness of the Indian navy that is beginning to present itself. In comparison to the PLA navy, Indian submarine forces are much smaller—estimated at only 14 in 2008. Nevertheless, India has embarked on an upgrade and modification of its current *Kilo* class submarines of Russian origin (*Sindhughosh* class) and the Type 209 German submarines (*Shishumar* class). India has begun the much-delayed construction of six French *Scorpene* submarines, the first of which may be commissioned in 2012. India is also considering the construction of a new class of advanced diesel submarines in collaboration with a foreign partner.[25]

As in China, India's surface fleet is undergoing a rapid transformation. In building a new generation of destroyers and frigates, India is beginning to move away from the traditional dependence on Russian-supplied ships to vessels jointly designed with Russia and built in India. The older generation *Rajput* (Kashin) and *Delhi* class destroyers are being replaced by more powerful *Kolkata* class destroyers that are being built in the Mazagon Docks. India also plans to buy and build new-generation frigates. To be called *Shivalik* class, these frigates are expected to bring a new punch to the navy. From the larger perspective, the modernization of the surface fleet involves four elements. As bigger ships, their endurance and reach make them suitable for blue-water missions. A second important element is the incorporation of stealth features into their design and construction. Third, all of them will have substantive computer and communication power that lets them become part of network-centric operations. Finally, most of these vessels are also being fitted with longer-range and more lethal cruise missiles of their own, including the supersonic *BrahMos*. These features, analysts argue, will lend the surface combatants to a strong interventionary role around the Indo-Pacific littoral.[26] Meanwhile, India is also focused on acquiring ships capable of amphibious operations. In early 2007, India acquired the former USS *Trenton* from the United States. It belongs to the *Austin* class landing platform dock ships that are meant to move troops and project force. India continues to purchase the smaller *Shardul* and *Magar* class ships meant for amphibious operations. It also has three fleet replenishment tankers. India is also embedding small units of the army with the navy, which could act as a kind of marine expeditionary force. Furthermore, the Indian navy is placing considerable emphasis on expanding its naval aviation as well as C4ISR capabilities. In terms of industrial production, Indian shipyards are humming with overflowing orders, and the new private-sector shipyard has deepened and expanded the industrial capabilities of India's shipbuilding sector. The government is under some pressure to devise a more effective policy for promoting private-sector participation in the production of naval equipment.

AIRCRAFT CARRIERS

Although the Chinese and Indian naval modernization efforts have a different tone and structure, their broad direction is similar—the creation of a large, balanced, and powerful navy that can operate far from the national shores. At the heart of such capability are the aircraft carriers, whose importance in Chinese and Indian naval modernization must be noted separately. India was the first Asian country to acquire aircraft carriers after the Second World War in a decision that went back to the late 1950s. India has operated two British-origin carriers, INS *Vikrant* (formerly HMS *Hercules*) and INS *Viraat* (HMS *Hermes*), since the 1960s. Given the larger problems with India's national security strategy and the navy's limited role in it, the Indian aircraft carriers could not be exploited to their full potential. Although the carriers played a modest role in the 1971 war and in the military confrontations with Pakistan in 1999 and during 2001–2002, there has been no shortage of public and professional questioning of the utility of investing in aircraft carriers.[27] It is only now, as part of a larger outward-looking maritime strategy that emphasizes blue-water missions, that the Indian carriers have become significant. Having operated aircraft carriers, however, is a tremendous advantage for India in relation to other Asian powers, in that such experience is so hard to come by. Unfortunately, though, for India the extraordinary delays in the acquisition of the third aircraft carrier from Russia (the *Gorshkov*) have meant that the Indian navy has had to contend with the frequent absence of a flattop from its operations. In a rare outburst, Admiral Sureesh Mehta, the Indian chief of naval staff, publicly questioned at the end of 2007 the commitment of the Russians to deliver the ship.[28] The admiral's charges were echoed in a 2009 report by India's auditor general.[29] India's focus, nevertheless, has been on completing the *Gorshkov* acquisition by resolving the outstanding issues with Moscow.

Central to India's fleet modernization plan is the ambition to have three aircraft carrier groups by 2020, with two carriers fully operational at any given time. The realization of this objective depends on the early commissioning of the *Gorshkov*, renamed *Vikramaditya*, and steady progress on the indigenous construction of two aircraft carriers. In early 2009 the keel was laid at the Cochin Shipyard for the construction of the first of the indigenous aircraft carriers. Originally conceived as an air-defense ship, the indigenous carrier is designed to displace around 37,000 tons and may not be ready to join the fleet before 2015. The third carrier design is considered more ambitious and aims to displace 64,000 tons, incorporate many advanced technologies, and enter service after 2017. During 2007–2008, there was considerable speculation that as part of its expanding defense relationship with India, the United States was offering the carrier USS *Kitty Hawk* after it is retired from the Seventh Fleet. While the Indian leadership might not be averse to acquiring supercarriers of the American kind, New Delhi is fully aware of the political and bureaucratic obstacles in both countries to such a transfer. The cost of acquiring an 80-aircraft air wing for an American carrier deck would have consumed much of the Indian navy's procurement budget for several years. In any case, during a visit to India in February 2008, the U.S. defense secretary at the time, Robert Gates, explicitly denied the speculation about the possible sale of the *Kitty Hawk* to India.[30] For the foreseeable future, the Indian navy will have its hands full in absorbing the *Gorshkov* and building the two indigenous carriers. There is no doubt that the three carriers would mark a huge improvement over India's current carrier capability and would give the Indian navy true blue-water potential.[31] The *Vikramaditya*, for example, has a range of nearly 14,000 nautical miles in comparison to the 5,000 nm range of the INS *Viraat*. Its complement of 16 MiG-29K aircraft, which have a range of 1,430 miles, offers a reach that the Indian navy did not have in the past. The indigenous aircraft carrier, too, has a range larger than that of *Viraat* at about 7,500 nm. It is also expected to carry 12 MiG-29s and have a STOBAR (short takeoff, barrier-arrested recovery) design. The third aircraft carrier will be larger than the indigenous aircraft carrier (37,000 tons) and will displace about 64,000 tons. The navy hopes to equip it with steam catapults, a technology currently found only in the U.S. and French navies.[32]

While India hopes to induct three aircraft carriers over the next decade, China is gearing up to introduce its first, which had its initial sea trial in August 2011. China's aircraft carrier decision, after years of debate among Chinese defense experts, veered toward closure in the middle of the 2000s.[33] There were some indications that China might be aiming at building either four or six aircraft carriers. According to one analyst, "One aircraft carrier may be symbolic, but four or six carriers is a new maritime strategy. In fact, it could presage the reorientation of the PLAN around Carrier Battle Groups (CVBGs), with the carrier at the heart of a constellation of supporting submarines, destroyers, and frigates—an amalgamation of power projection at its foremost. Such CVBGs are among the most impressive instruments of military power, in terms of sustained, far-reaching, and expeditionary offensive force."[34]

Like all other great powers in the past, China sees aircraft carriers both as a symbol of its military power and as a practical tool that can be put to use in the pursuit of national objectives in the realm of foreign and security policy far from its homeland. At the same time, China was careful not to undermine its broader narrative of "peaceful rise" and assurances that China's military modernization does not pose a threat to others. A Chinese general declared at the end of 2008 that "the question is not whether you have an aircraft carrier, but what you do with your aircraft carrier." For good measure, he added that "even if one day we have an aircraft carrier, unlike another country, we will not use it to pursue global deployment or global reach."[35] But nationalist clamor for aircraft carriers is growing at the popular level, and the discussion on aircraft carriers in the Chinese military and strategic community has become more robust.[36] While rejecting Western alarm about China's aircraft carriers, the nationalist newspaper *Global Times* argued that Beijing has the right to build carriers and that its naval power would be stabilizing rather than destabilizing: "The US is in possession of 11 aircraft carriers, and neighboring nations like India and South Korea have launched jumbo projects to build aircraft carriers. . . . China's ambition of building a blue-water navy is to pursue the basic right to develop, rather than maritime hegemony. The Chinese navy equipped with aircraft carriers and other advanced weaponry would be able to better help maintain regional stability and world peace . . . as much as other nations, China has the legitimate right to build up its naval force—including aircraft carriers."[37] While meeting with his counterpart, the Japanese defense minister, Yasukazu Hamada, in March 2009, Chinese General Liang Guanglie stressed that China is the only big nation that does not have aircraft carriers and stated that "China cannot be without aircraft carriers forever."[38] Balancing this assertion of the right to have an aircraft carrier, Admiral Wu Shengli, the navy commander, stated that "China will develop its fleet of aircraft carriers in a harmonious manner. We will prudently decide the policy [we will follow with regard to building aircraft carriers]. I am willing to listen to the views of experts from the navies of other countries and to seek opinions from our country."[39]

Until now, China has focused more relentlessly on assessing and targeting carriers of its main adversary, the United States, than on building its own. A central element of China's current naval modernization has been how to dent the impact of U.S. aircraft carriers in the western Pacific, especially in Taiwan-related contingencies, by targeting them with anti-ship cruise missiles and anti-ship ballistic missiles. Some experts believe that China's "recognition of the increasing vulnerability of carriers, particularly less-sophisticated versions such as China might develop, may thus retard Beijing's indigenous carrier development."[40] Yet, while China has stepped up its effort to limit the free movement of U.S. aircraft carriers in the western Pacific, the momentum behind its own carrier program had become relentless by the turn of the second decade of the twenty-first century. If China's earlier acquisition of older carriers, the HMAS *Melbourne* from Australia and the ex-Soviet carriers *Minsk*, and *Kiev*, was probably informed by the search for design knowledge, its work on the *Varyag*, bought from Ukraine in 1998, now appears to have moved China toward operational capability. *Varyag*, representing the largest and most advanced Soviet carrier design, has been used for pilot and deck-crew training and as a "test platform" for general research and development. China has shown interest in procuring Su-33 carrier-borne fighters from Russia. Since 2006, China and Russia have been in negotiations for the sale of 50 Su-33 Flanker-D fighters at a cost of up to $2.5 billion. While negotiations on the deal appear to have stalled, PLAN should not have a problem finding carrier-borne aircraft. China is reported to be training 50 pilots for carrier operations and has also secured cooperation from Brazil. The *Varyag*, while modestly capable, is likely to become "the centre piece of PLAN diplomacy, humanitarian operations, and disaster relief."[41]

Not everyone was impressed by the sea trials of the starter carrier in 2011.[42] Skeptics suggest that it will take a long time for PLAN to develop the skills of operating an aircraft carrier. They also point out that China's weaknesses in antisubmarine warfare, which is critical for protecting the carrier, have been enduring. They suggest that China's initial carrier operations will be modest rather than ambitious in making the carrier a vehicle for power projection. The building and commissioning of aircraft carriers will certainly underline the reality of China's emergence as a great power. But PLAN lacks the all-round capabilities to utilize the carrier as a vehicle for power projection.[43] Meanwhile, there are reports suggesting advances on the front of indigenous carrier construction. China's first new-construction aircraft carriers are expected to displace between 50,000 and 70,000 tons. (The *Varyag* has an estimated full-load displacement of about 58,500 tons.) A new Chinese carrier with a displacement of 50,000 to 70,000 tons might be able to operate an air wing of 30 or more aircraft, including vertical/short takeoff or landing airplanes and possibly conventional takeoff and landing airplanes.[44]

THE GREAT BASE RACE

No blue-water naval force can be sustained without critical infrastructure at home and far from one's own territory. As noted, Beijing and New Delhi have begun to build more powerful ships that are capable of undertaking blue-water missions. But power projection requires a significant improvement of the internal infrastructure as well as a reliable system of logistics that will let the forces operate at long distances. The inshore infrastructure must be capable of command and communications, active defense, stationing and berthing, training, technological and technical support, materiel supply, and cultural entertainment. What this means is that both China and India need to build "navy cities" that cater to a large system of systems. Offshore forward bases on islands far from the home waters need to be developed to accommodate facilities for intelligence, surveillance, reconnaissance, navigation and communication, ocean observation research, and meteorological forecasting. Since the new generation of ships consumes large amounts of materiel, logistics becomes more important in sustaining naval operations in the far seas. This in turn involves the potential creation of institutional arrangements for pre-positioning of fuel, munitions, equipment, and technical maintenance support in fixed forward locations or on floating logistical platforms.[45] While the development of inshore facilities is entirely a matter of generating synergy among geographic endowment, available financial resources, restructuring of organizational arrangements, and maritime policy initiatives, the creation of reliable offshore forward bases is tied intricately to diplomacy, foreign policy, and international politics.

While forward bases are central to sea power, organizing and sustaining them has been a major challenge for even the most powerful nations, especially since the age of empires. If the possession of far-flung territories made it easy for the great powers of the nineteenth century to project power through forward bases, projecting power needed a lot more effort in the second half of the twentieth century. If postcolonial nationalism pitted itself against the forward presence of the major powers, the intensified and global rivalry between the United States and the Soviet Union made forward bases critical for the national security strategy of these powers.[46] Our review in the first part of this chapter pointed to the traditional Chinese and Indian opposition to foreign military presence both as a general principle and as a matter of security concern in their own neighborhood. Today, both China and India are under increasing pressure to seek precisely such forward basing arrangements, on their own territories as well as on others'.

Both China and India have devoted considerable energies to the development of their strategic island territories and the creation of basing infrastructure.[47] The new Chinese naval base on Hainan Island has gotten worldwide attention after its satellite images appeared in the international media during 2008. Western analysts speculated that the base could hold up to twenty submarines, including a new type of nuclear-powered ballistic missile submarine, and future Chinese aircraft carrier battle groups, posing a challenge to long-standing U.S. military dominance in Asia.[48] India, meanwhile, has ended decades of neglect of its two island territories located strategically on its eastern and western flanks. On its eastern flank, India has strengthened its air and naval infrastructure, including the creation of an integrated Andaman and Nicobar Command that overlooks one of the world's busiest sea lanes at the mouth of the Strait of Malacca. India has also begun to use the Laccadive Islands to its west to monitor the sea lanes of the Indian Ocean with a new base for the launch of unmanned aerial vehicles. On the mainland, India has built a significant new naval base at Karwar, called INS Kadamba. India will shift the western naval command's infrastructure from the terribly congested Mumbai port to this new base farther south. Karwar will also host part of India's future fleet of nuclear submarines. Besides the INS Kadamba, India has been building a range of other facilities focused on air surveillance and satellite tracking and broadly relating to C4ISR.[49]

If China and India have embarked on a consequential inshore modernization of their infrastructure, their attempts to acquire bases and facilities useful for a forward military presence have begun to draw significant international attention. There has been a range of reports that India was setting up or seeking a variety of facilities (observation, research, tracking, reconnaissance, refueling, and replenishment) in such places as Mauritius, Seychelles, Madagascar, Oman, and Qatar on its western flank, Maldives and Sri Lanka in the south and in Burma, Singapore, and Vietnam on the east. While only sketchy reports have emerged, there is no doubt that seeking facilities and bases has now become an explicit part of India's naval and maritime strategy.[50] The need for bases was, of course, very much part of the founding vision of the modern Indian navy. K. M. Panikkar, who continues to inspire contemporary naval strategy, wrote in the middle of the last century about forward military presence:

If a steel ring can be created around India with air and naval bases at suitable points and if within this area so ringed, a navy can be created strong enough to defend its home waters, then the waters vital to India's security can be protected and converted into an area of safety. With the islands of the Bay of Bengal, with Singapore, Mauritius, and Socotra, properly equipped and protected and with a navy strong enough in its home waters, security can return to that part of the Indian Ocean which is of supreme importance to India.[51]

India's *Maritime Strategy,* for example, more modestly notes that ensuring a "presence on a regular basis in most areas of our interest, the capability to operate at considerable distances from the Indian coast is a prerequisite. . . . A major effort at improving the reach and sustainability of Indian naval forces is being undertaken currently."[52]

Although Beijing continues to deny its interest in acquiring a forward military presence, its recent interest in the maritime infrastructure development in Burma, Bangladesh, Sri Lanka, Pakistan, Maldives, Mauritius, and Seychelles has drawn concern in the United States and India.[53] Many international analysts question the wildly popular thesis on the "string of pearls"—or the presumed Chinese plans to acquire bases or facilities along the Indian Ocean sea lines of communication—by arguing that the current facilities are not military bases, but the proposition has acquired much currency in India.[54] A cautious assessment of China's counter-piracy operations since late 2008 argues that port calls in Salalah, Aden, Djibouti, and Singapore underline "PLAN's tentative yet very real steps away from home waters and into the global maritime domain."[55] Meanwhile, the signs of a formal debate in China on a forward presence and foreign military bases came to light in late 2009. An article published on the Chinese Defense Ministry website suggested that China might need to establish a "long-term supply base" near the Gulf of Aden. As international reaction rapidly set in, Beijing quickly distanced itself from the comments, and the Defense Ministry clarified that "an overseas supply base might be an option in the future, but it's not being considered at this time."[56] China's inherited policy rhetoric on nonintervention in the internal affairs of other nations and its traditional opposition to foreign military bases certainly appear to be stumbling blocks to formal agreements for logistical support to PLAN ships in the Indian Ocean. However, "legal nuance probably can be written into any agreement to ensure consistency with official policy . . . there is no reason to believe that China cannot and will not seek to achieve a balance between maintaining its policies and principles, on the one hand, and on the other adjusting to its growing place in the world."[57] The same could be said about the tension between the logic of India's own forward presence and its traditional foreign policy ideology. As their interests become global and the need to secure them pressing, Beijing and New Delhi are finding that many elements of their traditional worldview do not square with the imperatives of building blue-water navies. Recasting their foreign policy assumptions, then, will be critical for their emergence as great maritime powers.

Chapter Five

MARITIME NUCLEAR POWER

Nuclear issues have been central to many disputes between China and India and have long shaped their contestation. They are mainly about India's determination to achieve nuclear parity with China and Beijing's attempt to balance New Delhi by strengthening the nuclear and missile capabilities of Islamabad. Significant improvement in Indo-U.S. strategic relations during the years of the George W. Bush presidency has expanded the traditional China–India–Pakistan nuclear framework to include the United States. Nothing underlined this more than President Bush's civilian nuclear initiative that accepted India's nuclear exceptionalism, intensified military cooperation including the transfer of advanced conventional weapons, and made the broader decision to assist India's rise to great-power status. That much of this was animated by a desire in Washington to "hedge" against the rise of China is not in dispute. Nor was it much in doubt that Beijing perceived the move as directed against it and sought to scuttle the deepening Indo-U.S. rapprochement at multilateral forums such as the Nuclear Suppliers Group, or encourage the Indian communists to build up domestic opposition to it, or complicate it by promoting a nuclear deal with Pakistan similar to the India–U.S. nuclear initiative. Even more importantly, as India's nuclear-weapon capabilities began to steadily mature ten years after its self-declaration as a nuclear-weapon state, Beijing may find that it can no longer simply dismiss India's strategic weapons as being relevant only to the subcontinent. India's advances in nuclear delivery systems, missile defense, military, and civilian space programs all began to point to the prospect of a growing linkage between Chinese and Indian nuclear arsenals and deeper involvement of the United States in the equation. India's long-delayed advance on the front of naval nuclear propulsion in 2009 has lent an atomic dimension to their unfolding maritime rivalry.

Long decades ago, Chairman Mao reportedly told his naval commanders that they "must build a nuclear submarine in China even if it took ten thousand years." Indian leaders are not generally known for such earthy expressions of national political will. Yet, when he launched India's first indigenously built nuclear-powered submarine at the end of July 2009,[1] Prime Minister Manmohan Singh could have seen the parallel with China. The nuclear submarine, now christened *Arihant* (Sanskrit for "slayer of enemies"), had been in the works for nearly three decades. Widely known as the ATV, or Advanced Technology Vessel, the project suffered repeated technological, engineering, and organizational setbacks. It was the persistent political support and the navy's dogged pursuit that have now brought the project to its culmination. To be sure, there is considerable distance to go before *Arihant* is declared operational and viewed as a credible weapons platform. But there is no denying that unveiling the vessel marked a milestone for India on naval nuclear propulsion. It also set the stage for India's eventual deployment of some nuclear weapons at sea. Until now, only the five nuclear-weapon states recognized by the Non-Proliferation Treaty have had operational nuclear submarines. While India's achievement is significant, New Delhi is fully aware that India is well behind China in building conventional submarines, developing marine nuclear reactors, and mastering the technology of submarine-launched, nuclear-tipped ballistic missiles. Meanwhile, China itself is decades behind the United States in operating a credible nuclear navy. This chapter reviews the recent significant naval nuclear developments in India, puts them in a comparative perspective in relation to China, and speculates on their evolution. It offers a preliminary assessment of how India's emerging maritime nuclear capabilities might affect the Sino-Indian naval dynamic as well as the nuclear calculus of other great powers, especially the United

States. It also examines the potential impact of the Chinese and Indian naval nuclear capabilities on the security politics of the Indian Ocean and the western Pacific.[2]

THE DOCTRINAL CONTEXT

India's interest in a nuclear navy emerged out of the broader debate on atomic weapons in the late 1970s amid credible reports that Pakistan was close to acquiring nuclear weapons. Although it was China's first nuclear test in 1964 that set off the Indian nuclear debate and resulted in India's first nuclear test in May 1974, it was not until the late 1970s and early 1980s that New Delhi devoted serious attention to its nuclear strategy and policy.[3] As part of the many decisions that called for an intensified investment in a range of technologies related to the weaponization of India's nuclear option, New Delhi also decided to build an indigenous nuclear-propelled submarine as well as lease a nuclear submarine from the Soviet Union for training Indian naval personnel. At around the same time, in 1983, India launched the Integrated Guided Missile Development Program.[4] Sea-based missiles were, of course, way down the priority list of the program, which concentrated on the development of surface-to-surface ballistic missiles. Together the three decisions were critical for developing the Indian navy's nuclear dimension. When India announced its first draft nuclear doctrine in 1999, it emphasized two seemingly contradictory principles. One was that India would limit itself to a credible minimum deterrent and had no wish to embark on an arms race with any other country. At the same time, the doctrine declared that India will develop the classical "triad" of delivery systems. The triad refers to the deployment of nuclear weapons on bomber aircraft, land-based missiles, and submarine-launched missiles. Most Western analysts argued that building a triad is not compatible with the notion of minimum deterrence and pooh-poohed the prospect of India's building an underwater deterrent capability, the most difficult of the triad systems. Yet India's draft nuclear doctrine was quite clear that "India's nuclear forces will be effective, enduring, diverse, flexible, and responsive to the requirements in accordance with the concept of credible minimum deterrence. These forces will be based on a triad of aircraft, mobile land-based missiles and sea-based assets."[5] Whatever the limitation on its extant capabilities, India was quite clear that its nuclear arsenal would be balanced and not be trimmed to accommodate international criticism. In underlining its commitment to the development of sea-based nuclear delivery systems within the framework of a credible minimum deterrent, India was very much following the footsteps of China's nuclear evolution.

As the weakest of the then–nuclear-weapon powers that had to operate in an environment constrained by resources, managing the contradiction between the imperatives of credibility and minimalism was central to the conception and organization of the Chinese nuclear deterrent. Despite its conflicts with both the Soviet Union and the United States, China deliberately decided not to imitate the nuclear doctrine of the superpowers and chose instead to maintain a modest arsenal.[6] Some Western analysts of China's military argue that the nuclear logic has begun to change in Beijing and that we might see a significant expansion of its nuclear arsenal and a shift from the doctrine of "minimum deterrence" to one that is now called "limited deterrence." Others, however, question the evidence and argument that the Chinese arsenal is on the verge of a rapid expansion.[7] While China has subsisted for decades with a relatively small nuclear arsenal, it sought to build a balanced one. That is, from Beijing's perspective, a sea-based arsenal, despite all its technological challenges, must be built to make the Chinese deterrent credible and put it on an equal footing—if only symbolically and psychologically—with the other nuclear-weapon powers. Put simply, minimum deterrence did not mean that China would forgo certain elements of the nuclear triad. The Chinese political and military leaders were fully aware that a submarine carrying nuclear-tipped missiles was not just a symbol of technological advancement but, more significantly, would make Beijing invulnerable to any nuclear threats or blackmail.[8] For both China and India, sea-based nuclear weapons offer a secure second-strike capability. This was the context of Mao's exhortation that Beijing must do whatever it takes to build a nuclear submarine. That logic had equal appeal in New Delhi, which was "convinced that acquisition of a nuclear submarine will provide the most reliable deterrence [and] also give its navy a true blue-water status" and that "no country having a nuclear capability should be without a nuclear submarine."[9] India's official maritime strategy is quite explicit on this question. Pointing to the small size of the Indian nuclear arsenal, its emphasis on credible minimum deterrence, and the policy of no first use, the Maritime Strategy argues that "the most credible of all arsenals in a second strike is the nuclear-armed missile submarine."[10]

INDIA'S NUCLEAR NAVAL QUEST

Not too long after its first atomic test, India embarked on the development of three essential technologies for a nuclear submarine program—a marine reactor that can be integrated on a submarine platform, nuclear-tipped missiles that can be launched from underwater, and the operational skills to run a nuclear submarine. The program to build the platform, called the ATV, has been under way since the mid-1970s. The construction of a prototype has already taken more than three decades, highlighting the gap between India's nuclear strategic ambition and its industrial and technological capabilities. The difficult challenge in developing a nuclear reactor for a submarine is the small size of the reactor. This involves a lot more than simply scaling down the design of a traditional land-based reactor. Producing a small reactor requires sophisticated engineering skills. Although India's Department of Atomic Energy has been building power and research reactors since the 1960s, designing and building the reactor for the ATV was an entirely different ball game. For one, the design of the reactor must cope with very high-power densities in a small space. Reducing the size of the reactor core requires that it be run on enriched uranium. The higher the level of enrichment, the smaller the potential size. Unlike in the traditional reactors, the fuel for naval reactors is not made out of uranium oxide, but a uranium-zirconium metal alloy. The design aims at long life for the reactor without any fuel recharge. The long core life produces its own problems, however, when the fuel itself and the various materials at the heart of the reactor suffer radiation damage and become vulnerable to cracks. Accidents in naval nuclear reactors, while rare, tend to occur more often than in normal reactors. Therefore building a small, mobile, safe, and easy-to-use nuclear reactor has proved challenging to even the advanced countries. It was only in the 2000s that India's Department of Atomic Energy and its partners began to overcome many of the troubles of designing the reactor and have become confident about their designs.[11]

According to a variety of unconfirmed reports, the Indian navy has the authorization to build at least five nuclear submarines based on the ATV.[12]

The *Arihant* itself has been denoted as S-2 and is to be powered by a small reactor built by the Department of Atomic Energy in collaboration with the Defense Ministry's Defense Research and Development Organization and the navy. A former Indian naval commander says the 6,000-ton nuclear-powered submarine has a single, 85-megawatt reactor and carries a suite of 12 ballistic missiles.[13] The test bed reactor, built at the Indira Gandhi Center for Atomic Research in the Department of Atomic Energy complex at Kalpakkam outside Chennai, went critical in 2004. The highly enriched uranium fuel for the reactor was produced at the Rare Materials Project at Ratnahalli near Mysore in Karnataka. A delay in the supply of enriched uranium slowed down the launch of the *Arihant*. The cost of the program until mid-2009 was estimated at $3 billion.[14] For India, it was probably never a question of cost but of mastering an important strategic technology. It was also about a determination to catch up with China on the development of a sea-based deterrent.[15] The ATV project has brought both government agencies and the private sector into it. Larsen and Toubro, which has emerged as a major player in India's domestic private-sector shipbuilding industry and has been associated with the Indian nuclear and space programs, appears to have contributed significantly to the success of the ATV.[16] While much of the work on the ATV has been indigenous, India signed an agreement with Russia for the design and development of the nuclear submarine.[17]

The second element of India's maritime nuclear project is the development of an appropriate nuclear-tipped missile system for the submarines. Reports suggest that India is developing a number of naval missile systems for its sea-based deterrent.[18] The successful underwater test of a ballistic missile in 2008, called *Sagarika*, or K-15, with an estimated range of 700 kilometers (435 miles) seemed to give the basic test bed for a long-sought secure deterrent capability for India.[19] India is also reported to be developing a sea-launched cruise missile, called *Nirbhay*, that might be capable of delivering nuclear warheads up to a range of 1,000 km (621 miles) from a variety of platforms, including submarines.[20] India, however, will need longer-range missiles before it can claim a secure second strike capability against the Chinese nuclear arsenal.

Finally, the Russian decision to lease a *Charlie I* class nuclear submarine to India during 1988–1991 was an important catalyst in the evolution of the ATV. Russian crews reportedly operated the reactor and gave the Indian naval and scientific personnel valuable training in the management of a nuclear submarine.[21] Besides the training function, the *Chakra* became a valuable vehicle for developing indigenous capabilities in the design, maintenance, and operation of naval reactors. Cooperation with Russia has been revived with the Indian decision to lease *Akula* class submarines from Russia. The deal, announced in the early 2000s, involved Indian financing of the building of the boats to be leased. According to one report, the total cost of building two *Akula* class subs for India and the training of the crew was to be up to $2 billion.[22] Since then, there have been many difficulties in implementing the deal.[23] And the vessel that was to be sent to India had a major accident in November 2008. Amid a general political controversy in New Delhi over the reliability of Russia as an arms supplier, Moscow and New Delhi agreed to speed up the implementation of the deal. The *Akula* class submarines are believed to be quieter and deadlier than any other nuclear attack submarine in the Russian fleet.[24] The Indian navy formally received the first of the *Akula II* class nuclear submarines in early 2012.[25] Renamed INS *Chakra*, the vessel will be based at Vishakhapatnam on the east coast of India. While some Indian analysts question whether the *Chakra* is worth the cost and the wait, naval analysts underline its manifold significance in terms of generating the experience, personnel, and management procedures involved in the use of nuclear submarines.[26]

CHINA'S NUCLEAR FLEET

While the launch of the *Arihant* marked India's arrival in the nuclear maritime domain, its seaborne nuclear capability is a long distance away from becoming a credible force and is well behind China. Meanwhile, Beijing is trying to close its decades-long gap with the United States on underwater technologies. Given its international isolation immediately after the proclamation of the People's Republic, its conflict with the United States in the 1950s, the overwhelming superiority of the U.S. and Japanese navies in the western Pacific, and the variety of maritime territorial disputes with its neighbors in east and Southeast Asia, China has always emphasized the importance of submarines. Even in the current phase of its naval modernization, building advanced conventional submarines in large numbers has remained a priority for China.

Having declared itself a nuclear-weapon power after the first test in 1964, China has given considerable emphasis to building both fast-attack nuclear-powered submarines, known as SSNs, and nuclear-powered submarines equipped with ballistic missiles, or SSBNs. The Chinese political leaders, naval commanders, and the nuclear scientific establishment fully understood the significance of the twin development of the submarines. From 1965 to 1968, the Chinese military focused on the development of the experimental Type 091 *Han* class SSN. Although the turbulence of the Cultural Revolution had an impact on the program, the first *Han* class vessel was launched at the end of 1971. The same design was used to develop a separate SSBN (Type 092) of the *Xia* class. It is believed that not more than two operational *Xia* class SSBNs were built, and Western analysts estimate that only one has been operational since the mid-1980s. On October 15, 1985, China tested a JL-1 missile from the *Xia* class platform, but it was considered a failure.[27] As the Chinese intensified their efforts during the 1980s and 1990s to develop a credible SSBN, China was fortunate to have a strong naval commander, Admiral Liu Huaqing, who was determined to build a powerful nuclear force at sea. Admiral Liu, who is often called China's Mahan, was the leader of the armed forces during 1992–1998 and the powerful vice chairman of the Central Military Commission (1989–1997). During his stewardship, Liu sought to lay the foundation for a new generation of SSNs as well as SSBNs and had full political support.[28]

China launched its second-generation SSN, called the *Shang* class (also called Type 093) in 2002 and followed with a second vessel the next year. The first pictures of this submarine came into public view in 2008. Faster and stealthier and exponentially lethal, the *Shang* class submarines have the capability to operate in the Indian Ocean. Meanwhile, China is said to be developing a third-generation SSN, called Type 095. Five of these new subs are expected to join the Chinese fleet in the coming years. While they will give Chinese navy a strong punch, it is the *Jin* class (Type 094) SSBN that Beijing hopes will showcase its rise as a nuclear-weapon power. Western analysts assess that China may build five or six *Jin* class submarines in the coming years. Each will be equipped with 12 long-range ballistic missiles. The JL-2 missiles have an estimated range of at least 7,200 kilometers (4,500 miles) and are capable of carrying multiple warheads. The *Jin* class submarines in combination with the JL-2 missiles are expected to let China finally match Britain and France in terms of the technological sophistication of its nuclear arsenal and its credibility as a survivable second strike force.[29] Some Western assessments, however, suggest continuing difficulties with its SSBN program. The Pentagon's 2010 annual assessment of Chinese military power says, "The first of the new JIN-class (Type 094) SSBN appears ready, but the associated JL-2 SLBM [submarine-launched, nuclear-tipped ballistic missiles] appears to have encountered difficulty, failing several of what should have been the final round of flight tests. The date when the JIN-class SSBN/JL-2 SLBM combination will be effectively operational is uncertain."[30]

Western sources also assess that none of the Chinese nuclear-powered submarines equipped with ballistic missiles has sailed on deterrent patrol and that the missiles are not operational. Even if they are deployed close to China's own territory, the analysts suggest, the Chinese submarines are exposed and vulnerable to U.S. attack. "For its missiles to reach the continental United States, a Jin-class SSBN would need to deploy deep into the Pacific Ocean or the East China Sea through dangerous chokepoints. Regional targeting would be a different matter because the SLBMs would be able to reach Guam, all of India, and most of Russia (including Moscow) from port."[31] China is also reported to have difficulties in developing effective communication with SSBNs and instituting credible command and control systems. According to the Pentagon, "The PLA has only a limited capacity to communicate with submarines at sea, and the PLA Navy has no experience in managing a SSBN fleet that performs strategic patrols with live nuclear warheads mated to missiles. Land-based mobile missiles may face similar command and control challenges in wartime, although probably not as extreme as with submarines."[32]

MARITIME NUCLEAR DYNAMIC

As Beijing and New Delhi take their nuclear weapons to sea, they begin to have an impact on the strategic calculus of the other great powers and regional rivals. Although the Indian prime minister was careful to signal that the *Arihant* was not about aggressive designs against any state,[33] Pakistan greeted its launch with the predictable proposition that an arms race might be in the offing.[34] The indications are that Pakistan has plans to develop a sea-based deterrent of its own. There appears to be some expectation in Islamabad that Beijing will contribute to the development of Pakistan's sea-based deterrent. Analysts in Pakistan argue that the Russian support for the development of India's nuclear-powered submarine and the India–U.S. civilian nuclear initiative provide Pakistan "enough justification either to lease nuclear submarines or eventually develop its own, or both."[35] Pakistan and China, the analysts urge, must "plan [for] the training and subsequent lease of a nuclear-powered submarine."[36] Given China's earlier support for Pakistan's nuclear program, it might not be entirely outlandish to consider the probability of Beijing's leasing one of its nuclear submarines to Pakistan. In any event, international cooperation in military nuclear propulsion programs is not prohibited by the Non-Proliferation Treaty.[37] That is indeed the basis on which Russia has been cooperating with India on the nonexplosive military uses of nuclear energy.

Meanwhile, some naval analysts in India are aware that the Russian nuclear submarine technology is not the best in the world and are interested in alternative sources to build a credible fleet of nuclear-powered submarines. There are some reports that India might be looking at the prospects of acquiring French nuclear submarines, but the indications are that no approach has been made to Paris. Could the United States be a source for nuclear-powered submarines? That possibility appears remote for the moment. The India–U.S. civil nuclear initiative, unveiled by George W. Bush in July 2005, was rooted in an American domestic political consensus that Washington will not aid India's military nuclear capabilities and will limit any nuclear cooperation to civilian use.[38] It is not clear if the rapid expansion of the Chinese nuclear capability will eventually bring about U.S. assistance to India's maritime nuclear project. On the face of it, there is no sense of threat in Washington arising from India's nuclear-weapon capabilities. There are no signs of this debate in Washington at this stage, nor is India seeking such cooperation. Senator John McCain, who lost the 2008 presidential race to Barack Obama, seemed to endorse the U.S. transfer of nuclear-powered submarines to India in a 2010 speech. Defining a more purposeful agenda for future Indo-U.S. security cooperation, McCain said, "With political will on both sides, there is no reason why we cannot develop a joint U.S.-Indian concept of operations for both the Indian and Pacific Oceans. There is no reason why we cannot construct a network of intelligence sharing that creates a common picture of our common strategic challenges—on land, at sea, in space, and in cyberspace. . . . And there is no reason why we cannot work to facilitate India's deployment of advanced defense capabilities, such as nuclear submarines, aircraft carriers, missile defense architecture, as well as India's inclusion in the development of the Joint Strike Fighter."[39] As China's maritime nuclear capabilities grow and India takes the first steps toward building an underwater deterrent, U.S. efforts to balance China and boost India are adding to the complex nuclear multipolarity in the Indo-Pacific.[40]

IMPLICATIONS OF NUCLEAR MULTIPOLARITY

There is growing acknowledgment that the shift in the locus of atomic politics to Asia marks the emergence of the second nuclear age.[41] One element of the new nuclear age is the reality of a larger number of nuclear-weapon states shaping the balance in Asia. Unlike in Europe, where the British and French nuclear weapons did not materially alter the balance between the United States and the Soviet Union, the current dynamic in Asia is shaped by the presence of a larger number of nuclear-weapon powers. Since the 1990s, the number of declared-nuclear-weapon powers in Asia has doubled. India and Pakistan have consolidated their position as nuclear powers. The international community has failed to reverse the North Korean nuclear weapons program. Together the three have joined the United States, Russia, and China as the states shaping the Asian nuclear balance. As the United States and Russia draw down their nuclear forces and the Asian powers expand the size and sophistication of their atomic arsenals, the distribution of nuclear power in the Indo-Pacific is slowly but certainly changing. Traditional nuclear arms control, designed to stabilize the U.S.-Russian balance, seems largely incapable of addressing the challenge of constructing nuclear stability in Asia. Some of the new nuclear-weapon powers such as Pakistan and North Korea have not adhered to the traditional concepts of nuclear deterrence. This has raised the need to explore the different notions of nuclear utility in Asia.[42] As the balance, nuclear and conventional, between the United States and China begins to

SAMUDRA MANTHAN

evolve, new questions arise about the credibility of U.S. extended nuclear deterrence in Asia. In the past, the nuclear umbrella offered by the United States helped reduce the incentives for acquisition of nuclear weapons by its Asian allies—Japan, South Korea, Taiwan, and Australia. Questions about the credibility of U.S. extended deterrence as well as national nuclear options are now being widely discussed in Asia amid the rise of China and the emergence of a nuclear North Korea.[43] If Japan, South Korea, Taiwan, or Australia moves toward acquiring nuclear weapons or the United States holds them back by strengthening its extended deterrence, China's own nuclear calculus is bound to change, resulting in further destabilization of the Asian nuclear dynamic.[44] Asia's alliances face reorganization amid the new nuclear multipolarity. Some traditional special relationships have endured, and new ones are likely to emerge—these include China's nuclear ties to Pakistan, Beijing's reluctance to confront North Korea's nuclear proliferation, Russia's strategic technology transfers to both India and China, and the new nuclear warmth between Washington and New Delhi.

Beyond the flattening and broadening of the nuclear capabilities in the Indo-Pacific, the qualitative changes in the composition of the Asian nuclear arsenals are also consequential. On the face of it, China's development of a credible underwater deterrent, which provides a survivable and secure second strike capability, should help stabilize the nuclear dynamic between Beijing and Washington. Some analysts, however, warn that China's emphasis on building a powerful force of nuclear-powered submarines equipped with ballistic missiles could complicate the situation by limiting U.S. options for escalation in a cross-straits crisis involving Beijing and Taipei.[45] Other analysts suggest a direct link between China's SSBN force and its anti-access strategy vis-à-vis the United States. While China's underwater deterrent "augurs well for overall Sino-U.S. strategic stability, it may not be conducive to stable maritime interactions on the theater level. Meaningful deterrent patrols off Chinese shores will almost certainly solidify Beijing's protectiveness over and sense of entitlement to the China seas—thereby raising the stakes for access to the East Asian littoral."[46]

India's underdeveloped maritime nuclear capabilities are likely to remain relatively marginal to the U.S.–China maritime nuclear dynamic for many years to come. Yet, India has stakes in access to the South China Sea and will have to factor in the risks that emerging Chinese underwater capabilities have on India's growing profile in the western Pacific. What about the more direct impact of China's maritime nuclear capability on India's security calculus? Some Indian analysts see a limited effect in the near term but suggest long-term consequences in the context of India's potential conflict with Pakistan and China.[47] As reports about the likely deployment of Chinese nuclear submarines at Hainan emerged in 2008, there was considerable alarm in the Indian media.[48] Responding to the media reports, India's naval chief, Admiral Sureesh Mehta, said that "the rate of induction of nuclear submarines in the Chinese Navy is a more serious matter, rather than which base the boats operate from."[49] In a balanced assessment of the implications, a naval analysis sets out the list of potential Indian concerns: "The focus of China's SSBN program is clearly the United States and not India, but as the advanced SSBNs are inducted in sufficient numbers (about six), China is likely to disperse these boats all over, including in the Indian Ocean, to complicate America's strategic antisubmarine warfare and ballistic missile defense calculus. This would necessarily be accompanied by adverse implications for India's own security."[50] Gurpreet Khurana suggests that China could deploy the SSNs close to such choke points as the Strait of Malacca to prevent an interdiction of its energy and resource supplies. He speculates that China could leverage its underwater nuclear assets in the Indian Ocean to open a seaward front against India to coerce New Delhi in future military crises in the subcontinent.

The region's emerging missile defense capabilities, expanding military space potential, and increasing lethality of conventionally armed missiles have begun to impose additional layers of complexity on the unfolding nuclear multipolarity in the Indo-Pacific.[51] When the initial U.S. missile defense plans were announced by President Ronald Reagan in 1983, the reaction in China and India was quite similar, although their nuclear status was significantly different—Beijing was a recognized nuclear-weapon power; India was not. Beijing criticized missile defense for its potential to destabilize the deterrent relationship among the nuclear-weapon powers, including itself, and saw it as part of U.S. efforts to gain nuclear superiority over the Soviet Union.[52] India, for its part, saw missile defense as a trigger for a renewed nuclear arms race between the United States and the Soviet Union. Opposition to the deployment of space weapons became an important component of India's disarmament activism as reflected in its six-nation, five-continent peace initiative in the second half of the 1980s.[53] The similarity of Chinese and Indian perceptions would not, however, survive the second iteration of missile defense under President George W. Bush. India surprised itself and the world by becoming one of the few countries to welcome Bush's initiative on missile defense in May 2001. Bush, in turn, chose India as one of the few countries where he sent a special envoy to explain the importance of the initiative.[54] Since then, despite considerable skepticism, India has explored the prospects for missile defense cooperation with the United States.[55] Those familiar with the recent evolution of the Indian-U.S. partnership conclude that "New Delhi's decision in regards to missile defense [has] been intimately reflective of, and strongly linked to, the changing character of U.S.-Indian relations."[56] India has stepped up its own development and testing of missile defense systems. Since late 2006, India has conducted repeated tests of missile interception both within and outside the atmosphere.[57] By 2011, when India conducted the sixth round of its missile defense tests, its scientists were declaring that the program was maturing.[58] The head of the Indian DRDO claimed in 2012 that operational missile defense systems could be deployed on short notice to protect at least two Indian cities.[59] While India's current emphasis is on land-based missile defense systems, the Indian navy is said to be interested in sea-based missile defenses as its forces will have to cope with the proliferation of missiles in the Indo-Pacific littoral. There has been some initial discussion about the prospects for cooperation with the United States on maritime missile defense.[60]

Meanwhile, there has been a dramatic expansion of China's inventory of missiles, the political missions it has assigned to its missile forces, and the supportive military space capabilities that it has begun to acquire. China's development of an anti-ship ballistic missile, or ASBM, that can target U.S. aircraft carriers has triggered some alarm in the United States. The Chinese ASBM reportedly acquired initial operating capability in 2010.[61] Some see the combination of a long-range ballistic missile and a maneuverable reentry warhead as a "game changer" in the maritime security politics of the western Pacific.[62] It is not surprising that the Indian navy, which has begun to make sustained forays into the western Pacific, has expressed some concern. Responding to queries on India's views of the Chinese anti-ship ballistic missile, India's chief of naval staff, Admiral Nirmal Verma, said, "The areas in which it (ASBM) will be deployed in our area of operation [are] something we need to look at. And certainly we need to have something in place with respect to [an] ASBM-type of weapon and we will put it in place."[63]

For the Chinese army, the ASBM is only one element to limit U.S. access to Chinese waters. Others include the massive deployment of missiles targeting Taiwan and the U.S. bases in the western Pacific, and the development of C4ISR capabilities to track the movement of U.S. ships, including aircraft carriers. The United States has already taken a number of steps in response to the emerging Chinese attempt to limit the freedom of its naval forces in the western Pacific Ocean. These include assigning to the Pacific most of the Navy's *Aegis* cruisers and destroyers with ballistic missile defense capability—and home-porting some of those ships at Yokosuka, Japan, and Pearl Harbor; increasing the planned procurement quantity of SM-3 interceptor missiles with ballistic missile defense capability; and developing and procuring a sea-based, terminal-defense ballistic missile capability as a complement to the *Aegis* midcourse capability.[64] An action-reaction phenomenon involving missiles and defenses against them has begun to emerge in the western Pacific that could blur the distinction between conventional and nuclear missiles and generate greater instability in the region.[65] India and the eastern Indian Ocean could eventually become part of this dynamic, which has already begun to envelop China and the United States.

IMPACT OF MILITARY SPACE

Beyond missile defense, a range of space technologies is shaping the maritime strategies of China and India and reinforcing the competitive dimension between the two Asian giants. The extraordinary investments that China and India are making in their civilian space programs have been widely seen as reflecting the power of techno-nationalism in Beijing and New Delhi.[66] While China is way ahead of India in many aspects of its civilian space program, the notion of a space race between them has taken hold in the popular imagination.[67] If China's anti-satellite weapon tests in 2007 and 2010 surprised much of the world on the scope and pace of Beijing's military space effort, they also triggered new pressures on India to accelerate its own military space program.[68]

When it comes to the maritime domain, two dimensions of space technology prevail. One is to mobilize space and related technologies in the modernization of the navies and in addressing new maritime military missions; the other is to prevent and limit the use of space technology by one's potential adversaries. At this stage it might not be inaccurate to state that the Chinese and Indian policies are similar on the first objective and somewhat different on the second. On the first, the Chinese navy has made "informationalization" one of the central objectives of its maritime strategy.[69] As it recognized at the end of the Cold War that the U.S. military's superiority and effectiveness are rooted in America's lead in the development and application of information and communication technologies, the Chinese political leadership was determined to close the massive gap with the United States. As a consequence, "fighting wars under informatized conditions" became a guideline for China's armed forces.[70] The navy in turn was determined to invest in and modernize its capabilities in the area of command, control, communications, computers, intelligence, surveillance and reconnaissance—the so-called C4ISR. The naval leadership, too, recognized that it must look beyond the simple acquisition of advanced ships, submarines, and missiles and focus on integrating multiple platforms with their varied weapons systems and widely distributed sensors. This emphasis by China on transforming its C4ISR also fits in with the objectives of reducing or delaying U.S. access to the western Pacific and deploying the PLAN far from its shores. Because space technology is one of the keystone technologies of the C4ISR, China has decided to accelerate its military space program and combine it with the modernization of its naval forces. Although external observers continue to point to the enduring weaknesses of China's C4ISR capabilities, there is no denying its impressive advances in recent years and the real prospect for significant advances in the coming decades. Not surprisingly, the Indian navy has similar ambitions on leveraging space and information technologies to improve its effectiveness as a force through network-centric operations. India's maritime military strategy emphasizes the importance of military space and C4ISR technologies in the critical tasks of raising the navy's maritime domain awareness and improving its fighting skills.[71] As Admiral Arun Prakash, the former chief of the Indian naval staff, said, improved maritime domain awareness through C4ISR capabilities "increases synergy for command and control, resulting in superior decision-making and the ability to coordinate complex military operations over long distances, with the ultimate aim of obtaining overwhelming military advantage."[72]

China and India, however, display significant divergence in their attitudes toward the nature of space weapons, the aggressive use of space technologies, and the denial of space advantage to potential adversaries. Beijing seems quite unambiguous in moving toward a comprehensive articulation of a doctrine of space warfare, and its anti-satellite missile (ASAT) test is a clear signal. A growing number of American analysts are convinced that the ASAT test is part of a definitive Chinese "counter-space" strategy against the United States.[73] Although China has argued against the weaponization of space in general terms, its objective was to prevent the United States from deploying weapons in space. Opposition to space weapons, then, was not a matter of high principle but of limiting U.S. advantages through diplomacy and the force of international public opinion. The ASAT tests, however, underline the Chinese position that if and when space weapons become part of major power arsenals, Beijing should not and would not be found wanting. And Beijing would develop the full set of legal and political arguments that it would need to reinforce its future strategy of warfare in space. Meanwhile, space weapons have a more urgent salience for Beijing. It is looking for ways to convert the current U.S. dominance in space into a crippling weakness in the event of a conflict. By creating the capabilities to attack U.S. space assets, it is argued, China will be able to cripple the American armed forces and reduce their effectiveness. The most plausible scenario for this indeed is not an abstract one but the very central question of Taiwan. The Chinese strategic objective is to prevent the U.S. armed forces from interposing themselves into a conflict with Taiwan, or at least delay their arrival on the scene. Space warfare, then, is seen as crucial by Beijing in its mission of national unification and part of its anti-access strategy vis-à-vis the United States.[74]

India, in contrast, is more ambivalent in its articulation of the relationship between civilian and military space. The primary emphasis of India's space program until now has been on civilian uses. Over the past decade or less, New Delhi has indeed begun to apply its strengths to certain military uses, for example navigation, communication, and remote sensing.[75] But the Indian political leadership has been reluctant to articulate the case for a definitive military space program and to follow through with the necessary organizational changes that would allow its armed forces and security agencies to become full stakeholders in the national space strategy. This ambivalence is indeed similar to India's initial pious attitudes toward global nuclear disarmament and a reluctance to embark on explicit weaponization of its nuclear capabilities. Pointing to the dangers of a similar ambivalence toward military space, a leading Indian strategic thinker argues: "The [Indian] military feels that militarization followed by weaponization [of space] is inevitable; that questions of ethics and restraint should not be brought up, as they will only cripple defense preparedness. . . . How far are we prepared to go to mix realism with idealism? Swinging too far towards idealism may take us back to the days of proposing an NPT [and] eventually to keep out of it, to prevent being marginalized into a non-nuclear-weapon state."[76]

Despite the temptation of the Indian political leadership to moralize and avoid taking an explicit decision to develop a substantive military space program that involves both passive and aggressive military use of space, New Delhi may not be able to fudge for too much longer. The pressures from the armed forces are mounting for a more explicit military space policy, especially after the Chinese ASAT test.[77] The defense science community claims it has the capacity to demonstrate ASAT capability if there is a political decision.[78] While there were demands, especially from the Indian air force, to set up an aerospace command, the cautious defense leadership has set up a less ambitious "space cell" in the headquarters of the Integrated Defense Staff.[79] The space cell will coordinate space-related activities of different government agencies and is expected to come up with a doctrine on military space uses. In terms of the future, a leading space scientist offered a broad outline of the potential Indian response to the Chinese ASAT tests:

> In regard to China, its recent ASAT test does represent a threat to some of the space assets, especially those in the Sun-synchronous orbit like the IRS [Indian Remote Sensing satellite] and other orbits up to something like 1000 km altitude. . . . India joined many others in the international community in condemning the test and the fact that the debris could have some adverse implication for the IRS satellite was worrisome. This assumes even greater importance given the fact that India's space assets are considerable and likely to grow in future. What can India do to

safeguard itself? . . . Clearly, there are a number of defensive measures that could be adopted—manoeuvres, higher altitude operations, monitoring the space environment to identify potential problems, shielding against debris, radiation, etc. The other alternative is to take some preventive action. Taking active measures along with defensive measures to protect its assets is worth pursuing.[80]

Behind all the words of caution is the hint of a potential reordering of the Indian space program to take into account the emerging security challenges and to emulate China's adoption of an active security approach toward outer space.

There is one area in which China and India may remain on a divergent track—their attitudes toward cooperation with the current hegemon in the global commons, the United States. Despite the waxing and waning political relationship with Beijing since the late 1980s, the broad assumption in Washington was that China was unlikely to ever pose a threat to the United States, least of all to its command over the commons that is believed to be at the foundation of America's enduring primacy in the international system.[81] As late as 2005, leading American strategic thinkers were arguing that "China has not and probably cannot successfully challenge the United States in the naval and air global commons."[82] The U.S. policymakers were confident that Washington could lay down the terms for accommodating a rising China into the international system. This was the basis for the proposition that China must prove itself to be a stakeholder in the international system. Yet, the rapidity of China's rise and America's own difficulties in sustaining the unipolar moment have begun to shake the complacent confidence that Beijing poses no threat at all to the United States. By its behavior in the western Pacific and in outer space, China has begun to suggest it might acquire the capabilities to balance or even outplay the United States for short durations and in specific subregions. Some American analysts suggest that China's military modernization may be "designed to re-order the balance of power in China's favor by diminishing American strategic mobility and free access to Pacific waters, Pacific airspace, and the 'high terrain' of space and cyberspace. A good example of this is China's development of land-mobile anti-ship ballistic missiles. This anti-access capability is unprecedented anywhere in the world and has numerous implications for the U.S. Navy, probably best summarized as losing air and sea dominance—and perhaps control—in the Asian-Pacific region. This puts at risk American influence, regional security and alliance interdependence."[83]

Until recently it was also assumed that strategic stability between the United States and China was not threatened if at least three conditions were met: China does not challenge the U.S. dominance of the high seas; Washington accepts the relative improvement of Beijing's global position; and there is no conflict over Taiwan.[84] As we have noted, China's modernization of its nuclear forces and the expansion of its maritime nuclear and space capabilities are raising questions about the sustainability of these premises about the bilateral relationship. Doubts certainly have emerged on the previous expectations that China cannot or will not seek to undermine the American command of the commons.[85] Furthermore, the transformation of Chinese maritime nuclear forces is beginning to have an effect on the nature of U.S. alliances and the credibility of its extended deterrence in the Asia-Pacific region. This in turn has propelled a revaluation of U.S. maritime strategy in the Indo-Pacific and resulted in the decision to develop a new air-sea battle doctrine.[86] As we look closely at the nuclear and space dynamic in the Indo-Pacific region, it might well be that the United States over the longer term needs to strengthen its partnership with India in order to limit the Chinese challenge to its dominance over the seas. In the near term, India is unlikely to shape the nuclear, missile, and space contestation between the United States and China in the western Pacific. As India strengthens its capabilities in these areas and if U.S.-Indian maritime security cooperation expands, the nuclear and space dynamic will likewise expand to cover the Indo-Pacific region.

Having looked at the imperatives and features of the improving naval capabilities of India and China, we now turn to the expansion of New Delhi's maritime engagement with the Pacific and Beijing's rising profile in the Indian Ocean.

Chapter Six

INDIA'S PACIFIC AMBITIONS

Any suggestion that India might influence the balance of power in the western Pacific is met with surprise and skepticism from the community of diplomatic practitioners as well as regional experts in East Asia. Nearly two decades after the launch of its Look East policy, India is widely seen as marginal to the security of the Asia Pacific. Yet some of the recent scholarly work on India's international relations is beginning to explore the implications of India's growing economic, political, and military engagement with East Asia.[1] As the weakest of the major powers in Asia, India is understandably the least consequential for the ordering of Asia-Pacific security. Nevertheless, India's importance for security politics of East Asia is beginning to grow, albeit slowly. The debate on India's rise and its implications for the Asian and global balance of power centers around the new expectations and residual skepticism about the sustainability of India's recent impressive economic performance of around 8 percent annual growth rates during the first decade of the twenty-first century. If India can maintain this performance, its political and military weight in East Asia will undoubtedly improve. Also, in the past few years, India's Look East policy, launched in the mid-1990s, has matured. New Delhi has begun to expand the geographic scope as well as the substance of its Look East policy to cover the western

Pacific as an important area of strategic engagement. The expectations on India's rise have also begun to inject a new dynamism into India's relations with the great powers of Asia—the United States, China, and Japan. As a result, India may no longer be marginal to either the regional politics of East Asia or the great-power system that shapes the Asia-Pacific theater. That does not necessarily mean it has become either central or pivotal to Pacific Asian security, but India may be poised to affect the distribution of power in the western Pacific.

RECLAIMING THE EAST ASIAN TRADITION

Most Indian writers will be tempted to justify an Indian interest and role in the Pacific in terms of the grand sweep of civilizational links. Many of them would happily concur with the assessment that "in relationship to the Mongolian peoples and nations of Indo-China, Malaysia, Tibet, China and Japan, India stands as the sacred and revered source of some of their highest cultural attainments. Her fertile mind, through a thousand years of Brahmanical and Buddhist expansion, furnished archetypes and gave inspiration to literature, art, philosophy, religion and institutions in Mongolian Asia."[2] This assessment of the Indian influence in East Asia, from the early decades of the twentieth century, is now hugely contested, and there is no reason to venture into it.[3] Even a cursory examination of recent history would point to the strategic bonds that endure between India and East Asia. If regions are imagined communities, the perception that South and East Asia are two very different geopolitical entities, too, is of recent origin. It is quite easy to see how India's inward-looking policies from the 1950s and its deliberate de-globalization marginalized New Delhi in the Asian and Pacific regions. Since India turned outward and reintegrated itself into the global economy at the turn of the 1990s, it is logical to believe that its large size and immense economic potential would make it, eventually, an important factor in the structuring of the Asian economic and security order.

After early disappointments in trying to build Asian unity and lead the old continent on the world stage during the 1950s, India's political emphasis decisively turned global and multilateral. The presumed leadership of the Non-Aligned Movement gave India a stage to articulate its larger aspirations. But the focus on the Non-Aligned Movement coupled with the inward economic orientation meant that India could not sustain its primacy in Asia and the Indian Ocean littoral that it had achieved under the British Raj.[4] By the first decade of the twenty-first century, the wheel was close to turning full circle.

As Asia rediscovered itself in the twentieth century, powerful voices in the region were pointing to the enduring linkages among different subregions of Asia. Although there was never an accepted geographic definition of Asia, India was very much part of the early expression and popularization of Asian identity.[5] The very first ideas of "Asian unity" and the attempt to define a new "Asian identity" in the early years of the twentieth century came out of the dialogue between the Indian poet Rabindranath Tagore and the Japanese intellectual Okakura Tenshin at the two geographic extremes of Asia.[6] As the Indian national movement acquired traction in the period between the two World Wars, a strong sentiment favored the idea of independent India working for an "Eastern Federation" in Asia.[7] The armies of undivided India (nearly 750,000) pushed the Japanese troops out of Burma and took their surrender throughout Southeast Asia and made a decisive contribution to the Allied victory over Japan in Asia.

One of the early diplomatic acts of Jawaharlal Nehru was to host the Asian Relations Conference, the first conclave of modern Asian leaders, a few months before India's independence in 1947. In pursuit of Asian and Afro-Asian solidarity, Nehru also led the effort by the so-called Colombo Powers in organizing the Bandung Conference of 1955. (The "Colombo Powers" were the first to speak in the name of Asia and comprised three South Asian nations—India, Pakistan, and Ceylon, now Sri Lanka—and two Southeast Asian nations—Indonesia and Burma.)[8] That South and Southeast Asia were not always seen as separate geopolitical entities is underlined by the composition of the major Cold War alliance of the region, the Southeast Asia Treaty Organization, or SEATO, formed in 1954. Its members were Pakistan, Thailand, and the Philippines, in addition to the United States, United Kingdom, France, Australia, and New Zealand. Convenient political differentiation among regions at one moment becomes irrelevant or gets overtaken by new political imperatives and leads to the construction of new cartographies.

To be sure, newly independent India nursed the ambitions of sustaining the Raj legacy on regional security. Its early political activism in southern

Africa, the Middle East, and Southeast Asia, its large army, and the plans to build an ambitious navy all pointed to a strong Indian role in Asia. The notion that "Aden to Malacca" was India's sphere of influence was deeply rooted among post-independence foreign policymakers in New Delhi. In fact, the foreign policy assertiveness of India in the early Cold War years generated deep suspicion in some Western quarters that India might emerge as the "successor of Japan's Asiatic imperialism."[9] These fears, it turned out, were exaggerated. The enduring consequences of the subcontinent's partition, and the conflict with China over the Tibet boundary, tied India down to dealing with conflicts within its own neighborhood. India's insular socialist policies resulted not just in India's relative economic decline, but also in the erosion of historic trade links with neighboring regions in Asia. With no economic basis, India's relations with all the major powers, including the United States, Europe, Japan, and China, remained underdeveloped. As India drew closer to the Soviet Union in order to manage the regional balance of power within the subcontinent, its association with Moscow became increasingly disconcerting to even those countries that valued their traditional links with India. The Indian military, which had a long record of participating in wars beyond the subcontinent, was now bogged down in territorial defense. The foreign policy of nonalignment also meant that the Indian military shunned contact and cooperation with the outside world, including the Soviet Union. Although India's third-world activism meant taking positions on all global issues, these degenerated into mere posturing against one or both superpowers and an inability to come to the aid of friendly nations in conflict with their neighbors. Where India did take bold positions, as in Indochina in support of Vietnamese intervention in Cambodia, New Delhi was at odds with all the great powers (except Moscow) and the Association of Southeast Asian Nations, or ASEAN.[10]

It was only after the collapse of the Soviet Union and the end of the Cold War that India was compelled to base its approach to different regions more on national interest. India's new economic policies demanded a more focused outreach that emphasized trade and commercial cooperation. It also demanded a direct political approach to different regions of Asia, rather than the multilateral mechanisms of the G-77 and the Non-Aligned Movement. As India began to reorient its foreign policy after the

Cold War, the idea that much of Asia and the Indian Ocean formed its "extended neighborhood" began to take root.[11] As India's relations with Southeast Asia, Central Asia, the Persian Gulf, and the Middle East began to acquire a new dynamism, the old notion of reclaiming a security and political role from Aden to Malacca—so emblematic of Lord Curzon's British India—began to resurface.[12] Not surprisingly, the first regional initiative was toward Southeast Asia and was called the "Look East" policy. A voluminous literature outlining the origins and ideological underpinnings of India's Look East policy is already with us.[13] The urgent imperative was to be a part of the region's new economic dynamism and rebuild political relations with the rest of Asia that had frayed during the Cold War. Among all the subregions of Asia and the Indian Ocean littoral, Southeast Asia promised to be the most attractive in terms of political and diplomatic opportunities. In Central Asia, India was quick to reach out to the newly independent republics of the former Soviet Union. Yet its ability to influence developments there was constrained by the lack of direct geographic access. The oil-rich Persian Gulf was now right at the top of India's foreign policy agenda. But the overwhelming dominance of the United States in the Gulf and its extended conflicts with Iran and Iraq left little room for any major initiative by India. This was also true of the Middle East, where India now sought to generate greater balance between its ties with the Arabs and with Israel but hardly expected to play a major role in the region. India's significant interest in Africa (and eventually Latin America) had to wait until its economic growth accelerated and provided new options in the first years of the twenty-first century.

In contrast to all these regions, the greater coherence of ASEAN and the goodwill of countries like Singapore provided the opening for sustained Indian diplomacy in the region. While the steady expansion of economic links provided a new basis for India's cooperation with the region, it was the admission of India as an institutional partner of ASEAN that allowed New Delhi to develop an all-encompassing engagement with the region.[14] From the tentative sectoral dialogue partnership in the mid-1990s to a more affirmative nod to the membership of the East Asia Summit process in 2005, India's Look East policy advanced steadily and became one of the most organized components of its external relations. Besides a new level of political comfort at the highest levels, ASEAN offered a model for globalization just

when India was fighting the many demons in its mind about economic reform. This debt of gratitude was freely acknowledged by Manmohan Singh,
who was present at the creation of India's Look East policy as India's finance
minister and later, as prime minister, had the opportunity to elevate it to a
higher level. Speaking in 2006, he said,

> I must pay tribute to our East and Southeast Asian neighbors for shap-
> ing our own thinking on globalization and the means to deal with it.
> . . . In 1992 our Government launched India's "Look East" policy. This
> was not merely an external economic policy; it was also a strategic shift
> in India's vision of the world and India's place in the evolving global
> economy. Most of all it was about reaching out to our civilizational Asian
> neighbors.[15]

While ASEAN leaders held India's hand at a moment when the big ship
of the Indian state was turning and were prepared to experiment on the
prospects for a deeper economic relationship, they were wary, even at the
turn of the millennium, of a security entanglement with New Delhi. As
they prepared to launch the ASEAN Regional Forum in the early 1990s,
the ASEAN leaders explicitly told India not to press its case for membership; when New Delhi did anyway, its application was rejected.[16] ASEAN
leaders were concerned that India would bring the baggage of its difficult
problems with Pakistan and China into the organization. While India was
eventually admitted into the ASEAN Regional Forum in 1997, there was
an explicit understanding that India's role for the moment would be low
key and that a wider political and security relationship would be considered only after its economic interaction with the region expanded. As a
Southeast Asian analysis underlined the region's reservations about India:

> India remains effectively contained geopolitically in South Asia by Paki-
> stan and China. As long as this is so, its geopolitical impact on Southeast
> Asia will continue to be limited. To break out of this geopolitical im-
> passe, the emergence of an open, outward looking and dynamic econo-
> my is an essential condition, but not a sufficient one. Other important
> requirements may include diplomatic ingenuity and political will to re-
> solve disputes with Pakistan at an appropriate time and the continued
> maintenance of domestic political stability under secular conditions.[17]

Put another way, the doubts about India's internal stability, its capacity to emerge as an economic force, its geopolitical bind with Pakistan and China were all deeply entrenched in Southeast Asia. Therefore, security partnership with India could be considered only as a distant prospect. By 2005, however, this perception had eased considerably, reflected in ASEAN's decision to invite India—against the known reservations of China—into the East Asia Summit process. A whole host of factors, including India's superior performance, New Delhi's improved ties with Beijing, the warming of India's relations with the United States under the Bush administration, and the larger perception of a more purposeful Indian diplomacy, helped change the attitudes of the region toward security cooperation with India. Even before India was invited to join the East Asia Summit and giving legitimacy to the notion that New Delhi could be part of the region's security politics, New Delhi was integrating the Pacific into its conception of its extended neighborhood. As New Delhi began to recognize the new strategic opportunities coming its way amid the changing international perceptions of its economic performance, Prime Minister Atal Bihari Vajpayee also began to signal that India's Look East policy was not limited to Southeast Asia. In his Singapore Lecture in 2002, Vajpayee declared that geography and politics make India an important part of the Asia-Pacific community and that "it does not require formal membership of any regional organization for its recognition or sustenance."[18]

Soon enough, Vajpayee's foreign minister, Yashwant Sinha, was talking about a "second phase" in India's Look East policy.

> The first phase of India's Look East policy was ASEAN-centered and focused primarily on trade and investment linkages. The new phase of this policy is characterized by an expanded definition of 'East,' extending from Australia to East Asia, with ASEAN at its core. The new phase also marks a shift from trade to wider economic and security issues, including joint efforts to protect the sea-lanes and coordinate counter-terrorism activities. The military contacts and joint exercises that India launched with ASEAN states on a low-key basis in the early 1990s are now expanding into full-fledged cooperation.[19]

Sinha's successor at the Foreign Office, Natwar Singh, further developed the concept of India's interests in East Asia and the Pacific: "Developments in East Asia are of direct consequence to India's security and development. We are therefore actively engaged in creating . . . a paradigm of positive in-ter-connectedness of security interests. . . . We face the common threats of WMD proliferation, terrorism, energy shortage, piracy, to name a few."[20] In 2010, India joined the first conclave of the "ASEAN Defense Ministers Meeting Plus," and the Indian leaders were calling it a part of "the wider paradigm shift that characterizes India's Look East policy."[21] It was one thing for India to claim a security role in the Pacific, but entirely another for the region, which already had large number of institutions, to accept New Delhi as relevant, let alone a partner to help manage the security challenges in the region. That recognition and relevance came with the decision to offer India membership of the first East Asia Summit to be held at the end of 2005. The seeming incongruity of bringing India into an avowedly "East Asian" forum was explained by Singapore's Senior Minister Goh Chok Tong when he revealed some of the thinking that went into this decision in early 2005:

> With India's rise it will be increasingly less tenable to regard South Asia and East Asia as distinct strategic theaters interacting only at the margins. U.S.–China–Japan relations will still be important, but a new grand strategic triangle of U.S.–China–India relations will be super-imposed upon it. . . . Reconceptualizing East Asia holistically is [a] strategic imperative. . . . It would be shortsighted and self-defeating for ASEAN to choose a direction that cuts itself off from a dynamic India.[22]

EAST OF MALACCA

While the logic of rebalancing was beginning to create a new basis for East Asia's engagement with India, it was the Indian navy that underlined the future possibilities for New Delhi in the Pacific. Through a series of maritime forays throughout the first decade of the twenty-first century, the Indian navy made it quite clear that it did not have to explain that the separation of different theaters was entirely an intellectual exercise. The navy, after all, has no problem recognizing that the seas are connected to each other and that their separation is largely a political rather than geographical construct. The interconnectedness of the maritime universe meant the navy was well-positioned to fly the Indian flag in the Pacific and lay the basis for a long-term strategic engagement with the East Asian littoral. Shedding decades of military isolationism, India now opened up to service exchanges with major powers as well as regional actors in the Indian Ocean littoral.[23] Although its preliminary naval interaction with the United States got considerable international attention, India devoted special attention to military engagement with Southeast Asian nations. Its naval outreach to Southeast Asia was not a mere consequence of its new interest in the United States but part of an effort to develop its own independent security relationship with the region and demonstrate its capacity to project power.[24] Throughout the 1980s, India had confronted a growing suspicion of its maritime intentions as Southeast Asia reacted to its growing military, and especially naval, capabilities.[25] India had the immediate need to remove the misperceptions, rooted in Southeast Asia's wariness of India's strategic partnership with the Soviet Union. It has been argued:

> For New Delhi, getting in touch with Southeast Asian capitals directly, in order to establish contacts in defense matters, meant that it had cut itself off from the paradigm of derived relationships. The improvement in relations with Southeast Asia was not considered an upshot of the rapprochement with Washington. It thenceforth became a strategic objective in its own right, one that New Delhi intended to follow actively.[26]

The new outward orientation of the Indian navy steadily gathered momentum in the 1990s with wide-ranging bilateral and multilateral contacts. India began to expand its joint naval exercises with all the nations of Southeast Asia, stepped up its port calls in the region, and received ships from the region at its own ports.[27] The Indian navy also recognized the importance of contributing to the production and maintenance of "collective goods" in the Strait of Malacca and the western Pacific Ocean, especially after the events of September 11, 2001.[28]

It was the bold foray of the Indian navy into the South China Sea at the end of 2000 that drew regional attention to India's strategic ambitions east of the Strait of Malacca. Until then, it seemed that India was sticking to the claim that its maritime interests ranged from Aden to Malacca. It was widely presumed that this formulation meant that India might limit itself to the Indian Ocean and that it had no aspirations to play a larger role in the western Pacific Ocean. That China's neighbors were eager to welcome India highlighted the prospects for a new balance of power game in Asian waters. The mission also set the tone for frequent and wide-ranging naval exercises between India and the littoral states of the South China Sea.[29] Even as the Indian navy was seen as contesting China's influence in the region, New Delhi had no reason to give offense to Beijing and was quite eager to initiate simple joint exercises with the Chinese navy.[30] During 2002, the Indian navy undertook a high-profile mission to escort American warships participating in Operation Enduring Freedom through the Strait of Malacca. India was careful in responding to the Bush administration request and embarked on the mission only after informing the three littoral states, Indonesia, Malaysia, and Singapore.[31] At the end of 2004, when the tsunami struck, the Indian navy was quick to respond, on its own, to the disaster and later joined the navies of the United States, Japan, and Australia to provide relief in Southeast Asia. The Indian navy's impressive tsunami relief involved 32 ships in five different operations on the Indian coast, Maldives, Sri Lanka, and Indonesia. This signaled both the operational readiness of the Indian navy and its immense potential to contribute to future humanitarian and other contingencies in Southeast Asia.[32]

In 2005, the Indian aircraft carrier INS *Viraat* arrived for the first time in the ports of Southeast Asia—Klang in Malaysia, Singapore, and Jakarta in Indonesia—and transiting the Strait of Malacca. Even as the *Viraat* flaunted its carrier group to much interest in the region, the Indian naval leadership was diplomatic enough to emphasize cooperation with the littoral states rather than announce its own arrival as a great power. As he set out to meet the carrier group in the western Pacific, the Indian naval chief, Admiral Arun Prakash, said, "We have no intention of patrolling (unilaterally) the Malacca strait. We believe in working with the Singapore, Malaysian and Indonesian navies with whom we have joint programs."[33] Since then, coordinated patrolling with the littoral navies became the vehicle to express India's new commitments to the security of the Strait of Malacca. After decades of acting as a "lone ranger," the Indian navy steadily emerged as an important player in the construction of regional maritime security initiatives in the Strait of Malacca.[34] But the sustained expansion of India's naval engagement did not go unnoticed in China, which began to cast a wary eye on New Delhi's maritime ambitions east of the strait.

It did not take long for India to push its naval forays beyond the South China Sea toward the upper regions of the western Pacific. In the spring and summer of 2007, the Indian navy sailed all the way up to Vladivostok, the home port of the Russian Pacific Fleet, and conducted a series of bilateral and multilateral exercises with the United States, Japan, Russia, and China as well as a number of other nations. The decision to participate in the annual bilateral Malabar naval exercises with the United States in the western Pacific was a bold one and the first affirmation of India's determination to register its presence in northeast Asian waters. The move was made bolder by the first-ever trilateral exercise with the United States and Japan in Tokyo Bay. On the way in and out of the western Pacific, India conducted joint exercises with Singapore, Vietnam, and the Philippines.[35] A high-water mark of India's vigorous naval diplomacy in the first decade of the twenty-first century was participating in large-scale naval exercises with the United States, Japan, Australia, and Singapore in the Bay of Bengal in September 2007. These exercises featured a total of three aircraft carriers, 28 surface vessels, 150 aircraft, and more than 20,000 personnel and were conducted over five days.[36] If these exercises caught the eye of China and the world, they were bound to cause a political storm in India. Coming at a moment when the Indo-U.S. civil nuclear initiative had become a major political controversy, the exercises waved a red rag to the communist partners of the ruling coalition. While these exercises raised alarm about a potential "Asian NATO,"[37] India had no intention of forming such an alliance. The move was a professional initiative by the Indian navy, which saw it as a way of demonstrating its potential on the international stage. The demonstrations against the exercise by the communist parties put the Congress Party on the defensive, and the naval headquarters had to take a step back.[38] As a result, Malabar 2008 became a low-key affair that reverted to the bilateral format with the United States amid the political concern in New Delhi about the signals that multilateral naval exercises might send. But the logic of India's Pacific naval engagement would eventually prevail.

In the summer of 2009, the Indian navy ventured again into the Pacific Ocean to conduct trilateral exercises with the United States and Japan.[39] Malabar 2009, according to official U.S. sources, was about enhancing "interoperability" among the three navies and promoting regional stability in the Pacific. There was special focus on interdiction.[40] India's trilateral exercises planned for early April 2011 off Okinawa acquired a new political edge as they followed the intensification of China's maritime conflicts with Japan, the United States, and ASEAN during the previous months.[41] As Beijing noted the expanding scope and significance of the triangular maritime cooperation among Washington, Tokyo, and New Delhi, the Indian navy sought to maintain a measure of engagement with China. India participated in China's first fleet review at Qingdao during April 2009. The review was organized to mark the sixtieth anniversary of the founding of the People's Liberation Army Navy. The Indian chief of naval staff, Admiral Sureesh Mehta, who joined the celebrations, was keen to signal India's readiness to engage its Chinese counterpart in a substantive dialogue and on confidence building.[42] India's high-level participation in the sixtieth anniversary celebrations of PLAN's founding came on top of occasional port calls and simple naval exercises between the two nations throughout the decade.[43]

India's expanding maritime interest in this decade was not limited to the South China Sea and the upper reaches of the Pacific but also included Australia and the South Pacific. After a period of tension that followed Canberra's vigorous condemnation of New Delhi's nuclear tests in May 1998, Australia was quick to accept the changing weight of India on the Asian and international stage.[44] And as Indo-U.S. naval engagement began to move at a rapid clip during the presidency of George W. Bush, Australia sought to keep pace. In 2006, Australia and India concluded a pact on joint naval exercises in 2005 and a more comprehensive memorandum of understanding on maritime security cooperation in 2006.[45] And during the visit of Prime Minister Kevin Rudd to India in November 2009, both sides agreed to enhance their defense interaction, with a special emphasis on naval cooperation.[46] Indian analysts suggest the opportunities for a "quantum jump" in naval cooperation with Australia.[47] The United States, which welcomed India's naval cooperation, was encouraging similar cooperation with Australia.[48] The decision by Australia's Labor government at the end of 2011 to lift the ban against uranium sales to India and Canberra's enthusiastic welcome to the Obama administration's pivot to Asia amid Australian concerns about the rise of China have created a positive context for an India–Australia partnership.[49] Looking beyond Australia, the Indian navy has begun to make occasional forays toward the island states of Oceania and has invited New Zealand naval delegations to participate in the biennial Milan exercises in the Andaman Sea.[50]

EXPANDING SECURITY COOPERATION

Since the early 1990s, when India reconnected with ASEAN, India has steadily expanded security cooperation with the Southeast Asian neighbors. The absence of territorial disputes between India and the Southeast Asian nations and the perception among some in ASEAN that New Delhi could help contribute to the regional balance were two factors that made it easy to conceive of security cooperation. The end of the Cold War, during which ASEAN warily watched India's drift toward the Soviet Union, also provided a basis for a fresh look at bilateral security partnerships. Yet the construction of military engagement has been slow and incremental rather than dramatic. A firsthand account of India's Look East policy says that the "security consultations and defense cooperation between India and Southeast Asian countries at a bilateral level would require more intensive and focused interaction. The agendas are still not substantive enough."[51] As India began to devote greater attention to East Asia, its decisionmakers were soon claiming that "whereas the initial engagement was primarily economic, military cooperation has now emerged as a growing area of cooperation between India and its eastern neighbors. India is now generally perceived as a more serious and credible player in the regional and global balance of power."[52]

Malaysia, despite somewhat indifferent relations with India during the past two decades, had launched defense cooperation with India by signing a memorandum of understanding in 1993. In retrospect, it looks as if the agreement was driven less by a strategic convergence than by the Malaysian decision to acquire Russian fighter aircraft in the early 1990s. Since then, India has had a substantive military mission in Malaysia focused on training pilots and other air force personnel. India has assisted Malaysia in the maintenance and repair of equipment. In recent years, there has been some talk of India's selling BrahMos missiles to Kuala Lumpur. Malaysia is said to be keen on training to operate submarines. Both sides have recognized the possibilities for significantly upgrading defense collaboration.[53]

Although Malaysia was the first to initiate defense cooperation with India, it is Singapore that has gone the farthest. Training of Singapore military personnel expanded steadily and culminated in a more comprehensive arrangement in 2003, when a bilateral defense cooperation agreement was signed. Since then, India has given Singapore more convenient and wider access to training facilities in India. During Prime Minister Manmohan Singh's visit to Kuala Lumpur in October 2010, the two sides announced the framework for a strategic partnership that included intensified defense cooperation.[54]

Singapore was indeed the first country after the United States that New Delhi allowed to conduct joint exercises on Indian territory.[55] The collaboration is by no means a one-way street. Having acquired a niche position in global arms manufacturing, Singapore is well-positioned to participate in the modernization of India's armed forces as well as to take advantage of its complex restructuring.[56] Singapore has also developed some impressive capabilities in the production of such systems as advanced artillery guns and submersibles, items that are of enduring military value to India. Singapore's critical location in the Strait of Malacca at the confluence of the Pacific and Indian Oceans and its ready welcome to the Indian navy traversing the two oceans have been an important attraction to New Delhi. Singapore has emerged as the closest security partner of India in the East.[57]

Meanwhile, India itself is looking at the possibility of exporting arms, an area in which it had little success in the past. New Delhi, however, has begun to explore opportunities in Southeast Asia, which is emerging as a major market for weapons. As China builds up its own armed forces, many Southeast Asian countries have followed suit.[58] It is no surprise then that India and Indonesia are reportedly discussing the prospects of jointly producing weapons and military equipment. Ideas about equity tie-ups between companies on both sides in the defense sector have apparently been put on the table. These proposals have emerged out of the pursuit of security cooperation arising from the defense cooperation agreement signed in 2001. A joint declaration on strategic partnership issued in New Delhi in November 2005 said, "President Yudhoyono welcomed India's offer of cooperation with the Department of Defense of the Republic of Indonesia in the procurement of defense supplies, defense technologies, joint production and joint projects."[59] During Yudhoyono's visit to India in January 2011, the two sides expressed satisfaction at the progress in defense cooperation and announced the institutionalization of a biennial dialogue between the defense ministers.[60]

Vietnam has been an important focus of India's defense diplomacy in the western Pacific. The declaration on strategic partnership issued by the Indian and Vietnamese prime ministers in July 2007 said: "Recognizing the important role that India and Vietnam are called upon to play in the promotion of regional security, the two leaders welcomed the steady development of bilateral defense and security ties between their countries and pledged themselves to *strengthen cooperation in defense supplies, joint projects, training cooperation and intelligence exchanges*" (emphasis added).[61] During a visit to Vietnam in October 2010, the Indian defense minister, A. K. Antony, said India "will provide support to Vietnam to enhance and upgrade the capabilities of [the] Services in general and [the] Navy in particular" and "help Vietnam in its capacity building for repair and maintenance of its platforms."[62]

India's special relationship with Vietnam, of course, draws considerable international and regional attention, given their past security collaboration against China.[63] India's strategic relationship with Vietnam was indeed part of the problem between New Delhi and ASEAN during the 1980s. Much has indeed changed since then. Vietnam is now part of ASEAN and has vastly improved its relations with China since the 1980s. Yet the idea of Hanoi playing a key role in India's presumed efforts to balance China remains an alluring story in Asia, and at the center of this speculation is Vietnam's strategically located Cam Ranh Bay.[64] Some Indian defense analysts talk enthusiastically about gaining access to the deep water port and establishing a credible naval presence in the South China Sea. Some in the region fear that such a move might set off a conflict between China and India in the South China Sea. As an Australian skeptic has argued, "An Indian naval presence at Cam Ranh at the beginning of this decade would no doubt have been seen as confrontational by China and, perhaps more importantly, is unlikely to have been welcomed by the ASEAN states. It would have reflected an older Indian way of doing business with both China and ASEAN."[65] New Delhi is fully aware of the strategic potential of the relationship with Vietnam but is also aware of Vietnam's own sensitive relationship with China.[66] The India–Vietnam relationship is a work in progress, and rapid advances on security cooperation are likely to be determined by their respective imperatives to manage their special complex relationships with China.[67] As tensions mounted in 2010–2011 between Vietnam and China in the South China Sea, Delhi and Hanoi have stepped up their naval contacts and intensified negotiations on defense cooperation. India has also become more active in expressing its interest in the freedom of navigation in the South China Sea and the peaceful resolution of territorial disputes between Beijing and its maritime neighbors.

While India's defense relationships with all the regional actors are beginning to expand, it is New Delhi's security cooperation with the major powers that could be consequential to the balance of power in the Pacific. One of the more significant developments of our time in Asia has been the rapid expansion of India's military and security partnership with the United States during the eight years of the Bush administration (2001–2009). Although political controversy in India and diplomatic attention around the world have been riveted on the civil nuclear imitative, it is the less noticed but sustained progress on defense cooperation that promises to accelerate India's emergence as an influential factor in Pacific Asia. It might be recalled that at the beginning of his second term, President Bush had explicitly declared that one of his objectives was to "assist India to become a major world power in the twenty-first century."[68] Although a skeptical India took its time examining the gift horse of the nuclear initiative, New Delhi opened up bit by bit to a stronger defense partnership with Washington. The ten-year framework of defense cooperation signed by India and the United States in June 2005 laid out an ambitious framework for engagement on bilateral, multilateral, and global objectives.[69] This defining of political objectives for military cooperation was the first agreement of its kind that independent India ever signed. To be sure, there was some resistance from the Indian left, and the bureaucracy was not certain about the reliability of the United States as a defense partner. Key stakeholders in India, including its armed forces, however, recognized the value of military and defense industrial collaboration with the United States.[70]

Since 2005 the intensity and scope of Indo-U.S. military exercises have rapidly expanded. During 2006–2011, India bought a few major U.S. weapons platforms. These include the USS *Trenton* amphibious warfare ship to move troops, the C-130J military transport aircraft, the P-8 maritime reconnaissance aircraft, and the C-17 heavy lift transporter. The United States was also eager to win the mega contract for medium multi-role combat aircraft worth more than $10 billion and has mounted a heavy lobbying effort from President Obama himself.[71] But progress has been slow and incremental as India appeared hesitant about signing off on a range of enabling agreements that Washington argued were legal requirements for effective cooperation and the transfer of sensitive systems and technologies. India eventually agreed to sign an end-user monitoring agreement with the United States during Secretary of State Hillary Clinton's visit to New Delhi in July 2009. It was reluctant, however, to sign other agreements, such as the LSA (Logistics Support Agreement), CISMOA (Communications Interoperability and Security Memorandum of Agreement), and the BECA (Basic Exchange and Cooperation Agreement for Geospatial Information).[72] Despite these hurdles, there has been steady if slow expansion of bilateral engagement on arms transfers and defense industrial collaboration between the two countries. The door has opened for U.S. arms manufacturers, and this in turn has begun to increase New Delhi's negotiating leverage with its traditional suppliers in Russia, France, and Iran.[73] Meanwhile, the Indian private sector is eagerly looking forward to partnering with U.S. firms in developing supply chains for U.S. military equipment in India. Put simply, access to the U.S. defense market has the potential to accelerate the transformation of the Indian armed forces and defense industry. But the cumbersome process of India's defense management and arms acquisition and the burdensome U.S. regulations on advanced technology transfers have tended to limit the full potential of bilateral defense cooperation.[74] If India and the United States can fully leverage the potential of a bilateral defense connection, they will be in a position to stabilize the balance of power in the western Pacific. That the United States was prepared to open its military stores to India while continuing to deny arms sales to China and preventing its European allies from buying arms did not go unnoticed in Beijing.[75]

China's concerns about expanding Indo-U.S. defense cooperation acquired an extra edge as it saw Tokyo join Washington in the security outreach to New Delhi. Japan has been the last among the great powers of the world to sense India's rising power potential. But during the final years of the premiership of Junichiro Koizumi and the brief tenure of Shinzo Abe in the mid-2000s, Japan sought to define a new approach to India.[76]

Traditionally, India was not part of Japan's conception of Asia. In expanding its geographic definition of Asia to beyond Burma in the west and drawing India into a strategic partnership, Japan hopes it has a better chance of coping with the unfolding redistribution of power in Asia and establishing a stable balance of power in the region. India, in turn, sees huge strategic complementarities with Japan. To be sure, India's improved relations with the United States have made it easier for Tokyo to embark on a new relationship with New Delhi. Equally important is the fact that growing uncertainty in the Sino-Japanese relationship has had the same effect on Tokyo.[77] Sensing the new dynamic in Japan, India was quite happy to endorse Abe's proposal for greater political coordination among Asia's four leading democracies.[78] India was, however, quite conscious of potential Japanese backsliding, given the internal divisions in Japan and the depth of the Sino-Japanese relationship. India had no desire to present its emerging partnership with Japan as directed against China but was signaling the prospect of a deeper relationship with Tokyo and the political will to move at whatever speed the Japanese could muster. Prime Minister Manmohan Singh's visit to Tokyo in December 2006 unveiled the commitment to build a strategic partnership. He followed it up in October 2008 by signing a joint declaration on security cooperation similar to the one that Tokyo and Canberra had signed in 2007. These are the first security arrangements that Japan has undertaken outside of its alliance with the United States.[79] At the end of 2009, during the visit of Prime Minister Yukio Hatoyama to New Delhi, an action plan was unveiled to advance Japan–India defense cooperation.[80] Although the agreement merely lists the potential areas for security cooperation and identifies the mechanisms for their implementation, it has been considered a big step for Japan to take. It has signed only one similar declaration, with Australia. What is important to note, however, is the fact that Tokyo and New Delhi are steadily inching toward the construction of a security relationship, bringing their armed forces closer to each other, and cautiously undertaking joint military missions such as securing the sea lines of communication in the Indian Ocean and western Pacific.[81] In 2010, India and Japan held the so-called two plus two dialogue that brought together senior officials from their defense and foreign ministries.[82] While the Indian and Japanese leadership expressed satisfaction at the pace and direction of their security cooperation, there is residual skepticism about the political will and bureaucratic capacity to build consequential defense cooperation, especially in the context of the inevitable Chinese suspicion or hostility.[83]

As it expanded its defense interaction with Japan, India has also begun to focus on South Korea. Until the late 2000s, India's relations with South Korea were conspicuous for the lack of strategic warmth despite a deepening economic partnership. While India maintained a neutral stance on issues relating to the Korean Peninsula during the Cold War and beyond, Seoul had little incentive to engage India on political issues of central concern to it. As South Korea emerged as a major investor and trade partner in India from the 1990s and India became increasingly wary of North Korea's nuclear and missile links with Pakistan, a new context emerged to facilitate security cooperation between New Delhi and Seoul.[84] India invited the South Korean president, Lee Myung-bak, as the guest of honor for its Republic Day celebrations in 2010 and declared the establishment of a strategic partnership. Prime Minister Singh and President Lee agreed to intensify bilateral defense engagement and promote greater cooperation on maritime security.[85] This was followed by the first-ever visit by an Indian defense minister to South Korea and the signing of two defense agreements—one laying out a substantive program of military exchanges and the other on research, development, and co-production of weapons systems.[86]

From the early 1990s, when India launched its Look East policy, its relationship with East Asia has come a long way. While it continues to see ASEAN as the core of East Asia, India's interests have broadened to include the western Pacific as a whole. Although India's economic ties with East Asia are unlikely to ever become comparable to those of neighboring China, India's impressive economic growth has created a sound basis for India's relations with the Asia Pacific. In seeking to develop strategic partnerships with the United States, Japan, Australia, and South Korea, deepening political engagement with China, building security partnerships with key ASEAN states, and pursuing a vigorous maritime diplomacy, India has begun to create for itself some room for maneuver in the Western theater. India's future in the Pacific is not about matching the military weight of China in the littoral. It is about generating strategic options that did not previously exist for the littoral states of the western Pacific. If India continues to maintain high economic growth rates and builds on the framework for security cooperation that it has developed in the region, New Delhi's influence in the Pacific theater can only expand.

India's willingness to abandon its past unrealistic ambition about leading Asia, its deliberate choice to adopt a low-key role, its emphasis on pragmatic cooperation rather than ideological posturing, and its cooperative maritime strategy make it a potentially valuable security partner for many nations in Pacific Asia. While India's security interaction with East Asia and the Pacific has steadily risen, there is much concern in the region and beyond that New Delhi is not doing enough to build on the emerging opportunities. Officials and many leaders in ASEAN countries complain of India's episodic interest in the region and its inability to quickly follow through on agreements. Contrasting India's performance with China's purposeful engagement of the region, a senior Singaporean diplomat told U.S. officials in 2009 that "his stupid Indian friends" were "half in, half out of ASEAN."[87] Others reflect on the "fitful progress" in India's engagement with the East and its reluctance to become an agenda-setter in the region. India's Look East policy "has succeeded insofar as institutionalizing India's engagement with the Asia Pacific and bolstering New Delhi's claim to be a regional actor of consequence. But otherwise, this vaunted policy has failed to achieve its full potential."[88] Given India's inadequate capabilities on the military and diplomatic fronts and the cautious nature of its defense diplomacy, India's strategic footprint in the Pacific will expand only slowly and in fits and starts. China's profile in the Indian Ocean, meanwhile, is steadily rising. That is the focus of chapter 7.

Chapter Seven

CHINA EYES
THE INDIAN OCEAN

China's principal maritime preoccupations have been in the western Pacific—reunifying Taiwan, defending China's maritime territorial claims, and constraining the naval dominance of the United States. None of these concerns has gone away. Yet, the Indian Ocean might increasingly demand greater military attention from a rising China. Some analysts argue that "once it secures the East, Yellow and South China Seas to its satisfaction, Beijing will vector its nautical energies not eastward but toward the south and southwest, where its interests in energy security and economic development lie."[1] Although not everyone accepts this definitive assessment, most would agree with the proposition that while the Pacific imperatives are likely to remain predominant in the Chinese calculus, the Indian Ocean is beginning to acquire some strategic salience in Beijing.[2] Chinese analysts recognize the difficulties of operating in the Indian Ocean, such as extended lines of communication, critical choke points that control entry and exit to the ocean, the dominance of the United States in the littoral, and the growing capabilities of the Indian navy.[3] While the debate goes on about the relative weight of the two oceans in China's maritime strategy, Beijing's profile in the Indian Ocean has steadily risen since the mid-1990s and crossed a major threshold in late 2008 when China decided to send and sustain a naval contingent on anti-piracy missions in the Gulf of Aden.

As the world pays closer attention to China's rising profile in the Indian Ocean region, it is easy to conclude that Beijing's interests in this important littoral are recent and driven by its current concerns about energy security, growing dependence on the natural resources of the region, and the need to secure its sea lines of communication that facilitate China's massive trade with the Indian Ocean littoral and beyond with Europe. All these factors indeed are significant and will be discussed below. China's Indian Ocean strategy, though, must also be seen as driven by Beijing's sense of its own rise and its strategic imagination as a natural global power.[4] Despite the use of history to lend legitimacy to Beijing's current naval ambitions, there is no denying that China's engagement with the Indian Ocean goes back in time. Chinese government publicists often point to the seven voyages of Admiral Zheng He to the Indian Ocean in the early decades of the fifteenth century.[5] Many of these expeditions in the Ming era did stop at the ports of Sri Lanka, Kerala in the southwestern coast of India, the Gulf, and the east coast of Africa. More recently, China's interest in the Indian Ocean started coming into view from the mid-1980s, when its navy showed up in the Indian Ocean. On the face of it, there was no immediate reason for this naval foray. What it signaled was the consciousness in Beijing of the strategic importance of the Indian Ocean littoral. Although it enjoyed a positive relationship with the United States in the final years of the Cold War and its relations with India were improving, Beijing would not endorse the U.S. and Western dominance in the Indian Ocean, nor would it acquiesce in the notion that the Indian Ocean was "India's Ocean."

The Chinese naval warships made their first appearance in the Indian Ocean at the end of 1985. A two-ship squadron of the PLA Navy—a *Luda* class destroyer and a replenishment ship—had an extended foray in the Indian Ocean from November 1985 to January 1986. The squadron made port calls at Karachi in Pakistan, Colombo in Sri Lanka, and Chittagong in Bangladesh. According to one assessment, "The 1985 cruise demonstrated the PLAN's capability of operating in the IOR [Indian Ocean Region], began the process of familiarizing PLAN officers and men with the topography and hydrography of that region, and demonstrated Beijing's refusal to allow New Delhi a veto over China's military relations with countries of the Indian Ocean littoral."[6] In the second cruise in the Indian Ocean at the end of the 1980s, the PLAN training ship *Zheng He* carried two hundred cadets to Karachi, Mumbai, Chittagong, and Bangkok. The port call in Mumbai was a consequence of the slow normalization of Sino-Indian relations that was initiated in 1988 when Prime Minister Rajiv Gandhi visited China. If Beijing sought to reassure India that its outreach into the Indian Ocean was not aimed at India, the Indian navy was quite keen to check out the Chinese navy. As the Chinese naval missions into the Indian Ocean became a regular feature, the Indian strategic community began to assess the long-term implications for India's security.[7]

GOING WEST, FINDING SOUTH

Much of the Western and Asian writing on China's Indian Ocean policy tends to focus on the growing Chinese dependence on energy and resource trade with the Indian Ocean littoral and the need to protect the vital sea lines of communication. While this factor is real, India has a broader appreciation of China's Indian Ocean imperative: New Delhi sees China's coming into the Indian Ocean not just from the east through the Strait of Malacca, but also from the north. From the Indian perspective, the contemporary Chinese interest in the Indian Ocean is also driven by Beijing's enduring continental challenges. In the mid-1990s, China turned its gaze from organizing an economic miracle on its eastern seaboard to the challenges of development, stabilization, and national economic integration of its western regions. In the early phase of reform, Deng Xiaoping had argued famously in favor of letting some people (and regions) get rich first. Once the reforms began to produce dramatic results on the eastern seaboard, China had the resources to invest in massive developmental schemes of its remote western regions. The "Go West" strategy unveiled in the late 1990s by the Chinese Communist Party would begin to transform the vast underdeveloped regions of China that comprised six provinces (Gansu, Guizhou, Qinghai, Shaanxi, Sichuan, and Yunnan), five autonomous regions (Guangxi, Inner Mongolia, Ningxia, Tibet, and Xinjiang), and one municipality (Chongqing). These regions contain 71.4 percent of mainland China's area but only 28.8 percent of its population.[8] These regions were remote only in terms of contemporary political geography. They were once the very center of the Silk Road that connected China with South Asia, the Middle East, and the Mediterranean. If the rise of the maritime world steadily marginalized these regions, the evolution of the state system in inner Asia also made them "landlocked." China was now determined to reconnect them to the world.

China also recognized that successful development of its periphery required a new way of thinking about the security challenges it had faced for decades in its restive far western regions of Xinjiang, Tibet, and Yunnan. Beijing's answer was massive infrastructural development that promoted the internal as well as external market connectivities of Western China. "As against the previous era in which Tibet, Xinjiang and Yunnan were closed and national and ethnic conflicts there were sources of great insecurity, Beijing's new approach sees nationally and internationally integrated infrastructural development and pro-active open door policies as answers to the challenges of both security and modernization."[9] Beijing's project to develop western China and link it to the internal and external markets became one of the greatest projects undertaken anywhere in the world. Some have compared China's Go West strategy to the Russian expansion into the Far East and Siberia and the American opening of its far western regions in the nineteenth century. While the Russian and American territorial expansion ended on different coasts of the Pacific Ocean, all of China's western provinces are landlocked. Some of its neighbors in Central Asia were themselves landlocked, and some of them had to cross more than one country to access the sea. To the south, the subcontinent was a more attractive option to reach the oceans. The ports of South Asia—in Pakistan, India, and Burma—were the closest to western China and offered the shortest routes to the sea. Therefore, building transport corridors linking Xinjiang, Tibet, and Yunnan to the ports of South Asia became an integral element of China's Go West strategy.[10]

China's grand conception of transport corridors radiating out of its western frontiers marked the third stage in the modernization of transport infrastructure in Xinjiang, Tibet, and Yunnan. In the first phase, the 1950s, road building was given great emphasis by Mao Zedong, who wanted to make sure that these provinces inhabited by rebellious minorities were securely linked to the heartland. The second phase, in the 1960s and 1970s, involved the emergence of a transborder dimension, when China sought to expand its influence across borders with specific road projects. For example, the construction of a friendship highway with Nepal connecting Lhasa with Kathmandu was announced in 1961. It was part of a larger strategic effort to pry Nepal out of the British-Indian sphere of influence and claim its right to establish substantive political cooperation with New Delhi's South Asian neighbors.[11] The project was more political than economic in that China was not interested in trade and transborder economic cooperation. Similarly China's decision in 1964 to build the Karakoram Highway into Pakistan from its Xinjiang Province was also strategic in orientation. Its aim was to consolidate the political relationship with Pakistan and outflank India's positions on the Kashmir dispute.[12] The third phase of road building, in the 2000s, was far more sweeping in its conception and far more consequential for the economic, political, and strategic future of Asia. It is taking place in the context of China's economic globalization and an acute sense of strategic opportunities from pursuing economic regionalism. There was also a new self-assurance in how China thought of its sensitive spaces on the frontier being inhabited by restive minorities. In the past, China had locked down these spaces and guarded zealously against negative influences from across the frontiers. The emphasis was now on a forward policy that sought to secure its frontiers by influencing the regions across them. As China considered the benefits of linking its far western regions to the seas of the Indian Ocean, three transportation corridors through the subcontinent and its fringes would present themselves: one would reconnect Lhasa with Kolkata; the Pakistan corridor would integrate the Karakoram Highway with either Karachi or Gwadar on Pakistan's Makran coast; and the Irrawaddy Corridor through Burma would link Yunnan Province with the Bay of Bengal.

Lhasa to Kolkata

As world attention turned to the breathtaking Chinese project to build a rail link to Lhasa through the forbidding Tibetan plateau, international concerns were largely about the implications for the Tibetan struggle for autonomy, the dangers of increased Han migration into Tibet, the accelerated destruction of the unique Tibetan culture along with its deepening integration into the Chinese mainland, the complex engineering that went into making the railroad, and the railroad's impact on the fragile Tibetan environment.[13] Although these concerns were important, it is necessary to underline other important consequences—the end of Tibet's isolation from the rest of the world and the rediscovery of its historic role as the bridge between the subcontinent and inner Asia. The rail line was part of a massive expansion of the transport infrastructure in Tibet over the last many decades. From no real road mileage in the early 1950s when China moved in, Tibet in the first decade of the twenty-first century had close to 40,000 kilometers (24,900 miles) of road network that integrates Tibet within itself and links it to neighboring provinces.[14] The strategic decision to connect Tibet to its neighbors meant essentially the subcontinent. Unlike Xinjiang, which shares borders with many Central Asian nations as well as Pakistan, and Yunnan, which opens out to Burma and Southeast Asia, Tibet's borders are essentially with Nepal, Bhutan, and India.

The relatively small population of Tibet was concentrated in the eastern parts of the plateau that were integrated economically with the densely populated Eastern Gangetic Plains. After British India opened up Tibet in the early years of the twentieth century, all its basic necessities—including food and fuel—were largely imported from the Gangetic Plain. The historic Silk Road through the Chumbi Valley between Tibet and the southern slopes of the Himalayas was the lifeline that connected Lhasa to its closest port—Kolkata.[15] Until the late 1950s, when Beijing developed internal communication links with Tibet, the easiest access to Lhasa for the Chinese and the rest of the world was through Kolkata and from there northward to the Chumbi Valley. Not surprisingly, the resolution of the Sino-Indian dispute over Sikkim's integration into India in 2003 reopened this road at the Nathu La pass.[16] Although the route is not immediately amenable to significant traffic, the fact is that the rapid growth of the Chinese and Indian economies and the physical proximity of western China and South Asia opened the door for the exploration of many complementarities between the two regions.[17] Although Tibet itself has a small population, western China as a whole has close to 300 million people and the Gangetic Plain, which covers eastern India and Bangladesh, is one of the world's most populous regions. As China's transportation infrastructure in Tibet expanded rapidly and Beijing began to explore the extension of the road and rail links into Nepal and Bhutan, consternation in India has grown.[18] To be sure, the new infrastructure had created a stronger basis for the PLA to operate on its southwestern borders, and Chinese influence was bound to penetrate deeper and faster into the subcontinent. Just as India has been apprehensive about the implications of China's drive toward the subcontinent from the north, Beijing, too, is anxious about India's continuing influence north of the Himalayas at a moment when Tibet has become restive once more.[19] As renewed Sino-Indian tensions over Tibet express themselves on the long Indo-Tibetan border, the prospect of the Lhasa–Kolkata corridor is unlikely to become a reality. Nevertheless, the logic of Chinese infrastructural development is likely to play itself out by expanding the transport links between the Tibetan plateau and the Indo-Gangetic Plains. In early 2012, Beijing announced plans to extend its rail network in Tibet from Lhasa to Shigatse, close to the borders with Nepal and India.[20] India's own response to the infrastructural development has been to modernize and expand its own road and rail network in the regions bordering Tibet.[21] One way or another, it would seem that Tibet will edge closer to the Indian Ocean.

Kashgar to Karachi

If uncertain relations between Beijing and New Delhi slow down the process of linking western China with the Indian Ocean through Tibet, the strategic partnership between Beijing and Islamabad has accelerated the possibilities of constructing such an effective corridor between Kashgar in Xinjiang and the Pakistani ports in Balochistan—either at Karachi in Sindh Province or Gwadar in Balochistan Province. As part of the broader Go West strategy, China began to conceive of the historic city of Kashgar as a commercial and transportation hub that would link its Xinjiang Province with Central Asia and the subcontinent.[22] Well before the Tibet railway came into view, China had completed the construction of the South Xinjiang Railway line during the Ninth Five-Year Plan (1996–2000) and positioned the province for a massive integration with the mainland and the outside world.[23] As part of the effort to make Kashgar a hub for Central Asia, China considered plans to move the Xinjiang rail network into Pakistan and upgrade the old road network heading south across the Karakoram mountain range.

With the turn of the decade and the Tenth Five-Year Plan (2001–2005) came major Chinese decisions on modernizing the Karakoram Highway and building a greenfield port at Gwadar and a special emphasis on infrastructural development in Pakistan.[24] These two projects were part of a Chinese commitment to modernize the entire transport infrastructure inside Pakistan as well as transform China's connectivity with the region and the world. The Gwadar port—conceived, implemented, and funded largely by China—would be built in phases. The first phase was completed in 2006, and work on the second phase is reported to be in full swing. The port project was only one element of an ambitious geopolitical conception under which new road and rail networks would radiate outward from Gwadar and link up eventually with the upgraded Karakoram Highway. A northward rail line was to be built connecting Gwadar with Pakistan's main east-west rail line at Dalbandin and link the new port with the Iranian port of Bandar Abbas in the west, Karachi in the east, and Rawalpindi in the north. A two-lane highway would run all along the Makran coast to join the Indus Valley road and rail system. A road would also connect Gwadar with Chaman on the border with Afghanistan near Quetta. This in turn would tie into the garland road in Afghanistan, which connects all major cities in the nation and a northern spur that moves into Central Asia. "The Gwadar project combined with all the modernization of Pakistan's rail system will substantially enhance China's ability to move goods and people between its western regions via Pakistan to the Arabian Sea—and as importantly from Gwadar to Central Asia," a leading analyst of Chinese transborder projects in the region concluded.[25]

Beyond the upgrading of the transport links in and across Pakistan, China has become a major investor in a broad range of sectors within Pakistan, Afghanistan, and Iran. By combining major infrastructure projects with the development of natural resources (both petroleum and minerals) in the three countries and establishing special economic zones, China appears to have developed a comprehensive framework for emerging as a strategic player in southwest Asia and the Middle East and drawing the region into a tight embrace with western China.[26] For India, the more immediate concern has been Beijing's massive investments in the disputed regions of Jammu and Kashmir that are under the control of Pakistan. The Indian foreign minister, S. M. Krishna, called these projects "illegal."[27] They include the establishment of local transport links between Kashgar and Gilgit, the building of hydroelectric projects, and feasibility studies on extending the South Xinjiang Railway from Kashgar into Kashmir and from there toward Rawalpindi, where it would link into Pakistan's rail network.[28] Many other powers since the time of Alexander the Great dreamed of mastering the turbulent regions across the Hindu Kush mountains by developing new transport corridors, but few have succeeded. China, too, faces a number of problems, not least the insurgency in Balochistan, the political instability in Pakistan, the absence of modern state structures in Afghanistan, very difficult physical terrain that includes wide swaths of desert and some of the world's most forbidding mountain ranges, and above all the emerging tension between the Han and Uyghur Muslim population in Xinjiang seen in the rioting in the late 1990s as well as 2009.[29] Nevertheless, China may be well on its way to constructing a credible continental bridge linking Eurasia, western China, and the Indian Ocean.

The Irrawaddy Corridor

While the Kolkata corridor is unrealizable in the context of Sino-Indian distrust and the Kashgar corridor is making progress amid deepening partnership between China and Pakistan, the Irrawaddy Corridor linking Yunnan Province in southwestern China and the Indian Ocean through Burma has begun to take shape. Garver traces the origin of the Irrawaddy Corridor project to the mid-1980s.[30] It was a moment when China was just opening up its sensitive southwestern and western regions. Given the long border between Yunnan and Burma, it was only natural that China looked south to Burma in seeking a route to the Indian Ocean. But Rangoon, which was in a prolonged self-imposed isolation, was not ready for such big thinking. By the end of the 1980s, when Burma was going through a massive internal political convulsion, its military rulers sought to reengage the country with the world.[31] While the West shunned Burmese rulers for their brutal crushing of the pro-democracy movement, ASEAN, China, and India embraced Burma as a neighbor and without a reference to its reprehensible internal policies.[32]

As Burma joined the rest of Asia in pursuing outward-looking economic policies, its natural geopolitical significance began to emerge. Historically, Burma was a land bridge between India and Southeast Asia. That Burma is either the "backdoor" or the "southern gateway to China" is also deeply etched in the minds of students of war, peace, and geopolitics.[33] Although the Burma theater at the confluence of India, China, and Southeast Asia was critical for the defeat and rollback of the Japanese occupation of Asia during the Second World War, it steadily receded from the popular consciousness and is now known as the "forgotten war."[34] As socialist fervor gripped China, India, and Burma to different degrees in the postcolonial period, the region's strategic importance tended to fade from global strategic discourse. From the late 1980s, when China reached out to the Burmese rulers, Beijing had conceived its relationship with the southern neighbor in a strategic way and maintained a relentless focus on building an enduring partnership with Burma. It has been tempting in many quarters to see Burma as a mere supplicant of China. Such a view is entirely misplaced; since the late 1980s, Sino-Burmese cooperation has been a mutually beneficial arrangement.[35] The Burmese military consolidated its hold over the nation with the help of military, economic, and diplomatic assistance from Beijing. China, in return, won privileged access to Burma's rich natural resources and access as well to the Indian Ocean. Bilateral commerce reached $2.4 billion in 2007–2008, accounting for a quarter of Burma's foreign trade and a 60 percent increase over what it was three years earlier. Chinese companies have invested heavily in the country's manufacturing, mining, power generation, and energy sectors, and in 2008–2009 China emerged as Burma's number one investor, pumping $856 million into the country, or 87 percent of all foreign investment.[36]

At the heart of this relationship is the Irrawaddy Corridor. This is not a single project, but a combination of different forms of transportation—road, rail, and riverine—within Burma along the fluvial north-south axis that links up with new port infrastructure at the mouth of the river and on the western coast that looks into the Bay of Bengal. Over the past two decades, China has developed different elements of the Irrawaddy Corridor. China helped modernize the Burma Road (also known as the Stilwell Road), which was built by American engineers from northeastern India through northern Burma into southwestern China to supply the Chinese nationalist forces fighting the Japanese in the Second World War.[37] It has also helped upgrade parts of the Burmese railway system. Concurrently, China has been extending its railway network toward the Burmese border and has plans to expand it to the Arakan coast on the Bay of Bengal. Beijing hopes international assistance will help complete the remaining portion within China and the current railheads in Burma, since this stretch is part of the proposed Trans-Asian Railway. China has offered generous assistance to dredge the river in its middle portions and ease the movement of riverine traffic toward the south. China is also building two important ports—one at Kyaukphyu on the Indian Ocean coastline on the west and another at Thilawa, 40 kilometers south of Rangoon on the Irrawaddy Basin. By 2000–2001, the improvement of the different elements of the north-south corridor was beginning to move substantive traffic of goods from China to the Bay of Bengal. The building of the two major ports will also allow China to move goods brought from its industrial east coast up the Irrawaddy into northern Burma and southwestern China.[38] Few examples in contemporary international relations compare with China's determination to bind Burma to southwestern China. The political reforms in Burma that began to unfold in 2011 seemed to cast a shadow over the relationship with China. Responding to public pressure, the government of Burma canceled a hydropower project contracted with China. Coupled with the Western outreach to Burma, there has been much speculation about Beijing's losing its privileged position in the country.[39] While Burma's opening has given its rulers a more diverse set of foreign policy options, it is unlikely that the special relationship with China, rooted in history and geography, will simply disappear.[40]

THE "MALACCA DILEMMA"

For many in New Delhi's strategic community, Beijing's transport corridors through the subcontinent tend to reinforce the traditional suspicion that China seeks to encircle India in the subcontinent. Only a few in India might acknowledge the fact that whatever Beijing's motivations, its attempts to gain access to the Indian Ocean through the subcontinent are rooted in the logic of the economic development of its western regions. A broader perspective would also suggest that China's corridors through the subcontinent are similar to those that Beijing is developing in its other border regions. Beijing sought to boost economic development in many of its provinces by linking them with the nations across the border. The instruments for this were trans-frontier transportation links and organizations for subregional economic cooperation between China and different parts of East Asia. The rise of China and the consequential transborder economic integration are now part of the geoeconomic landscape of Asia.[41] Many outside observers did not see any significant or threatening geopolitical implications from China's purposeful pursuit of regional economic integration. The strategic communities across the region and in the United States viewed China's new policy as driven by the need to bring stability and security to the border provinces. According to one assessment, the fact that China's regional rail and road corridors were moving ahead in Southeast Asia "suggests acceptance and opportunism are winning out over fear and, on balance, the rewards of . . . [integration with China] . . . are perceived as greater than the risks."[42] But the security perceptions of these corridors altered significantly once the securitization of China's growing seaborne imports of energy began in both Beijing and other Asian capitals. As concerns on energy security mounted across the world in the first decade of the new century, China's transport corridors began to acquire a powerful maritime dimension and turned the focus onto the new importance of the Indian Ocean in the Chinese strategic calculus. This new interest was framed by the phrase "the Malacca Dilemma."

For millennia, the Malacca Strait has been one of the most important waterways to facilitate movement between the Pacific Ocean and the Indian Ocean. The Greco-Roman empires, the many kingdoms of India, and the Arab traders all used the waterway to trade with Southeast Asia and the western Pacific littoral. For the empires and kingdoms based in China, Java, Sumatra, and Malaya, the Malacca Strait was a valuable sea lane. Ports along its littoral became major entrepots for trade between the Indian and Pacific Oceans. Amid the decline of China, India, and the Arab world and the rise of Europe, the strait fell into the hands of the Portuguese, and later the Dutch and British. During the age of imperialism, the strait was further elevated as a critical link in trade between Europe, Africa, the Indian Ocean littoral, and the Asia Pacific. During the Cold War, it was seen as a critical choke point to prevent Russian ships and submarines from entering the Indian Ocean.[43] After the rapid growth of Japan and the broader East Asian miracle, the Malacca Strait acquired additional importance as an economic lifeline that brought natural resources to Japan, South Korea, and other "tiger" economies and the export of industrial goods from them to non-American destinations. The emergence of China as an economic giant rapidly transformed the strait into a pivotal geographic location. Today, about a third of international commerce travels through the Strait of Malacca. The deadweight of the ships traveling through the Strait of Malacca was around 46 billion tons in 2004 and is expected to rise to 6.4 billion tons in 2020. In recent years, piracy, terrorism, and natural disasters constituted much of the security concerns over the huge amount of trade going through the strait.[44] As China faced up to the implications of its rapidly increasing dependence on seaborne imports of energy, it was only a matter of time before Beijing securitized its vulnerabilities in the Strait of Malacca. Unlike the other actors in East Asia—Japan, South Korea, and the tiger economies—China was not going to rely entirely on the U.S. role as the provider of maritime security in the region. As the scale of these imports—both in absolute terms and as the share of its national energy needs—multiplied in an economy that grew at double-digit rates, Beijing began to devote political attention to it at the highest levels.[45]

The term "Malacca Dilemma" is attributed to President Hu Jintao. In a speech to a Chinese Communist Party conference in November 2003, Hu reportedly dwelled on the challenges inherent in supplying the nation's growing dependence on imported energy resources, which had to traverse the Indian Ocean and come into the Pacific through the Strait of Malacca. Hu apparently noted the U.S. dominance of the strait and its implications for China's energy security.[46] As the Chinese discourse began to focus on the Malacca Dilemma, the concerns in Beijing were not limited to the United States but also encompassed India. The growing U.S. naval cooperation with India and New Delhi's outreach to other countries were seen in China as underlining the potential danger. As one newspaper pointed out: "Oil is shipped from the Gulf via the Indian Ocean and the Strait of Malacca to China, Korea, and Japan. If another (power) holds the lifeline, the three importing countries will suffer severe blows. Because (the U.S.) strategy is to hold sway over the 'oil route,' the U.S. has in recent years showered attentions on India, Vietnam, Singapore, all of which lie on that route."[47] Some Chinese analysts argue that India "is trying to achieve military superiority at the entry and exit points of 'its' ocean: the straits of Malacca, Hormuz, and Bab-el-Mandeb, the Suez Canal, the Cape of Good Hope, and the Agalega

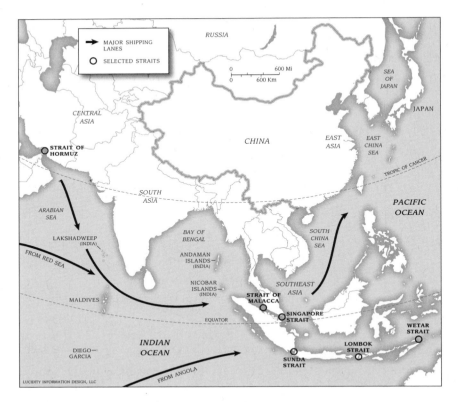

Figure 3. China's Indian Ocean Sea Lanes

Archipelago. . . . If bilateral relations between India and China should deteriorate, India could put China in a vulnerable position by choosing to play out disagreements in the Indian Ocean."[48]

For many Chinese analysts, the question was not merely about the intentions of its potential adversaries like the United States and India. It was about a profound geopolitical vulnerability amid the high national stakes in ensuring the reliable and uninterrupted flow of imported energy to sustain economic growth and prosperity at home. Even if the maritime intentions of the United States were benign, Chinese political leadership could not accept the proposition that Beijing could entrust its energy security to outside powers (see figure 3).

The Chinese policy evolution highlights a three-part solution to the Malacca Dilemma: "reducing import dependence through energy efficiencies

and harnessing alternative sources of power, investment in the construction of pipelines that bypass the Malacca Strait, and building credible naval
forces capable of securing China's SLOCs [sea lines of communication]."[49]
The first part of the solution is quite important but is clearly beyond the
remit of this volume and involves a whole range of complex issues relating to China's technical and political choices on its national energy mix.
The second part of the solution to the Malacca Dilemma reinforced the
importance of the transportation corridors that China had already begun
to build between western China and the subcontinent. The subcontinent
and Burma, as regions to the west of the Strait of Malacca, presented
themselves as the natural gateways for moving energy supplies into China.
Beijing also looked at a variety of options in Southeast Asia that would
link oil- and natural-gas-producing regions in Southeast Asia with China,
bypassing navigation through the Strait of Malacca.[50] A bold option was
to dig a navigable canal across the Kra Isthmus in southern Thailand that
would emerge as an alternative to the Strait of Malacca between the Bay
of Bengal and the western Pacific.[51] The idea of an Asian Panama canal
cutting through the Kra Isthmus dates to the late seventeenth century.
It has been repeatedly proposed and, given its excessive costs, repeatedly
discarded. According to some assessments, Beijing actively considered the
proposal but apparently balked at the estimated cost of more than $25
billion. Meanwhile, recognizing that much of the benefits of serving as a
transit between the Indian and Pacific Oceans currently accrue to Singapore, Thailand proposed the idea of a pipeline running across the isthmus
but underground. Much cheaper than a canal, such a pipeline could be
attractive not only to China, but also to Japan and South Korea, the other
major users of the Strait of Malacca. There were apparently some negotiations between Bangkok and Beijing to discuss what Thailand now termed a
"strategic energy land bridge."[52] But the high costs and a variety of political
difficulties have kept the project on hold.

In September 2010, China started the construction of parallel oil and
natural gas pipelines between the Kyaukphyu deep seaport on Burma's Arakan coast in the Bay of Bengal and Kunming in China's Yunnan Province
and probably beyond.[53] The 1,100-km (684-mile) gas pipeline will tap
into key blocks in Burma's energy-rich Shwe gas fields that were given to a
Chinese-led consortium in 2007 in a thirty-year lease. The pipeline project

itself was signed during the visit to Beijing in June 2009 by Maung Aye, the second-ranking general of the Burmese military regime. The project includes railway, road, and waterway construction, as well as upgrading the port at Kyaukphyu in Arakan State. Together the two decisions—on the supply of gas and the construction of the twin pipelines—mark the first successful Chinese effort at short-circuiting the Strait of Malacca. The twin pipeline project is expected to cost around $2.5 billion and will be borne by the Chinese companies. When the oil and gas pipelines are completed by 2013, according to China National Petroleum Corporation, Chinese tankers will dock at Kyaukphyu port to transport 0.6 million barrels every day from West Asia and Africa. The gas pipeline, meanwhile, will move about twelve billion cubic meters of gas annually to Kunming. The projects are expected to deliver anywhere between $30 billion and $55 billion to the Burmese regime over a period of thirty years. Burma's initial interest was in supplying the Shwe gas to India's remote northeast through Bangladesh, and the three countries began to negotiate on the terms of building a gas pipeline. During the prolonged deadlock between New Delhi and Dhaka on the terms of the pipeline, China made a counteroffer to move the gas to Yunnan and offered to pick up the cost of the twin pipeline project.

The pipeline project, however, has faced severe criticism from human rights groups and Burmese dissidents and pro-democracy activists who are trying to pressure China and the international community to stop or at least change the terms of the project.[54] Developments on the Sino-Burmese border after the deal was clinched also began to cast some shadow over the pipeline project. The growing number of clashes between ethnic Burmese groups and the central government and the flight of Chinese refugees from northern Burma into Yunnan created a bit of tension between Naypyidaw and Beijing.[55] As elsewhere, Beijing and its state-owned corporations have shown both the skill and the resolve to push through major energy projects notwithstanding international criticism and local opposition.[56]

THE "STRING OF PEARLS"

China's new discourse on the Malacca Dilemma did a lot more than raise the question of China's energy insecurity. It triggered a new debate on the fundamental objectives of China's naval and maritime strategy, bringing us to the third part of the solution. Although pipelines along the various transportation corridors west of Malacca are useful in reducing dependence on the strait, some Chinese analysts argue that they would not eliminate the problem of the vulnerability of seaborne energy imports:

> The Kra Isthmus canal, the Sino-Burmese and Sino-Pakistani oil pipelines would not be able to fundamentally avoid the impact of the navies of major powers. If the fleets of such powers directly intercept our tankers in the Persian Gulf, the Arabian Sea, or the Suez Canal . . . the above-mentioned three schemes would all become meaningless. Thus, before the Chinese navy's ocean-going squadrons can achieve some kind of force parity with the navies of major powers in the Indian Ocean, the security problem of China's oil transport routes and straits cannot be resolved.[57]

Some Western analysts, too, suggest that China's overland pipelines may largely be a "pipe dream," . . . "driven by a combination of a misunderstanding of global oil market mechanisms, incomplete assessment of security issues, and the lobbying by sectoral and local commercial and political interests." They add that "pipelines are more vulnerable to sabotage and military interdiction than seaborne shipping is. Projects (like the Burma–China pipeline) designed to help seaborne shipments bypass choke points are expensive, can be blockaded, and are themselves vulnerable to physical attack by non-state actors or other parties. Seaborne shipping, by contrast, is very flexible and can be routed around disruptions."[58]

Some Chinese analysts agree with this line of argument and look toward blue-water capabilities that allow Beijing to operate effectively in the Indian Ocean.[59] The ability to operate in distant waters, the Chinese naval strategists well understand, depends upon forward presence. Although Communist China has been opposed to foreign bases as a general principle, the importance of cultivating special maritime relationships was not lost on Beijing. A top Chinese navalist summed up Beijing's efforts in recent years:

> Through cooperation with nearby countries, during the 1990s, China constructed harbor wharves in the eastern Indian Ocean in Burma [and] cleared the Mekong waterways, in order to gain access to the sea in [China]'s southwest. In 2003, China leased a port in Russia's Far East and negotiated with Russia in an attempt to develop the mouth of the Tumen River. On the Makran seacoast of southwest Pakistan, China invested $1

billion to construct a deepwater port [at Gwadar], in order to establish a trade and transport hub for Central Asian nations and simultaneously expand China's geostrategic influence. For the past few years, China has provided aid to the South Pacific region and also strengthened economic and trade ties. Particularly since entering the World Trade Organization, [China] has strengthened economic and trade cooperation with Africa and the Caribbean region. These [achievements have] all contributed to the development of China's maritime geostrategic relationships.[60]

By the end of the first decade of the twenty-first century, however, there was an intensification of China's military diplomacy around the world, including in the Indian Ocean, and a more explicit Chinese debate on the need for and feasibility of a forward presence. In July 2009, Beijing announced that "China would comprehensively expand foreign military relations through initiatives such as: maintaining military attaché offices in 109 countries; annually sending more than 100 military delegations abroad and receiving more than 200 visiting military delegations; conducting high-level strategic consultations and professional and technical exchanges; and organizing study abroad exchanges for mid-grade and junior officers."[61] Later that year, there were some suggestions by Chinese officials that Beijing might be looking at establishing military bases, but those reports were quickly denied.[62]

Reviewing the increasing calls from a section of the Chinese strategic community for overseas basing facilities, some analysts caution against exaggerated conclusions about the emergence of Chinese bases around the Indian Ocean. "There is virtually no reason to suspect that China intends to establish a worldwide network of military bases that would give the PLA a global presence even approaching that of the United States, but some Chinese analysts clearly support establishing at least a limited number of facilities capable of supporting Chinese forces in areas deemed vital to China's expanding political and economic interests."[63] Quite clearly, China's anti-piracy mission off the coast of Somalia in 2009 has focused attention on the question of having adequate support facilities for sustained operations of the Chinese navy in distant waters. Even those Chinese analysts who call for foreign military bases are quite conscious of the sensitivities associated with Beijing's foreign policy traditions. Chase and Erickson conclude that an attractive alternative for Beijing may be "an approach similar to the 'places not bases' strategy put forward by the U.S. Pacific Command in the 1990s, in which China would have arrangements in place for access to key facilities in strategic locations while still refraining from establishing permanent military bases abroad." They add:

> The development of "places" would enable the PLAN to project power in key regions without necessitating a potentially controversial change in longstanding Chinese policy. Chinese analysts may also calculate that an approach centered on "places" would be less alarming to the United States, India, Japan, and other concerned regional powers. This is in part because support centers could presumably handle the requirements of non-war military operations—such as food, fuel, and maintenance and repair facilities—without the propositioned munitions and large-scale military presence typically associated with full-fledged overseas bases. For the same reasons, "places" would presumably be easier for host countries to accept, thus allowing China to more readily leverage its relationships with key countries in regions of strategic interest.[64]

Nevertheless, the proposition that China is determined to secure permanent footholds in the Indian Ocean gained ground, especially in India. The initial suggestion of a grand Chinese design came in a report on Asia's energy futures commissioned by the Pentagon.[65] Unlike the early analyses of China's search for access to the Indian Ocean, which were seen as relatively benign and motivated by the needs of development and security in its restive peripheries, the new assessments viewed it from the perspective of energy security and its links to maritime strategy. The new approach therefore unveiled an entirely different perspective on the Chinese activities in the Indian Ocean. The seemingly dispersed and unconnected Chinese activities now fell into a pattern that was called a "string of pearls"—a series of support centers along China's sea lines of communications in the Indian and Pacific Oceans. Put simply, "string of pearls" has become a catchphrase to describe China's growing geopolitical influence through efforts to gain access to ports and airfields, develop special diplomatic relationships, and modernize military forces that extend from the South China Sea through the Strait of Malacca, across the Indian Ocean, and on to the Arabian Gulf, the eastern coast of Africa, and the islands in the western Indian Ocean. "Each 'pearl' in the 'string of pearls' is a nexus of Chinese geopolitical influence or military presence. Hainan Island, with recently upgraded military facilities, is a 'pearl.' An upgraded airstrip on Woody Island, located in the Paracel Archipelago 300 nautical miles east of Vietnam, is a 'pearl.' A container shipping facility in Chittagong, Bangladesh, is a 'pearl.' Construction of a deepwater port in Sittwe, Burma, is a 'pearl,' as is the construction of a navy base in Gwadar, Pakistan. Port and airfield construction projects, diplomatic ties, and force modernization form the essence of China's 'string of pearls.'"[66] Although most of these facilities are currently civilian in nature, they certainly can assist future military operations of the PLA Navy. But in media headlines, "string of pearls," coined in the Booz Allen Hamilton study for the Pentagon, became a defining theme about Chinese maritime strategy in the Indian Ocean.[67] Some American analysts saw the pattern as a long-term strategy aimed at challenging U.S. naval hegemony in the South China Sea and the Indian Ocean, to deny the United States access to the region, to negate U.S. influence, and to intimidate neighbors into political accommodation.

Not everyone in the United States is alarmed by the thesis of a "string of pearls." While they see China's new imperatives and ambitions in the Indian Ocean, they believe Beijing is a long way from being able to defend its "pearls" against a potentially hostile power like the United States. Analyzing the case of the most talked about pearl, Gwadar in the Indian Ocean, two U.S. analysts argue that "Gwadar by no means represents a trump card for China, either in energy security or military terms. . . . Beijing's effort to outflank U.S. naval operations using an overland route might itself be outflanked in wartime. Should Washington direct the U.S. Navy to interdict Chinese petroleum shipments . . . cargoes bound for Gwadar, and thence for transshipment to China might never reach the Pakistani seaport in the first place. This would severely degrade its strategic value to Beijing."[68]

A more realistic basis than "pearls" to assess Chinese plans for a forward presence in the Indian Ocean is the pattern of Chinese naval operations in the Gulf of Aden since 2008. A review of Chinese port calls from late 2008 to mid-2010 suggested that "port calls for rest and replenishment by PLAN ships deployed for counter-piracy operations, negotiation of defense agreements, and military engagement through goodwill cruises and exercises show that a regional support network is already taking shape."[69] Unlike the initial speculation that characterized as a potential naval base every port that China financed or helped develop, this study helped

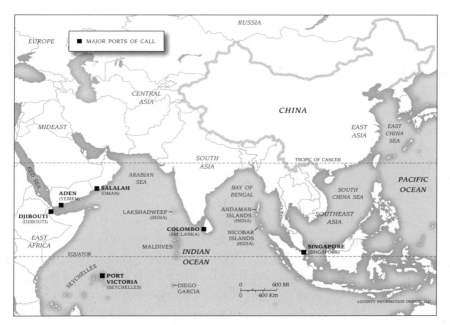

Figure 4. China's Indian Ocean Port Calls of Significance

focus on some locations—Singapore, Colombo, Karachi, Salalah, Aden, and Djibouti—that have turned out to be valuable for Chinese naval operations in the Indian Ocean (see figure 4). Regular access to all these places was indeed cemented by increased naval engagement and written agreements of varying kind with the host nations.

That the theme of a Chinese "string of pearls" gained ground so quickly within the Indian strategic community is not surprising. Unlike the United States, India could not take a relaxed view of China's rising maritime profile in the Indian Ocean littoral. India's history of conflict and rivalry with China meant that New Delhi was predisposed to treat China's growing naval presence around its waters with some wariness. At the same time, India's naval leadership was quite conscious of its own geographic and other advantages in the Indian Ocean and the many weaknesses that the Chinese navy had to overcome to become a credible player. But as China stepped up its military diplomacy in the Indian Ocean, the noise levels in New Delhi began to acquire a new edge in the summer of 2009.[70] For large sections of the Indian strategic community, the growing Chinese maritime activity in the Indian Ocean was part of Beijing's long-standing attempt at the "strategic encirclement" of India. It now had to confront a maritime dimension to the traditional jousting with China in and around the marches of the subcontinent. Traditionally Sino-Indian military tensions were concentrated on their long and contested land border. New Delhi's concerns about China were reinforced by Beijing's alliance with Islamabad in particular and all other South Asian neighbors in general. India was quite used to four decades of geopolitical wrestling around the Himalayas. Now the potential threat from the south seemed to ignite once again the "China threat" theory that had been subdued during the period of normalization between the two sides.

India's security dilemma with China has now been extended to the maritime domain. For many in the Indian strategic community, every advance that China makes in the Indian Ocean undermines India's own freedom of action in the waters adjoining the subcontinent. It was inevitable, then, that India would step up its own military diplomacy, which in turn is seen in Beijing as limiting China's right to access in the Indian Ocean. As a spiral of mistrust envelops New Delhi and Beijing, India's experienced decision-makers have sought to bring down the temperature and inject a measure of prudence into the debate. Shivshankar Menon, a former ambassador to China and foreign secretary and the national security adviser since 2010, regretted that the new debate on the Indian Ocean was being "framed solely in terms of a Sino-Indian rivalry. This is especially true of strategists in India and China themselves, though not of their governments. The terms in which the argument is presented are limited and would be self-fulfilling predictions, were governments to act upon them. Nor are they based on an examination of objective interests of the states concerned."[71]

Many in China, too, do not approach China's energy security challenge through the geopolitical or naval route. Many Chinese analysts have called for cooperative solutions as a redress to the Malacca Dilemma. One Chinese scholar argues that China's imports of energy should be seen as neither a vulnerability nor a threat. "The nature of China's relationship with the rest of the world can best be characterized as one of interdependence. The now common statement, 'China needs the world, and the world needs China,' is truer today than ever before. Establishing bilateral and multilateral negotiation and cooperation mechanisms helps to both routinize

130

constructive interaction as well as recognize the cost of non-cooperation. This is not a guarantee for success but it greatly lowers the possibility of vicious competition and military conflict. Oil diplomacy is simply not a zero-sum game."[72] He adds that the sea lines of communication and the world oil markets are international public goods and argues that participation in their maintenance is an important part of sustaining China's oil security. Other scholars point to the dangers of adopting military means to cope with the Malacca Dilemma. Potential backlash from the other powers and hedging by China's neighbors would complicate China's security environment and make it less secure.[73]

Even within the military establishment in China are those who argue that the "protection of China's international interests depends on more than just a strong navy." They maintain that the answer to China's problems of access to natural resources, the Malacca Dilemma, and sea lane security lies in pursuing international agreements, friendly diplomacy, and domestic reform.[74] A comprehensive analysis of China's internal debate on maritime strategy, however, points to the increasing emphasis among navalists to use the new economic arguments to make the case for higher budgetary support for the modernization of the PLA Navy. They underline the navy's important role in protecting and advancing China's national economic development. "There is a tendency to reverse the common logic of 'rich economy, strong army' . . . PLAN authors do acknowledge that a big economy allows the material basis for a strong army, but also assert that without a strong army, one cannot have a strong economy."[75]

Some Western analysts argue that China's concerns and its challenges to the other powers are likely to be concentrated in the western Pacific rather than the Indian Ocean. "It's not China's current limited ability to conduct distant water operations or its potential aircraft carrier development that should be a primary cause for concern, notwithstanding the understandable but exaggerated fears of India. Rather, it is the PLA's growing ability to deny access to East Asian seas in a crisis or conflict, and so to disrupt the security system led by [the] U.S. Pacific Command, that most threatens regional order and harmony at sea."[76] Other analysts concur with this argument. They concede that China's interests are expanding and becoming more international in nature but insist that recovering from a century of humiliation and ensuring domestic legitimacy remain the top priorities of

China's leadership.[77] With Washington's proclamation in 2011 of the U.S. pivot to Asia and the commitment to strengthen its military presence and political alliances in the region, it is likely that China's naval energies will remain focused on the western Pacific. Geography and political circumstance, then, are bound to constrain China's ability to establish a credible and sustainable forward naval presence in the Indian Ocean aimed at defending its growing economic and energy interests. This is not entirely dissimilar to the geographic constraints on India's role in the western Pacific. Nevertheless, the growing Chinese and Indian interest in waters far beyond their shores is leading to some political and diplomatic jousting in the Indo-Pacific littoral, and that is the focus of chapters 8 and 9.

CIRCLING THE STRATEGIC ISLANDS

As Beijing's interests in the Indian Ocean grow and New Delhi raises its profile in the Pacific, forward presence and support structures in other nations have become a new imperative for both countries' navies. The last chapter touched upon the notion of a "string of pearls" to describe China's search for access arrangements in the Indian Ocean. As noted, India, too, is not averse to acquiring facilities that will ensure naval operations far from the home territory. Throughout the history of warfare and statecraft, the need for secure access and bases in territories under the control of other entities was critical for the projection of force and the construction of empires. From the Peloponnesian War to the age of "Star Wars," gaining secure access to critical physical locations has been an important element in the strategies of the major powers. The Greeks, Romans, and Persians valued bases for controlling key access points and denying them to their adversaries. The earliest maritime powers in Venice, Portugal, Spain, and Holland set great store by them and fought for their possession. As the age of industrialization dawned and man's ability to master distances expanded, the value of bases did not decline. Instead, the control of coaling stations and critical choke points became even more important for the conduct of strategy. Mahan drew the attention of the American strategic community to the "demand for stations along the road, like the Cape of Good Hope, St. Helena, and Mauritius, not primarily for trade, but for defense and war; the demand for the possession of posts like Gibraltar, Malta, Louisburg, at the entrance of the Gulf of St. Lawrence, posts whose value was chiefly strategic, though not necessarily wholly so. Colonies and colonial posts were sometimes commercial, sometimes military in their character; and it was exceptional that the same position was equally important in both points of view, as New York was."[1]

ENDURING RELEVANCE OF ISLAND BASES

The British Empire, in organizing the dramatic expansion of global trade in the nineteenth century, was critically dependent on having a sustainable network of bases around the world that allowed its naval power to prevail.[2] As Kent Calder notes, "As geopolitical competition became global during the nineteenth and twentieth centuries, the nations that *lacked* extensive basing networks, while harboring great-power aspirations, such as Russia and Germany, clearly suffered as a consequence. Without broadly dispersed naval ports, coaling stations, and ultimately airfields, it was hard for them to meet military strategist Carl von Clausewitz's prescription for victory: Bring overwhelming force rapidly to bear."[3] The demise of empires in the middle of the last century did not in any way reduce the significance of foreign bases. During the Cold War, the United States and the Soviet Union competed vigorously for the acquisition of foreign bases and facilities. These were necessary not only for the projection of conventional military power, but also for the effective maintenance of the two superpowers' globally dispersed nuclear arsenals and supportive infrastructure. Within the American postwar defense system, basing arrangements consolidated alliances and promoted military burden sharing across the Atlantic and the Pacific. This military structure provided enduring stability under which dramatic expansion of global trade took place. The U.S. basing system also served the critical function of ensuring the secure flow of raw materials and energy resources from the developing world to the industrial heartland.

In the post–Cold War era, the U.S. wars in the Persian Gulf underlined the central importance of foreign bases for the pursuit of American national security strategy. The U.S. intervention and occupation in

Afghanistan needed sustained access to facilities in Pakistan and Central Asia and over-flight rights across many nations. In the nonconventional arena, too, the advent of missile defense and the military dependence on space assets demanded arrangements for deploying a range of instrumentation and facilities in other countries. Advances in technology did not obviate the need for bases, especially for force projection and the operation of modern naval forces, but the emergence of nationalism in the developing world tended to complicate the maintenance of bases and facilities in newly independent nations.[4] Opposition to bases also began to emerge to different degrees among the more solid American alliances in Europe and the Pacific. While this demanded significant readjustment of military dispositions, the case for forward deployment itself did not disappear from the American grand strategy. Although the literature on bases focuses on the American alliance system, little attention has been devoted to the discussion of the prospects that China and India could acquire military facilities. Our discussion on China's "string of pearls" and India's less overt approach to a possible "necklace of diamonds" is barely the first cut at understanding the prospects of such basing. Two important imperatives for forward basing—resource security and the ability to effectively operate close to the adversary's territory—are becoming important themes in the maritime discourse in China and India.

The early Indian navalists had no difficulty in seeing the importance of forward presence. K. M. Panikkar explicitly talked about the importance of India's constructing a steel ring of naval bases in Singapore, Sri Lanka, Mauritius, and Socotra.[5] As China and India mutate from postcolonial nations to rising powers, both are acutely conscious of the political controversy that surrounds the acquisition of bases on foreign soil and the deployment of troops in such facilities. As we discussed in earlier chapters, the ideological opposition to bases continues to be prominent in both countries. Yet, the recognition that they need to acquire bases and turnaround facilities is beginning to introduce a subtle shift in the positions of Beijing and New Delhi. In China there appears to be a new debate on foreign basing and on the terms and conditions under which it might be undertaken.[6] China and India seem to be interested in acquiring such facilities wherever they can along the sea lines of communication or critical choke points. Their focus is on strategic island states and territories, where it is relatively easier to acquire and operate facilities, rather than large littoral states where domestic opposition could complicate forward presence. Foreign military presence is subject to hostile nationalism. Both Beijing and New Delhi are conscious of potential hostility from the host nations to foreign bases, as seen in the pressure on the United States to withdraw from its major naval and air bases in the Philippines in 1992 amid popular opposition to them. The rising Asian powers are also aware that since the end of the Cold War, the United States, Russia, and France have continued to seek, wherever possible, bases, military facilities, access arrangements, and agreements to rotate troops in order to ensure a credible forward presence.[7] Bases remain in vogue not simply because of the pressure from the great powers. Many weak regimes continue to seek foreign military support. In 2009 Syria signaled its interest in offering a naval base to Russia, and Abu Dhabi offered one to France. Poor states like Djibouti consider foreign military bases a major source of revenue.[8]

Among the foreign military bases in the Indian Ocean, nothing comes close to comparison with the U.S. facilities in Diego Garcia. Acquired by the United States from Great Britain as it withdrew from the East of Suez at the turn of the 1970s, Diego Garcia has a fine harbor, is close to the east-west sea lines of communication, and is just over the horizon from the Persian Gulf. As Calder argues, Diego Garcia "has moved from obscurity to become one of the most strategically important bases on the earth, and yet one conspicuously and uniquely removed from the vagaries of base politics. Its emergence and expansion are testimony to the possibility of a way around the pitfalls that base politics so often otherwise imposes on military operations."[9] As retreating Britain granted independence to its Indian Ocean colonies in the mid-1960s, London got Mauritius to surrender its claim to the Chagos Archipelago in return for $8.4 million. In 1965, this island chain was combined with three islands that were detached from Seychelles to form the British Indian Ocean Territory. Created expressly for the defense of Anglo-American interests in the Indian Ocean, the territory, including Diego Garcia, was made available to the United States. Although many in the United Kingdom, Mauritius, and India protested the whole transaction, the controversy slowly faded away as the new base became one of the most important in the U.S. global network.[10] Since then, Diego Garcia has been at the heart of the U.S. maritime presence in the Indian Ocean during the Cold War and in the two decades since then.[11] Thanks to the emerging Sino-Indian maritime rivalry, the small Indian Ocean island states are now back in the limelight.

SEYCHELLES AND MAURITIUS

Chinese President Hu Jintao's brief stopover in Mauritius in February 2009, as part of his four-nation African tour, did not fit in with the widespread perceptions of Beijing's expansive resource diplomacy in Africa. As Hu prepared for his trip to Mali, Senegal, Tanzania, and Mauritius, Chinese officials were eager to counter the notion that China's African diplomacy was all about grabbing the continent's resources. Pointing out that the four African states on Hu's itinerary were not known for mineral wealth, Chinese officials insisted that Beijing's interest in Africa "isn't confined to energy and resources."[12] New Delhi had every reason to take Beijing at its word and wonder why Beijing was focusing so much attention on Mauritius, which had long been so close to India. Mauritius is not known for its natural resources, but its critical location in the western Indian Ocean. To be sure, India has watched warily as China's resource diplomacy in Africa unfolds. It is no secret that India has been chasing China's tail in its quest for equity oil and acquisition of mineral resources all around the world, including in Africa. New Delhi has also followed Beijing in giving a greater coherence to its diplomatic efforts in Africa. Following the first China–Africa summit in Beijing at the end of 2006, India organized a smaller version of its own Africa summit in New Delhi during April 2008 and followed up with another in Addis Ababa during May 2011. None of this competitive dynamic, however, captures the unfolding Sino-Indian rivalry in the western Indian Ocean. Although China's attempts to build maritime infrastructure in South Asia have received widespread attention, Beijing's competition with New Delhi for strategic influence in the important island states of the western Indian Ocean has not gotten similar attention. President Hu's two trips to Africa both terminated in the western Indian Ocean islands. The February 2007 trip concluded in Seychelles, and the February 2009 trip terminated in Mauritius. New Delhi could no longer ignore the Chinese strategic activism in the western Indian Ocean.

That the president of the world's most populous nation chose to show up, in quick succession, in two small countries—Seychelles (population: 85,000) and Mauritius (1.25 million)—speaks of the strategic significance of the two island territories. For centuries, these and other islands—Madagascar, Comoros, Reunion, and Socotra—have been critical links in the flow of goods and people across the Indian Ocean, from east and west and from north and south. In the colonial era, they acquired a military significance amid the efforts of European powers to control the sea lanes of the Indian Ocean. During the Cold War, the island territories of the western Indian Ocean were at the very heart of American power projection into the region. We have already referred to the continuing importance of the Diego Garcia naval base for U.S. maritime strategy. The French granted independence to Comoros but retained control over Reunion; they also maintained the second-largest naval presence in the Indian Ocean after the United States. Through the Cold War, the Soviet Union continually jockeyed for influence in Seychelles. Many of these island states were fragile and were easy targets for not just great-power intervention but also for attacks by small mercenary groups. As India geared up to limit the Chinese search for access in and around the South Asian waters, it was surprised to find Beijing's new thrust in the western Indian Ocean, especially toward Seychelles and Mauritius.[13] Although China's initiatives toward both these island territories were framed within Beijing's Africa policy, there was no mistaking the centrality of maritime considerations from the perspective in New Delhi. Traditionally, India has had rather strong political and security ties to the two island nations. The big question for New Delhi is whether it can sustain its privileged position there amid China's growing interest.

While New Delhi cannot prevent an intensification of economic and political cooperation between China and the western Indian Ocean island territories, it is aware that Beijing, by its own declaration, is keen to promote bilateral military and security cooperation with all the African states.[14] After years of avoiding international peacekeeping operations around the world, China is now stepping up its contribution to the operations, including those in Africa. There have been reports about China's growing arms transfers to the African states.[15] India, which already has close military and security ties with Mauritius and Seychelles, would not want to be outflanked by Beijing.[16] Concerns that Beijing might step in to supply arms to Seychelles compelled New Delhi to embark on a pre-emptive move in early 2005, when the Indian naval chief, Admiral Arun Prakash, presented the INS *Tarmugli*, a fast-attack craft, as a gift to the Seychelles coast guard. The Indian naval headquarters considered the request from Seychelles so urgent that it decided to pull the ship out of its own fleet barely three years after its commissioning.[17]

For the moment, though, India's economic and security cooperation with Seychelles is robust. India has trained large numbers of police and military personnel from Seychelles. A memorandum of understanding on defense cooperation was signed when Bhairon Singh Shekhawat, the vice president at the time, visited Seychelles in 2003. India had also given a few helicopters to Seychelles over the years. Indian naval ships routinely visit Seychelles. High-level visits between India and Seychelles have been frequent and have included a visit by Prime Minister Indira Gandhi way back in 1981. Despite all of those contacts over the years, China now is set to compete by bestowing intense, high-level political attention. Seychelles President James Michel was in Beijing in November 2006 to participate in the first China–Africa summit. Barely three months later, President Hu was on a return visit to Seychelles. Hu also made time for Seychelles at the Shanghai expo in the summer of 2010, where Michel was among the few leaders to meet with the Chinese president. Michel in turn saw Seychelles becoming a "bridge" between China and Africa.[18]

Given the small size of the Seychelles economy and the limited nature of its requirements, China has few difficulties in rapidly expanding its influence on the island state. New Delhi is closely monitoring Beijing's plans for Seychelles, including the possible search for oil and natural gas in its waters. Although the land area of Seychelles is only 435 square kilometers (168 square miles), it has an exclusive economic zone of nearly 1.3 million square kilometers (502,000 square miles). A few international oil companies are beginning to test the waters for hydrocarbons. Even more important from New Delhi's perspective is to prevent a major move by Beijing to sell arms or establish listening posts and monitoring stations on the island. There has been some speculation in the Seychelles political class that Beijing might be looking for precisely such arrangements on the island.[19] As China raised the bid for the affections of Seychelles, India began to intensify its own engagement with Seychelles in 2010. India received President Michel in June 2010 and underlined the importance of deepening all-around cooperation between the two countries, including in the arena of defense and security.[20] Soon after, India's foreign and defense ministers traveled to Seychelles within a fortnight of each other. The visit by the defense minister, A. K. Antony, was the first ever to Seychelles and affirmed the Indian commitment to the security of the island nation. This included grants worth $5 million for Seychelles defense projects and the provision of a new Dornier aircraft and two Chetak helicopters to boost maritime surveillance of Seychelles. Antony also promised that India would do more to improve the maritime capacity of Seychelles and train its security personnel.[21] China, too, has been eager to contribute to military capacity building in Seychelles and, not to be outdone, delivered two Y-12 aircraft for anti-piracy patrols and inter-island connectivity in June 2011.[22] Not much time elapsed after Antony's visit when the Chinese defense minister, Liang Guanglie, showed up in Seychelles in early December 2011. A few days later there were reports that Seychelles had offered China a base facility. Chinese officials denied there was any offer of a base but confirmed that Beijing was considering the Seychelles' offer of relief and resupply for the Chinese navy.[23] By early 2012, the president of Seychelles was in New Delhi meeting Prime Minister Manmohan Singh, reassuring him that there would be no military facilities for China in Seychelles and insisting that India will remain the main development partner for the island nation.[24] As a report in an Indian newspaper put it, Seychelles, like the rest of Africa, had "discovered the joys of balancing India and China."[25]

India's links with Mauritius are in fact deeper than those with Seychelles. Few other countries in the world are as intimately linked to India as Mauritius. Nearly 68 percent of its population is of Indian origin, and its people deeply value the relationship with the mother country. India's profile in every aspect of life in Mauritius remains significant and high.[26] China, too, has its historical links with Mauritius, as nearly 30,000 Mauritians are of Chinese descent. Beijing now appears determined to step up its relations with Port Louis, and President Hu's visit in February 2009 was an expression of that political will. In the first-ever visit to Mauritius by a Chinese head of state, President Hu announced a $260 million loan for the modernization and expansion of the airport in Port Louis and speeded up the completion of the $730 million special economic zone.[27] If the former represented Beijing's interest in picking up a stake in the infrastructure of the island nation, the latter is about taking full advantage of Mauritius as the gateway to Africa. The massive special economic zone project is expected to become a hub for Chinese commercial activity in Africa.[28] It is also the largest single injection of foreign capital into the island and is expected to generate up to 40,000 jobs and up to $200 million annually in exports. While Mauritius's bilateral trade and economic engagement with India is deeper and larger than that with China, President Hu's visit signaled that this advantage might not remain uncontested.

As India assesses China's rapidly rising profile in Mauritius, New Delhi would have every incentive to consolidate, expand, and protect its role as the principal security and military partner of Port Louis. Within years of its independence, Mauritius turned to New Delhi to secure its vast maritime estate. The Mauritius coast guard was established through Indian assistance, and India has regularly provided ships and helicopters to equip the force and officers to staff it under a defense cooperation agreement signed in 1974.[29] Indian naval ships conduct hydrographic surveys for Mauritius. Recent reports suggest that Mauritius has offered India a project to lease and develop tourist infrastructure on two of its islands called Agalega. Speculation abounds that this project would allow the Indian navy to develop an important facility in a critical location in the Indian Ocean.[30] More recently, as part of its growing effort to improve domain awareness, India has signed a memorandum of understanding with Mauritius to provide a coastal surveillance radar network. Under the agreement, India agreed to set up eight such systems in Mauritius, five of them on the main island and one each on the islands of Rodrigues, Agalega, and St. Brandon.[31] The system was commissioned in April 2011. The cost of this coastal radar network as well as a Dhruv helicopter delivered in November 2009 is covered by an Indian credit line to Mauritius. In early 2012, during a visit by Mauritius Prime Minister Navinchandra Ramgoolam to India, the two sides "agreed to strengthen cooperation to enhance security in the Indian Ocean region through jointly agreed programs of EEZ [exclusive economic zone] surveillance, exchange of information, capacity building and the development of an effective legal framework against piracy."[32] India also announced a fresh line of credit to Mauritius worth $250 million. Yet, at the same time that India has stepped up its engagement with Mauritius, the island nation is more than impressed with the speed, efficiency, and purposefulness of its bilateral cooperation with China.[33]

MALDIVES AND SRI LANKA

While Seychelles and Mauritius seem somewhat remote and do not attract much attention in the unfolding discourse on Sino-Indian rivalry, there is no missing the maritime power play between New Delhi and Beijing in Maldives and Sri Lanka. Both these island states are part of the South Asian Association for Regional Cooperation (SAARC) and have been quite close to India in both historical and political terms. Even more important, from the Indian perspective, New Delhi feels it has a measure of responsibility for the security of these small states. This special sense of obligation was seen in India's successful military intervention in 1988 to foil an attempted coup against the Maldivian government and an extended but failed military involvement in Sri Lanka to broker a peace in the nation's civil war during 1987–1990. These Indian interventions in quick succession raised the prospect of India's emergence as a major power amid the winding down of the Cold War, New Delhi's enduring burden of its Raj legacy as a regional security provider, the contradiction between its ideals and reality, and the gap between its resources and ambitions.[34] As China's rise began to envelop the subcontinent from the late 1990s and Beijing's interests in the Indian Ocean began to grow, Sri Lanka and Maldives became part of the traditional power struggle between India and China that played out for decades in the Himalayas and in Pakistan and Bangladesh. For Beijing, the location of Maldives and Sri Lanka along the sea lines of communication between Africa and the Persian Gulf on the one hand and China's East Coast on the other hand is seen as central to its resource security. With India sitting astride these sea lines of communication, the intensification of the competitive dynamic between New Delhi and Beijing in Maldives and Sri Lanka seemed inevitable.

The nearly 1,200 islands of Maldives, most of which are uninhabited, occupy a large and valuable piece of real estate in the Indian Ocean across the sea lines of communication. Although only a few islands were inhabitable, they drew the attention of the maritime powers during the colonial age as a location from where good watch could be kept over the main trading routes of the Indian Ocean. The islands experienced the standard pattern of changing imperial connections across the Indian Ocean—from the Portuguese to the Dutch and then on to the British, who by the late nineteenth century had made it a protectorate. But the British had no direct presence in the islands. During the Second World War, the British Royal Navy had built an airfield on Gan Island to serve its fleet air arm. The Royal Air Force took charge of the field in 1957 and used it as a way station between Britain and Singapore, where its Far East Air Force was based. Maldives thus became an important part of the British maritime network.[35] As the British withdrew from the East of Suez, an inward-looking India and its coastal navy had no strategic interest in Maldives except in an abstract sense of the island nation's being part of its sphere of influence in South Asia. The unstated assumption was that Maldives was a protectorate of India, much as it was in the British period. The occasion to test this assumption came in 1988, when India responded to the calls of the Maldivian government to put down a coup. Operation Cactus, in which all three services participated, was both quick and decisive in restoring order. In the years that followed, the India–Maldives bilateral relationship expanded, covering a wide range of areas from security cooperation to economic development.

The relative tranquility of Maldives began to be disturbed, from the Indian perspective at least, as Pakistan and China sought to contest the presumed Indian primacy in Maldives. The institutionalization of SAARC and the framework for regional cooperation opened up new opportunities for Pakistan to reach out to Maldives and build on their shared Islamic faith. Meanwhile, as China expanded its engagement of South Asia in the 1990s and looked toward the Indian Ocean at the turn of the century, it was inevitable that Maldives would draw Beijing's attention. The Chinese prime minister's visit to Malé in 2001 marked the substantive elevation of Maldives in the Chinese strategic calculus. As for Maldives itself, the internal order began to show strains as the long-ruling president, Maumoon Abdul Gayoom, became increasingly autocratic and a small dissident movement campaigning for democracy began to make its voice heard by the middle of the decade.[36] As the prodemocracy movement reached out to India, there was growing pressure on India to nudge Gayoom toward a political reconciliation. But by now, Gayoom, of course, had options that he did not have before. New Delhi, which was quite used to its land neighbors playing the China card against it, was now faced with a situation in which its maritime neighbors seemed ready to play the same game. As reports began to appear that China planned to lease a few islands from Maldives and turn some of them into a potential naval base, India chose to act.[37] Insisting that the Maldives' security dalliance with Pakistan and China was not acceptable, New Delhi signaled Malé that it was prepared to meet the island state's military needs, whatever they were. The Indian defense minister, Pranab Mukherjee, traveled to Malé in April 2006 to hand over a modern, 260-ton fast-attack craft to improve Malé's policing of its waters. An official press release issued on the eve of the visit described the importance of the island state for India: "India and Maldives share ethnic, linguistic, cultural and commercial links steeped in antiquity. . . . Maldives is a key member and partner of the Indian Ocean Region and it bestrides the strategic sea lanes of communication in this region. India is also assisting the Maldives Defense and Security authorities in their needs for training and defense equipment."[38] At the end of his visit, Mukherjee proclaimed India's determination to build a "privileged partnership" with Maldives.[39]

The Indian military assistance drew criticism from the prodemocracy movement in Maldives, which was apprehensive that Gayoom was successful in playing the China card against India. As the democracy movement gained momentum in 2008, India seemed to tilt this time in the other direction and nudge Gayoom toward reform. The denouement came toward the end of the year, when the opposition swept to victory against Gayoom in the election and power was transferred peacefully to Mohamed Nasheed.[40] Having played a role in easing Maldives's transition to democracy, India was quick to welcome the new leaders and use the moment to build a more solid partnership. Vice President Hamid Ansari was dispatched to attend the swearing-in ceremony of the new president in November 2008. As it warmed up to the friendly government in Malé, India decided to consolidate its special security relationship with Maldives under the new political dispensation. The top guns of India's bureaucratic establishment— National Security Adviser M. K. Narayanan, Foreign Secretary Shivshankar Menon, and Defense Secretary Vijay Singh—traveled to Maldives in July 2009 to work out a new framework of defense partnership. This came into view when the Indian defense minister, A. K. Antony, visited Maldives the following month. During that visit, the two sides announced that India would base two helicopters in Maldives for better surveillance of the ocean spaces around it, set up radar systems in all 26 atolls of the island nation and integrate them with India's own coastal radar network, and train the Maldivian security forces to operate the radar.[41] Unconfirmed reports talked about India's trying to reactivate the runway on Gan Island and establish a small but permanent military presence in the island nation.[42] As political reaction in Maldives warned the new president against handing over the national security to New Delhi, Antony took pains to clarify that the security partnership was being built on an "equal footing."[43] Subsequently, at the end of his visit to Maldives to attend the SAARC summit in December 2011, Prime Minister Manmohan Singh signed a comprehensive strategic partnership agreement with Maldives that sought to consolidate the expanding cooperation between New Delhi and Malé in the 2000s. Referring to the two governments' "unique geographic location" in the Indian Ocean, Article 5 of the agreement says they will enhance security cooperation "through coordinated patrolling and aerial surveillance, exchange of information, development of effective legal framework and other measures mutually agreed upon. They will intensify their cooperation in the area of training and capacity building of police and security forces."[44]

As India unveiled a treaty-like agreement with Maldives on the margins of the SAARC summit, China announced the opening of the Maldives Embassy in Beijing.[45] Irrespective of the timing, there is no question that Beijing will continue to promote its new interests in Maldives. That India's stepped-up defense diplomacy in Maldives was aimed at preempting any Chinese military advances in the island nation is not in doubt. It is also evident that the China question figured quite prominently in the political contestation between Gayoom and his opponents and the relationship between Malé and New Delhi. The successful democratic transition has certainly helped India to deepen its special security relationship with Maldives.[46] That does not mean, however, that Beijing will not continue its economic engagement and eye the possibilities for long-term military and security cooperation with Maldives. Even as Maldives deepened its security ties to India, the defense minister of the new government traveled to Beijing in early 2009 to signal that it was not hostile to China.[47] And as the Maldives president, Mohamed Nasheed, clarified during a visit to New Delhi in late 2009, he had no intention of playing the China card against India in the security domain—though he also made it clear that he is not averse to pursuing economic partnership with Beijing and that India should be able to differentiate between Malé's civilian and security cooperation with Beijing.[48] He pointed to the attractiveness of economic cooperation with China and implied that India should match it. Although Nasheed complained about Gayoom's playing the China card, it is quite obvious that Beijing is no longer a factor that could be ignored in Malé. Not only is the security dilemma real and rooted in the rivalry between New Delhi and Beijing, but it also opens up opportunities for small nations to gain by playing one against the other in the economic realm. When Nasheed was ousted from power in February 2012 and India quickly backed the new president, Mohamed Waheed, Nasheed said he had been under great pressure to sign a defense cooperation agreement with China but had refused and that the new rulers might tilt toward Beijing. At the same time, he reaffirmed Maldives's special relationship with India and said that New Delhi had no reason to worry about Malé's ties with Beijing.[49] The crisis nevertheless showed India's new clout in Maldives as all parties sought its help in managing the political convulsion as well as its responsibility to mediate between the new government and the opposition and prevent instability in the island nation. Nasheed traveled to Delhi in April 2012 to mobilize political support and was quickly followed by Waheed in May 2012. It also revealed, however, that the emergence of China is an important element in how the contending parties sought to develop leverage with India. The United States, in turn, worked closely with India to help defuse the crisis.[50]

The intersection between Sino-Indian rivalry and the internal dynamics and external orientation of the island states of the Indian Ocean seen in the case of Maldives also comes across in Sri Lanka. As the brutal civil war in Sri Lanka that endured for more than two decades moved toward a decisive confrontation in 2007, it was quite clear that India would inevitably be drawn into it. Less anticipated, however, was the extent to which China would be seen as a factor in the internal dynamics of Sri Lanka. As Sri Lankan armies raced toward cornering and defeating the seemingly invincible Liberation Tigers of Tamil Eelam during the summer of 2009, there was a widespread perception that Chinese military assistance and arms sales to Sri Lanka played a key role.[51] China's quest for maritime access in Sri Lanka seemed to many as lying at the heart of the new security partnership between Colombo and Beijing. The suggestion was that in letting China build a new port at Hambantota on the southern shores of Sri Lanka, Colombo was contributing to the maritime strategy of Beijing. Hambantota, lying halfway between the Strait of Malacca and the Persian Gulf, seemed a critical link in the Chinese quest to construct a "string of pearls" in the Indian Ocean. China, in return, seemed more than happy to offer decisive assistance in defeating the main source of internal security threat to Sri Lanka. China also seemed to cooperate with Pakistan in undermining Indian influence in Colombo and put an end to India's traditional claims of a veto over Colombo's right to engage in significant military cooperation with other powers.[52] For their part, both Colombo and Beijing insisted that Hambantota was a purely civilian facility and there was no question of China's establishing a naval base in Sri Lanka.[53] These denials did not in any way reduce the perception that a new Sino-Indian maritime dynamic was emerging in Sri Lanka and that Beijing was beginning to outsmart India in its own sphere of influence.[54]

There is no doubt that India has always taken seriously its role in the security of Sri Lanka. From New Delhi's perspective, Colombo was very much part of India's Raj legacy. Yet it was never easy for India to exercise a sense of dominance over Sri Lanka in a way that it might have in Bhutan or even influence it significantly as it did in Nepal. Sri Lanka had a well-developed elite that was fairly articulate in expressing its worldview. As part of a group of Colombo powers—including Burma, India, Indonesia, and Pakistan—Sri Lanka spoke up for much of Asia in the early postcolonial period. Its elite was certainly divided between those who were deeply anti-communist and pro-Western and others who outdid India on its nonaligned rhetoric and third-world radicalism.[55] Although India tended to be somewhat uncomfortable with either of Colombo's tendencies, there was little reason for India to be alarmed as there were no immediate direct security consequences for New Delhi. India's own engagement with Sri Lanka in the early decades after independence was refracted through the issue of the Tamil minorities in the island nation. That India had a large Tamil population of its own made the relationship between New Delhi and Colombo a unique one and made its policy acutely vulnerable to sentiments in Madras and Tamil Nadu. When the postcolonial tensions between Tamils and the Singhalese majority moved toward a civil war in the early 1980s, India's broader concern was largely domestic and bilateral. To the extent that external elements were involved, New Delhi's interest was in minimizing the role of Britain and the United States in Sri Lanka. This concern was reflected in the 1987 peace accord that New Delhi helped negotiate between the warring communities in Sri Lanka and in the troops that New Delhi sent to keep the peace between them. The agreement (explicitly) barred Sri Lanka from offering bases to third parties. India also took up with Colombo the question of Israeli arms supplies.[56]

Colombo had had good relations with Beijing for decades, and from New Delhi's perspective they were neither strategic nor threatening. All this began to change in the final years of the twentieth century as China stepped up its engagement with all the South Asian nations, including Sri Lanka.[57] The advances in China's engagement with Sri Lanka as part of Beijing's general outreach to the world acquired a new momentum and intensity in the first decade of the new century. By the middle of the decade, India was jolted into recognition of the strategic consequences of Chinese economic interaction with Sri Lanka and Beijing's expansive participation in the infrastructural development in India's southern neighbor. When reports of the Hambantota project began to surface in public, there was considerable concern in India. The project and associated infrastructure development raised concerns about Colombo's attitude and the larger Chinese grand design seen in conjunction with Chinese port-building activity in South Asia, including Gwadar in Pakistan and Sittwe in Burma.[58] China's Hambantota project—the two signed the agreement at the end of 2007—involved not only the construction of the port, but also a power project, facilities for major ship repair, modern transshipment systems, an oil refinery, and a bunkering facility—all sitting together just north of the Gulf–East Asia sea lines of communication. It also involved the development of an international airport at nearby Weerawila, construction of an international convention center, modernization of road links between Hambantota and the rest of the island, and construction of a new railway line. China would fund most of the development costs in a region of Sri Lanka that was home to the parliamentary constituency of President Mahinda Rajapaksa through concessional loans.[59]

That the Indian strategic elite was caught napping was evident from the reports that Colombo had first offered the port project to India, and it was New Delhi's typical inability to get its act together that pushed Colombo toward Beijing.[60] President Rajapaksa drove home this point when he declared that Colombo would have been happy to accept offers from India to develop a new port. He also insisted that the Hambantota project proposal was his initiative rather than Beijing's.[61] Although New Delhi seemed surprised at the discovery of Sri Lanka's importance for Chinese maritime strategy in the Indian Ocean, Beijing's interest in the "emerald island" goes back a long time. Chinese scholars never forget to point out that all of the Indian Ocean expeditions made by the great Chinese admiral Zheng He had stopped in Sri Lankan harbors. Sri Lankans, too, have been deeply conscious of the island's critical location on the maritime silk roads of the Indian Ocean and its role in the spread of Buddhism.[62] They underline the fact that Hambantota is right next to Godawaya, which was a major world port in the early centuries of the Christian era. In the postwar period, Beijing was acutely aware of the island's importance even when it had little seafaring activity. In 1963, China had signed a mutual maritime access agreement with Sri Lanka that allowed ships from the two countries to operate from each other's ports.[63] This generated some concern in New Delhi and London and also some political controversy within Sri Lanka, where opposition parties accused the government of surrendering Lankan sovereignty to China. In a period when Britain was still active in the Indian Ocean, London saw the agreement that allowed Chinese ships access to Sri Lankan ports as part of Beijing's strategy to reinforce its activism in Africa by acquiring a naval way station.[64] While those concerns were somewhat exaggerated, they have acquired a new resonance today. In the early 1970s, China had also given six fast-patrol craft to Colombo, signaling the kind of military diplomacy it could develop once it had material resources and strategic imperatives. By the early 1980s, a China that was reintegrating with the world found enough reasons to reach out to Colombo. As the ethnic conflict began to envelop the island nation in the early 1980s, Beijing started to take a larger interest. "While it is possible that Chinese policy toward Sri Lanka was driven by a desire for basing rights, it seems more probable that it was interested in denying such rights to the super powers. . . . China was primarily concerned about signs of Indian intervention, superpower machinations and the possibility that international stability would be upset."[65] By the first decade of the twenty-first century, as China turned to the sea and sought blue-water capabilities, Sri Lanka would naturally emerge as part of its new maritime contestation with India.

For India, the challenge of dealing with China's strategic foray into Sri Lanka got complicated with the collapse of the peace process that was launched in 2002 and Colombo's vigorous military offensive against the Tamil Tigers in 2007. On the one hand, there was the mounting pressure from Tamil Nadu to coerce Colombo into ending the offensive and resuming the talks with the Tamil rebels. On the other hand, New Delhi had no love lost for the Tamil Tigers, which successfully plotted the assassination of Prime Minister Rajiv Gandhi and was listed as a terrorist organization by the Indian government. At the same time, New Delhi was squirming at the fact that Colombo, in reaching out to Beijing and Islamabad for its arms supply, had solid new options in limiting New Delhi's influence. India was quite determined to protect its interests in the face of this difficult political bind. The national security adviser, M. K. Narayanan, reaffirmed India's Monroe Doctrine, arguing that Sri Lanka should respect India's sensitivities. "We are the big power in this region. Let us make it very clear. . . . We do not favor their going to China or Pakistan or any other country." This seeming diktat was modified by the proposition that the Indian national security adviser added: "We strongly believe that whatever requirements the Sri Lankan government has, they should come to us. And we will give them what we think is necessary."[66] As the civil war reached its climax amid the Indian general elections during the summer of 2009, New Delhi had successfully managed the competing pressures on its policy with some finesse. While continuing to urge restraint on the part of Colombo, New Delhi was quite happy to see the Tamil rebels defeated quickly and without having to look like India had contributed to the cause, given the perceived sentiments in Tamil Nadu. All indications are that India in fact played a key role in assisting Colombo, by providing a range of military help—from supplying warships and radar to sharing intelligence and choking off the sea routes of replenishment for the rebels—but would not want to advertise its role or claim credit for contributing to the defeat of the Tamil Tigers. In subtle public gestures, the Sri Lankan leaders were thanking India for its support without embarrassing New Delhi by arguing that it was fighting India's war against terror in Sri Lanka.

While recognizing India's internal constraints, Colombo valued China's support for its war effort against the rebels. Beijing reportedly exported ammunition, anti-tank guided missiles, rocket launchers and shoulder-fired surface-to-air missiles, deep penetration bombs and rockets, mortar ammunition, night vision devices, security equipment, tanks, F7G jets, naval vessels, radar, communication equipment, and other assistance to Sri Lanka. The Stockholm International Peace Research Institute's *Yearbook 2009* states that "between mid-2002 and mid-2007 Sri Lanka received at least $140 million worth of military equipment from China. A large part of this was probably for ammunition stockpiles, but it is also likely to have included small arms for the expanded Sri Lankan forces."[67] China has moved forward in building a broad-based political and economic relationship with Sri Lanka and has emerged as a champion of Sri Lanka's territorial integrity and as a partner that—in contrast to India—is not seen as interfering in its internal affairs. Unlike New Delhi, Beijing has also been bold in conceiving, promoting, and implementing megaprojects with strategic significance, such as the integrated development of Hambantota. While New Delhi has tended to emphasize its exclusive sphere of influence over Sri Lanka, Beijing has given Colombo larger political room in which to play by inviting it to join the Shanghai Cooperation Organization.[68] At a time when the United States, United Kingdom, and Europe press Colombo on human rights and treatment of the Tamil minority, China's position of noninterference and its support in the international forums is of considerable value to Sri Lanka. In return, China has gained a significant political position in Colombo, besides access to a very valuable location in the southern part of the island and rights for oil and natural gas exploration in the Gulf of Mannar, which separates Sri Lanka from the coastline of southern India.

The public agonizing over these developments in India, however, masks the significant expansion of India's own presence and influence in the island nation over the past decade. Trade between the two countries has boomed since the signing of a free trade agreement in 2000, and a more comprehensive economic partnership agreement has been inching toward completion. Indian capital has moved in significant quantities into Sri Lanka. Colombo boasts facilities that India would never offer to foreign countries. Indian oil companies are among the distributors of petroleum products on the island, and India also has won the contract for building and running an oil tank farm at the Trincomalee Port. India had in fact worked out a framework for deepening India's military links with Sri Lanka. It could not be ratified because of domestic concerns, but the lack of an agreement has been no obstacle to security cooperation with Colombo as Indian forces have forged significant cooperation at the ground level. Colombo has not been averse to a larger Indian strategic profile on the island; what has held India back is not so much the Chinese factor, but the burden of domestic politics in Tamil Nadu. Within this constraint, India has been able to pursue its interests in the island nation, although the notion of an exclusive sphere of influence may not be sustainable in the changed international conditions, especially the rise of China. Beijing's new interest in the Indian Ocean has certainly given Colombo greater maneuvering room vis-à-vis New Delhi. While the China card is useful, Sri Lankan leaders are likely to be careful not to push it too far;[69] after all, there is no way of overcoming India's geographic proximity to Sri Lanka. In November 2009, there were widespread reports that the Sri Lankan president feared a military coup by his army commander, General Sarath Fonseka, who led the Lankan forces in their victory against the Liberation Tigers of Tamil Eelam, and that he had asked the Indian army to stand by for assistance. While these reports have not been confirmed, they point to India's centrality in the security paradigm of Sri Lanka.[70] India warmly received President Mahinda Rajapaksa in 2010 and signaled its commitment to retain its special position in Sri Lanka.[71] The joint declaration issued on the occasion underlined India's commitment to participate more actively in infrastructure construction in Sri Lanka as well as to institutionalize bilateral defense cooperation.[72] While the Tamil factor did constrain India's ability to intervene in the conflict during 2007–2009 and limit the Chinese influence on the island, New Delhi can take satisfaction in the fact that Beijing and Islamabad have helped it achieve an objective—the destruction of the Tamil Tigers—that India was not in a position to realize on its own.

The Sino-Indian contestation for strategic islands is not limited to the four states—Mauritius, Seychelles, Maldives, and Sri Lanka—discussed in this chapter. It also extends to Madagascar, where both countries are trying to expand their influence. Both India and China are investing significantly in the exploitation of the natural resources of the island. New Delhi has activated a listening post in northern Madagascar that is expected to increase the domain awareness of the Indian navy and help it better contribute to the protection of the sea lines of communication in the Indian Ocean. This facility has been billed as the first of its kind that India has set up outside its territory.[73] Under construction since 2006 when India leased an island from Madagascar, it is part of New Delhi's plan to establish a radar network around the Indian Ocean and link it to India's maritime monitoring facilities.[74] According to media reports citing unidentified Indian officials, "With berthing rights in Oman and monitoring stations in Madagascar, Mauritius, Kochi, and Mumbai, the navy will effectively box in the region to protect sea lanes right from Mozambique and the Cape of Good Hope to the Gulf of Oman."[75] The Indian navy has already made its presence felt along the African coast with regular warship deployments to monitor piracy and terrorist movements. India also inked an agreement with Mozambique in 2006 to mount periodic maritime patrolling off its vast coast. In 2003, the Indian navy provided seaward protection for the African Union summit at Mozambique.[76] As Beijing catches up with India in its naval diplomacy in the island states of the Indian Ocean, it is New Delhi's turn to measure up to the rising Chinese profile in the Pacific islands. Although India has had a wide range of ethnic, cultural, and historical links with island states in recent centuries, it is China that has made waves with its bids to secure influence among the islands.[77] While some Western analysts consider Chinese influence in the region to be benign, others are deeply concerned at the unfolding decline in the traditional influence of the United States, France, Japan, Australia, and New Zealand and growing weight of Beijing.[78] Some of the talk of China's acquiring military facilities in the South Pacific Islands might be premature, but it has certainly spurred India into taking a more active interest in the affairs of the South Pacific, beyond its traditional concern for the ethnic Indian minority in Fiji. Thanks to the presence of its diaspora in the island states, India has always had a political and cultural interest in the South Pacific Islands. This also meant potential conflicts with the local regimes, as in the case of Fiji, where the internal tension between the indigenous population and the Indian communities constantly drew New Delhi into the South Pacific.[79]

As it noticed the steady expansion of the Chinese presence and influence in the South Pacific,[80] India recognized the importance of taking a strategic view of the region and not letting concerns with the diaspora become the main focus of its engagement with the region. Since the mid-1990s, India has expanded its diplomatic representation in the region. Since 2002, when India was invited to associate itself with the Pacific Islands Forum, New Delhi has begun an outreach that included occasional port calls and flag showing by the Indian navy.[81] India's involvement in the security politics of the South Pacific dates to the late eighteenth century under the East India Company.[82] As India develops its blue-water capabilities, it is inevitable that its navy will be drawn more actively into the South Pacific.

As we look to the future, it is reasonable to suggest that Beijing and New Delhi will both step up their efforts to sustain or gain significant influence in the strategic islands of the Indian and Pacific Oceans. China's approach has been to focus on building megaprojects that would be the basis for long-term access arrangements in the Indian Ocean. Beijing has embedded this in a broader framework of economic and political engagement of the small island states. India's emphasis, in contrast, has been on promoting operational collaboration with the armed forces of the islands. Building on elements of historic linkage, India has sought to forge interoperability with the fledgling maritime forces of the island states, provide them with naval hardware, and network them into India's own emerging system of domain awareness in the Indian Ocean. Looking beyond the bilateral, India has also been reported to promote a trilateral engagement with Sri Lanka and Maldives on maritime security issues. This process is led on the Indian side by its national security adviser.[83] In 2012, for the first time, India drew Mauritius, Seychelles, and Maldives into the biennial Milan naval exercises that were initially focused on the Southeast Asian neighbors as well as Sri Lanka and Bangladesh.[84]

It is not unreasonable to assume that China would want to emulate India in building a privileged relationship with the island states in the Indian Ocean. What remains unclear is how this Chinese search for greater influence might run into India's own efforts to deepen its exclusive security partnerships with these islands. Much the way Washington and Moscow were sucked into the internal conflicts of the countries they often wooed for strategic purposes, Beijing and New Delhi may find themselves circling each other in the small island states in order to protect their emerging high stakes. The worst moments for the Sino-Indian ties could come when an internal regime change is seen as altering the special security relationship with either Beijing or New Delhi or when an island nation overreaches in playing the two Asian giants against each other. Although such extreme scenarios are less likely in larger nations of the Indo-Pacific littoral, China and India are beginning to make a determined effort to improve their geopolitical standing and maritime positioning. Chapter 9 looks beyond the island states and examines the Sino-Indian contestation in the Arabian Sea, the Bay of Bengal, and the South China Sea.

Chapter Nine

CONTESTING THE LITTORAL

The interactive dynamic between the policies of China and India in various parts of the Indo-Pacific littoral plays out differently depending on the historical context of Chinese and Indian ties to these regions, the nature of the regional conflicts, and the role of other great powers, especially the United States. In chapters 6 and 7, we focused on the rising strategic profiles of India in the western Pacific and China in the Indian Ocean. In this chapter, we take up three specific subregions—the Arabian Sea, the Bay of Bengal, and the South China Sea—to assess the nature of competition between India and China. The Arabian Sea, which hosts the energy resources so desperately needed by both China and India, will be interesting to watch for signals of future Sino-Indian conflict. But they are muted today, given the American political and naval hegemony in the region and the long road ahead for Beijing and New Delhi to consolidate their current maritime outreach in the Persian Gulf and the Arabian Sea. In the Bay of Bengal, the contestation is sharper, given the traditional Indian primacy in these waters and Beijing's emerging ability to challenge it and China's deepening stakes in the Malacca Strait. In the South China Sea, the roles are reversed, with India trying to project itself onto an area where China has the natural advantage. The Indian forays into the western Pacific do not directly threaten China but could acquire some significance if China's relations with its maritime neighbors and the United States, which has been the dominant power in the western Pacific for decades, deteriorate in the coming years and if New Delhi is prepared for deeper military partnerships with the United States and Japan.

THE ARABIAN SEA

Ever since oil became the lubricant of the world economy, control of the Arabian Peninsula and its hydrocarbon resources has been a central element of the enduring Anglo-American primacy in international politics. As the British Empire declined and shed its strategic burdens in the East of Suez from 1967 onward, the United States stepped in to become the dominant power in the Gulf. Much like Russia contesting British hegemony in Persia during the Great Game of the nineteenth century, the Soviet Union tried to challenge the U.S. hegemony in the Gulf during the latter decades of the Cold War. Moscow found significant allies for some time but could not really threaten American primacy in the region in a real sense. After the Cold War, U.S. hegemony over the region seemed unquestionable; no other great power came anywhere close to its influence in the region. Two decades after the end of the Cold War, there is sense of military and political exhaustion in Washington from the prolonged and costly wars in Afghanistan and Iraq in the 2000s. U.S. dependence on oil imports from the Persian Gulf has begun to decline in the new century. As the United States realigns its internal resources and external commitments in the Arabian Sea and begins to devote greater attention to the challenges in the western Pacific, China and India have embarked on greater strategic activism in the littoral of the Arabian Sea. As China and India became the world's leading importers of crude oil, it was only natural that they would begin to devote greater diplomatic energies to the Gulf in the twenty-first century. Meanwhile, the Gulf states, too, have begun to talk about a Look East policy. They are keen to diversify their political and economic engagement beyond their traditional links to the Anglo-American powers and Western Europe. This was most dramatically underwritten by the visit of Saudi King Abdullah to China and India in January 2006. It was the first-ever visit by a Saudi monarch to China and the first to India in half a century. Although the United States and its Western allies continue to dominate the Arabian Sea, China and India are trying to raise their game in the Gulf by deepening their economic integration with the region and exploring strategic partnerships with key littoral states.[1]

Both Beijing and New Delhi have had historical links with Persia and the Arabian Peninsula. In the recent centuries, it is India that has had a more influential involvement in the region. In the colonial period, the British Raj in India was the organizer and protector of the state system in the Arabian Peninsula and the Persian Gulf.[2] Beyond the Gulf, throughout the northwestern quadrant of the Indian Ocean—the Red Sea, Gulf of Aden, and the littoral of East Africa—it was the government of India and not England that provided the men and materiel for securing this vital region through the nineteenth and early twentieth centuries. Many of these regions were in fact directly under the administrative supervision of the Raj.[3] The partition of the subcontinent, however, inevitably weakened and eventually undermined India's traditional role as the security provider on both sides of the Persian Gulf.[4] The unending conflict with Pakistan has also limited India's ability to sustain a leadership role in the Persian Gulf and the Middle East.

China's links to the Gulf and the Middle East go back centuries as overland and seaborne links between the two peaked at the zenith of the Chinese empire. As China declined in the modern period, its ties with the region inevitably frayed. If the rise of maritime capabilities in Europe undermined the significance of the Silk Road between China and the Middle East, European dominance of the seas ended what little hope there was for maritime links between China and the Gulf. Once a strong state emerged in China after the communist revolution in 1949, Beijing had no difficulty seeing the strategic importance of the Gulf and the Middle East. Despite deep ideological differences, China began to develop a framework to engage the region, and its special relationship with Pakistan played an important role. These were driven largely by considerations of the geopolitical balance of power and coping with the dynamics of great-power relations and their impact on China's southwestern periphery.[5]

Given their massive and ever-growing energy dependence on Gulf oil, which must be brought out through the Strait of Hormuz into the Arabian Sea before being shipped to either country, the phrase "Hormuz Dilemma" captures the new strategic interest of Beijing and New Delhi in the Persian Gulf. For the moment, the security of the Gulf in general and the Hormuz strait in particular rests with the United States and its navy. But there is no question that both China and India would want to address the Hormuz Dilemma by strengthening their own reach and influence in the Gulf.[6] With energy security at the top of their national security agendas, it is not surprising that both New Delhi and Beijing are devoting significant diplomatic, economic, and political energies to cultivating strategic links with the Gulf countries.[7]

Some in India have begun to argue that India needs a "Look West" policy—toward the Gulf—that is similar to the Look East policy that India had successfully developed for Southeast Asia in the early 1990s.[8] India formally announced its intent to pursue such a policy when Prime Minister Manmohan Singh ordered his cabinet in 2005 to intensify the economic and commercial engagement with the region:

> The Gulf region, like South-East and South Asia, is part of our natural economic hinterland. We must pursue closer economic relations with all our neighbors in our wider Asian neighborhood. India has successfully pursued a "Look East" policy to come closer to the countries of South-East Asia. We must, similarly, come closer to our western neighbors in the Gulf.[9]

The emphasis was on launching bilateral trade liberalization negotiations with the key Gulf states as well as multilaterally with the six-nation Gulf Cooperation Council (the six members of the GCC are Bahrain, Kuwait, Oman, Qatar, Saudi Arabia, and the United Arab Emirates). Trade between India and the GCC has gathered much momentum in the first decade of the twenty-first century. Besides remaining a major source of energy, the GCC as a collective has become India's largest trading partner in 2010–2011 (about $113 billion), well ahead of China, the United States, and the European Union. Indian expatriate labor (nearly six million) is the largest in the Gulf and contributes a significant share of India's foreign exchange remittances. The Indian private sector, too, has begun to invest in a big way in a range of projects in the Gulf. All of these factors set a new context for the strategic dialogue between India and the GCC.[10] India's accelerated engagement with the Gulf was made urgent in part by China's successful energy diplomacy in the Persian Gulf. The Chinese, in turn, were quick to notice the importance of India's Look West policy.[11]

Well before New Delhi's new relationship with the Gulf matured, the Indian navy recognized the importance of maritime engagement with the Gulf states. As part of its general outreach and the shedding of military isolationism from the early 1990s, the Indian navy raised the quality and intensity of its naval interaction with the Gulf states, which emphasized regular port calls, joint exercises, institutionalization of links with the naval forces of the region, and the implementation of long-term security cooperation agreements with the GCC states. Starting with the showing of the flag in the Gulf waters by the INS *Viraat* in March 1999, India's ship visits significantly expanded through the 2000s. During September and October 2004, New Delhi mounted a large expedition involving seven warships that called at ports in Oman, Bahrain, Iran, and the United Arab Emirates. The Chinese media described it as an effort by New Delhi to project its naval power in the sensitive Gulf region.[12] According to one count, during the period 2005–2007, India dispatched around 40 Indian naval vessels to the Gulf.[13] During August 2007, the Indian navy dispatched another five-ship flotilla into the Gulf with port calls at Muscat (Oman), Qatar, Abu Dhabi (UAE), Manama (Bahrain), and Al Jubail (Saudi Arabia).[14] Admiral Sureesh Mehta, who took charge of the Indian navy in early 2007, chose to travel to the Gulf in his first overseas visit as the chief of naval staff. He was underlining the new importance of protecting the flow of oil and trade through the various choke points of the Indian Ocean in cooperation with the major powers as well as the regional actors.[15]

With energy security looming large as a national security challenge, India has sought to define structured security cooperation with key Gulf states. Oman was the natural first choice, given the profound links that developed under the British Raj, when the Bombay provincial government was responsible for the Sultanate of Oman and Zanzibar. As a news release of the Indian government noted in 2009: "Till India became independent, military and economic support to the Sultanate of Oman was provided by the British from India. Oman's complete requirement of arms and ammunition as well as all military necessities were supplied from Indian ordinance factories, free of cost. Indo-Omani military relations were again revived when a protocol agreement was signed in 1972, leading to a three-year deputation of Indian Navy personnel to man Oman's navy in April 1973."[16] As India turned inward in the 1970s and abandoned many of its inherited functions of the Raj to provide security in the wider Indian Ocean littoral, its security ties with Oman became less significant. Since the early 1990s, India sought a purposeful renewal of the defense relationship, and Oman responded with enthusiasm. India launched annual naval exercises with Oman in 2003, and over the years the exercises have acquired greater sophistication. In 2006, they were complemented by the institutionalization of exchanges between the two air forces. The first India–Oman joint air force exercises, called "Eastern Bridge," was held in Oman during October 2009.[17] A year before the first air exercises, during the visit of Prime Minister Singh to Oman in November 2008, both countries made a commitment to deepen their security cooperation. This was reflected in expanded Indian training cooperation and arms sales with Oman. Muscat in turn has offered turnaround facilities for the Indian air force, significantly improving the operational reach of its aircraft on different missions in the Indian Ocean littoral. During the prime minister's visit to Muscat, New Delhi reportedly expressed its gratitude for Oman's willingness to offer berthing facilities for Indian ships operating in the Arabian Sea, most recently in the anti-piracy operations in the Gulf of Aden since October 2008.[18] Confirming the access agreements between the two countries, the ambassador of Oman told the Indian media in October 2009 that "Oman is keen to help the Indian Navy fight piracy. We have provided all the support to assist the Indian Navy, bearing in mind our force limitation, to ensure that fighting piracy is our common goal."[19]

Other countries in the region, too, have sought to deepen defense cooperation with India. For good reasons, Iran is very keen to step up security and naval cooperation with India; recognizing the sensitivities of Washington, India has deliberately kept naval exchanges with Iran limited. India held joint naval exercises with Iran in 2003 and 2006. "The recent exchange prompted some congressional criticism, but both the Bush administration and Indian officials insist the exchange emphasized mutual sports and entertainment activities rather than military technique."[20] India is also beginning to open up to greater military and naval cooperation with Saudi Arabia. Saudi ships tend to call on Pakistani ports frequently but had never sailed to India. That approach was changed in 2008 when Saudi naval vessels called on the Mumbai port. Indian ships in turn arrived on a friendly visit to Jeddah in 2009 and conducted a simple PASSEX (passing exercise).[21] These exchanges were part of the understanding on increased defense exchanges during King Abdullah's historic visit to India in January 2006. In February 2012, the first-ever visit by an Indian defense minister to Saudi Arabia occurred when A. K. Antony traveled to Riyadh. The two sides agreed to develop a comprehensive framework for deeper defense cooperation.[22] After decades of frosty bilateral relations, New Delhi and Riyadh have embarked on the construction of a potentially consequential security partnership.

During the prime minister's visit to Qatar in November 2008, the two sides signed a defense agreement that the media reported as a "landmark" development. Although no details of the pact were given, Indian news agencies reported that the agreement involves wide-ranging security cooperation that is just "short of deploying Indian troops" in the tiny Gulf kingdom. This was said to include substantive training, intelligence sharing, and cooperation in maritime security.[23] Senior officials in the Indian security establishment indicate that Qatar was quite keen to move toward a deeper understanding that could involve the semipermanent deployment of Indian naval units and security forces in the waters of the tiny Gulf nation. Ever cautious, however, India was emphasizing slow forward movement rather than steps that could upset other nations in the region.[24]

Although India has been hesitant to acquire or even debate in public about military naval bases in a traditional sense, its current maritime strategy has recognized the importance of access arrangements and turnaround facilities to facilitate naval operations in distant waters. As India stepped up its anti-piracy operations in the Gulf of Aden from October 2008, the need for secure access arrangements became even more important. More broadly, India's defense cooperation agreements with Oman and Qatar clearly reflect this trend line, where turnaround facilities become one part of a larger cooperation between New Delhi and its Gulf partners. India has also been interested in stepping up its cooperation with Djibouti, which is located deep in the Gulf of Aden and at the mouth of the Bab-el-Mandeb straits that is a choke point between the Red Sea and the Indian Ocean. European naval strategists during the colonial era had a deep appreciation of Djibouti's geopolitical significance.[25] And during the Cold War, the

United States and the Soviet Union competed for influence in Djibouti. Washington and Paris continue to maintain naval facilities on the island today. In the last few years, the Indian navy has increased the frequency of its port calls at Djibouti.[26] Since the growing concerns about piracy in the Gulf of Aden, Djibouti has become an attractive location for the foreign navies, including those of China and India, that started showing up, and it has been generally open to their using its facilities. In 2009, Japan signed access agreements for its naval ships and patrol aircraft at Djibouti and is providing significant economic assistance in return.[27]

Beyond Djibouti, India stepped up its activity in the Gulf of Aden and Red Sea area, participating frequently in naval exercises, including a series with Russia called INDRA and another with France called Varuna. Yemen and its Red Sea port of Aden have a very special place in the evolution of modern India. Occupied under British rule and developed as one of the coaling stations and trading entrepots for the Raj, Aden was a part of British India until 1937.[28] It was also the home for many Indian traders, and the founder of contemporary India's biggest corporation, Reliance Industries, Dhirubhai Ambani, cut his teeth in Aden. Many of these imperial arrangements became void after India's independence. As part of India's general post-independence retrenchment of its external security responsibilities, India's special relationship with Yemen waned as well. In recent years, a more outward-looking India has begun to focus on reviving the old relationship with Yemen. India's maritime ambitions are not limited to the southern end of the Red Sea. Through the 2000s, the Indian Navy has sought to expand its operations into the eastern Mediterranean through the Suez Canal. In 2004, after a deployment in the Gulf of Aden, four Indian naval ships made port calls in Egypt, Israel, Cyprus, and Turkey. What captured international attention was the navy's Operation Sukoon ("relief" in Hindi) in July 2006, when India deployed four ships to the coast of Lebanon to evacuate a large number of Indians and South Asians during a conflict between the Israeli Defense Forces and Hezbollah. Proud of its largest civilian evacuation effort, the naval headquarters in New Delhi declared: "The fact that Indian Naval warships are constantly 'on the beat,' so to speak, is what makes them readily available to be deployed in the best interests of the country, even in far-flung places. In keeping with this philosophy, the presence of these four Indian Naval warships in the vicinity was part of a regional deployment pattern that is increasingly becoming routine for the Indian Navy."[29] During the Libyan crisis in early 2011, the Indian Navy launched Operation Safe Homecoming to evacuate nearly 15,000 Indians from the North African country.[30]

China's continuing naval deployment in the Gulf of Aden since the end of 2008 was historic in many ways, and we discussed in chapter 7 its significance in terms of the changing direction of Beijing's maritime orientation, naval strategy, and doctrine. The Chinese Navy, however, is a long way from matching the current expansive operational engagement of the Indian Navy in the Arabian Sea, Red Sea, and the Gulf of Aden. As one of the littoral states of the Arabian Sea, India has enjoyed significant geographic, historical, and cultural links in the Persian Gulf and the Arabian Peninsula. China is making up for its disadvantages in the region through its larger economic clout, vigorous hydrocarbon diplomacy, and a political determination to build strategic links with the key nations of the Gulf. A study of the PLAN's port calls in the Gulf of Aden since it deployed there at the end of 2008 suggested that the Chinese debate on bases and facilities in the Indian Ocean was not an abstract one. Salalah in Oman, Aden in Yemen, and Djibouti have emerged as major ports of call for the Chinese naval deployments in the Arabian Sea and the Gulf of Aden. These ports indicate, the study says, "not only where the PLAN prefers to replenish its ships and rest its crews but also where it is likely to develop formal arrangements should it choose to do so." It adds that the "PLAN ships deployed to the Gulf of Aden have utilized Salalah more than any other port, with nineteen port calls through August 2010, and it can be argued that Salalah is already a 'place' for the PLAN in fact if not in name."[31] That China is gaining a foothold in Oman, a country that has been the closest to India in the Gulf, underlines the difficulties that New Delhi encounters in attempting to limit Beijing's maritime presence in the Indian Ocean.

Of special importance in the Chinese outreach to the Arabian Sea littoral has been its growing engagement with Iran. The expanding relationship covers the full range—from large-scale Chinese investments in the Iranian energy sector to the sale of missiles and military equipment, and from regional strategic coordination through the Shanghai Cooperation Organization to offering a measure of protection to Tehran from the West in multilateral forums including the UN Security Council.[32] Even as it embraced Iran amid Tehran's growing confrontation with the West, there is some speculation, somewhat premature, about Iran's offering military base facilities to China.[33] As it reached out to Iran, China has not neglected Iran's neighbors on the Arabian Peninsula. In the second half of the decade, China has stepped up the interaction with the Arab world in general, the GCC in particular, with a special emphasis on Saudi Arabia. As in Africa, so, too, in the Middle East, China has established a broad new framework for deepening all-round engagement with the Arab world. In collaboration with the Arab League in Cairo, China formed the China-Arab Cooperation Forum in January 2004 and since then has met at the level of senior officials and ministers to rapidly institutionalize energy, economic, and political cooperation.[34] At the subregional level, China is among the few countries with whom the Gulf Cooperation Council conducts a strategic dialogue. As the GCC countries seek to diversify their economic relationship beyond the traditional focus on the West, trade relations with China have boomed. Negotiations between the GCC and China on a free trade agreement are reported to be making progress.[35] The rapid expansion of the China–Saudi Arabia relationship in recent years has been one of the most important changes in the bilateral equations in the world. After a prolonged absence of diplomatic relations, Sino-Saudi relations have rapidly expanded since King Abdullah's visit to Beijing in January 2006. Hu Jintao made visits to Saudi Arabia in 2006 and 2009. Saudi Arabia has emerged as China's largest trading partner in the Middle East, with bilateral trade standing at nearly $42 billion in 2008. In 2009, China replaced the United States as the largest importer of Saudi petroleum and brought into relief the changing structure of the region's oil politics.[36] Few will question China's long-term interest in gaining influence in a region so vital to its energy security. What is not clear is how the pursuit of those interests might affect other powers. Although the U.S. navy welcomed China's maritime expedition into the Gulf of Aden in 2009 and has offered cooperation, Western doubts remain on whether Beijing is a partner or rival in the Arabian Sea, the Red Sea, and the Persian Gulf.[37]

While China's maritime forays into the Arabian Sea have gotten much international attention, Pakistan remains its main maritime partner in the region. Since the Kargil conflict in the summer of 1999 between India and Pakistan, during which India fully mobilized its naval forces in the

Arabian Sea, China and Pakistan have put a special emphasis on expanding their naval cooperation across the board. This has included the transfer of advanced naval arms, for example, in the induction in July 2009 of the first of the four F-22 frigates being built in China for the Pakistan navy.[38] China is also investing in the improvement of maritime infrastructure all across the Pakistan coast and improving its connections to the hinterland. In addition, the Chinese navy participates in the annual Aman naval exercises conducted by Pakistan in the Arabian Sea. Karachi has been a frequent port of call for the PLAN and is likely to emerge as an important facility for China in the future. Western analysts affirm that "for all the hype about Gwadar, it is far more likely that Beijing would send its warships to Karachi, Pakistan's largest port and primary naval base, if it were to seek a facility in Pakistan to support its forces." The analysts add that Karachi is well equipped to provide logistical and maintenance support for Chinese naval operations in the Indian Ocean.

> Substantial ship construction and repair facilities, including dry docks, are available at the Pakistan Naval Dockyard and the Karachi Shipyard and Engineering Works. Karachi is also where the Pakistan navy bases its Chinese-built F-22P frigates. . . . These warships, which most likely enjoy some degree of parts commonality with PLAN frigates, and extensive repair facilities, make Karachi a strong candidate as a friendly port where China would seek to repair any ships damaged operating in the Indian Ocean.[39]

While the Sino-Indian maritime competition emerges in the wider Arabian Sea littoral, the Pakistani coast is likely to emerge as an important arena for the maritime contest between the two Asian giants.[40]

At a broader level, as their interests grow in the Arabian Sea and the Middle East, China and India are finding it hard to cope with the sharpening contradictions in the region. As non-Western powers, both Beijing and New Delhi have sought to maintain some distance from the United States in the gathering confrontation between Washington and Tehran on the Iranian nuclear weapons program. Both countries have emphasized diplomatic solutions in resolving the nuclear question and have resisted Western pressures to cut off their economic links to Tehran amid the expanding unilateral U.S. and European sanctions against Iran's oil sector. While their stakes in energy cooperation with Iran are high, neither Beijing nor New Delhi is ready to make it the focus of an unwanted confrontation with the United States.[41] The political and diplomatic challenges for China and India become a lot worse as they are compelled to cope with the deepening divisions between Saudi Arabia and Iran and the widening conflict in the region between Sunni Arabs and Shi'i Iran. With high stakes in the energy relationship with both, Beijing and New Delhi are hard pressed to take sides. If the region's complexity has always tested great powers, China and India are getting their first bitter taste of pursuing their interests in the Middle East.

THE BAY OF BENGAL

The Bay of Bengal and the Andaman Sea host some of the world's busiest sea lines of communication at the entrance to the Strait of Malacca, the choke point that connects the eastern Indian Ocean with the western Pacific. The Andaman and Nicobar Islands form a long north-south stretch that provides a strategic perch to dominate the eastern Indian Ocean. As long as China, India, and Burma were looking inward, the Bay of Bengal seemed a backwater and attracted little strategic attention. Thailand and Indonesia, which form the eastern flank, were focused on regional integration in Southeast Asia from the early 1970s. The breakup of Pakistan in 1971 and the relative weakness of Bangladesh completed the marginalization of the Bay of Bengal littoral. All this began to change in the late 1980s, as China completed its first decade of reforms, India under Rajiv Gandhi began to bestir itself at home and abroad, and Burma emerged from isolation amid internal political turmoil. Since then the action-reaction dynamic between the Chinese and Indian policies has been quite strong in the Bay of Bengal and has expressed itself in two ways. One was the competition for influence within Burma, and the other was the gathering rivalry between the two sides for positions of advantage in the waters of the Bay of Bengal.

In the current debate on East Asian security, it is easy to forget that the imperial defense system of Great Britain in the eastern Indian Ocean and western Pacific relied on the vast resources of the united subcontinent. The armies of India, for example, played a decisive role in reversing the Japanese aggression of Southeast Asia during 1943–1945 and shaping the immediate postwar order in the East. As India headed toward partition, and the Congress nationalists refused to support the Anglo-American Cold War strategy in Asia, imperial defense planners in London invested heavily in Pakistan and its military. Pakistan's importance for postwar Western security in the so-called Northern Tier was behind its incorporation into the Central Treaty Organization (CENTO). At the same time, Anglo-American military strategists decided to bring Pakistan into the security framework of Southeast Asia. Drawing an undivided Pakistan into the Southeast Asia Treaty Organization underlined the relevance at least of its eastern half in the Anglo-American calculus of Southeast Asian security.[42] The liberation of East Pakistan in 1971 and the marginalization of the subcontinent as a whole from Asia in the 1970s meant Bangladesh was of little consequence for the security politics of the Indian Ocean.[43] Well before Beijing elevated its engagement of South Asia in the 1990s, China's influence was beginning to grow in Bangladesh, as Dhaka's ties with New Delhi began to fray amid the evaporation of the initial euphoria of India's support for the liberation of Bangladesh. Although Beijing had opposed the creation of Bangladesh, it now reached out to all the political segments in the country and had built up strong bipartisan support for the bilateral relationship with China. Engagement with China also gave more room for Dhaka, which chafed at being bordered by India on three sides. The enduring detritus of the partition meant there would always be significant opposition to full normalization of relations with India, and it made sense for any regime to play the China card vis-à-vis India.[44]

Through the 1990s there was a steady expansion of cooperation between China and Bangladesh, and it covered the full spectrum of issues, including the supply of arms. While India was irritated at Dhaka's China play and its unwillingness to move forward on bilateral cooperation with India, New Delhi was slow to sense the long-term strategic consequences of Beijing's outreach to Dhaka. New Delhi was more focused on its own border problems with Bangladesh and the fact that its eastern neighbor was emerging as a safe haven for radical Islamic extremists. New Delhi was also concerned about the rapidly expanding migration from across the border and was angered by the fact that many militant groups operating in India's northeast were taking shelter in Bangladesh. Nevertheless, there were calls from those dealing with Bangladesh in the Indian Foreign Office for a more strategic approach.[45] Over the years, the scale and depth of China's economic cooperation with Bangladesh began to eclipse the commercial ties between Dhaka and Delhi. In 2004, Beijing overtook New Delhi as the largest trading partner of Dhaka and has begun to race ahead.[46] Although Dhaka's trade deficits with Beijing were larger than those with New Delhi, China's constant political tending of the relationship and Bangladesh's need to stand up to "Indian hegemony" seemed to limit the space for New Delhi. Whatever might be the reasons for Dhaka's relaxed approach to Beijing and its anxious one toward India, it is quite evident that China had begun to overcome India's natural geographic advantages in Bangladesh. While China has no border with Bangladesh, India shares a frontier that is 4,096 kilometers (2,545 miles) long. Furthermore, Bangladesh was part of the Indian economic space until 1947, and the natural interdependence between divided parts of Bengal and the surrounding provinces of India is real. Yet, China was trying to reshape the regional economic geography through large investments in infrastructural projects and the development of transport corridors to link Bangladesh with southwestern China.[47] On top of it all, Delhi had to take note of the expanding military engagement between Dhaka and Beijing and a civilian nuclear cooperation agreement signed during a visit by Chinese Premier Wen Jiabao to Bangladesh in 2005.[48]

Sino-Bangladeshi military defense cooperation includes training of personnel, materiel support, and production and upgrading of equipment and armaments. Bangladesh's army, navy, and air force are predominantly equipped with Chinese military hardware—tanks and light tanks, frigates, patrol craft, and combat aircraft.[49] Over the years, the two countries have signed a number of protocols outlining cooperation in these areas. Consequently, China has emerged as the largest and most important provider of Bangladesh's military hardware and the training of the country's armed forces.[50] This arms supply relationship has been embedded in a broader framework for bilateral defense cooperation marked by agreements signed over the years. Cooperation in the defense sector is also underscored by the exchange of frequent high-level visits by leaders of the armed forces of both countries. While some Indians have seen this military cooperation as nonthreatening, others have begun to raise the alarm. The first school argues that "despite its increasing defense ties with China, Bangladesh is unlikely to pose a direct threat to India, but the latter cannot ignore the growing convergence of interests between Bangladesh and China."[51] Other Indian analysts, however, have expressed stronger concerns. "First, there are fears among the Indian military establishment that Dhaka may grant military basing rights to China, thus complicating India's security in the Northeast. . . . Second, there are concerns that Bangladesh may offer the Chittagong port for development to China, ostensibly for commercial purposes, but it could also be used for staging Chinese naval assets. This is to be expected and can be reasonably tied to the Chinese development of ports at Gwadar in Pakistan and Hambantota in Sri Lanka. Third, China will be able to monitor Indian missile testing conducted at Chandipur-on-sea near Balasore, Orissa, and also naval activity in the Andaman and Nicobar Islands in the Bay of Bengal."[52]

While some of these fears might seem exaggerated, India had no choice but to respond on two levels. First was the general attempt by India to re-vamp the very premises of its regional policy during China's rise. From the late 1990s, many liberals in India sought a good-neighbor policy to resolve long-standing political disputes with its neighbors and promote regional economic cooperation. Articulated strongly by Inder Kumar Gujral dur-ing his tenure as foreign minister and prime minister in 1996–1998, the approach found strong support among Gujral's successors. Both Atal Bi-hari Vajpayee of the Bharatiya Janata Party, or BJP, and Manmohan Singh of the Congress Party supported the essence of the so-called Gujral Doc-trine.[53] Unlike Gujral, who approached the neighborhood from the liberal perspective of peace and friendship, by the time Manmohan Singh came to power new economic and strategic underpinnings had emerged for the good-neighbor policy. As the Indian economy grew at a rapid pace, the logic of integrating the region now had a more practical basis. Sections of the permanent bureaucracy that were initially suspicious of the Gujral Doctrine were now recognizing that an Indian failure to reframe the ties with its neighbors would allow further Chinese penetration of what was India's natural hinterland and traditionally an exclusive sphere of influ-ence. India's concerns about Chinese penetration were so strong that New Delhi actively worked to bring Western powers into an observer role in the regional forum SAARC, when Pakistan and Bangladesh pressed for a more formal Chinese role in the subcontinent. The Indian foreign policy establishment was now articulating the notions of building a peaceful periphery, providing greater access to the Indian market through unilateral economic concessions if necessary, emphasizing the Indian "responsibility" to make its neighbors feel comfortable in their engagement with India, and working to deepen India's strategic links with the neighbors rather than merely objecting to their defense ties with Beijing.[54]

Translating this vision into reality with Bangladesh was not going to be easy. The profound internal divisions within Bangladesh, the political volatility, and the enduring burden of the partition meant that India had to work very hard to realize even minimal gains in the bilateral relationship. From the middle of the decade of the 2000s, New Delhi made a determined effort to transform the ties with Bangladesh. When the Bangladesh military imposed an emergency in January 2007 to suspend the electoral process amid major political violence, India did not condemn the move even though its traditional friends in Dhaka sought New Delhi's intervention. Instead, India signaled its readiness to do business with whoever was in power in Dhaka and made it clear it no longer had the desire to pick winners in Bangladesh. New Delhi made a special effort throughout the period to reestablish ties with the Bangladeshi army. The Bangladeshi army chief visited India in February–March 2008, and the visit was quickly reciprocated by his Indian counterpart in July–August 2008.[55] A similar process was initiated in 2009 between the two air forces. The Indian navy was ahead of the other two services and was quicker in recognizing the importance of reaching out to Bangladesh by drawing Dhaka into the ambit of India's new naval diplomacy and multilateral exercises in the Indian Ocean. The Indian naval chief traveled to Dhaka in 2005 and again in 2011 as part of a sustained effort to develop a cooperative maritime engagement with the Bangladeshi navy.[56]

In Bangladesh, the failed mutiny by a section of the paramilitary forces in March 2009 backed by extremists had shocked both civilian leaders and the army into recognizing the dangers of taking an attitude of benign neglect toward extremist groups operating inside its territory. New Delhi hoped that this might translate into more purposeful cooperation from Dhaka in confronting the sources of terrorism in the region. India has indeed recognized the strategic imperative of transforming the security ties with Dhaka. This was reflected in the very warm reception of the Bangladeshi prime minister, Sheikh Hasina, in New Delhi in January 2010. The declaration issued by the two leaders underlined the commitment to resolve all outstanding issues and lay the foundation for a durable partnership.[57] Prime Minister Manmohan Singh's return visit in September 2011 aimed at a big bang effort that would produce forward movement on river water sharing and market access, which was of interest to Dhaka, and overland transit, which was of major concern to New Delhi, with the hope of yielding a settled border that would benefit both. Lack of political consensus in India, however, postponed any agreements on sharing the Teesta and Feni rivers. And internal reservations in Dhaka resulted in deferring the agreements on transit. India, for its part, provided duty-free market access to Bangladeshi textile exports, and the two sides resolved all outstanding issues relating to their shared border. They also signed a comprehensive framework agreement for cooperation across the board.[58] While the visit fell short, it marked an expansive Indian political commitment to transform relations with Bangladesh. Although limiting Chinese military influence in Dhaka is not India's only motive, it has become an important one for New Delhi, which is aware of the possibilities of China's replaying in Bangladesh the very successful military diplomacy it pulled off in Pakistan. China may not supply nuclear weapons and missiles to Bangladesh, but even a modest military partnership between Beijing and Dhaka could severely complicate India's security environment. As an analyst notes:

> The Chinese approach of systematically nurturing and promoting diplomatic linkages with Bangladesh provides it with a number of strategic advantages against India. . . . (Beijing) will be in a position to link its electronic listening systems at Coco Island in Myanmar and the staging/listening systems in Bangladesh and [could then] monitor Indian naval and missile activity. Given the wide disparities in the India–Bangladesh naval order of battle, Bangladesh would be under pressure to open its facilities to the PLA Navy as a countervailing force against the Indian Navy. The prospect of Chinese ships and submarines operating in the North Andaman Sea would have serious repercussions for India's projection capabilities. This is sure to result in some aggressive counter-maneuvering by the Indian Navy, and the Indian naval response would be to execute a blockade and entanglement of Chinese naval assets in Chittagong.[59]

Although this is a worst-case scenario, India is waking up to the immense challenges that China might be able to pose if its outreach to Bangladesh remains uncontested by New Delhi. India has certainly begun to step up its own military engagement with Bangladesh. As it seeks to raise its game in Bangladesh, New Delhi is already deeply invested in the project to contest Chinese maritime and naval influence in Burma.

In chapter 7, we had surveyed the logic behind China's development of transport corridors between western China and the Indian Ocean through Pakistan and Burma. The prospect of a Chinese military naval presence at the mouth of the energy-rich Persian Gulf and on the western edges of the Malacca Strait did raise major concerns in New Delhi. India, however, was quite conscious of the fact that it was not in a position to significantly alter the dynamics of emerging Sino-Pakistan strategic cooperation in the maritime domain. It was also aware that China's rising naval profile in the Gulf might elicit responses from other great powers, especially the United States, which zealously guards its vital interests in the region. Burma was entirely different; there was no question of India's not joining a contest with China for influence in a state that had expansive borders with both the Asian giants. The contest would remain largely bilateral. The United States and Europe signaled that they had no strategic interest in Burma, only concerns about human rights and democracy after the collapse of the Berlin Wall and the Soviet Union. China and India, however, viewed Burma through the classical lens of geopolitics. Burma occupied a crucial territorial space—it offered Beijing access to the Indian Ocean and New Delhi a land bridge to East Asia and the western Pacific. During the Second World War, the Allies supported Chinese nationalist resistance to Japanese occupation from India. This included the building of the famed Burma Road—connecting the eastern subcontinent with China's Yunnan Province—by the American army engineers led by Gen. Joseph Stilwell. The Allies also ran air operations supporting the Chinese nationalists from bases in the northeastern parts of the subcontinent.

With Burma coming into the fold of the British Raj in the late nineteenth century and remaining a virtual protectorate after its separation from India in 1937, it seemed reasonable to presume that New Delhi would inherit the primacy of the Raj in Burma. Perceptive analysts such as K. M. Panikkar writing in the late 1940s did recognize that the Raj influence was premised on a weakened China in the first half of the twentieth century. He also understood that Burma's separation from India in 1937 couldn't be undone and called instead for a solid strategic partnership with Rangoon. A China on the rise, Panikkar argued in the early 1940s, would make Burma a contested zone between the two Asian giants. China's "mere existence as a great military power on the borders of Burma, and the increasing importance she will attach to the Burma Road and access to Rangoon, and the dynamics of Chinese population problems in relation to Burma and Malaya will create grave complications in Indian foreign policy."[60] Panikkar also argued that the Japanese occupation of Burma during the Second World War had shown the extraordinary strategic significance of the nation for the defense of both India and Southeast Asia.

> Burma in the hands of another Power would in the circumstances of modern air and naval power, be a serious menace to India. . . . Like other countries in East Asia Burma is in no position to defend herself. . . . Her defense therefore has to be related to India and considered in terms of Indian military problems . . . The defense of Burma is in fact the defense of India, and it is India's primary concern no less than Burma's to see that its frontiers remain inviolate. In fact no responsibility can be considered too heavy for India when it comes to the question of defending Burma.[61]

As one of the richest countries in emerging Asia, Burma quickly positioned itself as one of the new voices of Asia. Burma was one of the five "Colombo Powers"—along with Pakistan, India, Ceylon (now Sri Lanka) and Indonesia—constituting one of the first Asian groupings in the 1950s.[62] Intense Burmese nationalism, however, often put Rangoon at odds with both China and India. It would also emerge that the vast regions at the tri-junction of the three nations—regions that were never really under the effective sovereignty of any organized entity and were home to many tribal populations—would become restive. As ethnic conflicts spill across the borders, a basis had been created for mutual conflict among the three nation-states. Rangoon was wary of Chinese penetration in northern Burma and its attempts to foment rebellion;[63] at the same time, it was deeply resentful of the Indian population that was brought into the country and eventually expelled most of them.[64] But once Burma turned on itself in the 1960s after a military coup by General Ne Win, it had become

marginal to the strategic calculus of both China and India, which themselves had become inward-looking. All this began to change at the end
of the 1970s, when Burma hesitantly probed reestablishing relations with
its neighbors.[65] As Deng Xiaoping gained control of China and prepared
to open it up to the world, he visited Burma at the end of 1978 and laid
the foundation for a comprehensive engagement with Rangoon. In India,
Prime Minister Rajiv Gandhi, who was launching India on a new path in
the mid-1980s, also reached out to Burma. It was the elections in 1988
and their aftermath that brought about the dramatic transformation of the
internal and external context in Burma. The elections featured a resound-
ing triumph of pro-democracy forces led by Aung San Suu Kyi, but the
army refused to accept the verdict and reimposed military rule. Soon after,
the June 1989 turmoil in Beijing's Tiananmen Square invited sanctions
from the West and put an end to the warmth in the Sino-U.S. relations
forged in the battle against the Soviet Union in the final years of the Cold
War. If a shared sense of political isolation drew Beijing and Rangoon
together, India in the late 1980s found itself at complete odds with the
Burmese military regime. When Rajiv Gandhi made India the strongest
external supporter of Aung San Suu Kyi and her movement for democracy,
China became the most valuable partner for Burma's military regime. As it
watched Beijing's influence rapidly expand in the early 1990s, New Delhi
began a reconsideration of its hostility toward Rangoon. Soon enough,
New Delhi announced a policy of engaging Rangoon without endorsing
its repressive policies at home. Although the proponents of change cited
the importance of Rangoon's cooperation in securing the northeast against
many insurgencies there as well as Burma's importance as a land corridor
to Southeast Asia, the most important consideration, as usual, was balancing China.[66]

Not everyone in New Delhi was prepared to countenance the replace-
ment of India's moralpolitik in Burma with realpolitik. As India's foreign
and security establishments reached out to Rangoon in the early 1990s,
the president of India, K. R. Narayanan, whose wife was of Burmese origin, declared Aung San Suu Kyi the winner of the Jawaharlal Nehru Award
for International Understanding for the year 1993. This announcement,
which came right in the middle of a joint counterinsurgency campaign
between the Indian and Burmese armed forces during 1995, revived

Rangoon's distrust of New Delhi's intentions. Once the right-wing Bharatiya Janata Party took charge of the Indian government as part of a larger coalition with the National Democratic Alliance in 1998, most ambiguities in New Delhi were set to rest. Seeking more muscular foreign and national security policies, advisers of Prime Minister Vajpayee had no difficulty framing a more strategic approach toward Burma in terms of matching Chinese influence there and set about implementing the administration's approach purposefully. From the late 1990s, India began a vigorous effort to support infrastructure projects in Burma similar to those that China had launched. If Beijing was focused on developing north-south transport corridors, New Delhi's interest was in east-west corridors that linked eastern India with Southeast Asia through Burmese territory. Unlike the tentative engagement that began in the early 1990s, the Vajpayee government actively sought high-level political exchanges between the two sides, and visits by all top Indian and Burmese functionaries to each other's capital soon followed.[67]

The Indian response to China's rising profile in Burma was not limited to commercial, economic, and political engagement with Burma at the turn of the decade; it also included a military component. As China became the principal arms supplier to Burma from the late 1980s, India was soon compelled to craft a larger military response to Beijing's moves. The Chinese supplies to Rangoon included tanks, fighter planes, trainer and transport aircraft, radar, rocket launchers, and on the naval side, patrol vessels and a few frigates. India's supplies included a few weapons systems such as "Islander" surveillance aircraft, light artillery, and considerable amounts of nonlethal equipment—no match for the scale and scope of the Chinese military assistance. India has also been involved in servicing some of the Russian equipment that the Tatmadaw (the Burmese armed forces) had acquired. Despite the growing arms supply relationship between China and Burma, India did not seem alarmed about a potential change in the balance of power in the northeast, where the borders of China, Burma, and India meet. The Indian strategy appeared to be to stay in the Burmese field of external military acquisition rather than become an alternative supplier to China. The Indian emphasis was to build a long-term institutional relationship with the Burmese armed forces, promote high-level military exchanges, and intensify assistance in training and other operational aspects of modernizing the Burmese forces, which had been caught in a time warp.[68] The interests of the Indian internal security planners was in Burmese military cooperation in denying safe havens to Indian insurgent groups from the restive northeastern provinces and developing cooperation on border management. It was Sino-Burmese maritime cooperation that drew the most concern from the Indian security establishment as well as the public and elicited a strategic response from New Delhi.

As Chinese and Indian maritime interests began to overlap in the Bay of Bengal, Burma itself seemed little interested in the seas. From the perspective of Rangoon, its primary national security threats for decades have been internal threats from restive minority groups. Defeating them on the battlefield and integrating them into the nation had preoccupied the Burmese military for decades; as a consequence, there was little interest in building a naval force. Rangoon, therefore, was quite happy to take full advantage of the incipient Sino-Indian maritime rivalry to develop its moribund maritime infrastructure.[69] Although China had begun to supply naval equipment to Rangoon, the main concern for India was not a change in the order of battle in the Bay of Bengal. It was about the People's Liberation Army Navy's getting a long-term foothold in the Bay of Bengal. What seemed to agitate the Indian naval and maritime planners from the early 1990s were persistent reports that China was setting up a base facility for intelligence gathering or pre-positioning of arms in the Cocos Islands north of the Andaman and Nicobar island chain. While these reports gained ground across the region, closer analysis suggested that none of the claims of Chinese bases were based on reliable evidence. "In 2005, it was established to the satisfaction of the Indian government that there were no Chinese bases in the Cocos Islands, and probably never had been. Even so this myth has developed a life of its own and continues to distort analyses of Burma's foreign relations and the strategic environment of the Asia-Pacific region."[70] What was undeniable, however, was the open Chinese activity in the development of Burma's maritime infrastructure on the Arakan coast and Irrawaddy Delta. This in turn provoked a determined Indian naval diplomacy toward Burma.

A close examination of Chinese and Indian maritime activity in Burma suggests that "both Beijing and New Delhi appeared to have gained substantial advantages in Burma with regard to their Indian Ocean ambitions, but India seems to have got[ten] more than China in recent years." This assessment points to three major gains for India: "the right to berth and refuel in Burmese ports for Indian commercial vessels or warships; conducting joint naval operations with the Burmese Navy; and gleaning intelligence on the Chinese presence along Burma's coast so as to checkmate it."[71] While China did develop privileged access to the natural resources as well as the markets of Burma, the infrastructure it has developed there has not been for exclusive purposes. For example, the Thilawa Port developed by China to the east of the Irrawaddy Delta in the south has been used by other countries. Burmese rulers have been careful not to provide any privileged naval access to China at its ports. Indian naval vessels have been seen at Burmese ports often since 2002, when India appeared to have negotiated access to turnaround facilities in Burma. The Indian navy has frequently conducted joint naval maneuvers with its Burmese counterpart. Burmese ships have also visited Indian facilities in the Andamans. The naval interaction between Burma and China took a big step forward when two PLAN warships, part of a task force sent on anti-piracy duties in the Gulf of Aden, steamed into Thilawa to a warm reception in 2010.[72] The asymmetry in Burma's naval engagement with India and China—in favor of the former—was coming to an end.

As China's naval profile in the Bay of Bengal began to acquire a new depth, the strategic significance of the Andaman and Nicobar Islands came back into full view. Writing before India gained independence, K. M. Panikkar argued that "the defense of the long and open Indian coastline, not to speak of the active control of the Ocean, is possible only by having suitable island cover as advanced bases. The possession of the Andamans and Nicobars gives protection to the East coast and secures adequate control of the Bay of Bengal."[73] Pankikkar also urged India to end the neglect of its eastern island chain: "The Andamans can no longer be neglected as a group of islands suitable at best for the transportation of criminals and political offenders. Their development as suitable naval and air bases for the Indian navy and their reclamation and effective colonization are essential elements in a naval policy for India."[74] Yet neglect is what India did in the first decades after independence. Amid debates on the transfer of power and the interests of the Admiralty in London to retain control over Andaman and Nicobar Islands as well as other islands in the Indian Ocean, there was little interest or awareness in New Delhi about the importance of the island territories. It was Viceroy Mountbatten who insisted on retaining the islands with India and proposed negotiations with it over British use.[75] The impending tragedy of India's partitioning and the need to manage the new border problems created by it, further reduced the awareness of the Andaman and Nicobar Islands.

Thanks to the Kargil War of 1999 and the reform of the national security system that followed, the BJP government, with its greater interest in maritime affairs, ordered the establishment of the Andaman and Nicobar Command. It was also India's first joint military command that would exercise integrated control over air, naval, and ground forces in the region. Among the missions of the command were to suppress gun running and narcotics trafficking, prevent piracy, and establish and exercise authority over the 200-nautical-mile exclusive economic zone. Coming as it did in the wake of India's nuclear tests of 1998 and India's self-declaration as a nuclear-weapon state, the Andaman and Nicobar Command was also seen as important in strengthening India's nuclear deterrence. "In addition to the Andaman and Nicobar Islands' importance as forward bases for any sea-based Indian nuclear deterrent, these islands also have relevance for India in terms of the potential strengthening of its air-based nuclear deterrent vis-à-vis China. Campbell Airport on Great Nicobar is as near China's populated heartland as any airfield in India, and also affords aircraft a route to China that is over water (the South China Sea) and undefended compared with various trans-Himalayan avenues of approach."[76] Although unstated, one of the main objectives of the Andaman and Nicobar Command was to monitor and counter the emerging Chinese naval activity in the region. More broadly, the Andaman and Nicobar island chain would become the key to India's naval power projection in the eastern Indian Ocean, as the protector of the sea lines of communication at the mouth of the Strait of Malacca and as a naval complement to India's Look East Policy. As argued by an Indian naval officer, the augmentation of capabilities at the Andaman and Nicobar Command is necessary "to maintain good order in the extensive maritime zones of the far-flung island chain, though, of course, the imperative to deter China is also likely to have been the key driver."[77] For all the new awareness in New Delhi about the island chain, it is a long way from the integration of the Andamans into its maritime strategy. The establishment of the Andaman and Nicobar Command did not involve the permanent deployment of naval and air assets; nor has New Delhi outlined a bold geoeconomic vision for the island chain. But the Chinese pressure to do so might be relentless.[78]

In the coming years, the Bay of Bengal and the Andaman Sea are likely to loom larger in the maritime calculus of both China and India. Forming the hinge between the eastern Indian Ocean and the South China Sea, the waters of the Bay of Bengal and the Andaman Sea will become critical for security of the sea lines of communication in the Indo-Pacific. While the bilateral jockeying for position is likely to intensify, Beijing and New Delhi have begun to face a more complex regional environment amid the rapid political opening up of Burma during 2011 and the new Western outreach to the country. So long as Burma was isolated, Beijing and New Delhi enjoyed privileged economic and strategic positions in the country. An outward-looking Burma, increasingly engaged with the West and determined to regain its place in Asia and the world, will complicate the strategic calculus of Beijing and New Delhi. As large neighbors, China and India will always matter much to Burma. But located at the Asian crossroads and on the Indo-Pacific hinge, Burma will have an opportunity to set its own terms for engagement with Beijing and Delhi.[79]

THE SOUTH CHINA SEA

In chapter 6, we had explored at considerable length the Indian naval forays east of Malacca in the South China Sea and the broader western Pacific Ocean. At first look, the prevailing situation in the western Pacific would seem to be a mirror image of that in the Indian Ocean. While the United States is the dominant maritime power in both oceans, India has many natural advantages, located as it is at the very heart of the Indian Ocean. Chinese naval strategy in the Indian Ocean will have to come up against this reality as well as cope with such geographic difficulties as the choke points at all the major maritime entrances into the ocean and the long logistical lines that limit the effectiveness of its naval power in the Indian Ocean. East of Malacca, it is China that has the natural maritime advantage and it is India that has all the difficulties of entering the western Pacific and sustaining a credible presence. These advantages are somewhat neutralized by China's unresolved territorial disputes with its maritime neighbors in the South China Sea and the western Pacific. The hopes that these issues could be resolved peacefully faded since 2010, when China's assertiveness in the South China Sea and in its contested waters with Japan encountered a regional political backlash.[80] As China declared the South China Sea a core interest, U.S. Secretary of State Hillary Clinton, speaking at the ASEAN Regional Forum summit in Hanoi in July 2010, injected the United States into the dispute by declaring the U.S. interest in a peaceful resolution of the dispute and in the freedom of navigation in the South China Sea. President Barack Obama picked up the theme at the East Asia Summit in Bali, Indonesia, in November 2011 and confronted the Chinese premier, Wen Jiabao, on the issue. China in turn rejected third-party intervention and warned the United States and other powers not to meddle in its dispute over the South China Sea. Within the short span of 2011–2012, the South China Sea became a major issue of contention between Beijing and Washington.[81]

It is in this increasingly tense maritime setting that India finds itself. On the South China Sea issues, India has extended strong support to the principle of freedom of navigation and a peaceful resolution of the territorial disputes, in much the same manner as the United States. At the East Asia Summit in Bali in November 2011, India was among the overwhelming majority of members to express concerns on the South China Sea, despite a request from Wen Jiabao to Prime Minister Manmohan Singh not to raise the dispute.[82] Asked by Wen about India's interests in the South China Sea, Singh apparently responded by underlining that they were purely commercial and that China must settle its disputes in the waters in accordance with international law.[83] Beyond the diplomatic position at Bali, India was quite explicit in demonstrating its new interest in the South China Sea when it warmly received Vietnamese President Truong Tan Sang a few weeks before the East Asia Summit amid the growing tensions between Beijing and Hanoi. New Delhi reassured Truong of India's strong commitment to advance the defense and security partnership with Hanoi and its commitment to develop full spectrum cooperation in the hydrocarbon sector.[84] India's determination to pursue oil exploration in Vietnam's waters elicited much critical commentary from the Chinese media. Some comments suggested that India's actions were a response to China's growing presence in the Indian Ocean.[85] The idea that India is seeking a role in the South China Sea and the western Pacific to counter Beijing is not new. Ever since India launched its Look East policy in the early 1990s, there had been widespread speculation about the "China factor" in India's first post–Cold War diplomatic initiative. More recent analyses also argue that India's rising profile in East Asia and the Pacific is about India's search for parity with China.[86] Some even go to the extent of arguing that India's Pacific strategy is about a "counter-containment" of China. One assessment concludes that:

> India's engagement of ASEAN, its efforts to promote Vietnam as a bulwark against [the] Chinese sphere of influence, its developing military ties with both Australia and Japan, and last but not least, its forays into Mongolia, all point to the development of an ambitious Indian policy of counter-containment aimed at its Chinese neighbor.[87]

While the talk of counter-containment does not stand up to close scrutiny, India is increasingly being drawn into the security politics of the South China Sea. Vietnam has stepped up its efforts to encourage India to take on a larger role in the South China Sea as part of its effort to balance Beijing.[88] Washington, too, has been enthusiastic about a larger Indian role in the western Pacific. As she traveled from India to Southeast Asia to attend an ASEAN Regional Forum meeting in July 2011, Hillary Clinton underlined the American interest in a stronger partnership with India in the Asia-Pacific littoral: "The more our countries trade and invest with each other and with other partners, the more central the Asia-Pacific region becomes to global commerce and prosperity, and the more interest we both have in maintaining stability and security. As the stakes grow higher, we should use our shared commitments to make sure that we have maritime security and freedom of navigation."[89]

While India's current interest in the South China Sea has attracted much attention, the littoral is not a stranger to India's historical memory. Writing in the 1940s, when China was down and out, India's early navalists were quite clear about the potential future challenges from Beijing. But this concern was embedded in the larger notion that India's security perimeter extended to the western Pacific and South China Sea. K. M. Panikkar, for example, argued that India cannot secure the Indian Ocean without the ability of its naval forces to operate on the coastline of Indochina and exercise a measure of control over the Malayan Peninsula and Singapore, which sits astride the Strait of Malacca. He declared that the defense of the Indian Ocean from attacks originating in the western Pacific "must be based on the coastline of Indo-China and Thailand being in the hands of friendly powers. At no time can India or Britain permit their control by a single naval power. A renovated and triumphant China with her population irresistibly moving south from Tonkin to Singapore may become a greater menace to the defense of the Indian Ocean, than even Japan with her lines of communications extended so far from the sources of her power."[90]

In the post-independence years, as India marginalized itself from regional affairs, even the boldest of the strategists could raise the notion that Indian security interests extended from Aden to Malacca. After India fell out with China at the turn of the 1960s, balancing Beijing in Indochina became an important imperative of Indian foreign policy and its outreach to Vietnam and Indochina. In 2000, the defense minister at the time, George Fernandes, argued that India's maritime interests extend "from the north of the Arabian Sea to the South China Sea." It was the year when the Indian navy conducted its first naval exercises in the South China Sea with Vietnam. The Indian navy's document on maritime strategy has affirmed that while Singapore and the Strait of Malacca form a primary area of interest, the South China Sea is on the list of secondary areas of interest.[91]

As the Indian navy began to make repeated forays into the South China Sea, its strategy began to underline a number of reasons for the renewed Indian interest in the waters that Pankikkar called the "true Mediterranean of the Pacific."[92] First, as its trade with East Asia begins to overtake that with Western Europe, the Middle East, and Africa, India has begun to recognize the importance of its sea lines of communication not just in the Indian Ocean but also those in the western Pacific. Second, as an expanding navy with broad-based ambitions, the Indian navy sees the importance of maintaining the freedom of the high seas in the western Pacific. Much like China, which may not want to depend on the goodwill of the United States or India for the protection of its Indian Ocean sea lines of communication, India, too, would not want to totally depend on the United States or China for its maritime needs in the western Pacific. Third, India has concerns about the danger that Beijing could convert the

South China Sea into a "Chinese lake" by the forceful affirmation of its territorial claims. New Delhi has already encountered Beijing's objections to Indian companies exploring for oil in contracts with Vietnam.[93] Fourth, at the operational level, domain awareness in all areas of maritime interest has become a priority for the Indian navy, hence its desire to maintain a presence to track potential developments that could affect its security.[94] Finally, the Indian navy underlines the importance of a forward maritime presence and naval partnerships as critical to deter potential adversaries, for example, China in the South China Sea and western Pacific. As India's maritime military strategy says, "When dealing with a more capable adversary, deterrence can also be achieved by the formation of partnerships or coalitions/alliances, thereby combining capabilities of partner maritime forces, or presenting a picture of solidarity."[95]

Carving a role in partnership with regional and global navies in the South China Sea forms a modest but sustainable objective for India. At the same time, Indian navalists are acutely aware of taking on commitments in the South China Sea that can't be defended by current capabilities. Amid the assertion of Indian interests in the South China Sea during 2011, a former chief of naval staff, Arun Prakash, argued that "even if India is about to take a long overdue stand on principles, or adopt an assertive posture vis-à-vis China, a distant location like the South China Sea is hardly an ideal setting to demonstrate India's maritime or other strengths."[96] He underlined India's limitations in defending the oil drilling in the South China Sea by India's leading international oil company, OVL (Oil and Natural Gas Commission Videsh Ltd). Prakash adds that "at this juncture, it would be imprudent to contemplate sustaining a naval presence some 2,500 nautical miles from home to bolster OVL's stake in South China Sea hydrocarbons." India's security policymakers also are fully aware of the dangers of being drawn into an untenable confrontation with Beijing close to China's shores. While they appreciate the new diplomatic leverage coming their way in the South China Sea, they are unlikely to allow themselves to be pushed too far against Beijing.[97] India is quite clear that its exploration for oil in the contested waters of the South China Sea must be driven by commercial and not strategic considerations. OVL gave up in 2012 exploration in Block 128 it had acquired from Vietnam after drilling there did not produce satisfactory results. This did not mean India was acquiescing under political pressure from Beijing, as Delhi made it clear that its hunt for oil in the disputed waters of the South China Sea will continue.[98]

Despite much negative commentary in the Chinese press on India's activity in the South China Sea, the official responses in Beijing and by the policy research community have been guarded. Some Chinese analysts understand that the Southeast Asian nations have a natural interest in promoting a balance of power in the western Pacific and reach out to the United States, Japan, and India. According to Zhao Gancheng, "It is worth noting that the Indian military presence in the area is appreciated and welcomed by ASEAN in general. Explanation for the ASEAN attitude is based on the logic of balance of power. The guiding line of ASEAN security policy is to keep its autonomous and independent position as a regional bloc, and in the meantime, ASEAN welcomes all the other major powers to participate in regional security architecture, but not any single power to dominate."[99] While the Indian initiatives in the western Pacific are important, it might be exaggerated to call it "counter-containment of China." Instead, a more realistic assessment points to India's limitations—both internal and external—as well as the potential to contribute to the balance of power in the western Pacific.

> In pursuing strategic ties with nations that have traditionally had difficult relations with China—such as Vietnam, Indonesia, Japan, and the United States—New Delhi lends its military and economic power to a regional security order that can enhance stability in Asia by presenting Beijing with a series of structural constraints that may diffuse the negative aspects of China's rise and persuade it that attempts to dominate the region are unlikely to succeed.[100]

If one steps back to look at the Sino-Indian interaction across the Asian littoral, a number of broad trends stand out. During the first decade of the twenty-first century, the maritime interests and the naval profile of China and India increased in the Arabian Sea, the Bay of Bengal, the South China Sea, and the western Pacific. This trend is bound to continue as their economies, and their naval capabilities, expand. That China's maritime influence is rising faster than that of India is not in doubt. In the Arabian Sea, which holds much of the energy resources that both nations need, Beijing and New Delhi are just beginning to make their separate overtures. Although India is used to Sino-Pakistan strategic collaboration and has been concerned about the Gwadar port, the full implications of extending this partnership to the maritime domain remain unexplored. These trends have not conflicted in any significant manner. The Indian concerns, however, are growing in the Bay of Bengal, where Beijing is reaching out to Dhaka and China is establishing itself on the Burmese coast in order to address its presumed vulnerability to being choked off at the Strait of Malacca. Meanwhile, India's maritime activism has grown in the South China Sea and the Pacific, but it is not large enough to threaten Chinese interests in a fundamental way. As their weight begins to influence the Indo-Pacific maritime domain, and their naval footprints begin to intersect, China and India are likely to see increased mutual suspicions. China's entry into the Indian Ocean and India's into the western Pacific have, as described in this chapter, begun to revive notions of mutual encirclement that have long informed the Sino-Indian rivalry. Chapter 10 offers an exploration of possible pathways that might lead China and India away from potential maritime conflicts.

Chapter Ten

MITIGATING THE SECURITY DILEMMA

Chapters 8 and 9 explored the widening domain of Sino-Indian rivalry at the turn of the twenty-first century. In the past, the competition was largely limited to the subcontinent and was concentrated along and across the Great Himalayas that defined the long and contested frontier between the two Asian giants and expressed itself in their tensions over Pakistan. Writing at the end of the 1990s, John Garver noted the extension of this rivalry to the Indian Ocean littoral. "China's slow-paced push into [the] Indian Ocean between 1985 and 2001 is perhaps akin to its earlier establishment of the Sino-Pakistan *entente cordiale* or the Sino-Burmese strategic partnership. By slowly expanding its naval presence in the Indian Ocean, Beijing is trying to create a new status quo. New Delhi is resisting that process, in a methodical fashion and [with] a vigor not displayed by India when the Chinese partnerships with Pakistan and Burma were initially created."[1] Since then, as our own account suggests, the Sino-Indian contestation has become more widespread and intensive. It now encompasses all the major Indian Ocean island states as well as the basins of the Arabian Sea and the Bay of Bengal. The rivalry has also begun to encompass the Strait of Malacca, the South China Sea, and the western Pacific. The economic weight and military resources of both China and India have rapidly risen in the first decade of the twenty-first century. So have their great-power aspirations and the incentives to build blue-water navies. As the competition between the two rising powers in the Asian littoral gathers momentum, the question is whether the maritime competition between China and India leads to an inevitable conflict and if there are possibilities to mitigate it.

THE SECURITY DILEMMA

The security dilemma is about a political condition in which the attempt to increase the security of one nation alarms another. Seemingly prudent moves by one state are followed by similar moves by the other, leading to mutual tension, an arms race, and, more broadly, reduced security for both nations. Security dilemmas arise from the fact that there is no authority higher than the state in the international system and that each state is obliged to look after its own security. Unlike in domestic politics, where the state enjoys the monopoly on violence, enforces a set of laws, and mediates conflicts between different entities, states are on their own in the international system. The logic of security dilemma does not differentiate between the political nature of the governments locked in it. Even a liberal or peaceable state in general could generate fear and insecurity among other states that it is arming itself to achieve superiority and embark on military conquest. The other states respond in kind, and we have the basis for a vicious circle of competition, arms race, and likely conflict.[2]

This understanding of the security dilemma defined at the beginning of the Cold War led to an intense exploration of the opportunities and limits for political cooperation between states in a competitive relationship. Some scholars have pointed to the extreme difficulties, both political and psychological, of organizing cooperation under the security dilemma.[3] Others have pointed to the possibilities for mitigating and transcending the security dilemma in the current conditions of the world order.[4] What is of interest to us is the fact that studies of Sino-Indian relations since the middle of the last century have provided much evidence for the security dilemma at play. John Garver offers substantive evidence from the history of Sino-Indian relations from their first encounter as newly minted states in the late 1940s. For its part, India's insecurities about China have been driven by the Chinese aggression in 1962 and Beijing's sustained support to Islamabad, including in the area of nuclear weapons and missiles, to balance India in the subcontinent. More broadly, India is riled at China's relentless attempts at undermining New Delhi's primacy in the subcontinent and a deliberate policy of "encirclement." China is equally defensive, according to Garver. The sources of Chinese insecurity vis-à-vis India are the stability of Chinese control over Tibet and the security of China's sea lines of communication across the Indian Ocean. Garver points to the similarity between the Sino-Indian rivalry and the Soviet-American contestation in the Cold War:

> The metaphor of two scorpions in a bottle once used to describe USA–USSR relations during the mutual nuclear terror of the Cold War seems aptly applied to the Sino-Indian relationship today. Each country is fearful because of the inescapable proximity of the other and because of the shared ability to inflict great damage on the other. The state of play in the Sino-Indian relation is that Beijing is mobilizing pressure to compel New Delhi to acquiesce to an open-ended expansion of China's military links and security role in the [South Asian–Indian Ocean region]. New Delhi is mobilizing counter-pressure on China (via the Look East Policy) to compel Beijing to suspend, or roll back its deep and growing military involvement in the [South Asian–Indian Ocean region].[5]

That a "security dilemma" describes the current conditions between Beijing and New Delhi is not in doubt. Theorists of the security dilemma "recognize the difficulties" of mitigating it, but do not rule it out. They suggest that the security dilemma can be diminished by "policies providing for more peaceful relations."[6] It is also possible to conceive of factors that could mitigate the ineluctable evolution of a security dilemma into an overt conflict. These include political decisionmakers committed to moderation, synchronized diplomacy, wide-ranging cooperation, peaceful resolution of conflicts, and institutions of regional and international collective security. A close look at the development of Sino-Indian relations suggests that some of these mitigating factors have indeed begun to play themselves out in recent years. In fact, the normalization of Sino-Indian relations launched in the late 1980s was premised on the proposition that expanded engagement would reduce conflict and help resolve the long-standing territorial dispute. Two decades later, despite the dramatic expansion of bilateral cooperation, past conflicts have endured and new tensions have emerged amid the rise of both nations on the Asian and world stages.

The unexpected deterioration of Sino-Indian political relations during 2008–2011 showed the fragility of the two-decade-old rapprochement. At the highest levels, the Indian and Chinese political leaders have constantly asserted that they do not pose a threat to each other. The joint statement issued at the end of President Hu Jintao's visit to India in November 2006, for example, affirmed:

> Both sides agree that the relationship between India and China, the two biggest developing countries in the world, is of global and strategic significance. Both countries are seeking to avail themselves of historic opportunities for development. Each side welcomes and takes a positive view of the development of the other, and considers the development of either side as a positive contribution to peace, stability and prosperity of Asia and the world. Both sides hold the view that there exist bright prospects for their common development, that they are not rivals or competitors but are partners for mutual benefit. They agree that there is enough space for them to grow together, achieve a higher scale of development, and play their respective roles in the region and beyond, while remaining sensitive to each other's concerns and aspirations.[7]

Yet, in the years since that statement was issued, the management of their bilateral relationship has become more complex and challenging. Reflecting on the simultaneous rise of China and India, Shyam Saran, the former Indian foreign secretary and prime minister's special envoy, said the challenge was about arranging India's "relations with countries in our neighborhood and beyond in a manner that ensures our rise, and therefore the range of our options, while avoiding a clash with China . . . [at the] intersecting points." Saran went on to argue, "We should avoid being provocative, even while we seek to expand our own strategic space. Nervous articulations of a threat can trigger mirror-image and hostile perceptions on the other side. There is no inevitability of conflict with China."[8] Saran's successor as India's foreign secretary, Shivshankar Menon, spoke of the specific challenges of Sino-Indian relations in the maritime domain. He regretted that "much of the debate is framed solely in terms of India–China rivalry. This is especially true of strategists in India and China themselves, though not of their governments. The terms in which the argument is presented are limited and would be self-fulfilling predictions, were governments to act upon them. Nor are they based on an examination of [the] objective interests of the states concerned."[9] There is growing recognition among the Indian and Chinese governments that they must find a way to limit the potential for conflict in the maritime domain. Any diplomatic effort in that direction must necessarily be based on the experience of confidence building between the two sides since the late 1980s.

SINO-INDIAN CBMS

Until the 1980s, India and China tended to be dismissive of confidence-building measures as a tool of national security policy. As they watched the United States and the Soviet Union, as well as the North Atlantic Treaty Organization (NATO) and the Warsaw Pact, institute confidence-building measures during the period of détente, New Delhi and Beijing tended to sneer rather than applaud. India was an active participant in the global debates on peace and security ever since it acquired independence in the aftermath of the Second World War. New Delhi's voice on peace and security was given considerable hearing in both East and West. India's emphasis then was on "general and complete disarmament." It criticized arms control agreements as partial and unsatisfactory measures that diverted attention from the real goal of abolishing whole classes of weapons. China was even more ideological about arms control in the 1960s and mounted a special political offensive against superpower arms control as a reflection of its hegemonic aspirations. These attitudes changed in New Delhi and Beijing during the 1980s, when both countries began to see the value of confidence-building measures in limiting rivalries with other powers and in managing their own security. Both began to slowly adopt a few confidence-building measures as part of their security policies.[10] In the beginning, the process of adaption was slow as the conservatism of the security establishments questioned the utility of these confidence-building measures; nevertheless, by the end of the twentieth century, such measures were very much part of security planning in both Beijing and New Delhi.

In the case of Sino-Indian relations, the visit of Prime Minister Rajiv Gandhi to Beijing in December 1988 was critical in reframing the bilateral relationship after an extended period of hostility that followed the 1962 border war. India moved away from its earlier position that there can be no normalization of bilateral relations without resolution of the boundary dispute. The two sides agreed to embark on purposeful bilateral negotiations, simultaneously pursue normalization of bilateral relations, and institute a range of military confidence-building measures. This new approach opened the door for a steady expansion of bilateral contact, communication, and cooperation. As part of this effort, limited and low-level military exchanges were formalized in the 1990s. During Chinese Prime Minister Li Peng's visit to India in December 1991, the two sides agreed to establish new consulates in Shanghai and Mumbai, resume border trade at specific points on their land and contested border, and promote cooperation between their space programs. This was followed by two major military confidence-building agreements, one in 1993 during the visit of Indian Prime Minister Narasimha Rao to Beijing and the other in 1996 during the visit of Chinese President Jiang Zemin to New Delhi. The first was a broad outline of measures to realize peace and tranquility on the border pending resolution of the boundary dispute.[11] It included commitments to military restraint, frequent communication between local commanders, and the notion of pulling back troops from the border. The 1996 agreement fleshed this out in greater detail with specific measures for reducing military presence on the border, withdrawing offensive weapons, and limiting the size of military exercises and their prior notification.[12] All these measures were certainly useful in improving the contact and communication between the two sides at the middle and lower levels of the security establishments. But the substantive parts of the confidence-building agreements, such as withdrawal of forces and equipment, could not be implemented because of the lack of clarity on the alignment of forces on the ground. Without clarification of the Line of Actual Control on the ground or the definition of the boundary itself, there was no way the confidence-building measures tied to the alignment of the Line of Actual Control could be implemented. It did not really matter, because the overall tenor of the relationship in the 1990s was good: Both countries were focused on internal reforms and were keen to create a peaceful environment for economic growth, and their bilateral trade began to pick up momentum from the late 1990s.

The settlement of the dispute over Sikkim's integration into India during Prime Minister Atal Bihari Vajpayee's visit to China in June 2003 lifted a major burden on the bilateral relationship, and the two sides also agreed to engage in political negotiations to resolve the boundary dispute as opposed to the previous emphasis on legal and historical claims over it. The Indian defense minister, George Fernandes, once viewed with hostility in Beijing for his China threat theory, visited China at the height of the severe acute respiratory syndrome (SARS) crisis in 2003 to redeem his image in Beijing as a "China baiter." The appointment of special envoys, politically empowered, to meet frequently and settle the boundary dispute raised hopes all around for a breakthrough. The new mechanism quickly produced results. In April 2005, when Wen Jiabao visited New Delhi, agreement was reached on the political parameters and guiding principles for the settlement of the boundary dispute.[13] This was the first-ever formal agreement on the boundary dispute between Beijing and New Delhi. The declaration of a strategic partnership during the visit generated optimism about the possibilities of resolving the boundary dispute through a political approach and rapidly expanding the bases of the bilateral relationship. Within a year, during the visit of the Indian defense minister, Pranab Mukherjee, to China in May 2006, the two sides announced a consequential agreement on deepening and broadening their military engagement.[14] This included a pre-set calendar for defense exchanges at all levels, an annual defense dialogue at the level of vice ministers, and for the first time an identification of specific missions for their joint military exercises. These included anti-piracy, counterterrorism, search and rescue, and other areas of common interest. As a consequence, the first substantive military exercises between the two countries began in 2007. The two defense ministers declared that "strengthening effective contacts in the field of defense is of vital importance to enhancing mutual trust and understanding between their two armed forces, ensuring a peaceful environment in which they can pursue their respective national development objectives, and maintaining peace and stability in the region and the world at large."

In retrospect, though, the results from this expanding defense engagement present a mixed picture. Mounting tensions between the two countries over Tibet and the difficulties of ensuring peace and tranquility on the boundary during 2008–2010 showed the vulnerability of the Sino-Indian political and security relationship. The Indian media as well as the Chinese blogosphere made matters worse with intense and provocative nationalism that depicted the other side as a major threat. The carefully constructed normalization of Sino-Indian relations during the previous two decades appeared quite shaky during this time. At the turn of 2010 it was clear that military technical confidence-building measures alone were not enough to prevent the recrudescence of the mutual political mistrust and boundary tensions. Technical confidence-building measures of the kind China and India put in place for two decades function most effectively in the context of a positive political relationship and a stable military environment. From the late 1980s to the mid-2000s, there was reasonable stability and predictability in the Sino-Indian relationship, and the military confidence-building measures, although not very advanced, were contributing to the positive dynamic. When the environment began to deteriorate in the 2000s, the confidence-building measures could not prevent the downward slide in the relationship.

Four factors produced significant instability in the bilateral relationship in the mid-2000s. One was the modernization of the Chinese transport and communication infrastructure, including the rail link to Lhasa and the road networks all across Tibet and Xinjiang, which from the late 1990s significantly improved the logistics of the PLA in the border regions. According to the Indian army's assessments, the mobilization time for a two-battalion offensive by the PLA shrank from two weeks to one, a two-brigade assault from four weeks to two, and the mobilization of two divisions from ninety days to twenty.[15] As India woke up to the challenge, in its typically public sort of way, and began to respond with plans of its own to strengthen the border infrastructure, build roads to and along the China border, reactivate airstrips, and raise new troops, the sense of a military competition cut through the presumed sense of peace and tranquility on the border. Second, improved logistics of the PLA meant more aggressive patrolling on the border. From the Chinese perspective, this might have made sense given the ongoing boundary negotiations to determine possible territorial compromises between the two nations. In New Delhi, the aggressive Chinese patrolling translated into what the Indian establishment called "incursions" across the Line of Actual Control. Because there was no mutually agreed alignment of the Line of Actual Control, "intrusions" are common wherever the mutual perceptions of the line overlapped. The frequent media hype on the incidents of intrusion only added to the tension. A third factor that shook Sino-Indian relations in the late 2000s was the entirely unexpected revolt in Tibet in March 2008. Sino-Indian relations have always been sensitive to the internal situation in Tibet. When Tibet is tranquil, so are Sino-Indian relations. With Tibet restive just before the 2008 Olympics, China went into offensive overdrive around the world to limit its consequences and no more directly than in India, the home to the exiled Tibetan government. Since then China has tended to be more assertive about its claims on Arunachal Pradesh not just in bilateral forums but also in such multilateral forums as the Asian Development Bank, where India was seeking assistance for a project in Arunachal Pradesh. Finally, the Chinese attempt to undermine approval of the Indo-U.S. civil nuclear initiative at the Nuclear Suppliers Group in the fall of 2008 raised serious concerns in India about persistent Chinese hostility. For its part, Beijing had consistently viewed the nuclear deal as part of a larger Indo-U.S. strategic partnership to limit Chinese influence in Asia. In response, Beijing initially sought to extend a similar deal with Pakistan and used its friends within the Indian political spectrum to undermine it in the name of anti-imperialism.

The changed military and political realities in Tibet, the recrudescence of the territorial disputes on the Himalayan frontier, and the flux in balance of power politics involving the United States together seemed to escalate tensions in the summer and fall of 2009. The tensions culminated in the Chinese fusillades against India in November 2009 when his holiness the Dalai Lama visited the contested state of Arunachal Pradesh.[16] There were furious attempts to bring back a variety of confidence-building measures to de-escalate tensions. Thanks to open channels of diplomatic communication and political contact at the highest levels on the margins of various international conferences, the two capitals did not lose sight of the broader political challenge. On the military front, too, the two sides dispatched the military commanders responsible for the security of the border to visit each other and bring down the temperatures on the border.[17] Meetings also took place between the defense headquarters of the two countries when the Indian defense secretary visited Beijing in January 2010. The talks underlined the mutual commitment to step up contact between the two military establishments in an effort to rebuild mutual trust and confidence.[18]

Yet the political limitations of the Sino-Indian confidence-building process came into view when India suspended military exchanges with China in August 2010. New Delhi was responding to a Chinese decision to give a "stapled visa" to the Indian general leading the Northern Command, which includes the region of Jammu and Kashmir.[19] For nearly two years before that, India had begun to notice that Beijing was refusing to stamp visas on the passports of Indian citizens from the state of J&K. It offered instead visas on separate pieces of paper that were stapled to the passports. Indian immigration officials, in turn, prevented, where they could, passengers with stapled visas from boarding flights to China. It also advised its citizens from Jammu and Kashmir not to accept stapled visas from the Chinese Embassy and consulates in India. "It has come to the attention of [the] government of India that the embassy of the People's Republic of China in New Delhi and the Chinese consulates in Mumbai and Kolkata are issuing visas on a separate piece of paper 'stapled' to the passport (rather than pasted as is the usual practice), to certain categories of Indian nationals on the basis of their domicile, ethnicity and/or place of issue of the passport. Such paper visas stapled to the passport are not considered valid for travel out of the country," New Delhi said in travel advisory in November 2009.[20] This move was an internal administrative response to what New Delhi saw as a provocation from Beijing. When the Chinese policy on Kashmir visas touched on a top military commander of the Indian army, the government of India could no longer remain passive.

While the Chinese seemed surprised by India's deliberate escalation of the dispute, New Delhi had good reason to raise the stakes. India saw Beijing's practice of stapled visas as a departure from the apparent Chinese neutrality on the Kashmir dispute between India and Pakistan. Even in 1963, when Pakistan transferred a sliver of Jammu and Kashmir territory under its control to China, the bilateral agreement had declared that the final disposition of this territory would depend on a settlement between New Delhi and Islamabad.[21] China's stapled visas made it clear that Beijing was treating the J&K territories under India and Pakistan differently. By giving normal visas to Pakistani passport holders from Jammu and Kashmir, Beijing seemed to say that the state's territories administered by Islamabad were not in dispute while contesting India's sovereignty over J&K. Given the national neuralgia on the question of Jammu and Kashmir, New Delhi had no choice but to confront Beijing. India began to raise the issue at the highest political levels with Beijing, and the question of

Kashmir visas was at the top of the agenda when Wen Jiabao visited New Delhi in December 2010. After the meeting between Wen and Manmohan Singh, the Indian side seemed hopeful that China would abide by Wen's promise to resolve the question soon.[22] By the time Singh met the Chinese president, Hu Jintao, at the BRICS (Brazil, Russia, India, China, and South Africa) summit on Hainan Island during April 2011, the two agreed to put the Kashmir visa issue behind them and to resume defense exchanges.[23] There was nothing to suggest that China had reconsidered its policy on Jammu and Kashmir, but it did stop issuing stapled visas to Indian citizens from there. India in turn helped China save face by sending a military delegation in June 2011 headed by a general from its Northern Army command, one rank below that of the commander in chief who was denied a regular visa in 2010.

The entire episode, however, underlined the extreme vulnerability of the India–China confidence building to questions of territorial sovereignty. The very purpose of the military exchanges was to build greater trust and confidence between the two armed forces without prejudice to their specific territorial claims against the other. China's Kashmir visas underlined the difficulty of sustaining this principle and its political consequences. At Sanya, Singh and Hu agreed in principle to establish a "working mechanism for consultation and coordination on border affairs." India's national security adviser Menon explained that the mechanism will handle all issues relating to the maintenance of peace and security and explore new ways of cooperation at the borders.[24] The mechanism was formally unveiled in January 2012. It is expected to bridge the gap between the long-standing political commitment in both capitals to the maintenance of peace and tranquility on the border on the one hand and persistent incidents of low-level tension on the ground at the border on the other.[25]

BILATERAL NAVAL CONFIDENCE-BUILDING MEASURES

On the face of it, the prospects for naval confidence building, in contrast to those on the Himalayas, should be easier to accomplish given the absence of overlapping maritime territorial claims. As the Indian Ocean became a contested arena in the 2000s, both capitals recognized the need to structure confidence-building measures between the maritime and naval communities of the two countries. Naval confidence building has indeed had a long tradition in the history of modern international relations. In fact, one of the earliest forms of arms control as we know it today goes back to the Washington Naval Conference of 1921–1922, which produced an agreement among five major powers of the day—Britain, the United States, France, Japan, and Italy—to prevent a naval arms race after the First World War.[26] Naval confidence building differs from the confidence-building measures between land-based armed forces. This is because naval forces have distinct characteristics, mobility, flexibility, and long-range and potentially global reach. Operating in international waters, they are not separated by national boundaries. And unlike armies on the border that tend to be controlled quite tightly by headquarters, the naval forces leave greater room for initiative and leadership by the commander at sea. Navies also as a matter of routine tend to intersect with commercial and law and order imperatives at sea. All this provides for greater opportunities for contact and communication between navies. The distinctive character of the naval forces also presents a range of difficulties. Restrictions on size, technical and operational abilities, and movement demand trade-offs between a range of parameters on both sides that is not always easy to manage.

The Indian and Chinese navies have begun to explore possibilities for a variety of bilateral confidence-building measures. Ship visits and port calls have been the easiest ones the two sides could engage in. The earliest Indian ship visit to China was in 1958 when the Sino-Indian relationship was warm, and another visit took place in 1995 as part of the rapprochement launched in the late 1980s.[27] Chinese ships in turn had visited Indian ports from the late 1980s when the ships began to frequent the Indian Ocean. The naval chiefs of the two countries visited each other during the 2000s. The two sides also began to conduct simple exercises near each other's waters starting in 2003. As the frequency of Indian forays into the western Pacific and Chinese excursions in the Indian Ocean began to expand, it was quite convenient physically as well as politically for both sides to signal mutual goodwill through joint exercises of a simple kind. In 2009, as the Chinese navy celebrated the sixtieth anniversary of its founding at Qingdao Port, the Indian naval chief traveled to China and his naval contingent made an impressive representation at the fleet review in Qingdao.

The Chinese and Indian navies have barely begun to scratch the surface of possible bilateral naval confidence-building measures. One important possibility is the drafting of an "incidents at sea agreement." Such agreements, now being negotiated between various naval powers, are modeled on the U.S.-Soviet template. The U.S.-Soviet Incidents at Sea Agreement, signed in 1972, came at the apogee of arms control between the two nations during the era of détente. As the Soviet navy began to emerge as a credible force and demonstrate the capacity to project power, it came into frequent contact with the U.S. Navy, and the competitive dynamic between them began to generate maritime tension. The U.S.-Soviet Incidents at Sea Agreement provided for information exchange on various encounters between the two navies, a joint committee to review annually such incidents, and a framework to develop mutual understanding. The widespread assessment was that the agreement was a success.[28] Some naval analysts argue that the success of incidents at sea arrangements had a number of very specific reasons: mutuality of interest, involvement of only one governmental agency (navy-to-navy), absence of politics, a workable arrangement, and bilateralism.[29]

Skeptics would argue that it might be somewhat premature for China and India to consider naval confidence-building measures that Washington and Moscow agreed upon during the Cold War or similar arrangements of the kind China and the United States have begun to embark upon in the post–Cold War world. During the Cold War, the areas of naval operation between the Soviet and U.S. navies had a significant overlap all around the Eurasian land mass, especially in the waters of the northern Atlantic, Mediterranean, Black Sea, and the northern Pacific. The logic of nuclear deterrence in the Cold War added to the complexity of the naval situation, and the incidents at sea agreement provided a valuable tool for avoiding escalation due to incidents at sea. The U.S. and Chinese navies are now rubbing against each other in the western Pacific, and a series of incidents during 2008–2009 have underlined the importance of incidents at sea types of arrangements between Washington and Beijing. The two countries did sign a Military Maritime Consultative Agreement in 1998, and there was a resumption of military-to-military dialogue in 2009.[30] In contrast to the U.S.-Soviet and U.S.-Chinese situations, the overlap between the naval footprints of China and India is limited at present. The principal area of

Indian naval operations remains the Indian Ocean; for the Chinese navy, it's the western Pacific. This, however, does not mean there is no urgency for naval confidence building between the two naval forces. As the Indian navy goes into the South China Sea and the western Pacific more often and its Chinese counterpart shows up in the Indian Ocean on a more sustained basis, overlap between the areas can only increase. Although the intensity of this overlap might not be too high, the two navies are bound to run into each other more frequently. A naval incident in early 2009 points to one possible danger that could confront the Chinese and the Indian navies.

Shortly after the PLAN launched its first sustained naval operation in the Gulf of Aden at the end of 2008, Chinese media reported an incident. A report in the *South China Morning Post* from Hong Kong, citing mainland Chinese language media, said a Chinese naval unit and an Indian attack submarine were "locked in a tense stand-off" on January 15, 2009, in the waters near the Bab-el-Mandeb strait in the Gulf of Aden.[31] The report suggested that the Chinese ships "managed to force" an Indian *Kilo* class submarine to surface after a few rounds of maneuvering. The report went on: "The submarine tried to evade the Chinese warships by diving deeper. But the warships continued the chase . . . the Chinese ships sent an antisubmarine helicopter to help track the submarine, which had tried to jam the Chinese warship's sonar system. But the two destroyers eventually cornered the submarine and forced it to surface . . . the submarine had been trailing the Chinese ships since they had entered the Indian Ocean on the way to Somalia."[32] This triumphal account from Beijing was, not surprisingly, denied in New Delhi. India's naval headquarters denied that any of its submarines had surfaced in the Gulf of Aden and insisted that "nobody can force anybody to surface in international waters."[33] Senior naval officials in New Delhi, however, confirmed that its ships routinely monitor the movement of ships in the waterways of the Indian Ocean. China surely does the same thing in the East and South China seas. The veracity of the presumed encounter between the Chinese and Indian navies—many indeed have questioned it—is less important than the fact that it reportedly took place in the Gulf of Aden.

This in turn underlines the need for a credible set of arrangements between the two navies to promote mutual trust and confidence and keep any of these incidents from escalating into a major crisis in bilateral relations.[34]

In another reported encounter in the South China Sea in July 2011, an Indian ship sailing off the coast of Vietnam was warned by a caller identifying itself as the Chinese navy not to enter Chinese waters.[35] India denied the confrontation but confirmed that the Indian ship did receive a call on the radio from a voice identifying itself as the Chinese navy. According to the Indian account, the vessel moved on to Haiphong without any hindrance. While playing down the incident, New Delhi asserted India's right to "freedom of navigation in international waters, including in the South China Sea, and the right of passage in accordance with accepted principles of international law. These principles should be respected by all."[36] While the incident might have been overblown, it could be seen as a possible Chinese shot across the bow warning against the Indian navy's ambitions in the South China Sea. It also underlined the need for more maritime confidence building between India and China.[37]

TOWARD A MARITIME STRATEGIC DIALOGUE

Port calls, high-level naval exchanges, and exercises improve familiarity between the naval establishments and provide valuable channels of communication, but they do not generate the political space for a frank discussion of the conflict dynamic and the means to address mutual concerns and misperceptions. While the political leadership repeatedly affirms that they are not a threat to each other and that Asia is large enough to accommodate their aspirations and simultaneous rise, the strategic communities on both sides have nurtured adversarial images of each other. Alarmist views on each side have been amplified and broadcast by the noisy media in China and India. The traditional framework of a coded communication among a small set of people on either side in managing the Sino-Indian relationship has long become unsustainable. This framework is not capable of managing elite perceptions on either side, let alone shaping popular attitudes. Take, for example, how quickly the notion of "string of pearls" has come to symbolize in New Delhi the presumed Chinese maritime hostility. Similarly dark views of India's maritime cooperation with the United States have taken root in China. It has become axiomatic for many Chinese scholars that India might gang up with the U.S. Navy to choke Beijing's energy lifeline at the Strait of Malacca. To address the growing number of misperceptions about each other's strategic intentions in the Indo-Pacific, India and China agreed to launch a maritime security dialogue in April 2012, when foreign minister Yang Jiechi was in India.[38]

While the nature of the mechanism and its mandate is likely to evolve over a period of time, the Sino-Indian maritime engagement will have to address two important sets of issues. The first is the notion of exclusive spheres of maritime influence. In New Delhi the idea of Indian primacy in the subcontinent has had a powerful influence. The sense of primacy, however, was not limited to the land areas of the subcontinent but also extended to the waters of the Indian Ocean. The articulation of Indian primacy in the Indian Ocean going back to the early navalists of India such as K. M. Panikkar is a legacy from the Raj and has often been expressed along the lines of the U.S. Monroe Doctrine.[39] While the context and circumstances are different, the idea that the influence of other powers must be limited in the Indian Ocean has been an enduring theme of the post-independence Indian naval discourse from Jawaharlal Nehru, the first prime minister, to his more recent successors who have claimed that the sphere of Indian interest extends from the northwestern corners of the Arabian Sea to the South China Sea.[40] Whether or not New Delhi is in a position to enforce such a doctrine, it generates concerns in Beijing that India is inimical to China's pursuit of its interests in the Indian Ocean. An effort to undermine India's primacy in the region appears to Beijing to be a logical approach, which in turn rings alarm bells in New Delhi.

India, of course, is not alone in its seeming pursuit of its own Monroe Doctrine. Beijing's own policies point to the emergence of a Chinese Monroe Doctrine in East Asia and the Western Pacific. Beijing's long-standing emphasis on "Asia for the Asians" and its attempts to limit the influence of other great powers in the region is probably no different than the Monroe Doctrine. The Chinese navy's anti-access strategy, aimed at weakening the American naval presence in the western Pacific, and its assertive approach to territorial claims in the South China Sea, are seen by some as reflecting the aspirations for Beijing's hegemony in Asia. While many contest this view, others see this as a natural consequence of Chinese power. As Mearsheimer argues, "An increasingly powerful China is likely to try to push the United States out of Asia, much the way the United States pushed the European great powers out of the Western Hemisphere. We should expect China to come up with its own version of the Monroe Doctrine, as Japan did in the 1930s. . . . Why would China feel safe with U.S. forces deployed on its doorstep? Following the logic of the Monroe Doctrine, would not China's security be better served by pushing the American military out of Asia?"[41] As New Delhi and Beijing define their maritime approaches in terms of the U.S. Monroe Doctrine, the two would seem bound to step on each other's toes. "Unlike in the Western Hemisphere of the nineteenth century, which witnessed the rise of a single nautical hegemon that was remote from great power politics, two powers given to Monrovian thinking share a disputed land frontier, along with a past punctuated by intermittent conflict and warfare."[42] India and China, then, will need to constantly reassure each other that there is no intention to pursue hegemony in their neighborhood. Any attempt by either New Delhi or Beijing to construct an exclusive sphere of influence in the waters adjacent to them is bound to produce a reaction from the neighbors and the other great powers and create a coalition to thwart these ambitions.

That brings us to the second set of issues—the need to limit the misperception of each other's interests and the demonstration of some sensitivity to the concerns of the other. It is not often, for example, that one sees in the Indian discourse an acknowledgment of the many legitimate interests that China might have in the subcontinent and the Indian Ocean region. The general narrative is one of Beijing's hostile motives, a bias toward negative interpretation of the facts, and the reaffirmation of the fear of China's strategic encirclement of India. There is little effort in the Indian narrative to factor in the resource security imperatives of China and the naval consequences that might follow. This in turn boosts the negative perceptions of many Chinese analysts, who believe India will forever try to deny China access to the Indian Ocean. Unlike the current naval debates in New Delhi, K. M. Panikkar, who laid the foundation for an expansive naval vision for India at the turn of its independence, was prescient about the implications of the rise of China and the need for India to accommodate the legitimate interests of Beijing in the Indian Ocean. He argued that "the emergence of China as a first class Asiatic Power is one of the predictable results" of the Second World War and that its "status in world affairs will only grow with time."[43] Speaking about a regional arrangement for the Indian Ocean and Asia underwritten by the great powers after the war, Panikkar suggested that "in regard to Indo-China and Thailand," China "will have a special responsibility for defense. In regard to Burma, her interests are limited to the use of Rangoon as a free port and to maintenance of the Burma Road as an international highway. In respect of the defense of Singapore she will naturally have to share responsibility along with other powers."[44]

The question is not whether Panikkar's assessment of Chinese interests and the need to integrate them into any sustainable order in the Indo-Pacific have stood the test of the time. What is absolutely important, however, is the need for India to be realistic in the appreciation of China's interests and signal its sensitivity toward them. Some Indian decisionmakers are beginning to show that understanding in their formal statements about Chinese interests in the Indian Ocean. One of India's leading China hands, Shivshankar Menon,[45] speaking amid growing tensions between the two countries in 2009, rejected the notion that China had already acquired bases in the Indian Ocean, recognized that China has legitimate interests in energy security in keeping open the Indian Ocean sea lines of communication, and proposed cooperative security arrangements among the major powers.

> There are also Chinese interests involved. For China, as for India and Japan, her energy security is intimately linked to keeping the sea lanes open in the Indian Ocean. The threats to energy flows in the Indian Ocean come not from the major powers (such as India, the USA, China or Japan), all of whom have a shared interest in keeping these sea lanes working. . . . The immediate threats come from local instability and problems in the choke points and certain littorals, particularly the Strait of Hormuz and the Horn of Africa. These will not be solved simply by an application of military force, just as piracy off the Horn of Africa cannot be. This is a test of wisdom and is where China and other states can choose to be part of the solution rather than of the problem. My question is therefore: if energy and trade flows and security are the issues, why not begin discussing collective security arrangements among the major powers concerned?[46]

While sections of the Indian establishment are beginning to show greater realism in their understanding of China's interests in the Indian Ocean, the public discourse remains dominated by negative and hostile sentiment.

In China, too, as the Indian naval capabilities expand, the Chinese military community has begun to pay greater attention, and most of the commentary has been negative. A content analysis of *PLA Daily* and the journal *Modern Navy* from the mid-1990s to 2006 shows a sharp increase in the references to Indian naval developments. Chinese concerns include the perceived Indian ambitions to dominate the Indian Ocean, its increasing collaboration with the U.S. Navy, and the relative openness of Southeast Asian nations to expanding maritime engagement with India.[47] Other reviews highlight the prospect of India's potential alliance with the United States in blockading China's oil supply routes: "Chinese observers worry about India's dominant position astride China's most important oil SLOC [sea lines of communication]. Chinese naval and maritime affairs publications keenly follow Indian naval development; they are impressed by this development, especially in the realm of naval aviation, and fear that such capabilities could allow New Delhi to 'effectively prevent any outside great power's Navy from entering the Indian Ocean.'" The review of the debate goes on to say that Chinese analysts note India's "enhanced ability to project power to the east," establishment of the Andaman and Nicobar Command, "growing operational presence in the Andaman Sea and the Malacca Strait area, and increased exercises with the U.S. Navy." Some Chinese observers, according to this review, are concerned that "it is the fleets of the United States, Japan, and India that, together, 'invariably constitute overwhelming pressure on China's oil supply.'"[48]

Yet a close examination of potential scenarios suggests how difficult enforcing a blockade of oil supplies to China might be. "A distant naval energy blockade (say, in the Persian Gulf), though it could be conducted with low to moderate tactical risk with some navies' force structures, could probably not prevent the delivery of oil to China by means of alternative sea routes, falsified bills of lading, or transshipment of oil via third parties. Such a blockade will become even less feasible as China extends the reach and lethality of its naval and aerial forces. A close blockade (near the Chinese seaboard), on the other hand, would require large numbers of ships to operate in close proximity to the People's Republic of China's impressive and increasingly lethal anti-access weaponry, where they would be subject to attrition, with attendant escalatory risk. A blockade by convoy would also require a very large force structure, and a supply-side blockade of oil shipments to the PRC would only drive up prices for all global oil consumers."[49] Clearly the fear of outside powers choking off Chinese energy supplies feeds into a variety of bureaucratic politics inside the Chinese establishment. Those seeking new investments in pipelines, expanding the size of the navy, and a more assertive naval diplomacy have a clear interest in emphasizing the dangers of energy supplies being cut off and on the "Malacca dilemma." Others apparently are cautioning against an overdetermination of the threat to Chinese resource sea lines of communication. They point to the dangers of an aggressive Chinese maritime posture. A review of the Chinese debate on SLOC security says:

> Some Chinese analysts recognize the potential costs to China of a balancing reaction by neighbors and the United States, to a Chinese shift toward an extended SLOC-defense mission for the PLAN. Key strategic implications that could destabilize the Indian Ocean and western Pacific littoral regions might include regional naval power upgrades and alliance rebalancing to offset a more muscular and far-reaching Chinese naval presence. . . . India, Japan, the United States, Indonesia, Malaysia, and Australia would almost certainly bolster their own naval forces and would also likely seek to create security architectures more explicitly designed to contain China.[50]

The review goes on to add that some analysts emphasize the importance of working with other powers to deal with the challenges of energy and resource security and protection of the sea lines of communication. It cites Chinese analysts as saying that "Persian Gulf instability could harm China's interests significantly" and that "China must cooperate closely with India, South Korea and even Japan—which might otherwise join the United States against China in any conflict—in [the] energy sphere."[51] Clearly, protecting the sea lines of communication is a consequential but inconclusive debate in China. The debate is by no means monolithic, and that in turn opens the door for a positive maritime security dialogue with India.

As the economic stakes of China and India in the oceans steadily expand and the two sides proceed with the building of powerful navies, a substantive and open-ended dialogue between the two security establishments on maritime and naval issues has become an urgent imperative. While the public discourse is dominated by complete clarity and hostility—the Indian fear of Chinese encirclement and Beijing's apprehensions of India joining the United States in a naval blockade of Chinese resources—our analysis has shown considerable room for discussion if not cooperation. During the visit of Chinese Premier Wen Jiabao to New Delhi in December 2010, the two sides affirmed their shared interests in the Indian Ocean and agreed to cooperate in countering piracy in the Gulf of Aden.[52] This is probably the first time that New Delhi and Beijing spoke together about maritime security cooperation.

As China and India recognized the imperative of managing their potential conflicts in the Indian Ocean, the case for maritime confidence building became more urgent by the end of the 2000s. A number of naval incidents during 2010–2011 between China on the one hand and the United States, Japan, and the ASEAN members on the other underlined the gathering crisis of maritime security and the need for greater confidence building in the region.[53] While the need for more confidence building and greater engagement in the maritime domain of the Indo-Pacific is apparent, confidence-building measures alone are not going to be adequate. As a comprehensive assessment of the maritime security regime in Asia argues, significant differences exist among the major powers on the very concept of confidence building. "There is little likelihood," the report argues, that emerging security threats in the Indo-Pacific "will be profoundly reduced by the kinds of maritime cooperation and [confidence-building measures] widely advocated by Western scholars, leaders, and diplomats. It is understandable that governments are instead hedging their bets and building up their capabilities and partnerships against the possibility of worst-case scenarios, despite the obvious security dilemma risks inherent in this approach."[54] That in many ways brings us back to square one. Put simply, the unfolding maritime security dilemma between India and China cannot be mitigated through bilateral confidence-building measures alone. The Sino-Indian maritime dynamic will not be determined solely by the actions of New Delhi and Beijing directed at the other. The naval policy choices and decisions that China and India take in the coming years are likely to be shaped by the larger strategic environment in the Indo-Pacific.

Chapter Eleven

ORDERING THE INDO-PACIFIC

The last few chapters have focused on the overlapping maritime footprints of China and India as they venture beyond their home waters. We have examined the emerging maritime tensions between the two expressed in the form of a security dilemma and the possible ways in which it could be mitigated. While this narrow focus has laid bare the contours of the emerging Sino-Indian maritime rivalry, its evolution is likely to depend on other factors. As Beijing and New Delhi acquire, for the first time in centuries, the ability to exercise significant influence in their wider maritime neighborhood, the other great powers, their allies, and various independent actors will respond vigorously to the rise of China and India. It is this interactive dynamic that will shape the future order in Asia and its waters. This chapter begins with an assessment of how the rise of China and India has begun to alter many familiar geopolitical concepts. After positing the emergence of a new geopolitical theater now widely called the Indo-Pacific, the chapter assesses the three possible future orders in the region—cooperative security, a great-power concert, and a balance of power system.

TOWARD THE INDO-PACIFIC

A significant consequence of the rise of China and India as major powers is the need to reconceptualize many of the traditional geopolitical notions that have shaped international discourse for nearly a century. We began this volume by proposing that the seas of the western Pacific and the Indian Ocean must be seen as a single integrated geopolitical theater, the "Indo-Pacific." Our analysis in the rest of the tract has focused on the increasing ability of a rising China and India to influence large swaths of spaces around them in the Asian landmass and the Pacific and Indian Oceans. We have also noted the imperatives for the Chinese naval outreach to the Indian Ocean and the implications of India's rising profile in the western Pacific. Together these two trends are beginning to fashion the Indo-Pacific into a single geopolitical theater.

Unlike in the postwar years when the Western world put different regions of Asia into separate boxes and assumed there was little connection between them, the geopolitical theorists at the dawn of the twentieth century saw Asia as an integrated region. Mahan, for example, saw the geopolitical interconnections between Europe and Asia and speculated on the implications of Japan's rapid economic development, the political awakening in India, and the immense latent force of China. He argued that a broad stretch of Asia between the 30th and 40th parallels stretching from Asia Minor in the west to the Korean Peninsula in the east was the "debatable" and "debated" ground.[1] "Within this region, Mahan affirmed, "are to be found . . . the most decisive natural features, and also . . . political divisions the unsettled character of which renders the problem of Asia in the present day at once perplexing and imminent."[2] Few can quarrel with the proposition that many of the world's security challenges in the early twenty-first century are rooted in the Asian region identified by Mahan. Once you add Africa to Mahan's debatable and debated grounds in Asia, we have the framing of the Indo-Pacific for our times.

Mahan's concerns with expanding Russian power and Moscow's search for the seas in all directions in Asia, of course, paved the way for his successors to define the popular geopolitical conceptions of "Eurasia" and the relentless struggle between "sea power" and "land power." Halford Mackinder defined the contestation between the "pivot" area that included Russia,

Eastern Europe, and Central Asia and the rest of the "marginal" regions around the Eurasian landmass. Whoever controlled the pivot area, Mackinder averred, would dominate Asia.[3] While Mackinder emphasized the importance of land power, Nicholas Spykman argued that a coalition of maritime powers can defeat those dominant in the heartland by controlling the marginal regions in Eurasia.[4] From there came the visualization of an enduring geopolitical tension between the "heartland" and "rimland" in Eurasia. The rise of the United States as a great power at the turn of the twentieth century, and its unique capacity to dominate both the Atlantic and Pacific Oceans, helped sustain the strategic imagery of Eurasia and the role of the United States as the arbiter among the many powers of that vast space. The notion of a heartland in Eurasia gained some ground after the collapse of the Soviet Union and the contest among the major powers for influence in the newly independent republics in Central Asia, some of which are also rich in hydrocarbon resources. Russia's efforts to reclaim its influence in the so-called near abroad in the first decade of the twenty-first century, its collaboration with China in Central Asia, and Beijing's promotion of the Shanghai Cooperation Organization have also added to the general importance of the notion of Eurasia. But the notion of Eurasia's centrality in our geopolitical understanding of the world may not necessarily survive the rise of China and India and their growing maritime capabilities.

For all their insights on Asia and its influence on international politics at the turn of the twentieth century, the early geopolitical theorists could not escape the biases of their time. Mahan provided the intellectual basis for a rising America's imperial aspirations pursued so vigorously by Theodore Roosevelt.[5] Mackinder was, of course, representing the anxieties of a declining imperial power. With a keen sense of Britain's mounting financial troubles and deeply suspicious of Russia, Mackinder "looked into Britain's imperial future and the vision alarmed him. Britain, a relatively small country, was going to be outranked by states which controlled half continents. Sustaining the Royal Navy as a global force would become increasingly difficult economically, particularly if one power got control of the resources of Euro-Asia, 'The Geographical Pivot of History.'"[6] For Mahan and Mackinder, who stepped back to see Eurasia as a whole, managing the Russian power remained an important geopolitical preoccupation. Amid the rise of China and India, the growing maritime interests of their globalized economies, and the relative decline of Russia, the notion of Eurasia is increasingly yielding to the concept of the Indo-Pacific.

Unlike Mahan and Mackinder, Spykman, writing more than three decades later, was conscious, thanks to his focus on the emergence of large territorial units, of the prospect of China and India becoming part of the great-power constellation in the not-too-distant future.[7] That China and India were not autonomous players in world politics at the turn of the twentieth century meant the eastern and southern rimlands of Eurasia were important but passive grounds for geopolitical contest among the European powers and the United States. Japan was the only exception to the fact that Asia was largely under colonial rule, and once Japan was defeated in the Second World War and integrated into the U.S. alliance system, there were no powerful independent actors in the Asian rimland. China and India turned inward by the mid-1950s, choked off economic engagement with the rest of the world, and delayed their arrival on the world stage. After they opened up to the world—China in 1978 and India in 1991—it was a matter of time before they would become important elements of the regional balance of power. The defining region for China and India, however, is not Eurasia as traditionally conceived, but the Indo-Pacific. As China rose first and joined the East Asian miracle in the early 1990s,[8] it was commonplace to suggest that the world's economic gravity was shifting from the Euro-Atlantic to the Asia Pacific. India, which for long was not seen as part of Asia, let alone the Asia Pacific, began to challenge this perception when it started to grow rapidly at the turn of the twenty-first century. As the consequences of the rise of China and India radiate into the region, the sense of a permanent contest between the Eurasian rimlands and heartland looks less than credible. Some analysts, including Robert Kaplan, argue that Mackinder's separation of heartland and rimland in Eurasia is no longer sustainable.

> As the map of Eurasia shrinks and fills up with people, it not only obliterates the artificial regions of area studies; it also erases Mackinder's division of Eurasia into a specific "pivot" and adjacent "marginal" zones. Military assistance from China and North Korea to Iran causes Israel to take military actions. The U.S. Air Force can attack landlocked Afghanistan from Diego Garcia, an island in the middle of the Indian Ocean. The Chinese and Indian navies can project power from the Gulf of Aden

to the South China Sea—out of their own regions and along the whole Rimland. In short, contra Mackinder, Eurasia has been reconfigured into an organic whole.[9]

Others, however, question the new maritime emphasis of Kaplan and others on the Indo-Pacific or the "greater Indian Ocean" as a frame of reference to the new global geopolitics. They point instead to the emergence of a "horizontal Asia"—the expanding Chinese weight in inner Asia—amid the emergence of China and India as great powers.[10] The difference of emphasis might be less sanguine if we recognize that China and India would want to acquire both land power and sea power. With massive borders and growing interests in inner Asia, China has no reason to choose between land power and sea power. India is unlikely to take its eyes off its northern frontiers any time soon, given the unresolved boundary disputes with China and Pakistan. In addition, its aspirations for a role in inner Asia are deeply rooted in the memories of the Great Game in the nineteenth century and the origins of the Mughal empire beyond the Hindu Kush mountains. Meanwhile, the new maritime imperative will demand that India focus on the development of naval power. For the Europeans, there is a strong temptation to see the current struggles along the Indo-Pacific continuum as a power play in Eurasian waters.[11] But once you introduce Africa into the equation and take into account the importance of the continent's resources in sustaining Chinese and Indian economic growth, it might make more sense to go along with the notion of the Indo-Pacific. Put another way, Eurasia might be seen as the hinterland of the Indo-Pacific. As our own analysis in chapter 7 showed, China's horizontal expansion into inner Asia has included a vigorous strategy to connect, vertically, its far western marches with the Indian Ocean. There are also proposals to connect India overland to East Asia through rail and road networks cutting through Southeast Asia.[12] The United States is actively promoting India's "vertical" links with Central Asia through Afghanistan, despite Pakistan's reluctance to grant overland transit rights to India.[13] At the same time, Washington and Tokyo are also encouraging India to build "horizontal" links with Burma, Indo-China, and East Asia.

From our perspective, then, the Indo-Pacific is emerging as a recognizable geopolitical entity that connects the two great oceans and integrates the inner Asian regions to China and India. Given the expansive nature of this theater, it is difficult to imagine the emergence of a single security order for the whole region. For decades now, the United States has been the principal security provider in the Indian and Pacific Oceans. But the relative decline of the United States, its shrinking naval assets, the crisis that has enveloped its economy since the end of the 2000s, and its exhaustion from the Afghanistan and Iraq wars have naturally raised questions about the ability of the United States to sustain its traditional role in the two oceans. Meanwhile, the naval capabilities of many medium powers in the Indo-Pacific littoral are steadily growing. All these factors have induced an extraordinary geopolitical uncertainty. The United States has fought back against the perception of relative decline and the Obama administration has announced a strategy of "rebalancing" U.S. military forces toward Asia. Despite fiscal pressures at home, the United States has signaled its determination to remain a force to reckon with in the Indian Ocean and the Pacific by redeploying its forces, leveraging its technological strengths, building on its old and new partnerships, and developing new operational doctrines.[14] The following analysis examines three potential outcomes for ordering the Indo-Pacific in the changing regional context—cooperative security, the creation of a concert of Asian powers, and the likelihood of a balance of power system—and the developing attitudes in Beijing and New Delhi toward these orders.

TOWARD COOPERATIVE SECURITY

Many in Asia and the United States hope for collective or cooperative security arrangements in the Indo-Pacific. After the vigorous pursuit of unilateralism by the Bush administration, there has been much longing in the region for a stronger multilateral security architecture. Bush's successor, Barack Obama, has explicitly rejected the notion of balance of power and has sought relationships that transcend the traditional framework of power politics. In his first speech to the United Nations General Assembly in September 2009, Obama declared:

> In an era when our destiny is shared, power is no longer a zero-sum game. No one nation can or should try to dominate other nation[s]. No world order that elevates one nation or group of people over another will succeed. No balance of power among nations will hold. The traditional

the first Asian Relations Conference in 1947. But it had lost interest in the organization after a diplomatic debacle at Bandung in 1955, where Zhou Enlai outshone Nehru. India also was a reluctant partner when the South Asian Association for Regional Cooperation was formed in the early 1980s at the initiative of India's smaller neighbors.

Chinese and Indian attitudes toward multilateral organizations began to evolve as Beijing and New Delhi embarked on globalization (China from the late 1970s and India from the early 1990s) and recognized the virtues of regional economic cooperation. This new interest in multilateralism was especially prompted by the need to deal with the expanding Asian regionalism under the auspices of ASEAN.[22] The security establishments in India and China were naturally a little more reluctant than the rest of their systems in adapting to the possibilities of multilateralism.[23] In the age of globalization that also marked an end to India's long-standing defense isolation, the navy was first off the mark in exploring the possibilities of multilateral confidence-building measures. The one major exception to the isolation was India's substantive participation in international peacekeeping operations under the UN flag from the 1950s.[24] The Indian navy was in a sense rediscovering the multilateral maritime tradition that it was part of until the late 1950s. India participated in the annual British Joint Exercises off Trincomalee (JET) that brought a few Commonwealth navies (Pakistan and Sri Lanka) together until 1958.[25] In 1995 it took the initiative to hold the first multilateral naval exercises, called Milan, with neighboring countries to the east in the Bay of Bengal. The navies of Indonesia, Singapore, Sri Lanka, and Thailand joined the first naval conclave. The Milan exercises have been held in 1997, 1999, 2003, 2006, and biennially since then. Milan exercises were not held in 2001, when India was holding a major fleet review, or in 2005, when the region was recovering from the effects of the December 2004 tsunami. From four navies joining the Indian counterpart in 1995 the participating countries increased to eleven in 2008. Eight naval vessels from Australia, Bangladesh, Burma, Indonesia, Singapore, Sri Lanka, and Thailand joined Milan 2008; naval delegations from Brunei, Malaysia, New Zealand, and Vietnam arrived by air. In the 2008 exercise, an Australian ship was deployed for the first time.[26] At the seventh Milan exercises in 2010, eight Asia-Pacific navies— Australia, Bangladesh, Burma, Indonesia, Malaysia, Singapore, Sri Lanka, and Thailand—participated, and units from Brunei, the Philippines, Vietnam, and New Zealand observed. Besides discussions on maritime terrorism, piracy, humanitarian aid, and disaster relief, the participating naval units conducted exercises focused on sea lane security.[27] In Milan 2012, three important Indian Ocean island states, Maldives, Seychelles, and Mauritius, participated for the first time.[28] While Milan came to institutionalize the Indian navy's regional multilateralism, two other initiatives raised eyebrows around the world. India's coordination of the naval relief operations in Southeast Asia with the United States, Australia, and Japan in December 2004 and the multilateral naval exercises in the Bay of Bengal during September 2007 involving Singapore pointed to the possible strategic nature of India's new naval multilateralism. But the intensive negative reaction from the leftist parties at home and the concerns of China meant the Indian political leadership was going to be cautious rather than bold in embarking on strategic naval multilateralism.

Since the turn of the century, Beijing began to value participation in some multilateral military activities. Starting somewhat tentatively, China steadily expanded its participation in international peacekeeping operations under the auspices of the United Nations during the 2000s.[29] It was a little slower than India in embracing multilateral maritime diplomacy, not beginning bilateral naval engagement with many countries until the mid-1980s. The Chinese navy, which was not involved in the tsunami relief operations in 2004, slowly began to adapt to the requirements of multilateral military diplomacy. Bilateral military diplomacy turned the corner in 2003, when China dramatically stepped up its engagement with other nations.[30] By 2007, China's military diplomacy began to include a distinctive multilateral flavor. As China's defense white paper underlined in 2009: "In August 2007, within the framework of the [Shanghai Cooperation Organization], China, Russia, Kazakhstan, Kyrgyzstan, Tajikistan, and Uzbekistan held a joint counterterrorism military exercise in the Xinjiang Uygur Autonomous Region, China, and Chelyabinsk, Russia, focusing on the task of combating terrorism, separatism and extremism. This was the first time for the PLA to participate in a major land-air joint exercise outside the Chinese territory."[31] The new approach to multilateralism was also evident in the maritime domain. The white paper notes: "China has also conducted various forms of multilateral joint maritime training exercises with relevant countries, focusing on various tasks. In March 2007, China held the 'Peace-2007' joint maritime training exercise in the Arabian Sea with seven other countries, including Pakistan. In May 2007 China and eight other countries, including Singapore, conducted a multilateral joint maritime exercise in Singaporean waters within the framework of the Western Pacific Naval Symposium (WPNS). In October the same year China, Australia and New Zealand staged a joint maritime search-and-rescue training exercise in the Tasman Sea."[32] China has also begun to engage its Asian neighbors in an expansive multilateral defense dialogue on both traditional and nontraditional security threats. "China-ASEAN and ASEAN Plus Three (China, Japan and the Republic of Korea) cooperation in non-traditional security fields is developing in depth. At the China-ASEAN Summit and the ASEAN Plus Three Summit, held respectively in January and November 2007, China put forward a series of initiatives for strengthening cooperation in non-traditional security fields, and emphasized the importance of conducting institutionalized defense cooperation and military exchanges. China hosted the First China-ASEAN Dialogue between Senior Defense Scholars (CADSDS) in March 2008 and the Second ASEAN Plus Three Workshop on Disaster Relief by Armed Forces in June 2008."[33] The PLAN is indeed working with other navies in the Gulf of Aden since it deployed there at the end of 2008. Beijing has taken the initiative and participated in a range of efforts to coordinate the anti-piracy operations of the naval forces operating in the Gulf.[34]

Enhanced naval multilateralism on the part of India and China and their participation in various regional maritime and security forums have not necessarily brought them together or reduced their mutual misperceptions. Just as Beijing was concerned about the implications of India's multilateral exercises with the United States and other nations, New Delhi has warily watched China's maritime multilateralism. As a former Indian naval officer argues, "Chinese naval initiatives in the Indian Ocean have stirred considerable unease among some regional powers, particularly India, which has a tendency to perceive every Chinese move in the region as a step toward its strategic encirclement."[35] While these analysts see China's maritime multilateralism as a new tactic, other naval analysts are deeply concerned about the emerging Sino-Pakistan maritime nexus, especially China's participation in Pakistan's biennial Aman exercises that were launched in March 2007. Fourteen ships belonging to Bangladesh, China, France, Italy, Malaysia, the United Kingdom, and the United States took part. The exercises were held again in March 2009 on a much bigger scale.[36] Indian naval analysts saw the exercises as not only integrating the Pakistani navy into the Western maritime counterterrorism strategy but also facilitating greater naval interaction between China and the West under Pakistan's friendly auspices.[37]

At a broader level, mutual distrust between India and China on multilateral issues deepened in the 2000s despite the proclaimed desire for cooperation on global and regional issues and the hopes for coordination on issues relating to energy and maritime security. India's litany of complaints is well known; at the heart of it all was an inescapable political conclusion that New Delhi was running against Beijing's opposition in elevating India's global position.[38] New Delhi's quest for a permanent seat at the United Nations Security Council was stymied by Chinese resistance. Although Beijing made empathetic noises in bilateral meetings with Delhi, it ran a vigorous campaign to defeat the joint diplomatic effort by Brazil, Germany, India, and Japan to expand the Security Council's permanent membership.[39] And as ASEAN members debated the creation of a wider East Asian political forum, China opposed New Delhi's inclusion by questioning whether India really belonged to East Asia. India was nevertheless admitted into the East Asia Summit process when it was launched in 2005, thanks to strong support from Japan, Indonesia, and Singapore.[40] India has also been extremely wary of China's leadership role in the Shanghai Cooperation Organization, where Beijing was opposing full Indian membership (the forum was launched in 2001, and India has been an observer since 2005).[41] For New Delhi, Beijing's worst transgression was its attempt to undermine the U.S. effort to secure a waiver for India from the rules of the Nuclear Suppliers Group in 2008 as part of the implementation of the civil nuclear initiative. Although the Chinese reservations against the deal were known, New Delhi was not pleased.[42]

It was not just that India had grievances about China's hostility in multilateral forums. Beijing had its own list of Indian resistance to an expanding Chinese role in regional processes. As we discussed in chapter 1, India had long seen the subcontinent as its own sphere of influence and was loath to accept any Chinese penetration of the region. As China sought an

observer role in the South Asian regional forum SAARC, India did its best
to prevent it. The matter came to a head at the SAARC summit in Dhaka
at the end of 2005. As India pressed for the entry of Afghanistan into the
organization, Pakistan and Bangladesh made observer status for China a
precondition. New Delhi had no choice but to concede in the end, but it
managed to open the door for many other major powers, including the
United States and Japan, to join SAARC as observers.[43] New Delhi's opposition to Beijing's entry into the Indian Ocean Naval Symposium, an initiative launched by the Indian navy in 2008, fits into the same pattern. In
what has been seen as a major effort to cap India's now resurgent military
diplomacy, the navy convened a conclave of all the naval chiefs from the
Indian Ocean. Underlining the importance New Delhi attached to the initiative, the Indian prime minister, vice president, and the defense minister
all addressed a symposium on maritime security that was held along with
the naval chiefs' conclave. That China wanted to join the initiative but that
India was not ready to support its entry pointed to the persistent difficulty
of reconciling the Chinese and Indian perceptions of the maritime order
in the Indian Ocean.

For the Indian navy, the Indian Ocean Naval Symposium, or IONS,
initiative was indeed a culmination of its nearly two decades of outreach
in the Indian Ocean. According to an Indian naval officer, "Conceived
within the ambit of Article 52 of the UN Charter, inspired by the initial
successes of the ASEAN Regional Forum and modeled on the lines of
the West Pacific Naval Symposium (WPNS), IONS has the potential to
successfully coalesce the imagination of regional states, and serve as a valuable platform to synergize their resources and energies toward maintaining
'good order' in the Indian Ocean."[44] The IONS is not the first political
initiative in the Indian Ocean, but it is certainly the first Indian one. As
the Second World War was coming to an end, K. M. Panikkar called for
a multilateral mechanism to address the common interests of the Indian
Ocean region. He proposed creation of a "regional council" for the Indian
Ocean that would work under the incipient United Nations and its Security Council. The regional council centered on India, which, according to
Panikkar, "should work in close association with other powers having an
interest in the peace and security of the area." Panikkar suggested that the
council "should also devote itself to the general development of political

freedom, social consciousness, economic progress and betterment of living conditions of the masses."[45]

This proposal went nowhere, and India's multilateral focus on the Indian Ocean did not reemerge until the turn of the 1970s, when Britain announced its withdrawal from the East of Suez. While the idea of converting the Indian Ocean into a "Zone of Peace" gained much traction in the Indian foreign policy discourse, it was not an initiative from New Delhi. To be sure, there was vocal political support in New Delhi for the concept of an Indian Ocean Zone of Peace, which demanded that all "extra-regional" powers vacate their presence in the Indian Ocean. But the proposal itself came in the 1970s from more radical sections of the Non-Aligned Movement, especially Sri Lanka, and was a rejection of the theory of a "power vacuum" in the Indian Ocean after the British withdrawal from the East of Suez and an opposition to the emerging Soviet-American naval rivalry in the Indian Ocean. Leading Indian strategic analyst K. Subrahmanyam, who was close to policymakers at that time, suggested that Delhi merely went along with the Indian Ocean Zone of Peace proposal rather than actively promote it.[46] New Delhi was also an important member state of the Indian Ocean Rim Association for Regional Cooperation, or IOR-ARC, which was launched in 1997. India tended to be quite defensive about the IOR-ARC and its mandate, working actively to remove security-related issues from the organization's agenda.[47] The IOR-ARC has since drifted and become moribund like so many of the earlier initiatives in the Indian Ocean.[48] By 2011, as India began to focus on developing a comprehensive security framework for the Indian Ocean, the idea of reviving the IOR-ARC had gained some policy traction in New Delhi. Assuming the IOR-ARC chair at the end of 2011, India's external affairs minister, S. M. Krishna, emphasized India's political commitment to inject new life into the organization: "The Indian Ocean is of strategic importance to all our member nations. India is committed to take initiatives to address the contemporary challenges and developmental aspirations of all nations on its rim. We have taken a decision in the meeting to fully harness the potential of all IOR related institutions that have been established over the years."[49]

An India that was sensitive about discussing security issues in the multilateral arena until the late 1990s was launching by 2008 a security forum for the Indian Ocean all on its own. India's greater self-assurance and the rising profile of its navy did not necessarily guarantee the success of the Indian Ocean Naval Symposium initiative, as geopolitics inevitably intervened in the construction of the forum and there was no way of escaping the logic of Sino-Indian distrust in the making of a new security forum for the Indian Ocean littoral.

The objectives that India laid out for the Indian Ocean Naval Symposium were unexceptionable. These included promoting "a shared understanding of issues and concerns" bearing upon the maritime security of the Indian Ocean; strengthening "the capability of all nation-states of the Indian Ocean Region to address present and anticipated challenges to maritime security and stability"; constructing a "variety of trans-national, maritime, consultative and cooperative mechanisms"; and generating "interoperability" among the naval forces to provide "speedy, responsive, and effective humanitarian assistance and disaster-relief" throughout the Indian Ocean region.[50] Yet the moment India came toward a decision on which countries to invite to the first IONS symposium, it ran into political problems. India invited 33 countries, which according to New Delhi were members of the Indian Ocean littoral from a strict textbook geographic perspective.[51] In terms of great powers, France was in because of its territorial possessions in the Indian Ocean, but the dominant naval power of the region, the United States, was out. And the rising power China, with its rapidly increasing interests in the Indian Ocean, had also to be kept out. India had probably consulted Washington on why it had to be left out of the conference; the president of the U.S. Naval War College participated in the symposium, but no American (or Chinese) delegate was present in the naval chiefs' conclave.

Indian naval analysts clearly understood the implications of leaving out major powers like the United States and China. As Khurana argued, the Indian Ocean Naval Symposium "must be contextualized in terms of the larger Asian, and even global construct . . . The imperative to include extra-regional powers as observers in IONS stems from this rationale, besides the need to obviate suspicions and geopolitical schisms."[52] Even neutral observers were quick to recognize the danger of the Indian initiative being seen as self-serving amid a seeming Indian attempt to revive its old rhetoric against "extra-regional" powers. Sam Bateman, a leading naval analyst from Australia, pointed to one of the main difficulties facing the initiative:

"While the IONS is similar in concept to that of the WPNS, its implementation will be very different. The IONS lacks the political top cover that notionally is provided for the WPNS through APEC and the ASEAN Regional Forum. Its continued existence is likely to be entirely dependent on Indian funding and leadership. Potentially this defeats the purpose of a truly cooperative arrangement because India, as a consequence of providing most of the funding, will likely want firm control over IONS activities."[53] The discussions at the symposium underlined the many differences that had prevented the emergence of cooperative security mechanisms in the Indian Ocean. Above all, there was no escaping the question of where China stood in relation to the Indian initiative.[54] Beijing wasted no time in testing the proposition whether the Indian Ocean is India's ocean, putting in a request to be associated with the symposium in some form. The Indian Foreign Office had reportedly ruled that "there was no strategic rationale to let China be associated with IONS as it was strictly restricted to littoral states of the Indian Ocean."[55] China, however, is likely to persist with its diplomatic effort to open the door to its participation in future symposium gatherings.

Multilateralism, as we have seen in the preceding discussion, does not automatically guarantee a reduction of distrust among rival powers. The very process of constructing multilateralism and its rules is subject to geopolitical considerations, as we saw in the creation of the East Asia Summit, the expansion of the South Asian Association for Regional Cooperation, and the launch of the Indian Ocean Naval Symposium. More deeply, the regional security forums did not seem to have the capacity to resolve the core maritime disputes dividing the great powers on the UN Convention on the Law of the Sea or the territorial disputes between China and its neighbors. Sam Bateman points to a number of intractable "wicked problems." He writes that the "maritime security environment of the Asia Pacific is awash with wicked problems. These include different interpretations of the Law of the Sea, providing good order in regional seas, conflicting maritime claims, and managing the risks of greater naval activity in the region. These wicked problems may be distinguished from 'tame' security problems in the maritime security environment, such as piracy, humanitarian assistance, and the threat of maritime terrorism."[56] Warning that failure to address the wicked problems will escalate the current tensions into conflict, Bateman wonders if the Asian regional forums "can move beyond being 'talk-shops,' and whether mindsets can be changed with regard to how countries view the maritime domain."[57]

PROSPECTS FOR AN ASIAN CONCERT

One way of stabilizing the Indo-Pacific might be through a "concert" of great powers. The inspiration for the idea of a "concert" comes from the nineteenth century, when a small group of powers kept peace in Europe after the Napoleonic Wars. Could such a concert work in the contemporary context of Asia? A concert by definition privileges the relations among the great powers as the principal factor for stability within a defined geographic space. In its simplest manifestation, according to a recent definition, a concert "can be understood as an arrangement for managing power relations within a strategic system, involving an unusually high degree of voluntary consultation and restraint among the strongest countries." It adds that in a concert system, self-restraint derives from the expectation of balancing behavior by others and at least equally from shared interests or values and a common recognition that "the costs of war are not worth the potential gains."[58]

But many question the relevance of the European concert system to modern Asia or the Indo-Pacific. Amitav Acharya lists a number of reasons that the concert system might not work in Asia.[59] The first is that the European concert came in the wake of a cathartic and a systemic war in the early nineteenth century; Asia in contrast has avoided a great-power war for decades. Second, the European concert offered special privileges and responsibilities for great powers; this form of "tutelage" would not be acceptable to many large nations of Asia, which would oppose domination by any small group of great powers. Third, while shared interests in stability might facilitate a concert, the absence of shared political values, especially between China and the democratic powers, might undermine any potential concert in Asia. Fourth, significant territorial disputes between major powers—as between China and Japan and between China and India—might preclude an effective management of any concert. Finally, it would be difficult even to agree on which states should be members of a proposed concert. Robert Ayson argues that "a great power concert in Asia, however ineffective, is preferable to an Asia dangerously divided between two rival blocs, however internally effective these blocs may be. But for a flawed but still valuable concert to operate, almost all of the participating states would have to give up something. In other words, in order to win, one would have to lose."[60] The United States, for example, might have to give up its primacy in Asia, and China might have to temper its aspirations for regional dominance. Japan would have to come to terms with the reduced salience of the alliance with the United States, and the many medium-sized powers in Asia would have to accept the constraints imposed by an Asian concert. It is by no means clear if these conditions could be met in the coming years either in Asia or the Indo-Pacific.

But ideas similar to that of a concert have gained some ground in the academic literature as well as policy discourse in Asia. Jonathan Holslag talks of an "inclusive balancing" in the region and calls for American partnership with China on the one hand and Washington's stronger engagement with the other Asian powers—India, Japan, and Russia—on the other:

> Washington needs to engage all four regional powers simultaneously. Unlike counterbalancing, by using Taiwan as a fortress and fostering new alliances to contain China, inclusive balancing implies working with all the main players of the Asian system so that the multipolar order imposes sufficient costs to thwart military adventurism. Transcending different political systems, inclusive balancing seeks to give each player the scope to develop, resist military revisionism, address non-traditional threats, and protect an open trading system. Only such a posture will permit Washington to foster truly strategic military cooperation with China and to avoid the high costs of traditional containment and confrontation while also reassuring its traditional allies.[61]

Robert Kaplan has a similar vision for a concert that suggests that the United States expand security cooperation with China and deepen defense partnerships with India and Japan. He argues that the task of the U.S. naval strategy in the Indo-Pacific must be to "quietly leverage the sea power of its closest allies—India in the Indian Ocean and Japan in the Western Pacific to set limits on China's expansion." Kaplan is quick to add that "it will have to do so while seizing every opportunity to incorporate China's navy into international alliances; a U.S.-Chinese understanding at sea is crucial for the stabilization of world politics in the twenty-first century." "The goal of the United States," Kaplan concludes, "must be to forge a global maritime system that can minimize the risks of inter-state conflict while lessening the burden of policing for the U.S. Navy."[62]

Some Indian decisionmakers, too, have begun to recognize the importance of a concert-like mechanism to manage potential conflicts among rising China and India and the United States. Shivshankar Menon, who was India's top diplomat at the Foreign Office during 2006–2009 and the national security adviser since early 2010, has welcomed the notion of a great-power concert along and across the Asian littoral. Menon believes the shared maritime and energy security interests provide the major powers "a rare potential area of convergence" and that it could be the "starting point to build a flexible and adaptable Asian order."[63] While the notion of an Asian concert might not be under explicit discussion, India, China, and the United States are all engaged in bilateral consultations on Asian security issues, especially those relating to the maritime domain. Maritime security has begun to figure prominently in India's bilateral discussions with the United States, Japan, and key Asian nations. India and the United States embarked on an institutionalized dialogue about East Asia in 2010 and started a trilateral dialogue with Japan at the end of 2011. The United States also conducts trilateral dialogues with Japan and Australia as well as with Japan and South Korea. U.S. Secretary of State Hillary Clinton has proposed trilateral dialogue involving the United States, China, and India. Meanwhile, the United States and China launched a dialogue on security issues in the Asia Pacific in 2011 as part of their new strategic and economic dialogue.[64] While these moves do not add up to a formal concert, they have the potential to generate some agreements on shared interests among the major powers of the Indo-Pacific.

BALANCE OF POWER SYSTEM

In theory, a system of balance of power seeks to prevent any one great power among many from establishing primacy in a regional or global system. Equilibrium among the great powers is expected to provide the basis for stability and order. If the power of one state grows too rapidly, the system will adjust itself through two mechanisms—internal and external balancing.

Internal balancing involves the mobilization of domestic hard power re-sources—economic and military—to deal with presumed shifts in the balance of power. External balancing involves a realignment. While some states might align with the rising power, others are likely to band together against it. Still others could seek an alliance with another great power to reestablish equilibrium. The balance of power system has always had pow-erful critics, and there are a few in the Indo-Pacific who call for an explicit balance of power approach to stability in the region. The general critique of the balance of power system is that it is fundamentally unstable, will trigger arms races, and will eventually disintegrate amid the impossibility of managing the shifts in power distribution, leading to war and conflict. The balance of power theory was widely considered either outdated or ir-relevant to contemporary Asia. Indeed, the enormous lead of the United States over the other powers, the absence of great-power conflict, and the rapid advances in regional cooperation at the turn of the twenty-first cen-tury seemed to confirm that proposition. Yet by the end of the first decade of the new century, the politics of balancing seemed real amid the rise of China and India and perceived relative decline of the United States.[65]

Modern Asia has not had much experience with the construction and management of a classical balance of power system among roughly equal-size powers. While the Cold War had the look of a two-power balance, Asian security was essentially ordered by the United States. The United States has been the principal security provider in the western Pacific since the end of the Second World War and in the Indian Ocean from the mid-1970s. While the Soviet Union often challenged the primacy of the United States in the Indo-Pacific throughout the Cold War, it never became a genuine second pole in Asia as it did in Europe. China and India, which occasionally aligned with the Soviet Union or America, were too weak to make the power system in the Indo-Pacific a multipolar one. Beijing and New Delhi could alter the structure of Asian power only at the margins. In the past, both China and India explicitly rejected balance of power as an organizing principle for Asian security. Today, the notion of "balance of power" has begun to surface in the strategic vocabulary of the two nations. More broadly, as China rises rapidly, India emerges at a slower pace, and the perception of America's relative decline gains ground, the prospect for a genuine multipolar world might be at hand in Asia.[66]

Few governments in the region publicly acknowledge their interest in a new balance of power system, but all major actors are adapting to the changes in the regional power distribution. The United States is seeking to strengthen its traditional alliances in Asia with Japan, South Korea, Australia, the Philippines, and Thailand and is building new partnerships with India, Vietnam, and Indonesia. It is also reorganizing its force deployments in Eurasia with a greater emphasis on the Indo-Pacific region to reassure its Asian allies that the United States is there to stay despite pressure to cut defense budgets. The strategic defense guidance issued by President Obama in January 2012 asserted that "U.S. economic and security interests are inextricably linked to developments in the arc extending from the Western Pacific and East Asia into the Indian Ocean region and South Asia, creating a mix of evolving challenges and opportunities. Accordingly, while the U.S. military will continue to contribute to security globally, *we will of necessity rebalance toward the Asia-Pacific region*" (emphasis in the original).[67]

As the United States seeks to sustain its forward military presence in the Asia Pacific, China is acquiring military capabilities to expand its freedom of maneuver against the historical U.S. dominance of its waters. Beijing is stepping up its outreach to countries on its land and maritime peripheries and seeks to draw them into tighter economic partnership and greater political cooperation. As the tension between the U.S. determination to retain its primacy in the Asian littoral and the Chinese efforts to expand its influence on the maritime periphery plays out, India has sought to expand its own military and maritime capabilities. It has embarked on a defense partnership with the United States, expanded its security cooperation with major powers like Japan and regional actors like Vietnam, Indonesia, and Singapore, and extended military support to small but geopolitically critical states like Mauritius, Seychelles, and Oman. Meanwhile, many medium-size powers in the Indo-Pacific are rapidly building up their defense capabilities and reaching out to major powers for security partnerships. In its search for great-power equilibrium, the ASEAN invited India, Australia, and New Zealand to become founding members of the East Asia Summit in 2005. Facing a more assertive China, ASEAN in 2010 invited the United States and Russia into the East Asia Summit as well as the regional framework for defense consultations. All these trends point to active balancing strategies without formally identifying a specific threat from

China. Given the growing economic interdependence with China, which has emerged as the largest trading partner for most Asian countries as well as the United States, an explicit balancing strategy against China is indeed hard to construct. While the official reaction in China has been muted in response to the U.S. pivot to Asia, its strategic community has viewed the new American assertiveness as an attempt to revive Cold War politics in Asia and constrain China's freedom of action in its own neighborhood.[68]

Classical balance of power theory does not refer to the internal orientation of states. The major powers are expected to engage in balancing activity on the basis of relative shifts in power and perceived threats from the rising power. Yet in the current debate on Asian security order, building coalitions on the basis of shared political values has emerged as an interesting theme. The idea of democracies from Asia and the Pacific getting together had brief diplomatic traction during 2004–2007. The formal proposal for the "democratic quad" of Asia—the United States, Japan, India, and Australia—getting together to coordinate and cooperate in the promotion of regional stability had come from Japanese Prime Minister Shinzo Abe. The proposal reportedly had considerable support in sections of the Bush administration, especially the White House and the Vice President's Office.[69] After just one meeting of senior officials in the summer of 2007 and one joint naval exercise in the Bay of Bengal in the fall of 2007 that also included Singapore, the initiative folded. Political change in Japan and Australia, strong diplomatic protests from China, and Washington's desire not to offend Beijing seemed to limit the possibilities for a democratic quad. But the idea that democracies must band together remains a powerful idea in the U.S. political discourse. During the 2008 U.S. election campaign, some liberal Democrats and conservative Republicans proposed the idea of United States building a "concert" or "league" of democracies to address the challenges of the twenty-first century world. The idea has not had much effect on the foreign policy of the Obama administration. In calling itself realist, the administration has tended to avoid too much emphasis on either democracy promotion or human rights in the broad articulation of American foreign policy interests, most certainly in the case of China. As the reaction set in from the American strategic community, the Obama administration was under some pressure to bring issues relating to political freedom back into the discussion of American engagement with Beijing.

The idea of Asian democracies banding together was revived in a modest and tentative form, when India, Japan, and the United States launched a trilateral dialogue at the official level in December 2011.[70]

The notion of an alliance of democracies goes back in time. One of Mackinder's proposals was to "bind Britain and the Dominions into a League of Democracies with one fleet and one foreign policy. Encourage economic growth within the empire by a system of tariffs that promoted imperial trade."[71] More recent writings have sought to explain that the world maritime system—with its emphasis on political liberalism at home, free trade abroad, and muscular sea power—is an enduring part of the Anglo-Saxon tradition that goes back to the Dutch. The reference here to Anglo-Saxon tradition is not a racial culture but a strategic culture that focused on international commerce, defense of the global commons, and a capacity to manipulate global balances through projection of military power across the seas. It was a system that was developed by the Dutch, refined by Britain, and further developed by the United States.[72] Amid all the gloom and doom about the relative decline of American power, Mead does not see the rise of Asia threatening the future of the Anglo-Saxon maritime system. He argues that the emerging "complex strategic geometry of a changing Asia presents the United States with an extraordinary set of opportunities in the twenty-first century." Mead proceeds to make the logic of offshore balancing that is likely to work for America:

> From the classical point of view of maritime balancing powers like Britain and America, the first key feature of this situation is that it begins to look impossible for any single country realistically to aspire to an Asian hegemony. Not only does the United States stand offshore ready to build coalitions against any threatening power, the Asian powers look increasingly able to keep rough balance on their own. . . . Either India or China, *plus Japan*, is likely to be strong enough to make it unrealistic for the third power in the triangle to seek to dominate the other two (emphasis in the original).[73]

Pointing to the fact that in the past only Japan was able to contribute to the regional balance of power, Mead concludes that the rise of China and India may have created a condition that may have all the elements of a potentially stable balance of power.

While the prospect of a regional balance has gained some policy adherents, translating it into a credible structure may not be easy. In any event, the real world does not adhere to neatly structured concepts from political theory. Decisionmakers in China and India are likely to pursue all three ideas—cooperative security, an Asian concert, and balance of power—simultaneously. As they rise, China and India have become more open to regional cooperative mechanisms, but that doesn't mean they are ready to give up autonomy in pursuit of multilateralism. Both have taken an active interest in building multilateral institutions that they can influence. Beijing and New Delhi have also opened up to more formal consultations on maritime security issues with other great powers, in what could eventually amount to an Asian concert. At the same time, they have actively sought to balance each other in the Indo-Pacific. The vastness of the Indo-Pacific strategic space and their different strategic priorities—the Pacific for China and the Indian Ocean for India—means many subregional orders are likely to emerge. Despite its relative decline, the United States is likely to still have a dominant say in ordering both the oceans' spaces as well as defining the overarching security framework for the Indo-Pacific. The nature of the U.S. relationship with China and India and the unfolding dynamic between Beijing and New Delhi are likely to be the principal determinants of the future security order in the Indo-Pacific region. While many middle powers will have a bearing on the political evolution of the littoral, it is the United States that has the biggest influence on the emerging Sino-Indian contestation in the Indo-Pacific. It is to that triangular relationship we must turn in the next, concluding chapter of this volume.

Chapter Twelve

SAMUDRA MANTHAN

The story of *Samudra Manthan* is about the struggle between the gods and the demons for gaining control of ambrosia, or "amrit." The power play in this wonderful myth is continuously shaped by the almighty Lord Vishnu and supported by the rest of the trinity, Brahma and Shiva. The story begins when the gods go to Vishnu seeking to restore their power after losing a battle with the demons. Vishnu advises them to adopt a diplomatic approach and invite the demons into a joint venture to churn the oceans for ambrosia. Vishnu promises the gods that he will ensure that the demons will be denied the ambrosia. When the gods and demons seek a rope big enough to churn the oceans with mount "Mandhara," the Lord offers his own resting platform, the great snake "Vasuki." When they want to stop the mountain from sinking into the water, the Lord presents himself in the avatar of "Kurma," the great tortoise on which Mandhara could be placed. When the churning produces terrible poison, Vishnu instructs the gods and demons to seek the help of Lord Shiva, who drinks the poison but instead of swallowing it holds it in his throat. Finally, when the great churning produces the amrit, gods and demons begin to fight for control over the pot of elixir. When the demons gain control over the pot and the gods seek Vishnu's support, the Lord appears as "Mohini," the enchantress, tricks the demons to hand over the pot, and then distributes its contents to the gods. The story of *Samudra Manthan* invites a variety of interpretations—religious, spiritual, and philosophical. For our purposes here, it is about the fact that the incipient rivalry between China and India in the Indian and Pacific Oceans will be determined not merely by the logic of the Sino-Indian relationship. It will be influenced decisively by the kind of policies that the United States as the leading maritime power in the Indo-Pacific might adopt.

As a classical study on seapower and world politics points out, world powers have largely been ocean powers exercising command of the sea. It also contends that changes in the position of world leadership are associated with shifts in the distribution of seapower. All powers "with significant involvement in, and capable of acting upon, global politics, have also been seapowers."[1] A major question of our time, then, is about the regional and international consequences of the changing distribution of seapower, expressing itself most clearly in the Indo-Pacific. Great Britain's adaption to the rise of the United States at the turn of the twentieth century allowed a seamless transition toward a new leadership of the global maritime order. At the current juncture, the answers to the questions on whether and how the United States can accommodate the rise of Chinese and Indian naval power are open-ended.

As they lead more than two billion people to the seas, Beijing and New Delhi are bound to transform the world's maritime politics. The change will affect all major dimensions of the Indo-Pacific, including the balance of power in the region, exploitation of resources on its littoral and the seabed, and the maintenance of order and the protection of many public goods including the sea lines of communication. The United States and its Navy have performed most of these functions in the Pacific since the end of the Second World War and in the Indian Ocean since the withdrawal of the British from the East of Suez in the early 1970s. The rise of China and India and their growing impact on the Indo-Pacific will demand the re-framing of U.S. maritime policies in the Asian littoral. Our study has been focused on how the maritime policies of China and India and their naval ambitions are recasting the template of Sino-Indian relations. We have examined how their contestation along and across the Asian littoral has deepened the security dilemma and the problems of mitigating the mutual suspicion through bilateral and multilateral confidence-building measures. The ultimate outcomes from the Sino-Indian jousting in the Indo-Pacific are likely to be determined by the response of the United States to the simultaneous rise of China and India.

Whatever the eventual policy choices of the United States, an unanticipated "strategic triangle" is beginning to emerge among Washington, Beijing, and New Delhi. A strategic triangle by definition is a condition in which the policies of one have consequential effects on the ties between the other two on a sustained basis in time and space. Barring a brief period in the early 1960s, when the United States tilted toward India during the Sino-Indian conflict, there was little basis for imagining a triangular dynamic among the three nations. Throughout the Cold War, India was largely peripheral to the evolution of relations between China and the United States. It is only quite recently, during the years of the George W. Bush administration, that sections of the U.S. foreign policy community began to debate, somewhat skeptically, the notion of a strategic triangle involving China and India.[2] Very few in the American foreign policy community in recent decades have seen India as a consequential power outside the subcontinent. After the advent of the Bush administration's emphasis on promoting a "balance of power in Asia that favors freedom," scholarly and public interest in a triangular dynamic among the United States, China, and India has grown.[3] While no broad consensus exists in Washington on this issue, the steady rise of India has generated the prospect of a strategic triangle. Our focus here is to extract the essence of the triangular dynamic, now in great flux, and explore its potential impact on the Indo-Pacific.

AMERICAN DILEMMAS

During the Cold War, the economic expansion of Asia took place largely among America's allies and friends. While this growth did imply a relative American decline, Washington successfully met two of its most important strategic objectives—expansion of the liberal international economic order and containment of the Soviet Union. To be sure, the rise of China and India does provide economic benefits to the United States and brings nearly 2.5 billion people into the ambit of the liberal economic order. However, the emergence of China and India as economic powerhouses has begun to generate a new set of problems.[4] A growing perception in the United States that "relative gains" in the last couple of decades have gone largely in favor of China and increasingly in favor of India has resulted in strong second thoughts about globalization.[5] The rapid ascent of China, which is expected to overtake the United States in aggregate size by 2020, the economic slowdown in the West after the recent recession, and the vulnerabilities arising from the financial interdependence with China have deeply divided Washington on how best to cope with the new challenges. Unlike China, India is not seen as a proximate economic threat, given its slower growth rates and lesser dependence on exports. Yet New Delhi, like Beijing, is committed to strategic autonomy and independent foreign policy and has made it difficult for those in Washington seeking to partner with India in managing the rise of China. Given the growing weight of the Chinese and Indian economies, the United States can't deal with China in the manner in which it contained the Soviet Union, nor can it treat India the way it treats other friends and allies in Asia.

The contradictions are even sharper at the political level. The growth in Chinese military power and its increasing political influence on its Asian periphery have begun to raise fundamental questions about the future of U.S. primacy in Asia and the sustainability of its regional alliances. Here again, China is the main challenge for the United States, and India is a potential strategic partner. As Tellis argues:

> While the threat of a future power transition conditions American attitudes toward China today—attitudes that are likely to become more rivalrous and even hostile as Chinese power grows more comprehensively—India's potential to become a significant U.S. partner, either explicit or tacit, only increases. Given the proximity of the two Asian giants, China's rise could undermine India's security, autonomy, and standing, even before the United States is affected directly.[6]

Tellis goes on to argue that the mutual wariness between Washington and Beijing and the prospect of a power transition at the core of the global system "increases the strategic affinity between the United States and India in a way that is hard to replicate in the case of China and the United States." The idea of a "natural alliance" between India and the United States in response to China's rise is also reinforced by the shared democratic values between

New Delhi and Washington, in sharp contrast to Beijing's authoritarian political system. Yet the United States has found it difficult to privilege relations with India over those with China. Tellis points to the irony marking U.S. relations with China and India: "Despite fears and suspicions being greater in the U.S.–China relationship, this interaction has turned out to be the more important of the two dyads." In relation to China, the United States cannot afford a breakdown, because the consequences could be so disastrous for Washington and the world economy. In contrast, the engagement with India, Tellis argues, "while desirable and important, generally falls short of being compelling because neither Washington nor New Delhi has yet been able to deepen the relationship to a point where a failure of the partnership would end up costing both sides dearly."[7]

The U.S. dilemmas vis-à-vis China and India have been reflected in the shifting trendlines in Washington's engagement with Beijing and New Delhi since the turn of the century. The United States has tended to oscillate between different policies in response to the changing distribution of power in Asia and the Indo-Pacific.[8] One option has been to pick sides, à la *Samudra Manthan*, between China and India and move the balance between them in a preferred direction. The policy under George W. Bush has been widely seen as tilting toward India in order to limit the Chinese power in Asia. Robert Blackwill, who was George Bush's first envoy to India during 2001–2003 and had an important role in shaping the new partnership, explained how Bush saw China and India:

> President George W. Bush based his transformation of U.S.–India relations on the core strategic principle of democratic India as a key factor in balancing the rise of Chinese power. To be clear, this was not based on the concept of containing China. As you know, there is no better way to clear a room of Indian strategists than to advocate containing China. Rather, it centered on the idea that the United States and India in the decades ahead both had enormous equities in promoting responsible international policies on the part of China and that deep U.S.–India bilateral cooperation in that respect was in the vital national interests of both countries. It was with this strategic paradigm in mind that the Bush administration treated India with at least as much importance as China.[9]

The results of this new approach came into view as the United States sought to end India's prolonged atomic isolation through a civil nuclear initiative and a ten-year framework for defense cooperation, both signed in 2005. Yet it was quite clear that there was no widespread consensus within the U.S. foreign policy establishment on changing the nuclear rules—both domestic and international—exclusively for India. There was even less agreement that the Indo-U.S. engagement ought to be premised on the need to balance China. India was too wedded to strategic autonomy, some in the U.S. argued, for Delhi to align with Washington against Beijing. The search for a consensus in the United States meant diluting the terms of the civilian nuclear initiative and loading it with some conditionalities. This, in turn, reduced the strategic value of the deal in the eyes of the Indian establishment. Nevertheless, the civil nuclear initiative and expanding bilateral defense cooperation set the stage for a stronger partnership between Washington and New Delhi. The improved understandings with India did not mean the U.S. ties with China would go south. While Beijing was wary of the warming Indo-U.S. ties, the Bush administration succeeded in stabilizing the U.S. relationship with Beijing.

The Obama administration's initial approach to China, however, raised many concerns in India. New Delhi perceived the Obama administration as being far too deferential to China and nurturing the illusion that accommodating Beijing's core interests would make Beijing a preferred partner of Washington on all global and regional issues. This approach was reflected in the joint communiqué issued at the end of President Obama's visit to China in November 2009. While the Obama administration never used the term "G2," New Delhi believed that the significant intellectual support for the idea in Washington marked a change in the tone and tenor of the U.S. debate on China.[10] India feared that the antipathy among the Democrats and liberals to balance of power politics and the realism of others, who recognized the need to avoid confronting China amid the new weakness of the United States, marked a fresh turn in U.S. policy toward Asia.[11] India reacted strongly to the joint statement by Hu Jintao and Barack Obama that suggested a "supervisory" role for China in the maintenance of peace and order in South Asia.[12] Responding to the Indian protests,[13] Obama made amends a few days later when he hosted Prime Minister Manmohan Singh at the White House and affirmed India's role as a major "Asian power."[14] Since then, the United States has gone out of its way to reassure India of its commitment to build on the strategic partnership launched during the Bush years. But in New Delhi, Washington's dilemmas in dealing with China were too visible to miss.[15]

If President Obama began his tenure in the White House by trying to accommodate China, he was soon affirming the U.S. determination to sustain American primacy in Asia through a number of new initiatives. These included strengthening U.S. alliances in Asia, rebalancing the global military posture toward the Asia-Pacific, and devising a new operational doctrine to cope with the expansion of Chinese power. U.S. Defense Secretary Leon Panetta described India as the "lynchpin" of the new strategy: "We will expand our military partnerships and our presence in the arc extending from the Western Pacific and East Asia into the Indian Ocean region and South Asia. Defense cooperation with India is a linchpin in this strategy. India is one of the largest and most dynamic countries in the region and the world, with one of the most capable militaries. India also shares with the United States a strong commitment to a set of principles that help maintain international security and prosperity."[16] If Obama's pivot to Asia marked a significant turn in U.S. policy and seemed to reemphasize the strategic importance of India, Delhi was now acutely conscious of the volatility in U.S.-China relations and their sensitivity to the shifting power balance between Washington and Beijing. Skeptics in Delhi wonder if Washington will be able to sustain its new pivot to Asia and worry that the American temptations for a bilateral strategic understanding with China are real and enduring.

While the United States was debating the notion of a G2, the Chinese came up with their own idea on how to harmonize Beijing's interests with those of America. This involved the classical notion of "spheres of influence." In the telling of Admiral Timothy Keating, former U.S. commander in chief of the Pacific Command, a Chinese general, half in jest, offered a deal on separating the American and Chinese spheres of influence in the Indo-Pacific. "You, the U.S., take Hawaii East, and we, China, will take Hawaii West and the Indian Ocean. Then you will not need to come to the Western Pacific and the Indian Ocean, and we will not need to go to the Eastern Pacific. If anything happens there, you can let us know, and if something happens here, we will let you know," Keating recalled, according to an Indian reporter covering his discussions in India in May 2009.[17] While fanciful at one level, the idea of dividing up the Pacific into spheres of influence conforms to a long tradition in great-power politics. Nor is there a surprise that as a rising power China would want to push the U.S. naval presence farther away from its coastal waters and the first island chain that encloses them. The United States in turn is determined, at the current juncture, to maintain its forward naval presence in the western Pacific. If China's power rises rapidly and the domestic constraints on the U.S. ability to maintain its forward presence in Asia multiply, the case for America sharing the leadership with China or dividing the world into spheres of influence are likely to emerge as prudent policy alternatives in Washington.

"Offshore balancing" is yet another idea in the U.S. debate on the Indo-Pacific. Christopher Layne has argued that "other major powers in Asia—Japan, Russia, India—have a much more immediate interest in stopping a rising China in their midst than does the United States." He goes on to suggest that Washington has the "option of staying out of East Asian security rivalries (at least initially) and forcing Beijing's neighbors to assume the risks and costs of stopping China from attaining regional hegemony." He proposes that the United States can afford to "keep its forces in an over-the-horizon posture with respect to East Asia and limit itself to a backstopping role in the unlikely event that the regional balance of power falters." Layne insists that "by pulling back from its hegemonic role in East Asia and adopting an offshore balancing strategy, the United States could better preserve its relative power and strategic influence. It could stand on the sidelines while that region's great powers enervate themselves by engaging in security competition."[18] While the strategy of offshore balancing might be an attractive option that facilitates better balance between America's ends and means in the Indo-Pacific, it is an approach that has had little resonance in contemporary American strategic culture. But the changing debate on China in Washington during the Obama administration underlined a new reality. The strategy of offshore balancing would necessarily involve the contingency of the United States balancing India as well. This prospect is not forgotten in New Delhi, as sections of its strategic community refuse to forget the U.S. dispatch of the USS *Enterprise* during India's war to liberate Bangladesh. The Indian naval discourse, too, continues to maintain residual opposition to "external" forces in the Indian Ocean.

INDIA'S AMBIVALENCE

The United States is not the only power that is ambivalent about dealing with the other two elements of the strategic triangle. The ambivalence of India, as the weakest power among the three, is far more acute. During 1998–2008, the Indian political leadership was quite bold in first reaching out to the United States in search of reconciliation during the Clinton years and building on the opportunities offered by the Bush administration. But the implementation of the civil nuclear initiative and more broadly the building of a strategic partnership with the United States ran into immense political opposition in India from both ends of the political spectrum, the ideological left and the opportunist right. If the political purpose of the civil nuclear initiative was to slay the inherited demons of the past that prevented India and the United States from developing a security relationship, the very debate about its terms reinjected a toxic dynamic into the Indian political discourse on the relationship with the United States. Having expended much political capital to implement the civil nuclear initiative, the Manmohan Singh government, which returned to power in May 2009, has found it difficult to vigorously pursue a more ambitious agenda of strategic cooperation with the United States. In addition, the confidential documents released by WikiLeaks on the negotiations with the United States created a public atmosphere in New Delhi that was not conducive to bold moves toward the United States. New Delhi's inability to stop the Indian parliament from passing a law on civil nuclear liability that was not in tune with the international practice has made it difficult for private, including U.S., companies to take full advantage of the civil nuclear initiative. The narrow technical approach adopted by the Indian ministry of defense in the purchase of 126 fighter aircraft resulted in the exclusion of bids by two U.S. companies—Boeing and Lockheed. All these developments suggested that Indo-U.S. relations might have hit a plateau amid the lack of elite consensus within Delhi on how to move forward with Washington and generated considerable disappointment in sections of the American policy community.[19]

Meanwhile, the Obama administration's special outreach to China in the first year of its tenure made India aware of the new imperatives in Washington to find a modus vivendi with Beijing. Recognizing the U.S.

vulnerabilities vis-à-vis China, New Delhi was loath to be left hanging loose amid a potential Sino-U.S. condominium in Asia. Shyam Saran, the Indian prime minister's special envoy and an old China hand, pointed in February 2009 to

> an apparent willingness on the part of the U.S. to accommodate China's regional and global interests as a price to be paid for China refraining from tipping the U.S. into a full blown economic and financial crisis through its own policy interventions and, hopefully, supporting U.S. economic recovery. China is being invited to participate in the fashioning of new global governance structures and have a major voice in the management, if not resolution, of major regional conflicts.

While adding that Beijing had not yet shown its hand, Saran speculated on possible options for India in the new international context:

> It should be our objective to encourage the trend toward a more diffused and diversified international order. This fits in well with our own instinctive preference for a multipolar world, which includes a multipolar Asia. We will need to work with other powers who share this objective. Our effort should be to build coalitions on different issues of shared concern and not primarily rely on a more limited range of strategic relationships.[20]

Saran's simultaneous emphasis on a "multipolar world" and a "multipolar Asia" underlined the return of Indian wariness about too close an alignment with the United States and fears of Chinese dominance over Asia. Speaking a year later on the same subject, Saran was pleased that a potentially threatening G2 had not materialized but was insistent that India's policy is about "engaging with all major powers, but aligning with none."[21] Saran added that India's hedging strategy since the advent of the Obama administration had been successful. "The prospect for a Sino-US condominium has receded for the time being but there remains the opposite danger of growing tensions instead between the two countries. Neither condominium nor confrontation between the two is in India's interest."[22] As tensions between the United States and China rose during 2011–2012 and the Obama administration renewed the Bush emphasis on a strategic partnership with India, Delhi was reluctant to be seen at home or in Asia as aligning with the United States against China. The Indian defence establishment was eager to deepen bilateral defense cooperation with Washington but was reluctant to be drawn into the U.S. alliance system and expressed its discomfort at the growing confrontation between United States and China.[23]

If India was going to retain a measure of autonomy in dealing with the changing geopolitical landscape in Asia, reassuring Beijing that it would not join a U.S. alliance was an important element of New Delhi's strategy. The desire to avoid a confrontation with Beijing has not, however, ended India's many strategic dilemmas vis-à-vis China. In fact, many bilateral conflicts—relating to the boundary, Tibet, and Kashmir—intensified at the end of the 2000s. India's discomfort with China's rising power in the subcontinent has been matched by New Delhi's resentment at Beijing's attempts to limit India's international aspirations—whether it was in ending its nuclear isolation or becoming a permanent member of the UN Security Council. India's long list of political and security grievances against China have meanwhile acquired a new background—a rapidly expanding trade relationship that hit $74 billion in 2011. In India, the deepening economic partnership has created new and positive stakeholders in the nation's China policy, which traditionally has been dominated by the security establishment. In many ways, New Delhi's strategic dilemma vis-à-vis Beijing has begun to resemble that of the United States—how to benefit from China's economic rise and simultaneously limit the strategic consequences of Beijing's growing military power. Like the United States, India wants to prevent China from dominating Asia but would like to avoid the risks inherent in that strategy. India, however, has more difficulties than the United States in coping with a rising China. It is not only the weakest of the three powers, but also confronts all the vulnerabilities arising out of its geographic proximity to China. As U.S.-Chinese relations enter an uncertain phase, India finds itself torn between competing ideological impulses—enduring anti-Western nationalism, the rediscovery of Asianism, the attractions of non-alignment and neutralism, and the virtues of realpolitik.[24] Whatever the public debate on India's options toward the changing U.S.-China relationship may be, India's policy trajectory has largely followed the realpolitik impulse of engaging both Washington and Beijing, strengthening India's strategic capabilities in collaboration with the United States, finding ways to close the gap with China, avoiding a premature confrontation with Beijing, and exploring the possibilities for altering China's approach to India. There is no denying, however, the execution of this strategy is indeed difficult and that it often sends mixed signals to external and domestic audiences.[25]

CHINA'S HAND

Within the strategic triangle, there is no doubt that China's position has rapidly improved in the first decade of the twenty-first century. It has begun to close the strategic gap with the United States and widen the gap with India. Beijing has also drawn both countries into tighter economic interdependence, thereby limiting their political options of confronting China. This in turn has opened up room for Chinese assertiveness in the Indo-Pacific. Beijing has felt strong enough to reject Washington's outreach under Obama for a shared leadership of the world and felt free to confront the rest of Asia on a range of issues. To be sure, Beijing's worldview is not monolithic; its foreign policy elite is divided on how to deal with a changing world amid the rise of Chinese power.[26] Nor is China's foreign policy unconstrained by domestic political wrangling. Yet its actions in recent years vis-à-vis the United States underline a new sense of self-assurance and determination to set its own terms for engagement.

While China was wary of the American outreach to India, Beijing seemed quite confident about the limits to U.S.-India strategic partnership and its consequences for China. An editorial in China's *Global Times* in June 2009 acknowledged India's growing power potential but dismissed New Delhi's ability to leverage it in the bilateral relations with Beijing by avoiding a closer strategic partnership with the United States:

India can't actually compete with China in a number of areas, like international influence, overall national power and economic scale. India has apparently not realized this. Indian politicians these days seem to think their country would be doing China a huge favor simply by not joining the "ring around China" established by the U.S. and Japan. India's growing power would have a significant impact on the balance of this equation, which has led India to think that fear and gratitude for its restraint will cause China to defer to it on territorial disputes. But this is wishful thinking, as China won't make any compromises in its border dispute with India. And while China wishes to coexist peacefully with India, this desire isn't born out of fear.[27]

When Obama visited India in November 2010, he reaffirmed the U.S. commitment to a deeper bilateral strategic partnership, celebrated India's democratic virtues, endorsed India's full membership in the global non-proliferation regime, supported its candidacy for a permanent seat in the UN Security Council, and called on it to play a larger role in Asia and the Pacific. Obama's visit, however, did not ring alarm bells in Beijing. "The title of 'the biggest democratic nation' looks like a glass of red wine enjoyed together by India and the West. But it doesn't generate anything substantial that is of India's national interests. With a huge population and much work left to be done in developing the economy, perhaps India won't get too drunk to act superior in front of China, because such superiority will delight India much less than it delights the West."[28] Some Chinese analysts are also confident that while Obama's strategic power play with India might be real, it is not strong enough at this juncture to undermine the centrality of China in the American calculus. "Seemingly, the U.S. and India are right now singing a duet, echoing each other. Even so, it is too early to conclude that Obama would satisfy India's expectations better and more concretely than, say, the previous Bush administration. And it is absurd to say Obama's whirlwind tour to India is proof that the U.S. strategic focus has been shifted from Beijing to New Delhi."[29]

Visiting New Delhi a few weeks after Obama, the Chinese premier, Wen Jiabao, was keen to improve bilateral relations with India and address the immediate bilateral disputes relating to Kashmir visas and trade disputes. But on the big items of interest to India, there was little give from Wen. His support for India's permanent membership in the UN Security Council was lukewarm at best, and he made no mention of backing India's desire to become a full member of the nonproliferation regime. There was no pullback from the matching civil nuclear initiative that China had offered Pakistan following the one between Washington and New Delhi. Wen was the only major leader visiting India in the second half of 2010 who did not publicly call on Pakistan to eliminate the sources of international terrorism on its soil. While Wen's visit underlined the importance of the Sino-Indian relationship, it also brought into relief the growing convergence of interests in the Indo-Pacific between New Delhi and Washington and the difficulty of bridging the strategic differences between India and China.[30] On issues ranging from Kashmir to nonproliferation, from terrorism to India's global aspirations, Washington has become far more empathetic than Beijing to Delhi's core national security interests.

China, however, could alter its policies toward either India or the United States. It could accommodate the concerns of one or the other to preempt the deepening of the U.S.-Indian partnership. Although China had rejected the G2 concept in the early months of the Obama administration, Beijing could recalibrate its policy toward Washington if circumstances warrant it. For China, the question of a strategic partnership with the United States was not about the principle, but the terms. In mid 2012, China's top diplomat, State Councilor Dai Bingguo, who has been Beijing's major interlocutor with both Washington and Delhi, outlined his alternative to the U.S. G2 concept, the so-called "C2." Summarizing Dai's speech at the fourth round of the U.S.-China Strategic and Economic Dialogue in Beijing, the Ministry of Foreign Affairs said, "He pointed out that China and the U.S. are not seeking a G2 and will not dominate the world or engage in conflict or confrontation. But China and the U.S. can build a C2 to strengthen communications, coordination and cooperation and try to explore a brand new pattern of peaceful coexistence, close cooperation and common development."[31] China could also recraft its policy toward India and prevent tighter bonds between Delhi and Washington. China's strategic community often talks about India's strong identity as a non-aligned nation and its reluctance to subordinate its foreign policy autonomy to the United States. In a visit to New Delhi in early 2012, Dai teased his Indian interlocutors with the talk of a "golden era" at hand in the bilateral relations.[32]

CHURNING THE INDO-PACIFIC

The rapid rise of Chinese military power has put India and the United States in a challenging situation. On the one hand they need to draw closer to structure a sustainable balance of power in the Indo-Pacific. On the other hand, both New Delhi and Washington are apprehensive about provoking China and are tempted to find their own separate accommodation with Beijing. There could be a tipping point at which Beijing's growing assertiveness could compel India and the United States to abandon their current strategic inhibitions to build a solid operational security partnership in the Indian and Pacific Oceans. The impulse for this could emerge from the unfolding maritime dynamic in the Indo-Pacific. The expansion of Chinese naval capabilities, the slower accretion of Indian maritime strength and the pressures on the United States to maintain a substantive forward presence despite fiscal austerity at home underline the unfolding power-shift in the Indo-Pacific. The irony of the expansion of Asian navies at a time when their Western counterparts are shrinking has not been lost on historians.[33] Back in the fifteenth century, as China dismantled its maritime infrastructure, the West won the world through its naval rise. In the twenty-first century, a potential reversal of roles might be unfolding before our eyes. The scale and significance of the current redistribution of power and challenge of its peaceful management is put succinctly by Kaplan. He underlines the many power transitions in the Asian littoral since the West entered the waters of the Indian and western Pacific in the fifteenth century: from the Portuguese to the Dutch, from the Dutch to the British, and the British to American. "Therefore the peaceful transition away from American unipolarity at sea—and toward an American-Indian-Chinese condominium of sorts—would be the first of its kind. Rather than an abdication of responsibility, it will instead leave the Indian and Western Pacific Oceans in the free and accountable hands of indigenous nations for the first time in 500 years," Kaplan concludes.[34]

On the face of it, the common interests at sea should encourage New Delhi, Beijing, and Washington to develop either cooperative approaches to maritime security or at least agree on a division of labor in the vast Indo-Pacific theater.[35] But as the United States loses its dominance of the maritime commons, it might not be easy to structure a peaceful transition to an alternative system in the emerging multipolar world.[36] Nevertheless, the Obama administration signaled its interest in a trilateral dialogue with China and India. In a speech at Chennai in July 2011 welcoming a larger Indian role in Asia, Secretary of State Hillary Clinton said: "We are also committed to a strong, constructive relationship among India, the United States, and China. Now, we know this will not always be easy. There are important matters on which we all disagree, one with the other. But we do have significant areas of common interest. We could begin by focusing on violent extremism, which threatens people on all—in all of our countries. Ultimately, if we want to address, manage, or solve some of the most pressing issues of the twenty-first century, India, China, and the United States will have to coordinate our efforts."[37] India has welcomed this approach, by highlighting its own interests in a cooperative relationship with China. Speaking to an American audience in February 2012, the Indian foreign secretary, Ranjan Mathai, said,

> China is our largest neighbor, a major country in the Asia-Pacific region and a country with great global influence. We have considerable challenges in our relationship, but also enormous opportunities for mutually beneficial partnership at the bilateral and global levels. We will continue to invest in building a stable and cooperative relationship with China that is mutually beneficial, and also a source of regional stability and prosperity. There are a number of global and regional challenges on which India, China, and the United States must work together. We welcome the proposal Secretary Clinton made last July in New Delhi for a trilateral dialogue between India, China, and the United States.[38]

China has not responded positively to Clinton's proposal; the diplomatic assessment in Washington and New Delhi is that Beijing is not ready for such a forum and continues to treat its relationship with the United States as being in a category of its own.[39]

While the search for trilateral cooperation is likely to continue, maritime tension between China on the one hand and the United States and its allies and friends in the Western Pacific on the other hand began to boil over in 2010–2012. Chinese naval and fishing vessels sought to disrupt civilian and military activity of the United States, Japan, South Korea, the Philippines, and Vietnam. Beijing has also been more assertive in affirming its claims in territorial disputes with its neighbors. This has resulted in widespread doubts about the peaceful rise of China and deep concerns about its intentions. To be sure, China has its own historical narrative on the maritime territorial disputes with its neighbors. Beijing also has its own interpretation of the provisions of the UN Convention on the Law of the Sea in relation to freedom of navigation and the innocent passage of naval vessels in the territorial waters and the exclusive economic zones.[40] What matters is not so much the legitimacy of the Chinese claims and actions,

C. RAJA MOHAN

but its consequences for great-power balance in the waters of the western Pacific. Those can only get more negative, amid the U.S. affirmation of an interest in China's maritime disputes with its neighbors, an emphasis on the freedom of navigation in the waters of East Asia, and a political commitment to maintain a forward presence. Washington is strengthening its bilateral alliances, expanding its network of maritime partnerships, and deploying a larger portion of its forces to the Asian waters. With its growing naval capabilities and few direct quarrels with the United States, New Delhi is an attractive partner for the United States. Not surprisingly, Washington has called for greater Indian activism in the western Pacific and Indian Oceans.

At the same time, the maritime friction between Beijing and New Delhi has grown as China expands its influence in the Indian Ocean and India seeks to raise its profile in the Western Pacific. Beijing does not immediately threaten India's standing in the Indian Ocean, given the long logistical lines that China must develop, but its long-term intentions are a matter of concern to New Delhi. For now, India's focus has been on consolidating its natural strategic advantages in the Indian Ocean littoral. Sections of the Indian strategic community do see a small window of opportunity for establishing maritime security cooperation with China before a long-term threat materializes. Pointing to the current coexistence of the elements of convergence and divergence in the maritime interests of New Delhi and Beijing, an officer of the Indian navy argues that "since China's naval presence in the IO is relatively nascent the possible outcomes are nearly balanced in terms of their probability of occurrence. While preparedness and deterrence would remain the key pillars of India's maritime strategy, this presents an opportunity to create incentives for maritime cooperation. The window of opportunity would recede rapidly as China increases its national power in relation to India, and firms up its naval presence in the IO."[41] Although China and India have agreed to launch a maritime dialogue in 2012, it will be a while before it becomes substantive and productive.

New Delhi also has strategic aspirations to become a Pacific power and has stepped up its maritime engagement with the East Asian countries. As tensions rose in the South China Sea since 2010, India strongly affirmed its support to the principle of freedom of navigation in the contested

251

waters, signaled empathy with the Philippines, and declared its commitment to deepen the strategic partnership with Vietnam. Skeptics, however, point to the many geographic, material, and psychological constraints on New Delhi's current strategy in the Pacific. "In building relationships throughout the Asia Pacific, particularly with the United States and its allies, India would need to overcome the limitations of its traditionally defensive strategic thinking, which still work against its ability to project power and influence in the region."[42] The proposition that deeper partnership with the United States and its allies is critical to India's influence in the Pacific brings us to a deeper paradox. New Delhi is acutely aware of the reality of the widening strategic gap with Beijing (China's GDP and defense spending in 2011 were nearly four times that of India). New Delhi will find it increasingly difficult to match Beijing only through the mobilization of internal resources; it will need strong cooperation from the United States. But at the same time, a deeper military partnership with the United States has other consequences vis-à-vis China that are hard for New Delhi to ignore. As a result, there has been considerable strategic hesitation in New Delhi in regard to Washington.

Despite considerable advance in bilateral defense cooperation during the 2000s, India and the United States are some distance away from developing a consequential strategic partnership at the operational level in the Indo-Pacific. Admiral Robert Willard told the U.S. Congress in the early summer of 2011 that India's concerns for strategic autonomy were among the reasons for the underperformance of the bilateral defense cooperation. "The U.S.–India relationship remains challenged by a degree of suspicion fuelled by Cold War–influenced perceptions, complicated Indian political and bureaucratic processes, and the U.S.–Pakistan relationship," Willard said.[43] Besides New Delhi's problem with the U.S.-Pakistani relationship, India continues to find itself at odds with the United States in the Middle East, especially in relation to Iran. Given its large Muslim minority at home, India has always been unwilling to be on the American side in Washington's confrontations with the Muslim nations of the Middle East. As a series of crises erupted in the Middle East during 2011, India was reluctant to support Western intervention in Libya, the pressure on the Assad regime in Syria, and the U.S. and European sanctions against Iran. In the Middle East, India's default political positions are closer to those of Beijing than those of Washington. The Indo-U.S. divergence on the central conflict zone in the Indian Ocean—the Middle East—underlines the enduring political difficulties in constructing a comprehensive strategic partnership between Washington and New Delhi. Tellis points to the potential consequences of India's ambivalence:

> While the United States would undoubtedly value deeper cooperation—and in fact craves … it—India's traditional yearning for strategic autonomy, the inability of its leaders and elites to carry a consensus in favor of a stronger affiliation, and the failure of its government to pursue consistent and coherent policies vis-à-vis Washington—the travails of a postcolonial democracy in a complex society—all end up exposing India to greater risk in the face of rising Chinese power.

Although the idea of a strong maritime alliance with the West seems a recent and controversial idea in India, it can be traced back to India's formative years. Surveying the postwar situation on the eve of Indian independence, Panikkar, the early Indian navalist, emphasized the centrality of India's maritime interests and underlined the imperative of working with the West to improve its position:

> India is a maritime state with [a] predominance of interests on the sea. She is the one true Rimland, whose continental affiliations are comparatively negligible. From the continental point of view of Eurasia, she is only an abutting corner, walled off by impassable mountains. From the maritime point of view, she dominates the Indian Ocean. . . . To the maritime state system, India is invaluable. To the continental system she is unimportant.[44]

As he called for a long-term, treaty-based partnership between India and the West, Panikkar argued that the

> survival of the Rimland, which extends from Britain to Indonesia, depends on its organization as a close alliance of maritime states. Such an alliance means the creation of a Western bloc in Europe and with Great Britain in the center, and an organization of the Indian Ocean area with India as its center. . . . The alliance of a free and independent India with Britain is, therefore, not only of the utmost importance to the two countries, but also to the entire Rimland of the Eurasian continent.[45]

The partnership he calls for is comprehensive—political, economic, and military—and would involve British support for the emergence of India as an industrial and technological power. In the defense front, it would involve the integration of the defense of the Indian Ocean with that of India.

> The area of Indian defense should include all maritime interests this side of … Suez, and should extend to the Netherlands East Indies. The independence and integrity of the countries within this area should be a fundamental article of the political treaty between England and India. A joint declaration of the common interest in this area—an Indo-British Monroe Doctrine for the Indian Ocean region with a good neighbor policy toward the units—should be the first fruits of the alliance.[46]

Panikkar insists that "in regard to this area, Britain will not enter into agreements without the knowledge of India and her agreement."[47] He goes into the details of the potential division of labor within this alliance. "The organization of the military, air, and naval forces for the security of the region will be primarily the responsibility of India"; Britain will help train the forces and boost the war potential of India, and "will also make available to India the necessary naval and air bases within the region such as Socotra, Mauritius, and Penang which may be agreed upon as being necessary for joint defense."[48]

Panikkar's ambitious vision had little chance of being realized amid the partition of the subcontinent and the logic of the Cold War, which pitted India against Anglo-American power. The evolution of India's Cold War foreign policy discourse, which emphasized nonalignment as a philosophical principle and focused on an alignment with Moscow when it came to realpolitik, had no room for any conception of a security partnership with the West. Yet Panikkar's ideas appear to be coming back into play. Replace "Britain" with the "United States" and the "Indian Ocean" with the "Indo-Pacific," and we find the resonance of Panikkar's ideas for the contemporary Indo-U.S. engagement in the maritime domain. Panikkar's proposal that maritime states must work together is not very different from the kind of political impulses that guided the Bush administration's outreach to India in 2001–2008. While the defense relationship has stalled somewhat since then, there is no mistaking the fact that U.S.–Indian defense relations are at a much higher level than either Sino-Indian or Sino-American defense exchanges. Maritime security has figured as a major priority in the evolution of the bilateral relationship since the Bush years. In 2011, Washington and New Delhi began a new conversation on elevating their maritime security cooperation that includes an emphasis on joint operations that go beyond mere joint exercises, improving shared maritime domain awareness, assisting friendly nations in the littoral to improve their naval capabilities, and working together to promote maritime security.

Conditions for more accelerated Indo-U.S. maritime cooperation could emerge if New Delhi sheds its ambivalence toward Washington, the United States offers a more ambitious framework for maritime cooperation, and China overplays its hand with India. While New Delhi recognizes the importance of a partnership with the United States in balancing China, it remains concerned about being "played." Responding to the proposition that the United States must be a "sea-based balancer" and an "honest broker" between India and China, Shivshankar Menon said:

> Which major power would not like to play the role of balancer, given the chance? It's cheaper and easier and leaves the real work to the powers being balanced. For a superpower that is refocusing on Asia, but finding the landscape considerably changed while she was preoccupied with Iraq and Afghanistan, this would naturally be an attractive option. But is it likely that two emerging states like India and China, with old traditions of statecraft, would allow themselves to remain the objects of someone else's policy, no matter how elegantly expressed? I think not.[49]

While India's domestic politics and bureaucratic nitpicking in both capitals are indeed major concerns, the United States needs to redefine the framework of maritime cooperation with India. Panikkar's vision involved a very ambitious, independent role for India in the Indian Ocean in coordination with the West. The Indo-U.S. defense framework was conceived at the peak of the American unipolar moment in 2005. Readjusting it to the new realities in the Indo-Pacific will demand a different approach that will emphasize the rapid boosting of Indian naval capabilities, strengthen its ability to operate in distant corners of the Indo-Pacific, and provide a balance to China's maritime ambitions.

Enthusiasts for a stronger partnership with India in the United States have sought to address New Delhi's concerns about the implications of "interoperability" to India's sovereignty and strategic autonomy. Senator John McCain argues that "the opposite is true. The decision about *whether* to cooperate with the United States will always rest with India's democratic leaders; greater interoperability simply creates more options for *how* to cooperate if India chooses to do so" (McCain's emphasis). McCain goes on to propose that

> with political will on both sides, there is no reason why we cannot develop a joint U.S.-Indian concept of operations for both the Indian and Pacific Oceans. There is no reason why we cannot construct a network of intelligence sharing that creates a common picture of our common strategic challenges—on land, at sea, in space, and in cyberspace. There is no reason why India cannot post more officers at higher levels within PACOM and CENTCOM [United States Pacific Command and United States Central Command], with corresponding increases in representation for U.S. officers at India's commands. And there is no reason why we cannot work to facilitate India's deployment of advanced defense capabilities, such as nuclear submarines, aircraft carriers, missile defense architecture, as well as India's inclusion in the development of the Joint Strike Fighter.[50]

Washington and New Delhi might have to find exceptional solutions to move their defense cooperation to a higher level. The "political will" that McCain talks of can emerge out of either strong convictions of the leadership—as we saw in the case of George W. Bush in 2001–2009—or circumstances on the ground that help overcome ideological and other inhibitions for cooperation—as in Jawaharlal Nehru's request to President Kennedy for immediate and significant military assistance to cope with the Chinese attack on India's borders in 1962. Bush's sweeping vision for Indo-U.S. strategic cooperation was rooted in an assessment of the potential threat over the longer term from a rising China. New Delhi's own long-standing search for strategic parity with Beijing seemed to dovetail with the Bush vision. But there were big enough constituencies in both capitals that either questioned these perceptions or had other, more pressing, policy priorities. As a result, the construction of the bilateral relationship moved at a much slower pace than anticipated. But as China's power rose rapidly during the 2010s—some have called it China's golden decade[51]—Beijing's assertiveness toward Washington and New Delhi has been on the rise. There are good short-term calculations in both the United States and India to avoid a confrontation with China and deepen cooperation wherever possible. There are even better reasons for Washington and New Delhi to pool their resources in order to cope with the long-term consequences of a rising China.

At the same time, there is healthy recognition in Washington and New Delhi of the enormous difficulties in constraining Chinese power. Even as he called for a strong naval partnership with the West in the 1940s, Panikkar recognized the importance of addressing Beijing's concerns even at a time when China was in deep disarray. Nehru's decision to befriend Communist China was rooted in this recognition. After decades of demonizing China, many in India are today coming to terms with the need to address China's legitimate interests. In the United States, too, as concerns about a Chinese threat grow, there is an acute awareness of the dangers of confronting China, the need to befriend it and find a new basis for enduring cooperation. Just as former national security adviser Zbigniew Brzezinski was among the first to articulate the case for a G2, another foreign policy savant, former secretary of state Henry Kissinger, emphasized the importance of Sino-U.S. "co-evolution" in ensuring global stability in the twenty-first century.[52]

The real challenge for New Delhi and Washington will come in judging China's legitimate interests, how far they must go in accommodating these interests, and where they must draw a line. The judgments on these issues are contingent upon the international circumstances, domestic political dynamics, and the fluid nature of the consensus within the foreign policy elites in Washington and New Delhi. As China's position vis-à-vis India and the United States continues to improve, Beijing gains a decisive influence on the evolution of the strategic triangle. China could certainly tempt the United States into a modus vivendi—either through burden sharing or joint management—in the Indo-Pacific. Beijing could offer a genuine transformation of the ties with New Delhi—by resolving the boundary dispute with India, taking a more balanced approach to its relations with New Delhi and Islamabad, and agreeing to support India's larger global aspirations. It is also possible to visualize consultation and cooperation among Washington, Beijing, and New Delhi in the management of the Indo-Pacific maritime commons. There are no signs that Beijing is ready to make bold offers to either Washington and or New Delhi or invite them both into trilateral cooperation. Beijing also has options to retaliate against what it might construe as a joint effort by New Delhi and Washington to contain China.

The story of the *Samudra Manthan* has barely begun as the maritime imperatives of India, China, and the United States conflate in the Indo-Pacific. As in the myth of the *Samudra Manthan*, the evolution of the triangular dynamic between New Delhi, Beijing, and Washington would produce many fascinating twists and turns. For the moment, though, the interests of India and the United States might be in greater convergence than with those of China. New Delhi and Washington, however, have big problems translating that congruence into an effective coalition. China has more cards to play and is in a position to limit, delay, or disrupt the emergence of a strategic maritime partnership between Washington and New Delhi. Large democracies such as the United States and India often falter in coping effectively, and in time, with major national security challenges. But when confronted with major crises, they also surprise themselves and the world with resilience and resolve. The redistribution of seapower in the Indo-Pacific will surely test the political sagacity and strategic judgment of the leaders in Washington, Beijing, and New Delhi in the coming years.

Notes

CHAPTER ONE

1. For a succinct summary of the myth, see Ashok Kumar Bhattacharya, *A Pageant of Indian Culture: Art and Archaeology* (New Delhi: Abhinav, 1995), Chapter 5, 25–30. See also Eleanor Mannikka, *Angkor Wat: Time, Space and Kingship* (Honolulu: University of Hawaii Press, 2000).

2. See, for example, Robyn Meredith, *The Elephant and the Dragon: The Rise of India and China and What It Means for All of Us* (New York: W. W. Norton, 2008); David Smith, *The Dragon and the Elephant: China, India and the New World Order* (London: Profile Books, 2007); Clyde Prestowitz, *Three Billion New Capitalists: The Great Shift of Wealth and Power to the East* (New York: Basic Books, 2005); Tarun Khanna, *Billions of Entrepreneurs: How China and India Are Reshaping Their Futures and Yours* (Cambridge, Mass.: Harvard University Business School Press, 2008). Mohan Malik, *China and India: Great Power Rivals* (Boulder, Colo.: Lynne Rienner, 2011).

3. James R. Holmes and Toshi Yoshihara, "The Influence of Mahan upon China's Maritime Strategy," *Comparative Strategy*, vol. 24, no.1 (January 2005): 23–51; David Scott, "India's Grand Strategy for Indian Ocean: Mahanian Visions," *Asia-Pacific Review*, vol. 13, no. 2 (2006): 97–129.

4. K. M. Panikkar, *India and the Indian Ocean: An Essay on the Influence of Sea Power on Indian History* (London: Allen and Unwin, 1945). The title of his work was similar to Mahan's most popular work, published in 1890: *The Influence of Sea Power Upon History, 1660–1783.*

5. Satyindra Singh, *Blueprint to Bluewater: The Indian Navy, 1951–65* (New Delhi: Lancer, 1992).

6. David Muller, *China's Emergence as a Maritime Power* (Boulder, Colo.: Westview, 1983).

7. Iskander Rehman, "India's Future Aircraft Carrier Force and the Need for Strategic Flexibility," *IDSA Comment*, June 1, 2010 (New Delhi: Institute For Defence Studies and Analyses), available at www.idsa.in/idsacomments/IndiasFutureAircraftCarrier-ForceandtheNeedforStrategicFlexibility_irehman_010610; Richard Bitzinger, "Aircraft Carriers: China's Emerging Maritime Ambitions," *RSIS Commentaries*, 35/2009,

April 7. 2009; www.rsis.edu.sg/publications/Perspective/RSIS0352009.pdf; Reuters, "Factbox: China's Aircraft Carrier Ambitions," December 23, 2010, www.reuters.com/article/2010/12/23/us-china-defence-carriers-factbox-idUSTRE6BM0YG20101223.

8. See, for example, C. Raja Mohan, "India's Great Power Burdens," *Seminar*, no. 581, January 2008; see also Walter C. Ladwig III, "India and Military Power Projection: Will the Land of Gandhi Become a Conventional Military Power?" *Asian Survey*, vol. 50, no. 6 (November/December 2010): 1162–83. For a review of the Chinese debate, see Mark Burles and Abram Shulksy, *Patterns of China's Use of Force: Evidence from History and Doctrinal Writings* (Santa Monica, Calif.: Rand, 2000); Andrew Scobell, *China's Use of Military Force: Beyond the Great Wall and the Long March* (New York: Cambridge University Press, 2003); M. Taylor Fravel, "China's Search for Military Power," *Washington Quarterly*, vol. 31, no. 3 (Summer 2008): 125–41.

9. Indrani Bagchi, "Navy Action in Gulf of Aden Projects Indian Power on High Seas," *Times of India*, November 22, 2008; and Jonathan Adams, "China Projects Naval Power in Pirate Fight," *Christian Science Monitor*, December 30, 2008.

10. See David Scott, "Strategic Imperatives of India as an Emerging Player in Pacific Asia," *International Studies*, vol. 44, no. 2 (April 2007): 123–40; see also Harsh Pant, "India in the Asia-Pacific: Rising Ambitions with an Eye on China," *Asia-Pacific Review*, vol. 14, no. 1 (May 2007): 54–71.

11. Lee Jae-Hyung, "China's Expanding Maritime Ambitions in the Western Pacific and the Indian Ocean," *Contemporary Southeast Asia*, vol. 24, no. 3 (December 2002): 549–68; James Holmes and Toshi Yoshihara, "China's Naval Ambitions in the Indian Ocean," *Journal of Strategic Studies*, vol. 31, no. 3 (June 2008): 367–94.

12. Robert D. Kaplan, "Center Stage for the Twenty-First Century: Power Plays in the Indian Ocean," *Foreign Affairs*, vol. 88, no. 2 (March/April 2009): 18.

13. For example, see Paul Bracken, *Fire in the East: The Rise of Asian Military Power and the Second Nuclear Age* (New York: HarperCollins, 1999).

14. See David Lei, "China's New Multi-faceted Maritime Strategy," *Orbis*, vol. 52, no. 1 (Winter 2008): 139–57; see also Euan Graham, *Japan's Sea Lane Security, 1940–2004: A Matter of Life and Death?* (London: Routledge, 2005).

15. See Peter Cozens, "Some Reflections on Maritime Developments in the Indo-Pacific During the Past Sixty Years," *Maritime Affairs*, vol. 1, no. 1 (Winter 2005): 15–35; see also Stuart Kaye, *Freedom of Navigation in the Indo-Pacific Region* (Canberra: Sea Power Centre, 2008); see also James A. Boutilier, "Maritime Dynamism in Indo-Pacific Region," in *Lloyds MIU Handbook of Maritime Security,* edited by Rupert Herbert-Burns, Sam Bateman, and Peter Lehr (London: Taylor and Francis, 2009), 271–77; Michael Auslin, *Security in the Indo-Pacific Commons: Toward a Regional Strategy* (Washington, D.C.: American Enterprise Institute, 2010); Raoul Heinrichs, Justin Jones, and Rory Medcalf, *Crisis and Confidence: Major Powers and Maritime Security in Indo-Pacific Asia* (Sydney: Lowy Institute, 2011); John F. Bradford, "The Maritime Strategy of the United States: Implications for Indo-Pacific Sea Lanes," *Contemporary Southeast Asia*, vol. 33, no. 2 (2011): 183–208.

16. See, for example, Ellen L. Frost, *Asia's New Regionalism* (London: Lynne Rienner, 2008), especially Chapters 2 and 3. Chapter 2 (21–40) discusses the concept of "re-mapping Asia," and Chapter 3 (41–63) talks about the "legacy of maritime Asia."

17. Shinzo Abe, "Confluence of the Two Seas," speech at the Parliament of India, August 22, 2007, www.mofa.go.jp/region/asia-paci/pmv0708/speech-2.html.

18. In her widely noted essay highlighting the U.S. pivot to Asia in 2011, Secretary of State Hillary Clinton used the phrase, "Indo-Pacific"; see Hillary Clinton, "America's Pacific Century," *Foreign Policy*, November 2011, www.foreignpolicy.com/articles/2011/10/11/americas_pacific_century?page=full.

19. See the essay by former foreign secretary and special envoy to the prime minister, Shyam Saran, "Mapping the Indo-Pacific," *Indian Express*, October 29, 2011, www.indianexpress.com/news/mapping-the-indopacific/867004/0; for a skeptical view, see Rukmani Gupta, "India Puts the Indo in 'Indo-Pacific,'" Asia Times Online, December 8, 2011, www.atimes.com/atimes/South_Asia/ML08Df03.html.

20. For a comprehensive and insightful review of Sino-Indian relations, see John Garver, *Protracted Contest: Sino-Indian Rivalry in the Twentieth Century* (Seattle: University of Washington Press, 2001).

CHAPTER TWO

1. For a comprehensive review, see Tan Chung, ed., *Across the Himalayan Gap: An Indian Quest for Understanding China* (New Delhi: Indira Gandhi National Centre for the Arts, 1998); also Tan Chung, ed., *In the Footsteps of Xuanzang: Tan Yun-Shan and India* (New Delhi: Indira Gandhi National Centre for the Arts, 1999).

2. For a brief review, see William F. Kuracina, "Colonial India and External Affairs: Relating Indian Nationalism to Global Politics," *Journal of Asian and African Studies*, vol. 42, no. 6 (2007): 517–32.

3. See Premen Addy, "South Asia in China's Foreign Policy: A View from the Left," *Journal of Contemporary Asia*, vol. 2, no. 4 (1972): 403–14.

4. Guido Samarani, *Shaping the Future of Asia: Chiang Kai-shek, Nehru and China-India Relations During the Second World War Period* (Lund: Lund University, 2005); see also Avinash Mohan Saklani, "Nehru, Chinag Kai-shek and the Second World War," in *India and China in the Colonial World*, edited by Madhavi Thampi (New Delhi: Social Science Press, 2005), 167–83.

5. Stephen Hay, *Asian Ideas of East and West: Tagore and His Critics in Japan, China and India* (Cambridge Mass.: Harvard University Press, 1970); see also Sisir Kumar Das, "The Controversial Guest: Tagore in China," in Thampi, ed., *India and China in the Colonial World*, 85–125.

6. See for example the critical references to Nehruvian foreign policy legacy in "Indian hegemony continues to harm relations with neighbors," editorial in *People's Daily*, October 14, 2009, http://english.peopledaily.com.cn/90001/90780/91343/6783357.html.

7. Frederic A. Greenhut II, *The Tibetan Frontiers Question from Curzon to the Colombo Conference: An Unresolved Factor in Indo-Sinic Relations* (New Delhi: S. Chand, 1982).

8. Stratfor, "A Revival of Sino-Indian Tensions," June 13, 2009, available at www.realclearworld.com/articles/2009/06/a_revival_of_sinoindian_tensio.html; see also Jeff M. Smith, "The China-India Border Brawl," *Wall Street Journal*, June 24, 2009, http://online.wsj.com/article/SB124578881101543463.html.

9. David Scott, "The Great Power 'Great Game' between India and China: 'The Logic of Geography,'" *Geopolitics*, vol. 13, no. 1 (January 2008): 1–26.

10. See the declaration issued at the end of Prime Minister Manmohan Singh's visit to Beijing in early 2008: *A Shared Vision for the 21st Century of the People's Republic of China and the Republic of India*, January 14, 2008, available at www.fmprc.gov.cn/eng/wjdt/2649/t399545.htm.

11. See for example Jairam Ramesh, *Making Sense of Chindia: Reflections on China and India* (New Delhi: India Research Press, 2005).

12. Jeremy Moore, *The Pursuit of Asian Hegemony: A Comparison of Chinese and Indian Strategic Objectives and Containment Policies* (Robina, Queensland, Australia: Bond University, 2008).

13. There is a vast literature on the subject; the following are a few places where one could usefully begin: P. C. Chakravarti, *The Evolution of India's Northern Borders* (New Delhi: Asia Publishing House, 1971); Steven Hoffmann, *India and the China Crisis* (Berkeley: University of California Press, 1990); Parshotam Mehra, *The McMahon Line and After* (New Delhi: Macmillan, 1974); Neville Maxwell, *India's China War* (New York: Pantheon, 1970); Xuecheng Liu, *The Sino-Indian Border Dispute and Sino-Indian Relations* (Lanham, Md.: University Press of America, 1994).

14. Zheng Ruixiang, "Shifting Obstacles in Sino-Indian Relations," *Pacific Review*, vol. 6, no. 1 (1993): 63–70; see also Nancy Jetly, "Sino-Indian Relations: Old Legacies and New Vistas," *China Report*, vol. 30, no. 2 (1994): 215–23; Wang Hongyu, "Sino-Indian Relations: Present and Future," *Asian Survey*, vol. 35, no. 6 (June 1995): 546–54; Waheguru Pal Singh Sidhu and Jing-dong Yuan, "Resolving the Sino-Indian Border Dispute: Building Confidence through Cooperative Monitoring," *Asian Survey*, vol. 41, no. 2 (March/April 2001): 351–76.

15. Allen Carlson, "Constructing the Dragon's Scales: China's Approach to Territorial Sovereignty and Border Relations in the 1980s and 1990s," *Journal of Contemporary China*, vol. 12, no. 37 (November 2003): 677–98.

16. "The two sides agreed to each appoint a Special Representative to explore from the political perspective of the overall bilateral relationship the framework of a boundary settlement." See the declaration issued after Vajpayee's 2003 visit to China. "Declaration on Principles for Relations and Comprehensive Cooperation between the Republic of India and the Republic of China," Beijing, June 23, 2003, available at www.fmprc.gov.cn/eng/wjdt/2649/t22852.htm.

17. For the text of the April 2005 agreement, see "Agreement between the Government of the Republic of India and the Government of the People's Republic of China on the Political Parameters and Guiding Principles for the Settlement of the India-China

Boundary Question," New Delhi, April 11, 2005, available at www.hindu.com/the-hindu/nic/0041/indiachinatxt.htm.

18. Alka Acharya, "Course Correction: An Analysis of the Origins and Implications of the Sino-Indian Agreements of 2003 and 2005," *China Report*, vol. 47, no. 2 (May 2011): 159–71.

19. Based on author's conversation with senior Indian officials involved in the boundary negotiations during 2008–2009.

20. See, for example, John Garver, "The Unresolved Sino-Indian Border Dispute: An Interpretation," *China Report*, vol. 47, no. 2 (May 2011): 99–113.

21. For an informed Indian perspective, see Sujit Dutta, "Sino-Indian Diplomatic Negotiations: A Preliminary Assessment," *Strategic Analysis*, vol. 22, no. 12 (March 1999): 1821–34; See also Sujit Dutta, "Revisiting China's Territorial Claims on Arunachal," *Strategic Analysis*, vol. 32, no. 4 (July 2008): 549–81. For a recent Chinese perspective, see Junwu Pan, *Toward a New Framework for Peaceful Settlement of China's Territorial and Boundary Disputes* (Leiden: Martinus Nijhoff, 2009), 191–216.

22. Dawa Norbu, "Tibet in Sino-Indian Relations: The Centrality of Marginality," *Asian Survey*, vol. 37, no. 11 (November 1997): 1078–95; see also Steven Hoffmann, "Rethinking the Linkage Between Tibet and the China-India Border Conflict: A Realist Approach," *Journal of Cold War Studies*, vol. 8, no. 3 (Summer 2006): 165–94.

23. D. S. Rajan, "China: New Trends for Looking Beyond the Dalai Lama," *South Asia Analysis Group Paper* no. 2925 (Chennai: Chennai Centre for China Studies, November 2008).

24. For a recent analysis, see Warren W. Smith Jr., *China's Tibet? Autonomy or Assimilation* (Lanham, Md.: Rowman and Littlefield, 2008).

25. See John Garver, "China's Kashmir Policies," *India Review*, vol. 3, no. 1 (January 2004): 1–24.

26. See comments of the official spokesman of the Indian Foreign Office on October 1, 2009, available at www.mea.gov.in/mystart.php?id=530115198; for a Chinese view, see the forum on "China & Indian ruled Kashmir: How & What?" *Global Times*, November 27, 2009, http://forum.globaltimes.cn/forum/showthread.php?t=9473.

27. Saikat Datta, "The Great Claw of China," *Outlook*, February 7, 2011, www.outlookindia.com/article.aspx?270223; see also Pranay Sharma, "A Mandarin Riddle," *Outlook*, February 7, 2011, www.outlookindia.com/article.aspx?270226.

28. For a review of the early development of Sino-Pak relations see Anwar Hussain Syed, *China & Pakistan: Diplomacy of an Entente Cordiale* (Amherst, Mass.: University of Massachusetts Press, 1974).

29. See Rajat Pandit, "Army Reworks War Doctrine for Pakistan, China," *Times of India*, December 30, 2009, 1; see also Gurmeet Kanwal, "Defence Doctrine: Facing Up to War on Two Fronts," *Tribune*, March 4, 2010, www.tribuneindia.com/2010/20100304/edit.htm#6.

30. For a recent comprehensive review, see Thomas C. Reed and Danny B. Stillman, *The Nuclear Express: A Political History of the Bomb and Its Proliferation* (Minneapolis: Zenith Press, 2009).

31. See T. V. Paul, "Chinese-Pakistani Nuclear/Missile Ties and Balance of Power Politics," *Nonproliferation Review*, vol. 10, no. 2 (2003): 21–29.

32. Evan S. Medeiros, *Reluctant Restraint: The Evolution of China's Non-Proliferation Practices, 1980–2004* (Singapore: NUS Press, 2009).

33. Mark Fitzpatrick, *Nuclear Black Markets: Pakistan, A. Q. Khan and the Rise of Proliferation Networks: A Net Assessment* (London: International Institute of Strategic Studies, 2007).

34. Paul, "Chinese-Pakistani Nuclear/Missile Ties and Balance of Power Politics," 21–29.

35. See Bhaskar Roy, "China Unmasked—What Next?" South Asia Analysis Group Paper no. 2840, September 12, 2008, www.southasiaanalysis.org/papers29/paper2840.html; see also D. S. Rajan, "Indo-U.S. Nuclear Deal: China Harps on U.S. 'Containment' Theory," South Asia Analysis Group Paper no. 2781, July 25, 2008, www.southasiaanalysis.org/papers28/paper2781.html.

36. Ashley Tellis, "The China-Pakistan Nuclear 'Deal': Separating Fact from Fiction," *Policy Outlook* (Washington. D.C.: Carnegie Endowment for International Peace, July 16, 2010); Mark Hibbs, "The Breach," *Nuclear Energy Brief* (Washington D.C.: Carnegie Endowment for International Peace, June 4, 2010).

37. John Garver, "Sino-Indian Rapprochement and the Sino-Pakistan Entente," *Political Science Quarterly*, vol. 111, no. 2 (Summer 1996): 323–47; see also Garver's "China's South Asian Interests and Policies," paper presented before U.S.-China Economic and Security Review Commission, July 22, 2005, available at www.chinacenter.net/about/associates/home/docs/Garver_China_South_Asian_Policies.pdf; Robert Wirsing, "The 'Enemy of My Enemy': Pakistan's China Debate," Asia-Pacific Center for Security Studies, December 2003.

38. For a discussion see, Rajesh Basrur and Bommakanti Kartik, "The India-China Nuclear Relationship," *Strategic Analysis*, vol. 35, no. 2 (March 2011): 186–93.

39. Chien-peng Chung, *Domestic Politics, International Bargaining and China's Territorial Disputes* (London: Routledge, 2004), 117; See also Jonathan Holslag, "Progress, Perceptions and Peace in the Sino-Indian Relationship," *East Asia*, vol. 26, no. 1, 41–56.

40. Cited in David Scott, "Sino-Indian Security Predicaments for the Twenty-First Century," *Asian Security*, vol. 4, no. 3 (September 2008): 251.

41. See John Garver, "The Gestalt of Sino-Indian Relations," in *The Rise of China in Asia: Security Implications*, edited by C. Pumphrey (Carlisle, Pa.: Strategic Studies Institute, 2002).

42. See the speech of Foreign Secretary Shyam Saran, "Present Dimensions of Indian Foreign Policy," Shanghai Institute of International Studies, January 11, 2006, available at www.indianembassy.org/prdetail994/--%09--'present-dimensions-of-the-indian-foreign-policy'--address-by-foreign-secretary-mr.-shyam-saran-at-shanghai-institute-of-international-studies.

43. For a general discussion of Washington's anti-China moves in South Asia during the early years of the Cold War, see S. Mahmud Ali, *Cold War in the High Himalayas: The USA, China and South Asia in the 1950s* (New York: St. Martin's Press, 1999); for a detailed account of U.S.-Indian collaboration in Tibet, see Kenneth J. Conboy and James Morrison, *The CIA's Secret War in Tibet* (Lawrence: University Press of Kansas, 2002).

44. Rama Lakshmi, "For India, Tibet Poses Some Delicate Issues," *Washington Post*, April 2, 2008, A9, www.washingtonpost.com/wpdyn/content/article/2008/04/01/AR2008040102861.html.

45. For a general discussion, see Yufan Hao and Bill K. P. Chou, *China's Policies on Its Borderlands and the International Implications* (Singapore: World Scientific, 2010).

46. Sudha Ramachandran, "India Sweats Over China's Water Plans," Asia Times Online, May 1, 2010, www.atimes.com/atimes/South_Asia/LE01Df05.html; Ananth Krishnan, "On Rivers and Glaciers, India, China Walk on Thin Ice," *Hindu*, May 10, 2010, 12.

47. Rajeev Ranjan Chaturvedy, "India's Response to Chinese Road Building," *IDSA Comment* (New Delhi; Institute for Defence Studies and Analyses), September 14, 2006, www.idsa.in/idsastrategiccomments/IndiasResponsetoChineseRoadBuilding_RRChaturvedy_140906. See also Jyoti Malhotra, "Military Upgradation Plan along China Border Finally Takes Wing," *Business Standard*, June 17, 2009, 11.

48. For a discussion of China's strategy, see Robert D. Kaplan, "The Geography of Chinese Power," *Foreign Affairs*, May-June 2010; for an Indian perspective, see C. Raja Mohan, "The Return of the Raj," *American Interest*, vol. 5, no. 5 (May–June 2010): 4–11.

49. Yitzhak Shichor, "China's Central Asian Strategy and the Xinjiang Connection: Predicaments and Medicaments in a Contemporary Perspective," *China and Eurasia Forum Quarterly*, vol. 6, no. 2 (2008): 55–73; see also Michael Clarke, "'Making the Crooked Straight': China's Grand Strategy of 'Peaceful Rise' and Its Central Asian Dimension," *Asian Security*, vol. 4, no. 2 (2008): 107–42.

50. For a comprehensive discussion, see Marlene Laruelle and Sebastien Peyrouse, eds., *Mapping Central Asia: Indian Perceptions and Strategies* (London: Ashgate, 2011).

51. See James Bosbotinis, "Sustaining the Dragon, Dodging the Eagle, and Barring the Bear? Assessing the Role and Importance of Central Asia in Chinese National Strategy," *China and Eurasia Forum Quarterly*, vol. 8, no. 1 (2010): 65–81.

52. Joseph Y. S. Cheng, "The Shanghai Cooperation Organization: China's Initiative in Regional Institutional Building," *Journal of Contemporary Asia*, vol. 41, no. 4 (2011): 632–56; M. K. Bhadrakumar, "India Begins Uphill Journey with the SCO," Asia Times Online, March 25, 2009, www.atimes.com/atimes/South_Asia/KC25Df01.html.

53. Hillary Clinton, "Remarks at the New Silk Road Ministerial Meeting," New York, September 22, 2011, www.state.gov/secretary/rm/2011/09/173807.htm; Praveen Swami, "India Backs 'New Silk Road' in Central Asia," *Hindu*, September 24, 2011.

54. For a nuanced view of India's attitudes to the major powers beyond the traditional arguments of non-alignment, see Harsh Pant, *Contemporary Debates in India's Foreign and Security Policy: India Negotiates Its Rise in the International System* (New York: Palgrave, 2008).

55. Swaran Singh, *China-Pakistan Strategic Cooperation: Indian Perspectives* (New Delhi: Manohar, 2007).

56. For a more detailed analysis see C. Raja Mohan, "How Obama Can Get South Asia Right," *Washington Quarterly*, vol. 32, no. 2 (April 2009): 173–89.

57. See Harsh Pant, "The Pakistan Thorn in China-India-U.S. Relations," *Washington Quarterly*, vol. 35, no. 1 (Winter 2012): 83–95.

58. For an optimistic assessment of Sino-Indian relations from a civilizational perspective, see David Camroux, "Asia . . . Whose Asia? A 'Return to the Future' of a Sino-Indic Asian Community," *Pacific Review*, vol. 20, no. 4 (December 2007): 551–75.

59. See, for example, John Garver, "Chinese-Indian Rivalry in Indochina," *Asian Survey*, vol. 27, no. 11 (November 1987): 1205–19; see also Ramesh Thakur, "India's Vietnam Policy, 1946–1979," *Asian Survey*, vol. 19, no. 10 (October 1979): 957–76.

60. Zhao Hong, "India and China: Rivals or Partners in Southeast Asia?" *Contemporary Southeast Asia*, vol. 29. no. 1, April 2007, 121–42.

61. See for example David Scott, "Strategic Imperatives of India as an Emerging Power Player in Pacific Asia," *International Studies*, vol. 44, no. 2 (April 2007): 123–40.

62. Shivshankar Menon, "Developments in India-China Relations," speech at the Chinese Embassy, New Delhi, January 9, 2012, available at www.mea.gov.in/mystart.php?id=530118876.

63. Dai Bingguo, "A Brighter Future When China and India Work Hand in Hand," *Hindu*, January 16, 2012.

64. You Ji, "Dealing with the Malacca Dilemma: China's Effort to Protect Its Energy Security," *Strategic Analysis*, vol. 31, no. 3 (May 2007): 467–89; see also Marc Lanteigne, "China's Maritime Security and the 'Malacca Dilemma,'" *Asian Security*, vol. 4, no. 2 (2008): 143–61.

CHAPTER THREE

1. K. M. Panikkar, *India and the Indian Ocean: An Essay on the Influence of Sea Power on Indian History* (New York: Macmillan, 1945).

2. For a classic modern work on Zheng He, see Louise Levathes, *When China Ruled the Seas: The Treasure Fleet of the Dragon Throne, 1405–1433* (New York: Oxford University Press, 1994).

3. James R. Holmes and Toshi Yoshihara, "Soft Power at Sea: Zheng He and Chinese Maritime Strategy," *U.S. Naval Institute Proceedings*, vol. 132, no. 10 (October 2006): 34–39.

4. See, for example, Gavin Menzies, *1421: The Year China Discovered the World* (New York: Perennial, 2004).

5. Arun Prakash, "The Rationale and Implications of India's Growing Maritime Power," in *India's Contemporary Security Challenges*, edited by Michael Kugelman (Washington, D.C.: Woodrow Wilson Center, 2011), 81–82.

6. Wang Gungwu, "The Rise of China: History as Policy," in *History as Policy*, edited by Ron Huisken and Meredith Thatcher (Canberra: ANU ePress, 2007), 62.

7. For a survey of the continental and maritime traditions in China, see John K. Fairbank, ed., *The Cambridge History of China, Vol. 12, Republican China 1912–1949, Part I* (Cambridge: Cambridge University Press, 1983), 1–27.

8. Sanjay Subrahmanyam, ed., *Maritime India* (New Delhi: Oxford University Press, 2004).

9. Hermann Kulke and Dietmar Rothermund, *A History of India*, 3rd ed. (London and New York: Routledge, 1998), 197–200.

10. John Curtis Perry, "Imperial China and the Sea," in *Asia Looks Seaward: Power and Maritime Strategy*, edited by Toshi Yoshihara and James R. Holmes (Westport, Conn.: Praeger, 2008), 19.

11. Jadunath Sarkar, *India Through the Ages* (Calcutta: Orient Longman, 1993), 45. Sarkar's grand survey was published originally in 1928.

12. The relationship between the two is well developed in Percival Spear, *India, Pakistan and the West* (London: Oxford University Press, 1948).

13. Wang Gungwu, "The Rise of China: History as Policy," in Huisken and Thatcher, eds., *History as Policy* (Canberra: ANU ePress, 2007).

14. See Bruce Swanson, *Eighth Voyage of the Dragon: A History of China's Quest for Sea Power* (Annapolis, Md.: Naval Institute Press, 1982).

15. For a discussion of partition and India's early territorial conflicts, see Graham Chapman, *The Geopolitics of South Asia* (London: Ashgate, 2003).

16. For an easy grasp of the unformed territoriality of independent India, see the first few chapters of Ramachandra Guha, *India after Gandhi: The History of World's Largest Democracy* (London: Macmillan, 2007).

17. Integrated Headquarters, Ministry of Defense, Government of India, *Freedom to Use the Seas: India's Maritime Military Strategy* (New Delhi: Ministry of Defense, 2007), 15.

18. For a good modern summary of Mahan's thought, see Margaret Tuttle Sprout, "Mahan: Evangelist of Sea Power," in *Makers of Modern Strategy: Military Thought from Machiavelli to Hitler*, edited by Edward Mead Earle (Princeton: Princeton University Press, 1943).

19. Banyan, "Chasing Ghosts," *Economist* blog, June 11, 2009, www.economist.com/world/asia/displaystory.cfm?story_id=13825154.

20. See James R. Holmes and Toshi Yoshihara, "The Influence of Mahan upon China's Maritime Strategy," *Comparative Strategy*, vol. 24, no. 1 (2005): 23–51; David Scott, "India's 'Grand Strategy' for the Indian Ocean: Mahanian Visions," *Asia-Pacific Review*, vol. 13, no. 2 (November 2006): 97–129.

21. Ni Lexiong, "Sea Power and China's Development," *People's Liberation Daily*, April 17, 2005; translated for U.S. China Economic and Security Review Commission, www.uscc.gov/researchpapers/translated_articles/2005/05_07_18_Sea_Power_and_Chinas_Development.pdf.

22. Figures from the World Bank, available at http://data.worldbank.org/indicator/TG.VAL.TOTL.GD.ZS.

23. Integrated Headquarters, Ministry of Defense, Government of India, *Freedom to Use the Seas: India's Maritime Military Strategy* (New Delhi: Ministry of Defense, 2007), 10.

24. For a comprehensive discussion, see David Lei, "China's New Multi-Faceted Maritime Strategy," *Orbis*, vol. 52, no. 1 (Winter 2008): 139–57.

25. For a discussion of the origins and implications of the crisis, see Suisheng Zhao, ed., *Across the Taiwan Strait: Mainland China, Taiwan and the 1995–1996 Crisis* (New York: Routledge, 1999); see also Andrew Scobell, "Show of Force: Chinese Soldiers, Statesmen, and the 1995–96 Taiwan Strait Crisis," *Political Science Quarterly*, vol. 115, no. 2 (Summer 2000): 227–46.

26. For a discussion see Ashley Tellis, "India's Naval Expansion: Reflections on History and Strategy," *Comparative Strategy*, vol. 6, no. 2, 185–219.

27. For a general discussion of some of these issues, see L. Alan Winters and Shahid Yusuf, eds., *Dancing with Giants: China, India, and the Global Economy* (Washington, D.C.: World Bank, 2007).

28. See, for example, Eurasia Group, "China's Overseas Investments in Oil and Gas Production," paper prepared for the U.S.-China Economic and Security Review Commission (New York: Eurasia Group, 2006), www.uscc.gov/researchpapers/2006/oil_gas.pdf; see also Shaofeng Chen, "Motivations Behind China's Foreign Oil Quest: A Perspective from the Chinese Government and the Oil Companies," *Journal of Chinese Political Science*, vol. 13, no. 1 (2008): 79–104; Shebonti Ray Dadwal and Uttam Kumar Sinha, "Equity Oil and India's Energy Security," *Strategic Analysis*, vol. 29, no. 3 (July–September 2005): 521–29; Tanvi Madan, "India's International Quest for Oil and Natural Gas: Fueling Foreign Policy?" *India Review*, vol. 9, no. 1 (January-March 2010): 2–37.

29. See, for example, Gabriel Collins, Andrew Erickson, Lyle Goldstein, and William Murray, *China's Energy Strategy: The Impact on Beijing's Maritime Policies* (Annapolis, Md.: Naval Institute Press, 2008); Roland Dannreuther, "China and Global Oil: Vulnerability and Opportunity," *International Affairs*, vol. 87, no. 6 (November 2011): 1345–64; see also Gurpreet S. Khurana, "The Maritime Dimension of India's Energy Security," *Strategic Analysis*, vol. 31, no. 4 (July 2007): 583–601; Amit A. Pandya, Rupert Herbert-Burns, and Junko Kobayashi, *Maritime Commerce and Security: The Indian Ocean* (Washington, D.C.: Stimson Center, 2011).

30. Michael T. Klare, *Resources Wars: The New Landscape of Global Conflict* (New York: Henry Holt, 2002).

31. For an illustrative analysis, see Stein Tønnesson and Åshild Kolås, *Energy Security in Asia: China, India, Oil and Peace* (Oslo: International Peace Research Institute, 2006); S. Philip Sen, "Crouching Tiger, Hidden Dragon: India, China and the Dynamics of Energy Security," in *The Globalization of Energy: China and the European Union*, edited by Mehdi Pervezi Amineh and Yang Guang (Leiden: Martinus Nijhoff, 2010), 139–78; Geoffrey Kemp, *The East Moves the West: India, China and Asia's*

Growing Presence in the Middle East (Washington, D.C.: Brookings Institution Press, 2010).

32. Andrea Goldstein, Nicolas Pinaud, Helmut Reisen, and Xiaobao Chen, *The Rise of China and India: What's in It for Africa?* (Paris: Organization for Economic Cooperation and Development, 2006); Harry Broadman, *Africa's Silk Road: China and India's New Economic Frontier* (Washington, D.C.: World Bank, 2007). See also Padraig Carmody and Francis Owusu, "Competing Hegemons? Chinese versus American Geo-Economic Strategies in Africa," *Political Geography*, vol. 26, no. 5 (June 2007): 504–24; Ian Taylor, *Unpacking China's Resource Diplomacy in Africa*, Working Paper no. 19 (Hong Kong: Center on China's Transnational Relations, Hong Kong University of Science and Technology, 2007).

33. You Ji, "Dealing with the Malacca Dilemma: China's Effort to Protect Its Energy Security," *Strategic Analysis*, vol. 31, no. 3 (May 2007): 467–89; see also Marc Lanteigne, "China's Maritime Security and the 'Malacca Dilemma,'" *Asian Security*, vol. 4, no. 2 (2008): 143–61.

34. Zhang Wenmu, "Sea Power and China's Strategic Choices," *China Security* (Summer 2006): 20; www.wsichina.org/cs3.pdf.

35. See Shivshankar Menon, "Maritime Imperatives of India's Foreign Policy," *Maritime Affairs*, vol. 5, no. 2, 15–21.

36. Ibid., 21.

37. See his address to Combined Commanders Conference, New Delhi, October 18, 2006; available at www.outlookindia.com/printarticle.aspx?232868.

38. For a fine analysis of forward basing during the Cold War, see Robert E. Harkavy, *Bases Abroad: The Global Foreign Military Presence* (New York: Oxford University Press, 1989).

39. For a discussion on the criteria, see A. W. Singham and Shirley Hune, *Non-Alignment in an Age of Alignments* (London: Lawrence Hill, 1986).

40. See, for example, K. M. Panikkar, *India and the Indian Ocean: An Essay on the Influence of Sea Power on Indian History* (London: Macmillan, 1945); see also Keshav B. Vaidya, *The Naval Defence of India* (Bombay: Thacker, 1949.)

41. See, for example, David Lai, "Chinese Military Going Global," *China Security*, vol. 5, no. 1 (Winter 2009): 3–9; available at www.washingtonobserver.org/pdfs/DavidLai.pdf; for India, see Rajat Pandit, "Navy Steams to Foreign Shores to Build Bridges, Project Power," *Times of India*, May 31, 2009, http://timesofindia.indiatimes.com/articleshow/msid-4598351,prtpage-1.cms.

42. For a critical review of the literature, see Andrew Selth, "Burma, China and the Myth of Military Bases," *Asian Security*, vol. 3, no. 3, 2007, 279–306.

43. The phrase China's "string of pearls" first appeared in U.S. media citing a technical study commissioned by the Pentagon; see Bill Gertz, "China Builds Up Strategic Sea Lanes," *Washington Times*, January 18, 2005.

44. See Steven Forsberg, "India Stretches Its Sea Legs," *Proceedings of the U.S. Naval Institute*, vol. 133, no. 3 (March 2007): 38–42; see also Sudha Ramachandran,

"India's Quiet Sea Power," Asia Times Online, August 2, 2007, www.atimes.com/atimes/South_Asia/IH02Df01.html.

45. Ni Lexiong, "Sea Power and China's Development," *People's Liberation Daily*, April 17, 2005; translated for U.S. China Economic and Security Review Commission, available at www.uscc.gov/researchpapers/translated_articles/2005/05_07_18_Sea_Power_and_Chinas_Development.pdf.

46. Ibid.

CHAPTER FOUR

1. Nitin Pai and Sushant Singh, "Deciding on Use of Force," *Mint*, November 19, 2008; www.livemint.com/2008/11/19002154/Deciding-on-use-of-force.html.

2. Zhang Haizhou, "Experts Debate China's Role in Somalia Mission," *China Daily*, December 12, 2008, www.chinadaily.com.cn/world/2008–12/12/content_7297675.htm.

3. For a brief review of China's international peacekeeping activity, see Bonny Ling, "China's Peacekeeping Diplomacy," International Relations and Institutions, China Rights Forum, no. 1 (2007), http://hrichina.org/public/PDFs/CRF.1.2007/CRF-2007–1_Peacekeeping.pdf. See also Yin He, *China's Changing Policy on UN Peacekeeping Operations* (Stockholm: Institute for Security and Development Policy, 2007).

4. For a substantive discussions, see Bates Gill and Chin-Hao Huang, "China's Expanding Peacekeeping Role: Its Significance and the Policy Implications," SIPRI Policy Brief, Stockholm International Peace Research Institute, February 2009.

5. This illustrative list is from Aaron L. Friedberg, "'Going Out': China's Pursuit of Natural Resources and Implications for the PRC's Grand Strategy," *NBR Analysis*, vol. 17, no. 3 (September 2006): 26.

6. David Lai, "Chinese Military Going Global," *China Security*, vol. 5, no. 1 (Winter 2009): 4–5.

7. Information Office of the State Council of the People's Republic of China, *China's National Defense in 2008* (Beijing: January 20, 2009); www.china-un.org/eng/gdxw/t534184.htm.

8. Alan Bullion, "India and UN Peacekeeping Operations," *International Peacekeeping*, vol. 4, no. 1 (Spring 1997): 98–114.

9. For a succinct review of the Indian army's deployment in the Indian Ocean region, see Thomas R. Metcalf, *Imperial Connections: India in the Indian Ocean Arena, 1860–1920* (Berkeley and Los Angeles: University of California Press, 2007), 69–101.

10. For a brief overview, see Daniel P. Marston and Chandar S. Sundaram, eds., *A Military History of India and South Asia: From the East India Company to the Nuclear Age* (Bloomington: Indiana University Press, 2008).

11. For a firsthand account from an Indian official involved in the decisionmaking, see S. Jaishankar, "2004 Tsunami Disaster: Consequences for Regional Cooperation,"

paper presented at the 26th Annual Pacific Symposium, Asia Pacific Democracies: Advancing Prosperity and Security, June 8–10, 2005, www.ndu.edu/inss/symposia/Pacific2005/jaishankar.pdf.

12. The text of the agreement reprinted as Annexure I in C. Raja Mohan, *Impossible Allies: Nuclear India, United States and the Global Order* (New Delhi: India Research Press, 2006), 285–88.

13. C. Raja Mohan, "Playing the Great Game: India's Interventionist Future," *India & Global Affairs*, vol. 1, no. 1 (January–March 2008): 78–90.

14. Integrated Headquarters, Ministry of Defense (Navy), Government of India, *Freedom to Use the Seas: India's Maritime Military Strategy* (New Delhi: Ministry of Defense, May 2007), 11.

15. Significant literature has recently emerged on the changing profile of the two navies. See, for example, James R. Holmes and Toshi Yoshihara, *Chinese Naval Strategy in the 21st Century: The Turn to Mahan* (New York: Routledge, 2008), and James R. Holmes, Andrew C. Winner, and Toshi Yoshihara, *Indian Naval Strategy in the Twenty-First Century* (New York: Routledge, 2009). See also David G. Muller, *China as a Maritime Power* (Boulder, Colo.: Westview Press, 1983); Bernard D. Cole, *The Great Wall at Sea: China's Navy Enters the Twenty-First Century* (Annapolis, Md.: Naval Institute Press, 2001); Satyindra Singh, *Blueprint to Bluewater: The Indian Navy 1951–65* (New Delhi: Lancer, 1992); and Rahul Roy-Chaudhury, *Sea Power and Indian Security* (London: Brassey's, 1995).

16. Ronald O'Rourke, *China Naval Modernization: Implications for U.S. Navy Capabilities—Background and Issues for Congress* (Washington, D.C.: Congressional Research Service, February 3, 2011).

17. David Lague, "Chinese Submarine Fleet Is Growing, Analysts Say," *New York Times*, December 5, 2008, www.nytimes.com/2008/02/25/world/asia/25iht-25submarine.10349022.html.

18. Ronald O'Rourke, *China Naval Modernization: Implications for U.S. Navy Capabilities-Background and Issues for Congress* (Washington, D.C.: Congressional Research Service, February 3, 2011).

19. Bernard D. Cole, *The Great Wall at Sea: China's Navy Enters the Twenty-First Century* (Annapolis, Md.: Naval Institute Press, 2001).

20. Huang Jing, "The PLA Navy: Expanding into Uncharted Waters," presentation at the RSIS-NMF Seminar on "Between Rising Naval Powers: Implications for Southeast Asia of the Rise of Chinese and Indian Naval Power," Singapore, November 18–19, text of Power Point obtained from the author.

21. L. C. Russell Hsiao, "PLAN East Sea Fleet Moves Beyond First Island Chain," *China Brief*, vol. 10, no. 9 (April 29, 2010): 1–2.

22. Edward Wong, "China Navy Reaches Far, Unsettling the Region," *New York Times*, June 14, 2011, www.nytimes.com/2011/06/15/world/asia/15china.html.

23. Isabelle Saint-Mézard, "India's Naval Ambitions: The Emergence of a Major Power in the Indian Ocean and Beyond," presentation at the Institute of South Asian Studies,

Singapore, November 26, 2008; see also David Scott, "India's 'Grand Strategy' for the Indian Ocean: Mahanian Visions," *Asia-Pacific Review*, vol. 13, no. 2 (2006): 97–129.

24. See Rahul Roy-Chaudhury, "The Limits to Naval Expansion," in *Securing India: Strategic Thought and Practice*, edited by Kanti Bajpai and Amitabh Mattoo (New Delhi: Manohar, 1996).

25. "Indian Navy Seeks to Acquire Six More Submarines," *India Defense,* September 28, 2008, available at www.india-defence.com/reports-4029; see also Manu Pubby, "NextGen diesel submarines to be built in Indian shipyard," *Indian Express*, July 15, 2010, 6.

26. James R. Holmes, Andrew C. Winner, and Toshi Yoshihara, *Indian Naval Strategy in the Twenty-First Century* (New York: Routledge, 2009), 86.

27. Dean Mathew, "Aircraft Carriers: An Indian Introspection," *Strategic Analysis*, vol. 23, no. 12 (March 2000): 2135–58.

28. Sandeep Unnithan, "Battle over Gorshkov," *India Today*, December 7, 2007, http://indiatoday.intoday.in/index.php?issueid=116&id=2289&option=com_content&task=view&sectionid=36.

29. K. V. Prasad, "CAG Picks Holes in Gorshkov Acquisition," *Hindu*, July 25, 2009, www.hindu.com/2009/07/25/stories/2009072556341100.htm.

30. "U.S. Not Offering *Kitty Hawk* to India: Gates," Rediff News Online, February 28, 2008, www.rediff.com/news/2008/feb/28kitty.htm.

31. David Scott, "India's Drive for a 'Blue Water' Navy," *Journal of Military and Strategic Studies*, vol. 10, no. 2 (Winter 2007–2008).

32. James R. Holmes, Andrew C. Winner, and Toshi Yoshihara, *Indian Naval Strategy in the Twenty-First Century* (New York: Routledge, 2009), 83–84.

33. For a review of the debate in China, see Andrew S. Erickson and Andrew R. Wilson, "China's Aircraft Carrier Dilemma," *Naval War College Review*, vol. 59, no. 4 (Autumn 2006): 13–45.

34. Richard Bitzinger, "Aircraft Carriers: China's Emerging Maritime Ambitions," *RSIS Commentaries* 35/2009 (Singapore: S. Rajaratnam School of International Studies, April 7, 2009), http://www3.ntu.edu.sg/rsis/publications/Perspective/RSIS0352009.pdf.

35. Quoted in J. David Goodman, "A Chinese Aircraft Carrier: Not If, but When," *New York Times*, November 17, 2008, http://thelede.blogs.nytimes.com/2008/11/17/a-chinese-aircraft-carrier-not-if-but-when.

36. For a review, see Robert Ross, "China's Naval Nationalism: Sources, Prospects, and the U.S. Response," *International Security*, vol. 34, no. 2 (Fall 2009): 46–81.

37. "Time to Prepare for China's Aircraft Carrier," *Global Times*, March 11, 2010, http://opinion.globaltimes.cn/editorial/2010–03/511703.html.

38. Wang Jianfen and Nie Ligao, "Japan Defense Minister's China Visit a Sign of Warming Relations," *China Daily*, March 23, 2009, www.chinadaily.com.cn/china/2009–03/23/content_7607571.htm.

39. Cited in U.S. Defense Department, *Military and Security Developments Involving the People's Republic of China* (Washington, D.C., 2010), 48.

40. Andrew S. Erickson, "Can China Become a Maritime Power?" in *Asia Looks Seaward: Power and Maritime Strategy*, edited by Toshi Yoshihara and James R. Holmes (Westport, Conn.: Praeger International, 2008), 90.

41. Ibid., 90–91.

42. For a discussion, see Andrew S. Erickson, Abraham M. Denmark, and Gabriel Collins, "Beijing's 'Starter Carrier' and Future Steps: Alternatives and Implications," *Naval War College Review*, vol. 65, no. 1 (Winter 2012): 14–54; David Lai, "China's Aircraft Carrier: The Good, the Bad, and the Ugly," October 27, 2011, www.strategicstudiesinstitute.army.mil/index.cfm/articles/chinas-aircraft-carrier/2011/10/27; Trefor Moss, "Decoding China's Aircraft Carrier," *Diplomat*, August 13, 2011, http://the-diplomat.com/2011/08/13/decoding-china's-aircraft-carrier.

43. Gary Li, "Towards a Blue Water Future: China's Aircraft Carrier Programme," *RUSI Brief* (London: Royal United Services Institution), July 10, 2009.

44. Ronald O'Rourke, *China Naval Modernization: Implications for U.S. Navy Capabilities—Background and Issues for Congress* (Washington, D.C.: Congressional Research Service, February 3, 2011).

45. Nan Li, "The Evolution of China's Naval Strategy and Capabilities: From 'Near Coast' and 'Near Seas' to 'Far Seas,'" *Asian Security*, vol. 5, no. 2 (May 2009): 161.

46. See Robert Harkavy, *Bases Abroad: The Global Foreign Military Presence* (New York: Oxford University Press, 1989).

47. Donald L. Berlin, "The 'Great Base Race' in the Indian Ocean Littoral: Conflict Prevention or Stimulation?" *Contemporary South Asia*, vol. 13, no. 3 (September 2004): 239–55.

48. "China's New Naval Base Triggers U.S. Concerns," Agence France-Presse, May 12, 2008, http://afp.google.com/article/ALeqM5gRqO2xhQzglbp4Cums3qh3MO07Yw.

49. For a broad review, see Donald L. Berlin, "India in the Indian Ocean," *Naval War College Review*, vol. 59, no. 2 (2006): 58–89.

50. David Scott, "Indian 'Footprints' in the Indian Ocean: Power Projection for the 21st Century," *Indian Ocean Survey*, vol. 2, no. 2 (2006): 1–26; see also Steven Forsberg, "India Stretches Its Sea Legs," *US Naval Institute Proceedings*, vol. 133, no. 3 (March 2007): 38–43.

51. K. M. Panikkar, *India and the Indian Ocean: An Essay on the Influence of Seapower on Indian History* (London: George Allen and Unwin, 1945), 15.

52. Integrated Headquarters, Ministry of Defense (Navy), Government of India, *Freedom to Use the Seas: India's Maritime Military Strategy* (New Delhi: Ministry of Defense, 2007), 81.

53. Christopher J. Pehrson, *String of Pearls: Meeting the Challenge of China's Rising Power across the Asian Littoral* (Carlisle, Pa.: Strategic Studies Institute, U.S. Army War College, July 2006), www.strategicstudiesinstitute.army.mil/pdffiles/PUB721.pdf.

54. Harvir Sharma, "China's Interests in the Indian Ocean RIM Countries and India's Maritime Security," *India Quarterly*, vol. 57, no. 4 (2001): 67–88; Gurpreet S. Khurana, "China's 'String of Pearls' in the Indian Ocean and Its Security Implications," *Strategic Analysis*, vol. 32, no. 1 (January 2008): 1–39.

55. Daniel J. Kostecka, "Places and Bases: The Chinese Navy's Emerging Support Network in the Indian Ocean," *Naval War College Review*, vol. 64, no. 1 (Winter 2011): 75.

56. For a review of the Chinese debate, see Michael S. Chase and Andrew S. Erickson, "Changes in Beijing's Approach to Overseas Basing?" *China Brief*, vol. 9, no. 19 (September 24, 2009); Jesse Karotkin, "PLAN Shapes International Perception of Evolving Capabilities," *China Brief*, vol. 10, no. 3 (February 4, 2010): 4–7; Ian J. Storey, "China Debates the Need for Overseas Bases," *Straits Times*, April 29, 2010, www.iseas.edu.sg/viewpoint/ijs29apr10.pdf.

57. Daniel J. Kostecka, "Places and Bases: The Chinese Navy's Emerging Support Network in the Indian Ocean," *Naval War College Review*, vol. 64, no. 1 (Winter 2011): 75.

CHAPTER FIVE

1. "PM Launches Arihant in Visakhapatnam," *Times of India*, July 27, 2009, 1; Amitav Ranjan and Shishir Gupta, "All Set for a Quiet Launch of India's First Indigenous N-Sub," *Indian Express*, July 8, 2009, 1; see also Rajat Pandit, "N-sub's Here in 10 Days," *Times of India*, July 17, 2009, 11.

2. The literature on this subject is somewhat sparse. See Donald L. Berlin, "The Indian Ocean and the Second Nuclear Age," *Orbis*, vol. 48, no. 1 (Winter 2004): 55–70; see also Lawrence Prabhakar, Joshua Ho, and Sam Bateman, eds., *The Evolving Maritime Balance of Power in the Asia-Pacific: Maritime Doctrines and Nuclear Weapons at Sea* (Singapore: World Scientific, 2006); C. Raja Mohan, "Coming to Terms with a Nuclearizing Asia: Restoring and Reorienting the Non-Proliferation Regime," in *Security through Cooperation: Furthering Asia Pacific Multilateral Engagement*, edited by Brian Job, CSCAP Regional Security Outlook, 2007 (Singapore: CSCAP, 2007), 19–28.

3. For a history of India's nuclear-weapon program, see George Perkovich, *India's Nuclear Bomb: The Impact on Global Proliferation* (Berkeley, Calif.: University of California Press, 2002).

4. For a recent review of India's missile and space program, see Harsh V. Pant and Bharath Gopalaswamy, "India's Emerging Profile in Space," *RUSI Journal*, vol. 153, no. 5 (October 2008): 66–71.

5. "Draft Report National Security Advisory Board on Indian Nuclear Doctrine," August 17, 1999, available at http://nuclearweaponarchive.org/India/nuclear_doctrine_aug_17_1999.html.

6. For a review of China's minimum deterrent posture, see Jeffrey Lewis, *The Minimum Means of Reprisal: China's Search for Security in the Nuclear Age* (Cambridge, Mass.: MIT Press, 2007).

7. For a recent discussion of some of these issues, see Paul J. Bolt and Albert S. Willner, eds., *China's Nuclear Future* (Boulder, Colo.: Lynne Rienner, 2006); see also M. Taylor Fravel and Evan S. Medeiros, "China's Search for Assured Retaliation: The Evolution of Chinese Nuclear Strategy and Force Structure," *International Security*, vol. 35, no. 2 (Fall 2010): 48–87.

8. For the history of China's development of an underwater nuclear deterrent, see John W. Lewis and Xue Litai, *China's Strategic Seapower: The Politics of Force Modernization in the Nuclear Age* (Stanford, Calif.: Stanford University Press, 1994).

9. Vijay Sakhuja, "Sea-Based Deterrence and Indian Security," *Strategic Analysis*, vol. 25, no. 1 (April 2001): 31.

10. Integrated Headquarters, Ministry of Defense, Government of India, *Freedom to Use the Seas: India's Maritime Military Strategy* (New Delhi: Ministry of Defense, 2007), 76.

11. T. S. Subramanian, "Reactor for Nuclear Submarine Fully Operational," *Hindu*, August 18, 2006, 7.

12. For a comprehensive survey of public sources, see The Federation of American Scientists, "The Indian SSN Project: An Open Literature Analysis," available at www.fas.org/nuke/guide/india/sub/ssn/part01.htm.

13. Vijay Shankar, "Force Planning to Shape India's Maritime Space: The Nuclear Dimension," *Defense and Security Alert*, vol. 3, no. 3 (December 2011): 24.

14. Varun Sood and James Lamont, "India Set to Launch Nuclear Submarine," *Financial Times*, July 9, 2009, www.ft.com/cms/s/0/c4d49e94–6c1e-11de-9320–00144feabdc0.html.

15. Rajat Pandit, "India Worried about China's Growing N-Sub Prowess," *Times of India*, May 6, 2008, 1.

16. Among the more informative reports is Rahul Bedi, "India's Nuclear Powered Submarine Project Moves Ahead," *Tribune*, May 19, 2007, 9; see also "We Played a Vital Role in Arihant: L&T," *Business Standard*, July 27, 2009, www.business-standard.com/india/news/we-playedvital-role-in-arihant-l/365017.

17. Premvir Das, "INS Arihant: A Watershed Moment," *Business Standard*, July 30, 2009, www.business-standard.com/india/news/premvir-das-ins-arihantwatershed-moment/365321.

18. Robert S. Norris and Hans M. Kristensen, "Nuclear Notebook: Indian Nuclear Forces, 2008," *Bulletin of the Atomic Scientists*, vol. 64, no. 5 (November 2008): 38–40.

19. Ibid.

20. See "Sagarika/K-15/Shourya/Nirbhay: Weapons of Mass Destruction," GlobalSecurity.org, www.globalsecurity.org/wmd/world/india/sagarika.htm.

21. This Western claim is apparently based on Russian sources. See Nuclear Threat Initiative, "India Submarine Capabilities," June 22, 2011, www.nti.org/analysis/articles/india-submarine-capabilities.

22. "Project 971 Shuka-B Akula Class," GlobalSecurity.org, www.globalsecurity.org/military/world/india/s-akula.htm.

23. Vera Ponomareva, "Nuclear Subs on Lease from Russia to India," August 16, 2005, Bellona Foundation website, www.bellona.no/en/international/russia/nuke-weapons/nonproliferation/39412.html.

24. "India-Bound Russian Nuke Sub Repaired, Resumes Sea Trials," RIA Novosti, July 10, 2009, available at http://sify.com/news/fullstory.php?a=jhkp4bebdeb&title=India_bound_Russian_nuke_sub_repaired_resumes_sea_trials.

25. Rajat Pandit, "India Becomes 6th Nation to Join Elite Nuclear Submarine Club," *Times of India*, January 24, 2012, 11; see also Harry Kazianis, "India Leases Russia Nuke Sub," *Diplomat*, January 2, 2012, http://the-diplomat.com/flashpoints-blog/2012/01/02/india-leases-russia-nuke-sub.

26. Pravin Sawhney and Vijay Shankar, "Is the Navy's Newest Sub Worth the Price?" *Hindu*, January 25, 2012, 9.

27. Ta-Chen Cheng, "The Evolution of China's Strategic Weapons," *Defense and Security Analysis*, vol. 22, no. 3 (September 2006): 248–49.

28. Andrew S. Erickson and Lyle J. Goldstein, "China's Future Nuclear Submarine Force: Insights from Chinese Writings," *Naval War College Review*, vol. 60, no. 1 (Winter 2007): 56–60.

29. Andrew S. Erickson and Michael S. Chase, "An Undersea Deterrent?" *U.S. Naval Institute Proceedings*, vol. 135, no. 6 (June 2009): 36–41.

30. U.S. Defense Department, *Military and Security Developments involving the People's Republic of China* (Washington, D.C.: 2010), 34.

31. Robert S. Norris and Hans M. Kristensen, "Nuclear Notebook: Chinese Nuclear Forces, 2010," *Bulletin of the Atomic Scientists*, vol. 66, no. 6 (November/December 2010): 137.

32. U.S. Defense Department, *Military and Security Developments Involving the People's Republic of China* (Washington, D.C.: 2010), 34.

33. "PM's Remarks on the Occasion of the Launch of the Advanced Technology Vehicle," *Visakhapatnam*, July 26, 2009, www.pmindia.nic.in.

34. "India's Nuclear Submarine to Trigger Arms Race: Pak Navy," *Dawn*, July 27, 2009, 1.

35. Muhammad Azam Khan, "S-2: Options for the Pakistan Navy," *Naval War College Review*, vol. 63, no. 3 (Summer 2010): 98.

36. Ibid., 99.

37. James Clay Moltz, "Closing the NPT Loophole on Exports of Naval Propulsion Reactors," *Nonproliferation Review*, vol. 6, no. 1 (Fall 1998): 108–14.

38. For a review of the origins of the India-U.S. nuclear deal, see C. Raja Mohan, *Impossible Allies: Nuclear India, United States, and the Global Order* (New Delhi: India Research Press, 2006).

NOTES

39. See John McCain's speech to the Carnegie Endowment for International Peace in Washington, D.C., November 2010, http://carnegieendowment.org/2010/11/05/senator-john-mccain-on-future-of-u.s.-india-relationship/1sd6.

40. For a comprehensive assessment of the Asian nuclear situation, see Muthiah Alagappa, ed., *The Long Shadow: Nuclear Weapons and Security in 21st Century Asia* (Singapore: National University of Singapore Press, 2009).

41. Paul Bracken, "The Structure of the Second Nuclear Age," *Orbis*, vol. 47, no. 3 (Summer 2003): 399–413.

42. The discussion here draws from Christopher P. Twomey, "Asia's Complex Strategic Environment: Nuclear Multipolarity and Other Dangers," *Asia Policy*, no. 11 (January 2011): 51–78.

43. Richard C. Bush, "The U.S. Policy of Extended Deterrence in East Asia: History, Current Views, and Implications," Arms Control Series, no. 5 (Washington, D.C.: Brookings Institution, February 2011).

44. For insights into the nuclear debates among U.S. allies and friends in Asia-Japan, South Korea, Taiwan, Australia, and ASEAN, see Muthiah Alagappa, ed., *The Long Shadow: Nuclear Weapons and Security in 21st Century Asia*, 347–478; see also Rod Lyon, *A Delicate Issue: Asia's Nuclear Future* (Canberra: Australian Strategic Policy Institute, 2009).

45. For a discussion of the Chinese motivations behind its SSBN force, see Andrew S. Erickson and Michael S. Chase, "An Undersea Deterrent?" *U.S. Naval Institute Proceedings*, vol. 135, no. 6 (June 2009): 36–41.

46. Toshi Yoshihara and James R. Holmes, *Red Star over the Pacific: China's Rise and the Challenge to U.S. Maritime Strategy* (Annapolis, Md.: Naval Institute Press, 2010), 148.

47. Srikanth Kondapalli, "The Chinese Threat in the Indian Ocean," Rediff News Online, May 8, 2008, www.rediff.com/news/2008/may/08guest.htm.

48. Shishir Gupta, 'Chinese N-Submarines: Cabinet Security Panel to Meet, Navy Chief to Brief NSA Narayanan," *Indian Express*, May 4, 2008, www.indianexpress.com/story/305072.html.

49. Manu Pubby, "China's New N-Submarine Base Sets Off Alarm Bells," *Indian Express*, May 3, 2008, http://indianexpress.com/story/304797.html.

50. Gurpreet S. Khurana, "China's New Submarine Base at Hainan: Analyses of Recent Media Reports," *Strategic Analysis*, vol. 32, no. 5 (September 2008): 714–15.

51. See Kurt Campbell and Jeremiah Gertler, *The Paths Ahead: Missile Defense in Asia* (Washington, D.C.: Center for Strategic and International Studies, March 2006).

52. John Garver, "China's Response to the U.S. Strategic Defense Initiative," *Asian Survey*, vol. 26, no. 11 (November 1986): 1220–39.

53. For an Indian critique, see Rakesh Gupta, ed., *SDI: Aims, Implications, and Responses* (New Delhi: Panchsheel, 1988); see also D. R. Goyal, *Nuclear Disarmament: The Six-Nation Initiative and the Big Power Response* (New Delhi: Sterling, 1987).

54. For an initial review of the impact of missile defenses in India and its neighborhood, see Chris Gagné and Michael Krepon, eds., *The Impact of U.S. Missile Defenses on Southern Asia* (Washington, D.C.: Henry L. Stimson Center, 2002).

55. See Stephen Burgess, "India's Emerging Security Strategy, Missile Defense and Arms Control," INSS Occasional Paper no. 54 (Colorado Springs: U.S. Air Force Academy, 2004); for a skeptical review, see Rajesh Rajagopalan, "Missile Defenses in South Asia: Much Ado about Nothing," *South Asian Survey*, vol. 11, no. 2 (September 2004): 205–17.

56. For a comprehensive account from an insider, see Ashley J. Tellis, "The Evolution of U.S.-Indian Ties: Missile Defense in an Emerging Strategic Relationship," *International Security*, vol. 30, no. 4 (Spring 2006): 151.

57. See Martin Sieff, "A Giant Leap Forward for Indian Missile Defense," December 1, 2006, www.spacewar.com/reports/A_Giant_Leap_Forward_For_Indian_Missile_Defense_999.html; Ajai Shukla, "The Untold Story of India's Missile Defense," Rediff online, January 30, 2008, www.rediff.com/news/2008/jan/30missile.htm; "India Tests 'Swordfish' Radar with Successful Missile Defense Test," March 6, 2009, available at www.domain-b.com/aero/mil_avi/miss_muni/20090306_successful_missile.html; Bharath Gopalaswamy, "Missile Defense in India," *Bulletin of the Atomic Scientists*, February 27, 2009, available at www.thebulletin.org/node/5947; see also A. Vinod Kumar, "A Phased Approach to India's Missile Defense Planning," *Strategic Analysis*, vol. 32, no. 2 (March 2008): 171–95.

58. T. S. Subramanian and Y. Mallikarjun, "Interception Missile Test-Fired Successfully," *Hindu*, March 7, 2011, 1.

59. Press Trust of India, "Missile Defence Shield Ready: DRDO Chief," *Hindu*, 11.

60. Vijay Sakhuja, "Asian Navies Gear Up for Ballistic Missile Defense at Sea," *South Asia Defense and Strategic Review*, April 11, 2010, www.defstrat.com/exec/frmArticleDetails.aspx?DID=235.

61. Yoichi Kato, "China's Anti-Ship Missile Is Nearly Operational," *Asahi Shimbun*, August 26, 2010, www.asahi.com/english/TKY201008250379.html.

62. Andrew S. Erickson and David D. Yang, "On the Verge of a Game-Changer," *Proceedings of the U.S. Naval Institute*, vol. 135, no. 5 (May 2009).

63. Press Trust of India, "China's ASBM Program Matter of Concern: Navy Chief," December 2, 2010, http://news.outlookindia.com/item.aspx?703459. See also Vinod Anand, "PLA Navy's Anti-Ship Ballistic Missile: Challenge to India," Vivekananda International Foundation, New Delhi, January 18, 2011, www.vifindia.org/article/2011/january/18/PLA-Navy-Anti-Ship-Ballistic-Missile-Challenge-to-India.

64. Ronald O'Rourke, "China Naval Modernization: Implications for U.S. Navy Capabilities—Background and Issues for Congress," *CRS Report for Congress* (Washington, D.C.: Congressional Research Service, May 29, 2009), RL33153, 23.

65. For a detailed discussion, see Yoshihara and Holmes, *Red Star over the Pacific*, 45.

66. C. Raja Mohan, "Space: Asia's New Military Frontier," *Straits Times*, December 22, 2007.

67. Jeremy Page, "India Takes On Old Rival China in New Asian Space Race," *Times Online*, June 20, 2008, available at www.freerepublic.com/focus/f-news/2034657/posts; see also Mary Hennock, "The Real Space Race Is in Asia," *Newsweek*, September 19, 2008, www.newsweek.com/id/160037.

68. Bharath Gopalaswamy, "The Science and Politics of an Indian ASAT Capability," *Space Policy*, vol. 26, no. 4 (November 2010): 229–35.

69. See the sections on the Navy and other passing references in Information Office of the State Council of the People's Republic of China, *China's National Defense in 2008* (Beijing: January 20, 2009), www.china-un.org/eng/gdxw/t534184.htm.

70. Andrew S. Erickson and Michael S. Chase, "Information Technology and China's Naval Modernization," *Joint Forces Quarterly*, no. 50 (2008): 24–30.

71. Integrated Headquarters, Ministry of Defense, Government of India, *Freedom to Use the Seas: India's Maritime Military Strategy* (New Delhi: Ministry of Defense, 2007), 57–70.

72. Arun Prakash, "A Vision of India's Maritime Power in the 21st Century," *Air Power Journal*, vol. 3, no. 4 (October-December 2006): 560.

73. Ashley J. Tellis, "China's Military Space Strategy," *Survival*, vol. 49, no. 3 (Autumn 2007): 41–72; for a contestation of this view, see Michael Krepon, "China's Military Space Strategy: An Exchange," *Survival*, vol. 50, no. 1, (2008): 157–98.

74. Larry M. Wortzel, "The Chinese People's Liberation Army and Space Warfare," *Astropolitics*, vol. 6, no. 2 (2008): 112–37.

75. Jacob Chiriquí, "Military Applications of India's Space Program: The Military Surveillance and Reconnaissance System" (New Delhi: Institute of Peace and Conflict Studies, June 20, 2006), www.ipcs.org/article_details.php?articleNo=2043.

76. Raja Menon, "Strategic Space," in *Space Security and Global Cooperation*, edited by Ajey Lele and Gunjan Singh (New Delhi: Academic Foundation, 2009), 86.

77. Jasjit Singh, "New Space for Arms Race," *Indian Express*, January 27, 2007; Sudha Ramachandran, "India Enters the Space Race," Asia Times Online, February 6, 2007, www.atimes.com/atimes/South_Asia/IB06Df01.html; Gavin Rabinowitz, "Indian Army Wants Military Space Program," Associated Press, June 17, 2008, www.msnbc.msn.com/id/25216230/wid/7279844; Radhakrishna Rao, "Chinese Threat to Indian Space Assets," domain-b.com, January 29, 2009, www.domain-b.com/aero/20090129_indian_space.html.

78. Manu Pubby, "Can Show Anti-Satellite Capability If Govt Gives Nod: DRDO Chief," *Indian Express*, April 21, 2012, www.indianexpress.com/news/can-show-antisatellite-capability-if-govt-gives-nod-drdo-chief/939594/0.

79. "Now, Space Cell to Keep an Eye on China's Plans," *Times of India*, June 11, 2008, 11.

80. K. Kasturirangan, "The Emerging World Space Order: An Indian Perspective," in Lele and Singh, eds., *Space Security and Global Cooperation* (New Delhi: Academic Foundation, 2009), 40.

81. For the relationship between hegemony and command of the commons, see Barry R. Posen, "Command of the Commons: The Military Foundation of U.S. Hegemony," *International Security*, vol. 28, no. 1 (Summer 2003): 5–46.

82. Michael May, "The U.S.-China Strategic Relationship," *Strategic Insights*, vol. 4, no. 9 (September 2005).

83. Paul S. Giarra and Michael J. Green, "Asia's Military Balance at a Tipping Point: America's Deterrent Is Shrinking in the Region," *Wall Street Journal*, July 17, 2009, http://online.wsj.com/article/SB124776820445852755.html.

84. Michael May, "The U.S.-China Strategic Relationship," *Strategic Insights*, vol. 4, no. 9 (September 2005).

85. James R. Holmes and Toshi Yoshihara, "China and the Commons: Angell or Mahan?" *World Affairs*, vol. 168, no. 4 (Spring 2006): 172–91.

86. Jan van Tol et al., "AirSea Battle: A Point-of-Departure Operational Concept" (Washington, D.C.: Center for Strategic and Budgetary Assessments, 2010); for a critique, see Thomas P. M. Barnett, "Big-War Thinking in a Small-War Era: The Rise of the AirSea Battle Concept," *China Security*, vol. 6, no. 3 (November 2010): 3–11.

CHAPTER SIX

1. For a comprehensive review of India's security engagement with East Asia, see David Brewster, *India as an Asia Pacific Power* (New York: Routledge, 2012); see also Walter C. Ladwig III, "Delhi's Pacific Ambition: Naval Power, 'Look East,' and India's Emerging Influence in the Asia-Pacific," *Asian Security*, vol. 5, no. 2 (2009): 87–113; Lisa Curtis, "India's Expanding Role in Asia: Adapting to Rising Power Status," Heritage Foundation Backgrounder, no. 2008, February 20, 2007 (Washington, D.C.: Heritage Foundation); David Scott, "Strategic Imperatives of India as an Emerging Player in Pacific Asia," *International Studies*, vol. 44, no. 2 (April 2007): 123–40; Harsh V. Pant, "India in the Asia-Pacific: Rising Ambitions with an Eye on China," *Asia-Pacific Review*, vol. 14, no. 1 (May 2007): 54–71; Lakhvinder Singh and Changsu Kim, "India's Recent Foreign Policy Initiatives and Implications for East Asian Security," *Korean Journal of Defense Analysis*, vol. 17, no. 3 (2005): 128–50.

2. E. S. Craighill Handy, "The Renaissance of East Indian Culture: Its Significance for the Pacific and the World," *Pacific Affairs*, vol. 3, no. 4 (April 1930): 362–69.

3. See, for example, Susan Bayly, "Imagining 'Greater India': French and Indian Visions of Colonialism in the Indic Mode," *Modern Asian Studies*, vol. 38, no. 3 (July 2004): 703–44.

4. For a summary of India's crucial role as the fulcrum of regional security in the Eastern and Western parts of Asia, see Peter John Brobst, *The Future of the Great Game: Sir Olaf Caroe, India's Independence and the Defense of Asia* (Akron: University of Ohio Press, 2005).

5. For a review of the historic debate on the changing concept of Asia, see Anthony Milner and Deborah Johnson, "The Idea of Asia," in *Regionalism, Subregionalism and*

APEC, edited by John Ingleson (Melbourne: Monash Asia Institute, 1997), 1–19; see also David Camroux, "Asia … Whose Asia? A 'Return to the Future' of a Sino-Indic Asian Community," *Pacific Review*, vol. 20, no. 4 (December 2007): 551–75.

6.   See Rustom Bharucha, *Another Asia: Rabindranath Tagore and Okakura Tenshin* (New Delhi: Oxford University Press, 2006); see also Stephen Hay, *Asian Ideas of East and West: Tagore and His Critics in Japan, China, and India* (Cambridge, Mass.: Harvard University Press, 1970).

7.   T. A. Keenleyside, "Nationalistic Indian Attitudes Towards Asia: A Troublesome Legacy for Post-independence Indian Foreign Policy," *Pacific Affairs*, vol. 55, no. 2 (Summer 1982): 210–30.

8.   See William Henderson, "The Development of Regionalism in Southeast Asia," *International Organization*, vol. 9, no. 4 (November 1955): 463–76; see also Russell H. Fifield, *The Diplomacy of Southeast Asia: 1945–1958* (New York: Harper, 1958).

9.   A U.S. State Department assessment in 1950, quoted in Baldev Raj Nayar and T. V. Paul, *India in the World Order: Searching for Major-Power Status* (Cambridge: Cambridge University Press, 2003), 119.

10.   For a discussion of India's policy toward Southeast Asia until the late 1980s, see Mohammed Ayoob, *India and Southeast Asia: Indian Perceptions and Policies* (London: Routledge, 1990).

11.   David Scott, "India's 'Extended Neighborhood' Concept: Power Projection for a Rising Power," *India Review*, vol. 8, no. 2 (2009): 107–43.

12.   See C. Raja Mohan, *Crossing the Rubicon: The Shaping of India's New Foreign Policy* (New Delhi: Viking, 2003), 204–36.

13.   Two of the most illuminating works are Kripa Sridharan, *The ASEAN Region in India's Foreign Policy* (Aldershot: Dartmouth Publishing Company, 1996), and Christophe Jaffrelot, "India's Look East Policy: An Asianist Strategy in Perspective," *India Review*, vol. 2, no. 2 (2003): 35–68.

14.   For a recent comprehensive review of India's Look East policy and Southeast Asian response, see Tan Tai Yong and See Chak Mun, "The Evolution of India-ASEAN Relations," *India Review*, vol. 8, no. 1 (2009): 20–42.

15.   Prime Minister Manmohan Singh's address to Asia Society Corporate Conference, Mumbai, March 18, 2006, available at www.rediff.com/money/2006/mar/18asoc.htm.

16.   For the initial difficult period of the Look East policy, see J. N. Dixit, *My South Block Years: Memoirs of a Foreign Secretary* (New Delhi: UBS Publishers, 1996), 264–71.

17.   Daljit Singh, "The Geopolitical Interconnection between South and Southeast Asia," in *India and ASEAN: The Politics of India's Look East Policy*, edited by Frederic Grare and Amitabh Mattoo (New Delhi: Manohar, 2001), 38; for an Indian view expressing concern that the focus on the East might be a distraction from the enduring security threats to New Delhi from the northwest, see Zorawar Daulet Singh, "Should India 'Be East' or Be Eurasian?" *Strategic Analysis*, vol. 36, no. 1 (January 2012): 1–5.

18. Atal Bihari Vajpayee, "India's Perspectives on ASEAN and the Asia-Pacific Region," Twenty-first Singapore Lecture, Institute of Southeast Asian Studies, April 9, 2002, www.iseas.edu.sg/vajpayee.pdf.

19. Yashwant Sinha's speech at Harvard University, September 29, 2003, excerpts available at http://meaindia.nic.in/speech/2003/09/29ss09.htm.

20. Inaugural Address to the Seventh Asian Security Conference, Institute of Defense Studies, New Delhi, January 27, 2005, www.idsa.in/node/1553.

21. External Affairs Minister S. M. Krishna's "Inaugural Address at the India-ASEAN Delhi Dialogue III," New Delhi, March 3, 2001, www.mea.gov.in/mystart.php?id=530117332.

22. "Reconceptualizing East Asia," keynote address by Senior Minister Goh Chok Tong at the official launch of the Institute of South Asian Studies, Singapore, January 27, 2005, http://app.mfa.gov.sg/internet/press/view_press_print.asp?post_id=1241.

23. Rahul Roy-Chaudhury, "The Role of Naval Diplomacy in India's Foreign Policy," Foreign Service Institute, *Indian Foreign Policy*, vol. 2 (New Delhi: Konark, 1998), 194–206; see also Vijay Sakhuja, "Naval Diplomacy: Indian Initiatives," Bharat Rakshak Monitor, vol. 6, no. 1 (July–August 2003), available at www.bharat-rakshak.com/MONITOR/ISSUE6–1/Sakhuja.html.

24. See Walter C. Ladwig III, "Delhi's Pacific Ambition: Naval Power, 'Look East,' and India's Emerging Influence in the Asia-Pacific," *Asian Security*, vol. 5, no. 2 (2009).

25. G. V. C. Naidu, "The Indian Navy and Southeast Asia," *Contemporary Southeast Asia*, vol. 13, no. 1 (June 1991): 74–80; Pervaiz Iqbal Cheema, "Indian Naval Buildup and Southeast Asian Security," *Contemporary Southeast Asia*, vol. 13, no. 1 (June 1991): 87–95; Derek da Cunha, "Major Asian Powers and the Development of the Singaporean and Malaysian Armed Forces," *Contemporary Southeast Asia*, vol. 13, no. 1 (June 1991): 57–71; P. Lewis Young, "India's Nuclear Submarine Acquisition: A Major Step Towards Regional Dominance?" *Asian Defense Journal* (November 1988): 4–18.

26. Isabelle Saint-Mézard, *Eastward Bound: India's New Positioning in Asia* (New Delhi: Manohar, 2005), 293.

27. Rahul Roy-Chaudhury, "The Role of the Navy in India's Security Policy," *Contemporary South Asia*, vol. 2, no. 2 (1993): 151–64.

28. Gurpreet S. Khurana, "Cooperation Among Maritime Security Forces: Imperatives for India and Southeast Asia," *Strategic Analysis*, vol. 29, no. 2 (April–June 2005): 295–316.

29. For an overview, see David Scott, "Strategic Imperatives of India as an Emerging Player in Pacific Asia," *International Studies*, vol. 44, no. 2 (April 2007): 126–28.

30. Stratfor, "India Challenges China in South China Sea," April 26, 2000, available at www.atimes.com/ind-pak/BD27Df01.html; see also Josy Joseph, "Navy Hails Successful South China Seas Visit," Rediff News Online, October 17, 2000, www.rediff.com/news/2000/oct/17spec.htm.

31. Sudha Ramachandran, "India Signs On as Southeast Asia Watchdog," Asia Times Online, April 5, 2002, www.atimes.com/ind-pak/DD05Df01.html; see also Gurpreet S. Khurana, "Safeguarding the Malacca Straits," IDSA (Institute for Defense Studies

and Analyses) Comment, January 5, 2005, www.idsa.in/idsastrategiccomments/Safe-guardingtheMalaccaStraits_GUKhurana_050105.

32. For an official account of the Indian Navy, see www.indiannavy.nic.in/tsunami.htm. See also Vijay Sakhuja, "Indian Naval Diplomacy: Post-Tsunami," February 8, 2005 (New Delhi: Institute for Peace and Conflict Studies), www.ipcs.org/article/navy/indian-naval-diplomacy-post-tsunami-1640.html.

33. Sujan Dutta, "Navy Touches Up Friendly Face," *Telegraph*, July 23, 2005, 4.

34. See Donald L. Berlin, "India in the Indian Ocean," *Naval War College Review*, vol. 59, no. 2 (Spring 2006): 58–89.

35. See C. Raja Mohan, "East Asian Security: India's Rising Profile," *RSIS Commentaries*, 81/2007 (Singapore: RSIS), July 30, 2007.

36. "Malabar 2007: India, United States, Japan, Australia, Singapore Begin Massive 5–Day Naval Exercises," *India Defense*, September 3, 2007, www.india-defence.com/reports-3519; Gurmeet Kanwal, "Ex Malabar 2007: The Great Game in the Indian Ocean," *Opinion Asia*, September 12, 2007, www.claws.in/index.php?action=details&m_id=17&u_id=7; Gurpreet S. Khurana, "Joint Naval Exercises: A Post-Malabar-2007 Appraisal for India," IPCS Brief (New Delhi: Institute of Peace and Conflict Studies), no. 52, September 2007.

37. Praful Bidwai, "Five-Nation Drill Presages Asian NATO?" September 8, 2007, Antiwar.com, www.antiwar.com/bidwai/?articleid=11574.

38. P. S. Suryanarayana, "No Evil Design Behind Proactive Naval Exercises: Admiral Mehta," *Hindu*, May 21, 2007, 1.

39. P. S. Suryanarayana, "India and the East Asian Maritime Domain," *Hindu*, April 1, 2009, and "Rising Profile as a Maritime Power in East Asia," *Hindu*, May 2, 2009.

40. Matthew White, "U.S., India, Japan Increase Interoperability During Malabar 2009," U.S. Navy, April 29, 2009, www.navy.mil/search/display.asp?story_id=44843.

41. Sandeep Dikshit, "Japan to Take Part in India-U.S. Naval Exercises Again," *Hindu*, February 16, 2011, 1. Tokyo had to pull out of these exercises at the last minute because of the relief effort in the wake of the massive tsunami that hit Japan in March 2011.

42. For a discussion on the prospects of such a dialogue, see C. Raja Mohan, "Sino-Indian Naval Engagement," *ISAS Brief* (Singapore: Institute of South Asian Studies), no. 103, April 16, 2009, www.isasnus.org/events/backgroundbriefs/104.pdf.

43. P. S. Suryanarayana, "India, China Discuss Anti-Piracy Cooperation," *Hindu*, May 31, 2009, 1.

44. See Sandy Gordon, *Widening Horizons: Australia's New Relationship with India* (Canberra: Australian Strategic Policy Institute, 2007); Rory Medcalf, *Problems to Partnership: A Plan for Australia-India Strategic Ties* (Sydney: Lowy Institute, November 2009). For a more skeptical view, see David Brewster, "Australia and India: The Indian Ocean and the Limits of Strategic Convergence," *Australian Journal of International Affairs*, vol. 64, no. 5 (November 2010): 549–65.

45. David Scott, "Strategic Imperatives of India as an Emerging Player in Pacific Asia," *International Studies*, vol. 44, no. 2 (April 2007): 132–33.

46. "India-Australia Joint Declaration on Security Cooperation," New Delhi, November 12, 2009, www.mea.gov.in/mystart.php?id=530515310.

47. Shishir Upadhyaya, "India–Australia Relations: Scope for Naval Cooperation," New Delhi, National Maritime Foundation, December 4, 2009, www.maritimeindia.org/sites/all/file/pdf/Commentary04Dec09.pdf.

48. Hamish McDonald, "U.S. Seeks Naval Roles for Australia, India," *Sydney Morning Herald*, October 30, 2010, www.smh.com.au/world/us-seeks-naval-roles-for-australia-india-20101029-177ja.html.

49. See Sandy Gordon, "Behind Australia's India Uranium Sale Decision," November 21, 2011, www.eastasiaforum.org/2011/11/21/behind-australia-s-india-uranium-sale-decision; see also Greg Sheridan, "Call for Indo-U.S. security pact with Canberra," *Australian*, November 4, 2011.

50. "Indian Navy: Year End Review, 2010," Indian Navy, Ministry of Defense, December 29, 2010, www.marinebuzz.com/2010/12/29/indian-navy-year-end-review-2010.

51. Sudhir Devare, *India and Southeast Asia: Towards Security Convergence* (Singapore: Institute of Southeast Asian Studies, 2006), 208.

52. Rajiv Sikri, "India's Foreign Policy Priorities in the Coming Decade," ISAS Working Paper (Singapore: Institute of South Asian Studies), no. 25, September 25, 2007.

53. P. S. Suryanarayana, "India, Malaysia to Step Up Defense Ties," *Hindu*, January 8, 2008, www.hindu.com/2008/01/08/stories/2008010856131200.htm. See also Vivek Raghuvanshi, "India, Malaysia Strengthen Defense Relations," *Defense News*, August 18, 2008, 7.

54. "Joint Statement on the Framework for the India-Malaysia Strategic Partnership," Kuala Lumpur, October 27, 2010, www.mea.gov.in/mystart.php?id=530516603; see also Amit Singh, "India-Malaysia Strategic Relations," *Maritime Affairs*, vol. 7, no. 1 (Summer 2011): 85–105.

55. For a firsthand account of the defense agreement, see Chak Mun, *India's Strategic Interests in Southeast Asia and Singapore* (Singapore: Institute for South Asian Studies, 2009), 130. See also G. V. C. Naidu, "Whither the Look East Policy: India and Southeast Asia," *Strategic Analysis*, vol. 28, no. 2 (April-June 2004): 331–46.

56. Ron Matthews and Curie Maharani, "Singapore's Arms Sale to UK: A Defense Export Breakthrough," *RSIS Commentaries* (Singapore: RSIS), no. 1, January 2, 2009, www.rsis.edu.sg/publications/Perspective/RSIS0012009.pdf.

57. For a comprehensive review, see David Brewster, "India's Security Partnership with Singapore," *Pacific Review*, vol. 22, no. 5 (December 2009): 597–618; see also Sinderpal Singh and Syeda Sana Rahman, "India-Singapore Relations: Constructing a 'New' Bilateral Relationship," *Journal of Contemporary Southeast Asia*, vol. 32, no. 1 (April 2010): 70–97.

58. Richard A. Bitzinger, "The China Syndrome: Chinese Military Modernization and the Rearming of Southeast Asia," RSIS Working Paper (Singapore: RSIS), no. 126, May 2, 2007.

59. See Joint Declaration between the Republic of India and the Republic of Indonesia," New Delhi, November 23, 2005, www.mea.gov.in/mystart.php?id=530510388.

60. "Vision for India-Indonesia New Strategic Partnership over the Coming Decade," New Delhi, January 25, 2011, www.mea.gov.in/mystart.php?id=530517097. For an Indian assessment of the bilateral relationship, see Pankaj Jha, "India-Indonesia: Emerging Strategic Confluence in the Indian Ocean Region," *Strategic Analysis*, vol. 32, no. 3 (May 2008): 439–58.

61. For the text of the declaration, see "Vietnam, India Issue Joint Declaration on Strategic Partnership," July 7, 2007, available at www.nanotech-now.com/news.cgi?story_id=23706. For an analysis, see C. Raja Mohan, "The Importance of Being Vietnam," *Indian Express* (New Delhi), July 10, 2007.

62. See Press Information Bureau, Government of India, "India and Vietnam to Expand Defense Cooperation Covering All Three Services," New Delhi, October 13, 2010, available at http://pib.nic.in/newsite/erelease.aspx?relid=66302.

63. John Garver, "Chinese-Indian Rivalry in Indochina," *Asian Survey*, vol. 27, no. 11 (November 1987): 1205–19.

64. Ian Storey and Carlyle Thayer, "Cam Ranh Bay: Past Imperfect, Future Conditional," *Contemporary Southeast Asia*, vol. 23, no. 3 (December 2001): 452–73.

65. David Brewster, "India's Strategic Partnership with Vietnam: The Search for a Diamond on the South China Sea?" *Asian Security*, vol. 5, no. 1 (January 2009): 41.

66. C. Raja Mohan, "The Importance of Being Vietnam," *Indian Express*, July 10, 2007, 10.

67. Pankaj K. Jha, "India-Vietnam Relations: Need for Enhanced Cooperation," *Strategic Analysis*, vol. 32, no. 6 (November 2008): 1085–99.

68. "Background Briefing by Administration Officials on U.S.-South Asia Relations," U.S. Department of State, March 25, 2005, www.fas.org/terrorism/at/docs/2005/StatePressConfer25mar05.htm.

69. For the text of the agreement, see "New Framework for the U.S.-India Defense Relationship," June 28, 2005, C. Raja Mohan, *Impossible Allies: Nuclear India, United States, and the Global Order* (New Delhi: India Research Press, 2006), 285–89.

70. For a discussion of the initial domestic resistance to Indo-U.S. defense cooperation and government's management of it, see Mohan, *Impossible Allies*, 99–130.

71. For a primer on the deal and the competition, see Ashley J. Tellis, *Dogfight! India's Medium Multi-Role Aircraft Decision* (Washington, D.C.: Carnegie Endowment for International Peace, 2011).

72. For an informed discussion, see Bethany Danyluk, "Perceptions and Expectations of the India-U.S. Defense Relationship," in *India's Contemporary Security Challenges*, edited by Michael Kugelman (Washington, D.C.: Wilson Center, 2011), 119–31.

73. James Lamont, "U.S. Agrees Sales of Weapons to India," *Financial Times*, July 20, 2009, www.ft.com/cms/s/0/663e6e04–7507–11de-9ed5–00144feabdc0.html.

74. Sunil Dasgupta and Stephen P. Cohen, "Arms Sales for India: How Military Trade Could Energize U.S.-Indian Relations," *Foreign Affairs*, March/April 2011.

75. For a review of Chinese press commentary, see D. S. Rajan, "China Worried over U.S.-India Military Cooperation," Rediff News Online, September 24, 2009, http://news.rediff.com/column/2009/sep/24/china-worried-over-us-india-military-cooperation.htm.

76. Chietigj Bajpaee, "Strategic Interests Pull Japan and India Together," Power and Interest News Report, February 16, 2007.

77. See Teresita Schaffer and Vibhuti Hate, "India, China and Japan," South Asia Monitor, no. 102, January 3, 2007, www.csis.org/media/csis/pubs/january2007_india-china-japan.pdf.

78. See C. Raja Mohan, "Japan and India: The Making of a New Alliance?" *RSIS Commentaries*, August 27, 2007; see also C. Raja Mohan, "Asia's New 'Democratic Quad,'" *ISN Security Watch*, March 19, 2007, www.isn.ethz.ch/news/sw/details.cfm?ID=17383.

79. Thomas S. Wilkins, "Japan's Alliance Diversification: A Comparative Analysis of the Indian and Australian Strategic Partnerships," *International Relations of the Asia-Pacific*, vol. 11, no. 1 (2011): 115–55.

80. "Joint Declaration on Security Cooperation between India and Japan," Tokyo, October 22, 2008, http://pib.nic.in/release/release.asp?relid=44047; "Action Plan to Advance Security Cooperation Based on the Joint Declaration on Security Cooperation between Japan and India," New Delhi, December 29, 2009, www.mea.gov.in/mystart.php?id=530515442.

81. For a discussion of some of the possibilities, see Gurpreet S. Khurana, "Security of Sea Lines: Prospects for India-Japan Cooperation," *Strategic Analysis*, vol. 31, no. 1 (January 2007): 139–53; see also G. V. C. Naidu, "Ballistic Missile Defense: Perspectives on India-Japan Cooperation," *Strategic Analysis*, vol. 31, no. 1 (January 2007): 155–77.

82. Sandeep Dikshit, "India-Japan Ties Enter Strategic Sphere," *Hindu*, July 4, 2010, www.thehindu.com/news/national/article498924.ece; see also Ministry of External Affairs, "India-Japan 2+2 Dialogue," Press Release, New Delhi, July 6, 2010, www.mea.gov.in/mystart.php?id=530216045.

83. Sourabh Gupta, "Japan-India Maritime Security Cooperation: Floating on Inflated Expectations?" May 11, 2010, www.eastasiaforum.org/2010/05/11/japan-india-maritime-security-cooperation-floating-on-inflated-expectations.

84. David Brewster, "India's Developing Relationship with South Korea: A Useful Friend in East Asia," *Asian Survey*, vol. 50, no. 2 (March/April 2010): 402–25.

85. "India-Republic of Korea Joint Statement: Towards a Strategic Partnership," New Delhi, January 25, 2010, www.mea.gov.in/mystart.php?id=530515523.

86. Press Information Bureau, Government of India, "India and South Korea Sign Two Landmark MoUs to boost Defense Cooperation," New Delhi, September 3, 2010, http://pib.nic.in/newsite/erelease.aspx?relid=65522.

87. Singapore's ambassador-at-large, Tommy Koh, quoted in the U.S. cables (WikiLeaks); see P. S. Suryanarayana, "Singapore Official's Unflattering Comment," *Hindu*, December 13, 2010.

88. Walter C. Ladwig III, "India's Unfinished Asia Pivot," *Wall Street Journal, Opinion Asia*, January 25, 2012.

CHAPTER SEVEN

1. James R. Holmes and Toshi Yoshihara, "China's Naval Ambitions in the Indian Ocean," *Journal of Strategic Studies*, vol. 31, no. 3 (June 2008): 367.

2. David Lei, "China's New Multi-Faceted Maritime Strategy," *Orbis*, vol. 52, no. 1 (Winter 2008): 139–57.

3. For a review of the Chinese debate, see European Council on Foreign Relations and Asia Center, *China's Sea Power: Reaching Out to the Blue Waters* (Paris: March 2011).

4. Jonathan Holslag, "Embracing Chinese Global Security Ambitions," *Washington Quarterly*, vol. 32, no. 3 (July 2009): 105–18.

5. See, for example, Louise Levathes, *When China Ruled the Seas: The Treasure Fleet of the Dragon Throne, 1405–1433* (New York: Oxford University Press, 1996); see also Tansen Sen, "Maritime Interactions between China and India: Coastal Maritime Power in the Indian Ocean," *Journal of Central Eurasian Studies*, vol. 2 (December 2010): 1–42.

6. John Garver, *Protracted Contest: Sino-Indian Rivalry in the Twentieth Century* (Seattle: University of Washington Press, 2001), 44.

7. See Chintamani Mahapatra, "Chinese Navy: Development and Diplomacy," *Strategic Analysis*, vol. 12, no. 8 (November 1988): 865–78; Jasjit Singh, "Growth of Chinese Navy and Its Implications for Indian Security," *Strategic Analysis*, vol. 10, no. 12 (March 1990).

8. For a comprehensive discussion of the origins of the project, see David S. G. Goodman, ed., *China's Campaign to "Open up the West": National, Provincial and Local Perspectives* (New York: Cambridge University Press, 2004); see also Y. M. Yeung and Shen Jianfa, eds., *Developing China's West: A Critical Path to Balanced National Development* (Hong Kong: Chinese University Press, 2004).

9. Sujit Dutta, "China's Rise and Implications for South Asia," unpublished seminar paper (New Delhi: Institute of Defense Studies and Analysis, 2006), 3.

10. For a comprehensive and insightful account, see John Garver, "Development of China's Overland Transportation Links with Central, Southwest and South Asia," *China Quarterly*, no. 185 (March 2006): 1–22.

11. Shen-Yu Dai, "Peking, Kathmandu and New Delhi," *China Quarterly*, no. 16 (1963): 86–98.

12. Hermann Kreutzmann, "The Karakoram Highway: The Impact of Road Construction on Mountain Societies," *Modern Asian Studies*, vol. 25, no. 4 (October 1991):

711–36. See also Mahnaz Ispahani, *Roads and Rivals: The Political Uses of Access in the Borderlands of Asia* (Ithaca, N.Y.: Cornell University Press, 1989).

13. For an early and oppositional framing of the issues by the exiled Tibetan movement, see *Crossing the Line: China's Railway to Lhasa, Tibet* (Washington, D.C.: International Campaign for Tibet, 2003); for a popular rendering of various issues, see Abrahm Lustgarten, *China's Great Train: Beijing's Drive West and the Campaign to Remake Tibet* (New York: Henry Holt, 2009).

14. The author's interview with senior officials of the government of Tibet Autonomous Region in Lhasa during June 2005; see C. Raja Mohan, "Many Roads to China's Tibet Policy," *Indian Express*, June 20, 2005, www.indianexpress.com/storyOld. php?storyId=72949.

15. For an insight, see Tina Harris, "Silk Roads and Wool Routes: Contemporary Geographies of Trade Between Lhasa and Kalimpong," *India Review*, vol. 7, no. 3 (July–September 2008): 200–22.

16. Jabin T. Jacob, "The Qinghai-Tibet Railway and Nathu La: Challenge and Opportunity for India," *China Report*, vol. 43, no. 1 (January 2007): 83–87.

17. For an optimistic view of the possibilities, see Tarun Khanna, "China+India: The Power of Two," *Harvard Business Review*, December 2007, http://hbr.org/product/china-india-the-power-of-two/an/R0712D-PDF-ENG.

18. See, for example, Dawa Norbu, "Chinese Strategic Thinking on Tibet and the Himalayan Region," *Strategic Analysis*, vol. 32, no. 4 (July 2008): 685–702.

19. D. S. Rajan, "China: Military Media Attacks on India-A Tibet Issue Fallout?" South Asia Analysis Group, Paper no. 2650, March 28, 2008, www.southasiaanalysis. org/%5Cpapers27%5Cpaper2650.html.

20. Ananth Krishnan, "China's Rail Network to Touch India's Border," *Hindu*, January 18, 2012; see also Vijay Sakhuja, "China's Strategic Advantage in Nepal," *China Brief*, vol. 11, no. 11 (June 17, 2011).

21. James Lamont, "China's Progress Provokes Border Envy in India," *Financial Times*, January 3, 2010, www.ft.com/cms/s/0/28211170–f875–11de-beb8–00144feab49a. html#axzz1GPrushS4.

22. See D. S. Rajan, "Kashgar as Hub in Central and South Asia Economic Groupings," South Asia Analysis Group, Paper no. 1494, August 10, 2005, www.southasiaanalysis.org/%5Cpapers15%5Cpaper1494.html; see also Michael Clarke, "'Making the Crooked Straight': China's Grand Strategy of 'Peaceful Rise' and its Central Asian Dimension," *Asian Security*, vol. 4, no. 2 (2008): 107–42.

23. For useful assessments, see Yueyao Zhao, "Pivot or Periphery? Xinjiang's Regional Development," *Asian Ethnicity*, vol. 2, no. 2 (September 2001): 197–224; Witt Raczka, "Xinjiang and Its Central Asian Borderlands," *Central Asian Survey*, vol. 17, no. 3 (1998): 373–407; Nicolas Becquelin, "Staged Development in Xinjinag," *China Quarterly*, no. 178 (2004): 358–78.

24. Sumita Kumar, "The China-Pakistan Strategic Relationship: Trade, Investment, Energy, and Infrastructure," *Strategic Analysis*, vol. 31, no. 5 (September 2007): 757–90.

25. John Garver, "Development of China's Overland Transportation Links with Central, Southwest and South Asia," *China Quarterly*, no. 185 (March 2006): 10.

26. For a discussion of China's transport networks, see Geoffrey Kemp, *The East Moves West: India, China, and Asia's Growing Presence in the Middle East* (Washington, D.C.: Brookings Institution Press, 2010), 64–102.

27. Pranab Dhal Samanta, "More Than Troops, Chinese Projects in PoK Worry India," *Indian Express*, September 5, 2010, 1; "Chinese Participation in PoK Projects Illegal: India," *Indian Express*, October 29, 2009, 5.

28. B. Raman, "China in Pakistan-Occupied Kashmir," C3S Paper no. 340 (Chennai: Chennai Center for China Studies, August 28, 2009), www.c3sindia.org/pakistan/796; see also Syed Fazl-e-Haider, "Pakistan Acts to Guard China's Interests," Asia Times Online, September 4, 2009, www.atimes.com/atimes/South_Asia/KI04Df03.html; Preeti Bhattacharji, "Uighurs and China's Xinjiang Region," Council on Foreign Relations Backgrounder, July 6, 2009, www.cfr.org/publication/16870.

29. See, for example, Robert Kaplan, "Pakistan's Fatal Shore," Atlantic Online, May 2009, www.theatlantic.com/doc/200905/kaplan-pakistan; Ziad Haider, "Baluchis, Beijing, and Pakistan's Gwadar Port," *Georgetown Journal of International Affairs*, vol. 6, no. 1 (Winter/Spring 2005): 95–103, www.stimson.org/images/uploads/research-pdfs/GWADAR.pdf; Tariq Mahmud Ashraf, "Afghanistan in Chinese Strategy Towards South and Central Asia," *China Brief*, vol. 8, no. 10 (May 13, 2008).

30. John Garver, "Development of China's Overland Transportation Links with Central, Southwest and South Asia," *China Quarterly*, no. 185 (March 2006): 11–14.

31. For a recent survey of political and economic development in Burma, see Christina Fink, *Living Silence: Burma Under Military Rule* (New York: Zed Books, 2001); Myat Thein, *Economic Development of Myanmar* (Singapore: Institute of Southeast Asian Studies, 2004); Thant Myint-U, *The River of Lost Footsteps: A Personal History of Burma* (New York: Farrar, Straus and Giroux, 2008).

32. For a review of the regional and international politics of Burma, see Mya Than, *Myanmar in ASEAN: Regional Cooperation Experience* (Singapore: Institute of Southeast Asian Studies, 2005); Donald M. Seekins, "Burma-China Relations: Playing with Fire," *Asian Survey*, vol. 37, no. 6 (June 1997): 525–39; Wayne Bert, "Burma, China and the USA," *Pacific Affairs*, vol. 77, no. 2 (Summer 2004): 263–82; Renaud Egretau, *Wooing the Generals: India's New Burma Policy* (New Delhi: Authors Press, 2003).

33. Frank Outram and G. E. Fane, "Burma Road: Back Door to China," *National Geographic*, vol. 78, no. 5 (November 1940): 629–58; Owen Lattimore, "China Opens Her Wild West," *National Geographic*, vol. 82, no. 3 (September 1942): 337–67; John Leroy Christian, "Burma: Where India and China Meet," *National Geographic*, vol. 84, no. 4 (October 1943): 489–512. Joseph E. Passantino, "Kunming: Southwestern Gateway to China," *National Geographic*, vol. 88, no. 2 (August 1945): 137–68.

34. Christopher Bayly and Tim Harper, *Forgotten Armies: Britain's Asian Empire and the War with Japan* (London: Penguin, 2005).

35. For an insightful piece, see Poon Kim Shee, "The Political Economy of China-Myanmar Relations: Strategic and Economic Dimensions," *Ritsumeikan Annual Review*

of International Studies, vol. 1 (2002): 33–53, www.ritsumei.ac.jp/acd/cg/ir/college/
bulletin/e-vol1/1–3shee.pdf.

36. Ian Storey, "Emerging Fault Lines in Sino-Burmese Relations: The Kokang Incident,"
China Brief, vol. 9, no. 18 (September 10, 2009): 1–3.

37. Donovan Webster, *The Burma Road: The Epic Story of the China-Burma-India Theater
in World War II* (New York: Farrar, Straus and Giroux, 2003); see also Barbara W.
Tuchman, *Stilwell and the American Experience in China, 1911–45* (New York: Macmillan, 1970).

38. John Garver, "Development of China's Overland Transportation Links with Central,
Southwest and South Asia," *China Quarterly*, no. 185 (March 2006): 11–14.

39. Brian Spegele, "Myanmar, China Face Off over Halted Dam Project," *Wall Street
Journal*, October 3, 2011; Edward Wong, "U.S. Motives in Myanmar Are on China's
Radar," *New York Times*, November 29, 2011.

40. Maung Aung Myoe, *In the Name of Pauk-Phaw: Myanmar's China Policy Since 1948*
(Singapore: Institute of Southeast Asian Studies, 2011).

41. For a substantive analysis, see Xiangming Chen, *As Borders Bend: Transnational Spaces
in the Pacific Rim* (New York: Rowman and Littlefield, 2005); for details on various
Chinese transportation projects toward East and Southeast Asia, see Zhang Yunling,
ed., *Development of China's Transportation Infrastructure and International Connectivity*, ERIA Research Project Report 2009, no. 7–5 (March 2010), www.eria.org/pdf/
research/y2009/no7–5/all_files.pdfsino_india_pacific_ch_7_v4.docx.

42. Christopher Jasparro, *Paved with Good Intentions? China's Regional Road and Rail Connections* (Honolulu: Asia-Pacific Center for Security Studies, December 2003), 2.

43. For a history of the Strait of Malacca, see Donald B. Freeman, *The Straits of Malacca:
Gateway or Gauntlet?* (Montreal: McGill University Press, 2003); see also Yaacov Vetz-
berger, *The Malacca-Singapore Straits: The Suez of Southeast Asia* (London: Institute
for the Study of Conflict, 1982).

44. See, for example, Graham Gerard Ong-Webb, ed., *Piracy, Maritime Terrorism and
Securing the Malacca Straits* (Singapore: Institute of Southeast Asian Studies, 2006).

45. For an early discussion of the strategic implications of China's growing energy insecu-
rity, see Philip Andrews-Speed, Xuanli Liao, and Roland Dannreuther, *The Strategic
Implications of China's Energy Needs*, Adelphi Papers, no. 346 (London: International
Institute of Strategic Studies, 2002); see also Ingolf Kiesow, *China's Quest for Energy:
Impact on Foreign and Security Policy* (Stockholm: Swedish Defense Research Agency,
2004).

46. For a broad discussion of the issues, see Zhong Xiang Zhang, "China's Energy Security, the Malacca Dilemma, and Responses," *Energy Policy*, vol. 39, no. 2 (December
2011): 7612–15; Andrew B. Kennedy, "China's New Energy-Security Debate," *Survival*, vol. 52, no. 3 (June-July 2010): 137–58; Marc Lanteigne, "China's Maritime Security and the 'Malacca Dilemma,'" *Asian Security*, vol. 4, no. 2 (May 2008): 143–61;
You Ji, "Dealing with the Malacca Dilemma: China's Effort to Protect its Energy
Supply," *Strategic Analysis*, vol. 31, no. 3 (May 2007): 467–89; Ian Storey, "China's
'Malacca Dilemma,'" *China Brief*, vol. 6, no. 8 (April 12, 2006).

47. "U.S.-Indian Alliance against China," editorial in *Ming Pao* daily, August 17, 2005, quoted in James R. Holmes and Toshi Yoshihara, "China's Naval Ambitions in the Indian Ocean," *Journal of Strategic Studies*, vol. 31, no. 3 (June 2008): 18.

48. European Council on Foreign Relations and Asia Center, *China's Sea Power: Reaching Out to the Blue Waters* (Paris: March 2011), 3.

49. Ian Storey, "China's 'Malacca Dilemma,'" *China Brief*, vol. 6, no. 8 (April 12, 2006).

50. See Xuengang Zhang, "China's Energy Corridors in Southeast Asia," *China Brief*, vol. 8, no. 3 (February 4, 2008); see also Ian Storey, "New Energy Projects Help China Reduce Its 'Malacca Dilemma,'" *Opinion Asia* (Singapore: Institute of South East Asian Studies, May 14, 2007).

51. For a recent technical study of the proposal, see Rajesh Thapa, Michiro Kusanagi, Akira Kitazumi, and Yuji Murayama, "Sea Navigation, Challenges and Potentials in Southeast Asia: An Assessment of Suitable Sites for a Shipping Canal in the South Thai Isthmus," *GeoJournal*, vol. 70, no. 2–3 (October 2007): 161–72.

52. See Busakorn Chantasasawat, "Burgeoning Sino-Thai Relations: Heightening Cooperation, Sustaining Economic Security," *China: An International Journal*, vol. 4, no. 1 (March 2006): 86–112, http://muse.jhu.edu/journals/china/v004/4.1chantasasawat.pdf.

53. Graeme Jenkins, "China Building Pipelines to Carry Burmese Oil," *National Post*, January 15, 2008, available at www.biwako.shiga-u.ac.jp/eml/Ronso/387/Kim.pdf; Carl Mortished, "China Secures Gas from Burmese Waters in $5.6 Billion Deal," *Times*, August 26, 2009; "Construction of Sino-Myanmar Pipeline Starts," *China Daily*, September 10, 2010, www.chinadaily.com.cn/china/2010–09/10/content_11288046.htm.

54. See, for example, Shwe Gas Movement, *Corridor of Power: China's Trans-Burma Oil and Gas Pipelines* (Chiang Mai, Thailand: 2009).

55. Brian McCartan, "China, Myanmar Border on Conflict," Asia Times Online, September 10, 2009, www.atimes.com/atimes/Southeast_Asia/KI10Ae01.html; Ian Storey, "Emerging Fault Lines in Sino-Burmese Relations: The Kokang Incident," *China Brief*, vol. 9, no. 18 (September 10, 2009); see also Tom A. Peter, "China Issues Rare Rebuke after Burma Border Clashes," *Christian Science Monitor*, August 30, 2009, www.csmonitor.com/World/terrorism-security/2009/0830/p99s01–duts.html.

56. Antoaneta Bezlova, "China Pushes Burma Pipelines Amid Criticism," Inter Press Service, September 9, 2009, available at http://us.oneworld.org/article/366625–china-pushes-burma-pipelines-amid-criticism; see also Matthew E. Chen, "Chinese National Oil Companies and Human Rights," *Orbis*, vol. 51, no. 1 (Winter 2007): 41–54.

57. Liu Jianping and Feng Xianhui, "Going Global: Dialogue Spanning 600 Years," *Liaowang* (July 11, 2005): 14–19, translation from FBIS-CPP10050719000107.

58. Andrew S. Erickson and Gabriel B. Collins, "China's Oil Security Pipe Dream," *Naval War College Review*, vol. 63, no. 2 (Spring 2010): 91–92.

59. European Council on Foreign Relations and Asia Center, *China's Sea Power: Reaching Out to the Blue Waters* (Paris: March 2011); see also David Walgreen, "China in the

Indian Ocean Region: Lessons in PRC Grand Strategy," *Contemporary Strategy*, vol. 25, no. 1 (March 2006): 55–73.

60. Xu Qi, "Maritime Geostrategy and the Development of the Chinese Navy in the 21st Century," *Naval War College Review*, vol. 59, no. 4 (Autumn 2006): 58.

61. U.S. Defense Department, *Military and Security Developments Involving the People's Republic of China* (Washington, D.C.: 2010), 8.

62. "China Rules Out Naval Base Now," *China Daily*, January 1, 2010, 1.

63. Michael S. Chase and Andrew S. Erickson, "Changes in Beijing's Approach to Overseas Basing?" *China Brief*, vol. 9, no. 19 (September 24, 2009).

64. Ibid.

65. Juli MacDonald, Amy Donahue, and Bethany Danyluk, *Energy Futures in Asia*, Booz Allen Hamilton report sponsored by the Director of Net Assessment, Department of Defense (Washington, D.C.: November 2004).

66. Christopher J. Pehrson, *String of Pearls: Meeting the Challenge of Rising Power across the Asian Littoral* (Carlisle, Pa.: Strategic Studies Institute, U.S. Army War College, July 2006).

67. Bill Gertz, "China Builds Up Strategic Sea Lanes," *Washington Times*, January 18, 2005, 1.

68. James R. Holmes and Toshi Yoshihara, "China's Naval Ambitions in the Indian Ocean," *Journal of Strategic Studies*, vol. 31, no. 3 (June 2008): 379–80.

69. Daniel J. Kostecka, "Places and Bases: The Chinese Navy's Emerging Support Network in the Indian Ocean," *Naval War College Review*, vol. 64, no. 1 (Winter 2011): 60.

70. For a brief review of the hysteria in Delhi during the summer of 2009, see B. Raman, "India-China: Dangerous Hysteria," South Asia Analysis Group, paper no. 3398, September 8, 2009, www.southasiaanalysis.org/papers34/paper3398.html; Shekhar Gupta, "Stop Fighting the 1962 War," *Indian Express*, September 18, 2009, www.indianexpress.com/news/stop-fighting-the-1962–war/518975; Ishan Tharoor, "Why India Sees a Chinese 'Red Peril' on Land and Sea" *Time*, September 20, 2009, www.time.com/time/world/article/0,8599,1924884,00.html.

71. Shivshankar Menon, "Maritime Imperatives of Indian Foreign Policy," lecture at the National Maritime Foundation, New Delhi, September 11, 2009, www.maritimeindia.org/pdfs/SMenon.pdf, 5.

72. Zha Daojiong, "Energy Interdependence," *China Security*, no. 3 (Summer 2006): 11.

73. Shaofeng Chen, "China's Self-Extrication from the 'Malacca Dilemma' and Its Implications," *International Journal of China Studies*, vol. 1, no. 1 (January 2010): 1–24.

74. For a frequency and content analysis of these issues in Chinese military writings, see M. Taylor Fravel and Alexander Liebman, "Beyond the Moat: the PLAN's Evolving Interests and Potential Influence," in *The Chinese Navy: Expanding Capabilities, Evolving Roles*, edited by Phillip C. Saunders, Christopher D. Yung, Michael Swaine, and Andrew Nien-Dzu Yang (Washington, D.C.: National Defense University Press, 2011), 74.

75. Ibid., 76.

76. Chris Rahman, "China's Maritime Strategic Agenda," *Policy Analysis*, no. 60 (Canberra: Australian Strategic Policy Institute, April 2010).

77. Ryan Clarke, *Chinese Energy Security: The Myth of the PLAN's Frontline Status* (Carlisle, Pa.: Strategic Studies Institute, 2010).

CHAPTER EIGHT

1. Cited in Reynolds Peele, "The Importance of Maritime Choke Points," *Parameters* (Summer 1997): 61–74, https://carlisle-www.army.mil/usawc/Parameters/97summer/peele.htm.

2. For a comprehensive review, see Robert Harkavy, *Strategic Basing and the Great Powers, 1200–2000* (London: Routledge, 2007).

3. Kent E. Calder, *Embattled Garrisons: Comparative Base Politics and American Globalism* (Princeton, N.J.: Princeton University Press, 2007), 7–8.

4. Catherine Lutz, ed., *The Bases of Empire: The Global Struggle against U.S. Military Posts* (New York: New York University Press, 2009).

5. K. M. Panikkar, *India and the Indian Ocean: An Essay on the Influence of Seapower on Indian History* (London: George Allen and Unwin, 1945), 84–95.

6. Michael S. Chase and Andrew S. Erickson, "Changes in Beijing's Approach to Overseas Basing?" *China Brief*, vol. 9, no. 19 (September 24, 2009).

7. See, for example, Zdzislaw Lachowski, "Foreign Military Bases in Eurasia," SIPRI Policy Paper no. 18 (Stockholm: Stockholm International Peace Research Institute, 2007); Andrew Hansen, "The French Military in Africa," *Backgrounder* (New York: Council on Foreign Relations, 2008).

8. "Russia plans navy bases in Libya, Syria, Yemen: Report," Reuters, January 16, 2009, http://af.reuters.com/article/topNews/idAFJOE50F0LO20090116; Matthew Saltmarsh, "France Opens First Military Bases in the Gulf," *New York Times*, May 26, 2009; Aly Verjee, "Forward Operating Base Djibouti," Security Sector Reform Resource Center, July 27, 2011, www.ssrresourcecentre.org/2011/07/27/forward-operating-base-djibouti.

9. Kent E. Calder, *Embattled Garrisons*, 183–84.

10. For a full account, see David Vine, *Island of Shame: The Secret History of U.S. Military Base on Diego Garcia* (Princeton, N.J.: Princeton University Press, 2008); see also Vytautas B. Bandjunis, *Diego Garcia: Creation of the Indian Ocean Base* (San Jose: Writer's Showcase, 2001).

11. Andrew S. Erickson, Walter C. Ladwig III, and Justin D. Mikolay, "Diego Garcia and the United States' Emerging Indian Ocean Strategy," *Asian Security*, vol. 6, no. 3 (2010): 214–37.

12. The statement on the eve of the visit by Chinese Assistant Foreign Minister Zhai Zun in Beijing, February 6, 2009; see "FM: Energy Co-Op Only Part of Sino-Africa

Co-Op," Xinhua, February 6, 2009, http://news.xinhuanet.com/english/2009–02/06/content_10775342.htm.

13. C. Raja Mohan, "Beijing is Testing Strategic Waters in India's Backyard," *Indian Express*, January 30, 2007, 1; C. Raja Mohan, "Circling Mauritius," *Indian Express*, February 11, 2009, 13.

14. See "China's African Policy," *People's Daily*, January 2006, http://english.peopledaily.com.cn/200601/12/eng20060112_234894.html.

15. Ian Taylor, "Arms Sales to Africa: Beijing's Reputation at Risk," *China Brief*, vol. 7, no. 7 (May 18, 2007); see also Andrei Chang, "China Expanding African Arms Sales," UPI Asia, January 26, 2009, available at www.freerepublic.com/focus/f-news/2171826/posts.

16. Alex Vines and Bereni Oruitemeka, "India's Engagement with the African Indian Ocean Rim States," Africa Programme Paper no. 1/08 (London: Chatham House, 2008).

17. Author's conversations with senior naval officials in New Delhi, March 2005.

18. "Seychelles at Shanghai World Expo 2010," *Nation*, May 3, 2010, www.nation.sc/imprimer.php?art=19329.

19. The founding president of Seychelles, James R. Mancham, has been warning for years about Chinese penetration into Seychelles and urging the U.S. to devote greater attention to island states. For an Indian assessment of Chinese interests in the region, see Vidhan Pathak, "China and Francophone Western Indian Ocean Region: Implications for Indian Interests," *Journal of Defense Studies*, vol. 3, no. 4 (October 2009): 79–102.

20. India Ministry of External Affairs, "Visit of the President of Seychelles to India," New Delhi, June 4, 2010, available at www.mea.gov.in/mystart.php?id=550315827.

21. India Ministry of Defense, "India and Seychelles Agree to Expand Cooperation for Maritime Security in IOR," July 19, 2010, available at http://pib.nic.in/newsite/erelease.aspx?relid=63345.

22. Sarabjeet Singh Parmar, "Island Hopscotch in the Indian Ocean Region," *IDSA Comment*, December 15, 2011, www.idsa.in/idsacomments/IslandicHopScotchintheIndianOceanRegion_ssparmar_151211.

23. "China, Seychelles to Boost Bilateral Ties," Xinhua, December 3, 2011, http://news.xinhuanet.com/english2010/china/2011–12/03/c_131286266.htm; Jeremy Page and Tom Wright, "Chinese Military Considers New Indian Ocean Presence," *Wall Street Journal*, December 14, 2011; Li Xiaokun and Li Lianxing, "Navy looks at offer from Seychelles," *China Daily*, December 13, 2011, www.chinadaily.com.cn/china/2011–12/13/content_14254395.htm.

24. India Ministry of External Affairs, "Prime Minister's Meeting with President of Seychelles," New Delhi, February 2, 2012, available at www.mea.gov.in/mystart.php?id=190018971.

25. Indrani Bagchi, "India's Big Push for Africa, Indian Ocean Strategy," *Times of India*, February 1, 2012, 11.

26. For an official Indian review of the bilateral ties with Mauritius, see "India-Mauritius Relations," February 2012, available at www.mea.gov.in/mystart.php?id=50044499.

27. Richard Lough, "China Signs $260 mln Airport Deal With Mauritius," Reuters India, February 17, 2009, http://in.reuters.com/article/asiaCompanyAndMarkets/idINLH32372920090217?sp=true.

28. "Mauritius-China: 'Gateway to Africa' Aim," *Africa Research Bulletin*, vol. 45, no. 2 (February 16–March 15, 2008): 17733.

29. See the Official Indian review, n. 26.

30. Siddhartha, "India Eyes an Island in the Sun," *Times of India*, November 26, 2006, 1.

31. "Visit of MoS Dr. Shashi Tharoor to the Republic of Mauritius," November 4, 2009, available at http://indiahighcom-mauritius.org/visit_MOS.php.

32. India Ministry of External Affairs, "Joint Statement on the Occasion of the State Visit of the Prime Minister of Mauritius," New Delhi, February 7, 2012, available at www.mea.gov.in/mystart.php?id=530518986.

33. James Lamont, "China Makes Foray into Mauritius," *Financial Times*, January 25, 2010.

34. See, for example, Mohammed Ayoob, "India as a Regional Hegemon: External Opportunities and Internal Constraints," *International Journal*, vol. 46, no. 3 (Summer 1991): 420–48; Anirudha Gupta, "A Brahmanic Framework of Power in South Asia?" *Economic and Political Weekly*, vol. 25, no. 14 (April 7, 1990): 711–14; Devin Hagerty, "India's Regional Security Doctrine," *Asian Survey*, vol. 31, no. 4 (April 1991): 351–63.

35. For an account of Maldives's emergence as an independent nation in 1965 and its early political evolution, see Urmila Phadnis and Ela Luithui, *Maldives: Winds of Change in an Atoll State* (New Delhi: South Asia Publishers, 1985).

36. V. S. Sambandan, "A Cry for Democracy," *Frontline*, vol. 21, no. 20 (September 25, 2004). See also Sucharita Sidhanta, "Maldives: Is Gayoom's Government Getting More Autocratic?" South Asia Analysis Group, Paper no. 1195, December 20, 2004, www.southasiaanalysis.org/papers12/paper1195.html.

37. Sudha Ramachandran, "Maldives: Tiny Islands, Big Intrigue," Asia Times Online, April 7, 2006, www.atimes.com/atimes/South_Asia/HD07Df01.html.

38. For the official press release issued by the government of India, see "Pranab to Visit Maldives Handing over of Fast Attack Craft," April 13, 2006, available at http://indiannavy.nic.in/pres04.htm.

39. See the official Indian press release, "India and Maldives to Develop a Privileged Partnership: Pranab Mukherjee," Press Information Bureau, New Delhi April 17, 2006, http://pib.nic.in/newsite/erelease.aspx?relid=17153.

40. Jyoti Malhotra, "Maldives Opposition Lobbies India's Support for Democracy," *Mint*, July 22, 2008, 1; see also Stephen Zunes, "The Power of Protest in the Maldives," December 2, 2008, available at www.opendemocracy.net/india/article/stephen_zunes/maldives_nonviolent_conflict; Andrew Buncombe, "Maldives Celebrates as Dictator Is Voted Out," *Independent*, October 30, 2008.

41. Manu Pubby, "India Bringing Maldives into Its Security Net," *Indian Express*, August 13, 2009, 1.

42. Sujan Dutta, "Navy Eyes Maldives: Counter to China's 'String of Pearls' Plan," *Telegraph*, August 20, 2009.

43. For the official Indian statement on Antony's visit to Maldives, see "India and Maldives Agree to Step Up Defence Cooperation, India and Maldives Are Equal Partners," New Delhi, August 20, 2009, http://pib.nic.in/newsite/erelease.aspx?relid=52038.

44. Indian Ministry of External Affairs, "Framework Agreement on Cooperation for Development between India and Maldives," November 12, 2011, available at www.mea.gov.in/mystart.php?id=530518529.

45. Associated Press, "China Opens Embassy in Maldives," *Guardian*, November 11, 2011.

46. Jyoti Malhotra, "Maldives, Mauritius New Centers of Sino-Indian Rivalry," *Business Standard*, September 11, 2009.

47. Xinhua, "China Vows to Expand Military Cooperation with Maldives," February 19, 2009.

48. Jyoti Malhotra, "There is a Maldivian Link to 26/11," interview with President Nasheed, *Business Standard*, October 25, 2009, 1.

49. Manu Pubby, "Week Before Ouster, Faced Pressure to Sign Defense Deal with China: Nasheed," *Indian Express*, February 15, 2012, 1; Press Trust of India, "Delhi Has Special Place, Should Not Worry about Beijing," *Hindustan Times*, February 17, 2012, 1.

50. Press Trust of India, "India, U.S. Working Together on Maldives: Nuland," *Asian Age*, February 18, 2012, 5.

51. Peter Popham, "How Beijing Won Sri Lanka's Civil War," *Independent*, May 23, 2009, www.independent.co.uk/news/world/asia/how-beijing-won-sri-lankas-civil-war-1980492.html.

52. Jeremy Page, "Port in a Storm: How Chinese Billions Funded Army's Battle to Break Tigers," *Times*, May 2, 2009; Dan Murphy, "Briefing: Indian Ocean as new strategic playing field," *Christian Science Monitor*, July 3, 2009, www.csmonitor.com/World/Asia-South-Central/2009/0703/p12s01–wosc.html.

53. Goh Sui Noi, "China Not Planning Sri Lanka Naval Base," *Straits Times*, June 24, 2009.

54. Mahdi Darius Nazemroaya, "Indian Ocean Great Power Confrontation: Geopolitics of the Sri Lankan Civil War," *Sri Lanka Guardian*, October 29, 2009, www.srilankaguardian.org/2009/10/indian-ocean-great-power-confrontation.html; "India Encircled by China's String of Pearls?" Tamil News Network, July 29, 2009, www.tamilnewsnetwork.com/tamilnewsnetwork.com/post/2009/07/29/India-encircled-by-Chinae28099s-string-of-pearls.aspx.

55. Shelton U. Kodikara, *Foreign Policy of Sri Lanka: A Third World Perspective* (New Delhi: Chanakya, 1982).

56. For a comprehensive account, see K. M. De Silva, *Regional Powers and Small State Security: India and Sri Lanka, 1977–90* (Washington, D.C.: Woodrow Wilson Center Press, 1995).

57. Swaran Singh, *China-South Asia: Issues, Equations, Policies* (New Delhi: Lancers, 2003).

58. See B. Raman, "Gwadar, Hambantota and Sitwe: China's Strategic Triangle," South Asia Analysis Group, Paper no. 2158, March 6, 2007, www.southasiaanalysis.org/%5Cpapers22%5Cpaper2158.html; see also Sudha Ramachandran, "China Moves into India's Backyard," Asia Times Online, March 13, 2007, www.atimes.com/atimes/South_Asia/IC13Df01.html.

59. For a short Sri Lankan official summary of the project, see "Hambantota: The New Hub of Development," Current Affairs Sri Lanka, March 12, 2007, www.priu.gov.lk/news_update/Current_Affairs/ca200703/20070312hambantota_new_hub_development.htm.

60. Author's conversations with officials from the Indian Embassy, Colombo, January 2007.

61. See his interview with *Time* magazine in 2009: Jyoti Thottam, "The Man Who Tamed the Tigers," *Time*, July 13, 2009, www.time.com/time/world/article/0,8599,1910095,00.html.

62. Senake Bandaranayake et al., *Sri Lanka and the Silk Road of the Sea*, 2nd ed. (Colombo: Sri Lanka Institute of International Relations, 2003).

63. See Amal Jayawardane, ed., *Documents on Sri Lanka's Foreign Policy: 1947–65* (Colombo: Regional Center for Strategic Studies, 2005), 200–207.

64. Ibid.

65. James Manor and Gerald Segal, "Causes of Conflict: Sri Lanka and Indian Ocean Strategy," *Asian Survey*, vol. 25, no. 12 (December 1985): 1184.

66. "Center Considering Unified Command for Armed Forces," *Hindu*, June 1, 2007, 1.

67. *SIPRI Yearbook 2009: Armaments, Disarmament and International Security* (Stockholm: Stockholm International Peace Research Institute, 2009), 316.

68. Ameen Izzadeen, "Sri Lanka Drifts Closer to the East," Asia Times Online, June 18, 2009, www.atimes.com/atimes/South_Asia/KF18Df02.html.

69. "Lanka, China Unlikely to Ink Defense Pact: Rohitha Bogollogama," *Daily News & Anaylsis* (Mumbai), October 25, 2009, www.dnaindia.com/world/report_lanka-china-unlikely-to-ink-defence-pact-rohitha-bogollagama_1302944.

70. Jeremy Page, "Sri Lanka's President Rajapaksa 'Feared Coup' after Defeat of Tamil Tigers," *Times*, November 14, 2009, www.timesonline.co.uk/tol/news/world/asia/article6916618.ece.

71. Mian Ridge, "Why India Embraces Sri Lanka's Rajapaksa in First Postwar Visit," *Christian Science Monitor*, June 10, 2010, www.csmonitor.com/World/Asia-South-Central/2010/0610/Why-India-embraces-Sri-Lanka-s-Rajapaksa-in-first-postwar-visit.

72. India Ministry of External Affairs, "India-Sri Lanka Joint Declaration," June 9, 2010, available at www.mea.gov.in/mystart.php?id=530515869.

73. Manu Pubby, "India Activates First Listening Post on Foreign Soil: Radars in Madagascar," *Indian Express*, July 18, 2007, 1.

74. Sudha Ramachandran, "Delhi All Ears in the Indian Ocean," Asia Times Online, March 3, 2006, www.atimes.com/atimes/South_Asia/HC03DfO2.html.

75. Manu Pubby, "India Activates First Listening Post on Foreign Soil: Radars in Madagascar," *Indian Express*, July 18, 2007.

76. For a comprehensive account, see Alex Vines and Bereni Oruitemeka, "India's Engagement with African Indian Ocean Rim States," Africa Programme Paper no. 1/08 (London: Chatham House, April 2008), www.chathamhouse.org.uk/publications/papers/view/-/id/607.

77. Tamara Renee Shie, "Rising Chinese Influence in the South Pacific: Beijing's 'Island Fever,'" *Asian Survey*, vol. 47, no. 2 (March/April 2007): 307–26; see also Thomas Lum and Bruce Vaughn, "The Southwest Pacific: U.S. Interests and China's Growing Influence," CRS Report for Congress (Washington, D.C.: Congressional Research Service, July 2007).

78. Paul Buchanan, "China Steps into Pacific Power Vacuum," Pacific Islands Report, East-West Center, September 17, 2009, available at http://archives.pireport.org/archive/2009/September/09–18–cm.htm.

79. For a review, see Carmen Voigt-Graf, "Transnationalism and the Indo-Fijian Diaspora: The Relationship of Indo-Fijians to India and its People," *Journal of Intercultural Studies*, vol. 29, no. 1 (February 2008): 81–109.

80. Terence Wesley-Smith, *China in Oceania: New Forces in Pacific Politics* (Honolulu: East-West Center, 2007); Fergus Hanson, *The Dragon in the Pacific: More Opportunity than Threat* (Sydney: Lowy Institute, 2008); Jian Yang, "China in the South Pacific: Hegemon on the Horizon?" *Pacific Review*, vol. 22, no. 2 (May 2009): 139–58.

81. Shubha Singh, "Reaching out to the South Pacific," *Frontline*, vol. 19, no. 20, October 12–25, 2002, www.hindu.com/thehindu/fline/fl1920/stories/20021011008305900.htm.

82. John M. Ward, *British Policy in the South Pacific, 1796–1893* (Sydney: Australasian Publishers, 1948).

83. Jayanth Jacob, "India Begins Trilateral Talks to Check China," *Hindustan Times*, December 20, 2011, 1.

84. S. Anandan, "Nirmal Verma: Today's Oceans Are Maritime Highways Linking Nations," *Hindu*, February 5, 2012, 10.

CHAPTER NINE

1. For a detailed analysis, see Geoffrey Kemp, *The East Moves West: India, China, and Asia's Growing Presence in the Middle East* (Washington, D.C.: Brookings Institution Press, 2010).

2. James Onley, *The Arabian Frontier of the British Raj: Merchants, Rulers, and the British in the Nineteenth-Century Gulf* (New York: Oxford University Press, 2007).

3. Robert Blyth, *The Empire of the Raj: Eastern Africa and the Middle East, 1858–1947* (New York: Palgrave Macmillan, 2003).

4. For early insights into the strategic consequences of the partition for the security of the Gulf, see Olaf Caroe, *Wells of Power: The Oil Fields of South Western Asia* (London: Macmillan, 1951).

5. Yaacov Vertzberger, *China's Southwestern Strategy: Encirclement and Counterencirclement* (New York: Praeger, 1985).

6. Yitzhak Shichor, "Blocking the Hormuz Strait: China's Energy Dilemma," *China Brief*, vol. 8, no. 18 (September 22, 2008).

7. Ed Blanche, "Enter the Tiger and the Dragon: India and China Move into the Arabian Sea to Protect Their Energy Lifelines to the Middle East," *Middle East*, April 1, 2009, available at www.thefreelibrary.com/_/print/PrintArticle.aspx?id=198169975.

8. See, for example, C. Raja Mohan, "India's Look West Policy," *Hindu*, June 17, 2004; C. Raja Mohan, "Nine Ways to Look West," *Indian Express*, January 8, 2007; Prasanta Kumar Pradhan, "Accelerating India's 'Look West' Policy in the Gulf," *IDSA Issue Brief* (New Delhi: Institute for Defense Studies and Analysis, February 3, 2011), www.idsa.in/system/files/IB_IndiaLookWestPolicy.pdf.

9. "PM Launches Look-West Policy to Boost Cooperation with Gulf," Press Release, New Delhi, July 27, 2005, available at http://pib.nic.in/newsite/erelease.aspx?relid=10534.

10. For a comprehensive recent review of India's relations with the Gulf, see Samir Pradhan, "India's Economic and Political Presence in the Gulf: A Gulf Perspective," in Gulf Research Center and Nixon Center, *India's Growing Role in the Gulf: Implications for the Region and the United States* (Dubai: 2009), 15–39.

11. See Chietigj Bajpaee, "India, China locked in energy game," Asia Times Online, March 17, 2005, www.atimes.com/atimes/Asian_Economy/GC17Dk01.html; see also "India to Adopt 'Look West Asia' Policy," *People's Daily*, August 24, 2005, http://english.people.com.cn/200508/24/eng20050824_204224.html.

12. Xinhua, "India Deploys Warships in Gulf Region," September 12, 2004.

13. David Scott, "India's 'Extended Neighborhood' Concept: Power Projection for a Rising Power," *India Review*, vol. 8, no. 2 (2009): 133.

14. Ibid. Unless otherwise specified, many of the following details are largely from Scott, who gives a comprehensive account of India's maritime diplomacy and the power projection efforts in recent years.

15. See Atul Aneja, "Navy Chief for Enhanced Ties with UAE," *Hindu*, February 8, 2007, 1; see also B. Raman, "Indian Navy Begins to Look West," South Asia Analysis Group, Paper no. 2128, February 9, 2007.

16. "Indian Ambassador, IAF Observer, and Commander RAFO Visit IAF Contingent in Oman," Press Information Bureau, New Delhi, October 28, 2009, www.pib.nic.in/release/rel_print_page1.asp?relid=53650.

17. "Indo-Oman Air Exercise-Eastern Bridge to Foster Defense Cooperation Ties," Press Information Bureau, New Delhi, October 14, 2009, www.pib.nic.in/newsite/erelease.aspx?relid=53179.

18. Sandeep Dikshit, "India, Oman to Step Up Defense Ties," *Hindu*, November 10, 2008.

19. Sandeep Dikshit, "India, Oman Still Studying Undersea Pipeline," *Hindu*, October 30, 2009.

20. K. Alan Kronstadt and Kenneth Katzman, *India-Iran Relations and U.S. Interests* (Washington, D.C.: Congressional Research Service, August 2006), 5.

21. Indo-Asian News Service, "Saudi Arabian Warships on Maiden Visit to India," New Delhi, July 25, 2008; K. S. Ramkumar, "Saudi-Indian Naval Drill Today," *Arab News*, May 25, 2009.

22. Ghazanfar Ali Khan, "Joint Team to Prepare Road Map for Saudi-India Defense Cooperation," *Arab News*, February 15, 2012, http://arabnews.com/saudiarabia/article575809.ece.

23. Press Trust of India, "India, Qatar Ink Key Defense Cooperation Pact," November 10, 2008 http://news.outlookindia.com/items.aspx?artid=12199; see also Vinod Mathew, "Security Pact with Qatar Gives India Gulf Toehold," *Indian Express*, November 12, 2008.

24. Author's conversation with Indian officials, New Delhi, December 2008.

25. Charles W. Koburger Jr., *Naval Strategy East of Suez: The Role of Djibouti* (New York: Praeger, 1992)

26. Scott, "India's 'Extended Neighborhood' Concept," 134.

27. See Alex Martin, "First Overseas Military Base Since WWII to Open in Djibouti," *Japan Times Online*, July 2, 2011, www.japantimes.co.jp/text/nn20110702f2.html. For the text of the Japanese agreements with Djibouti, including the Status of Forces Agreement, see the official website of the Ministry of Foreign Affairs of Japan, www.mofa.go.jp/region/Africa/djibouti/index.html.

28. John M. Willis, "Making Yemen Indian: Rewriting the Boundaries of Imperial Arabia," *International Journal of Middle East Studies,* vol. 41, no. 1 (January 2009): 23–38.

29. See the official account of Operation Sukoon at www.indiannavy.nic.in/sukoon.pdf.

30. Press Trust of India, "'Operation Safe Homecoming' Draws Towards a Close," March 10, 2011, available at http://news.outlookindia.com/items.aspx?artid=714685.

31. Daniel J. Kostecka, "Places and Bases: The Chinese Navy's Emerging Support Network in the Indian Ocean," *Naval War College Review*, vol. 64, no. 1 (Winter 2011): 65.

32. For a comprehensive analysis of the emerging Sino-Iranian relationship, see John Garver, *China and Iran: Ancient Partners in a Post-Imperial World* (Seattle: University of Washington Press, 2006.)

33. Kaveh L. Afrasiabi, "A China Base in Iran?" Asia Times Online, January 28, 2009, www.atimes.com/atimes/Middle_East/JA29Ak03.html; see also Christina Lin, "China's Persian Gulf Strategy," *China Brief*, vol. 9, no. 21 (October 2009).

34. "Chinese, Arab Senior Officials Hold 6th Meeting for China-Arab Cooperation Forum," Beijing, June 23, 2009, available at www.mfa.gov.cn/eng/wjdt/wshd/t569 478.htm.

35. For a review, see John Calabrese, "Peaceful or Dangerous Collaborators? China's Relations with the Gulf Countries," *Pacific Affairs*, vol. 65, no. 4 (Winter 1992–93): 471–85; Julian Madsen, "China's Policy in the Gulf Region: From Neglect to Necessity," *Power and Interest News Report*, October 27, 2006; Michael Thorpe and Sumit Mitra, "Growing Economic Interdependence of China and the Gulf Cooperation Council," *China & World Economy*, vol. 16, no. 2 (March-April 2008): 109–24.

36. Jad Mouawad, "China's Growth Shifts the Geopolitics of Oil," *New York Times*, March 19, 2010, www.nytimes.com/2010/03/20/business/energy-environment/20saudi.html; see also "China exceeds U.S. to become Saudi Arabia's Top Oil Importer," *Global Times*, February 23, 2010, http://business.globaltimes.cn/china-economy/2010–02/507404. html.

37. Flynt Leverett and Jeffrey Bader, "Managing China-U.S. Energy Competition in the Middle East," *Washington Quarterly*, vol. 29, no. 1 (Winter 2005–06): 187–201; John Keefer Douglas, Matthew B. Nelson, and Kevin Schwartz, "Fueling the Dragon's Flame: How China's Energy Demands Affect its Relationship in the Middle East," paper presented to U.S.-China Economic and Security Review Commission, U.S. Congress, Washington, D.C., September 14, 2006; Jon B. Alterman, "China's Hard Choices on Iran," *World Politics Review*, October 14, 2009, available at www. worldpoliticsreview.com/articles/4443/chinas-hard-choices-on-iran; Yitzhak Shichor, "Blocking the Hormuz Strait: China's Energy Dilemma," *China Brief*, vol. 8, no. 18 (September 22, 2008).

38. "First Chinese-Built Frigate Inducted into Pakistan Navy," *Dawn*, July 31, 2009, www.dawn.com/wps/wcm/connect/dawn-content-library/dawn/the-newspaper/ front-page/first-chinesebuilt-frigate-inducted-into-pakistan-navy-179.

39. Daniel J. Kostecka, "Places and Bases: The Chinese Navy's Emerging Support Network in the Indian Ocean," *Naval War College Review*, vol. 64, no. 1 (Winter 2011): 71.

40. Itamar Lee, "Deepening Naval Cooperation between Islamabad and Beijing," *China Brief*, vol. 9, no. 13 (June 24, 2009), available at www.jamestown.org/single/?no_ cache=1&tx_ttnews%5Btt_news%5D=35173.

41. For a discussion of the Chinese and Indian dilemmas, see John W. Garver, "Is China Playing a Dual Game in Iran?" *Washington Quarterly*, vol. 34, no. 1 (Winter 2011): 75–88; Harsh V. Pant, "India's Relations with Iran: Much Ado about Nothing," *Washington Quarterly*, vol. 34, no. 1 (Winter 2011): 61–74.

42. K. B. Sayeed, "Southeast Asia in Pakistan's Foreign Policy," *Pacific Affairs*, vol. 41, no. 2 (Summer 1968): 230–44.

43. For an account of the strategic dynamics of the creation of Bangladesh and its immediate geopolitical aftermath, see G. W. Choudhury, *India, Pakistan, Bangladesh, and the Major Powers: Politics of a Divided Subcontinent* (New York: Free Press, 1975).

44. For an overview, see Sucheta Ghosh, *China-Bangladesh-India Tangle Today: Towards a Solution?* (New Delhi: Sterling Publishers, 1995).

45. Deb Mukharji, "Bangladesh," in J. N. Dixit, ed., *External Affairs: Cross-Border Relations* (New Delhi: Roli Books, 2003), 189–212.

46. Sreeradha Datta, "Bangladesh's Relations with China and India: A Comparative Study," *Strategic Analysis*, vol. 32, no. 5 (September 2008): 766.

47. Sharif M. Hossain and Ishtiaque Selim, "Sino-Bangladesh Economic Relations: Prospects and Challenges," *BIISS Journal*, vol. 27, no. 4 (October 2006): 354–55.

48. Anand Kumar, "Bangladesh's Quest for Nuclear Energy," *IDSA Comment*, October 17, 2007 (New Delhi: Institute for Defense Studies and Analyses), www.idsa.in/idsastrategiccomments/BangladeshsQuestforNuclearEnergy_AKumar_171007.

49. Subhash Kapila, "Bangladesh-China Defense Cooperation Agreement's Strategic Implications: An Analysis," South Asia Analysis Group, Paper no. 582, www.southasiaanalysis.org/papers6/paper582.html.

50. Urvashi Aneja, "China-Bangladesh Relations: An Emerging Strategic Partnership?" IPCS Special Report (New Delhi: Institute of Peace and Conflict Studies, 2006).

51. Sreeradha Datta, "Bangladesh's Relations with China and India: A Comparative Study," *Strategic Analysis*, vol. 32, no. 5 (September 2008): 764–65.

52. Vijay Sakhuja, "China-Bangladesh Relations and Potential for Regional Tensions," *China Brief*, vol. 9, no. 15 (July 23, 2009), 11.

53. Padmaja Murthy, "The Gujral Doctrine and Beyond," *Strategic Analysis*, vol. 23, no. 4 (July 1999): 639–52.

54. For a comprehensive analysis see C. Raja Mohan, "India's Regionalism: The Third Wave," *Quaderni di Relazioni Internazionali*, no. 7 (June 2008): 71–89.

55. To capture the sense of change, see the following three papers from the South Asia Analysis Group during 2008. They are all available at www.southasiaanalysis.org: Subhash Kapila, "Bangladesh-India Strategic Partnership: The Imperatives," Paper no. 2765, July 11, 2008; Subhash Kapila, "Bangladesh: Visit of Indian Army Chief Significant," Paper no. 2778, July 23, 2008; Anand Kumar, "Indo-Bangladesh Relations: Visit of Indian Foreign Secretary," Paper no. 2291, July 9, 2007.

56. C. Raja Mohan, "Military Diplomacy: Admiral Nirmal Verma in Bangladesh," *Indian Express*, April 4, 2011, www.indianexpress.com/news/military-diplomacy-adm-nirmal-verma-in-bang/771441.

57. "Joint Communiqué," New Delhi, January 12, 2010, available at www.mea.gov.in/mystart.php?id=530515482.

58. "Joint Statement on the Occasion of the Visit of the PM of India to Bangladesh," September 7, 2011, www.mea.gov.in/mystart.php?id=190018210.

59. Vijay Sakhuja, "China-Bangladesh Relations and Potential for Regional Tensions," *China Brief*, vol. 9, no. 15 (July 23, 2009): 12.

60. K. M. Panikkar, *The Future of South-East Asia: An Indian View* (London: George Allen and Unwin, 1943), 35–36.

61. Ibid., 43–45.

62. Frank N. Trager, *Burma: From Kingdom to Republic: A Historical and Political Analysis* (Westport, Conn.: Greenwood Press, 1976).

63. John H. Badgley, "Burma's China Crisis: The Choices Ahead," *Asian Survey*, vol. 7, no. 11 (November 1967): 753–61.

64. Nalini Ranjan Chakravarti, *The Indian Minority in Burma: The Rise and Decline of an Immigrant Community* (New York: Oxford University Press, 1971).

65. William L. Scully and Frank N. Trager, "Burma 1979: Reversing the Trend," *Asian Survey*, vol. 20, no. 2 (February 1980): 168–75.

66. David I. Steinberg, "Myanmar as Nexus: Sino-Indian Rivalries on the Frontier," *Studies in Conflict and Terrorism*, vol. 16, no. 1 (1993): 1–8; Andrew Selth, "Burma and the Strategic Competition between China and India," *Journal of Strategic Studies*, vol. 19, no. 2 (June 1996): 213–30.

67. K. Yhome, *India-Myanmar Relations (1998–2008): A Decade of Redefining Bilateral Ties* (New Delhi: Observer Research Foundation, 2009).

68. Renaud Egreteau, *Wooing the Generals: India's New Burma Policy* (New Delhi: Authors Press, 2003).

69. C. S. Kuppuswamy, "Myanmar: Sandwiched between China and India and Gaining from Both," South Asia Analysis Group, Paper no. 2574, January 31, 2008, www.southasianalysis.org/%5Cpapers26%5Cpaper2574.html.

70. Andrew Selth, "Burma's Coco Islands: Rumors and Realities in the Indian Ocean," Working Paper no. 101 (Hong Kong: Southeast Asia Research Center, City University of Hong Kong, November 2008): 2.

71. Renaud Egreteau, "India and China Vying for Influence in Burma: A New Assessment," *India Review*, vol. 7, no. 1 (January-March 2008): 44.

72. Wai Moe, "Chinese Warships Make First Visit to Burma," *Irrawaddy*, August 30, 2010, www.irrawaddy.org/article.php?art_id=19334; see also Ben Arnoldy, "China Warships Dock in Burma, Rattling Rival Naval Power India," *Christian Science Monitor*, August 30, 2010, www.csmonitor.com/World/Asia-South-Central/2010/0830/China-warships-dock-in-Burma-rattling-rival-naval-power-India.

73. K. M. Panikkar, *India and the Indian Ocean: An Essay on the Influence of Seapower on Indian History* (London: George Allen and Unwin, 1945), 93.

74. K. M. Panikkar, *The Strategic Problems of the Indian Ocean* (Allahabad: Kitabistan, 1944), 18.

75. Raja Menon, "Isle of Contention," *Indian Express*, September 29, 2009, 11.

76. Donald L. Berlin, "The 'Great Base Race' in the Indian Ocean Littoral: Conflict Prevention or Simulation?" *Contemporary South Asia*, vol. 13, no. 3 (September 2004): 242.

77. Gurpreet S. Khurana, "China-India Maritime Rivalry," *Indian Defense Review*, vol. 23, no. 4 (October-December 2009), http://indiandefencereview.com/2009/04/china-india-maritime-rivalry.html.

78. Shyam Saran, "India's Foreign Policy and the Andaman & Nicobar Islands," Port Blair, September 5, 2009, available at www.maritimeindia.org/pdfs/Shyam_Saran_Address.pdf; see also Pushpita Das, "Securing Andaman and Nicobar Islands," paper presented at the Institute for Defense Studies and Analyses, New Delhi, July 9, 2010.

79. For a discussion of Myanmar's geopolitical possibilities, see Thant Myint-U, *Where China Meets India: Burma and the New Crossroads of Asia* (New York: Farrar, Straus and Giroux, 2011).

80. For a general background, see Ralf Emmers, *Geopolitics and Maritime Territorial Disputes in East Asia* (London: Routledge, 2009); Min Gyo Koo, *Island Disputes and Maritime Regime Building in East Asia: Between a Rock and Hard Place* (New York: Springer, 2010). See also Michael D. Swaine, "China's Assertive Behavior, Part One: On 'Core Interests,'" *China Leadership Monitor*, no. 34 (Winter 2011): 1–25; Michael D. Swaine and M. Taylor Fravel, "China's Assertive Behavior, Part Two: The Maritime Periphery," *China Leadership Monitor*, no. 35 (Summer 2011): 1–27.

81. For an American view, see Patrick Cronin, ed., *Cooperation from Strength: United States, China and the South China Sea* (Washington, D.C.: Center for a New American Security, 2012); for a review of the Chinese debate, see Sarah Raine, "Beijing's South China Sea Debate," *Survival*, vol. 53, no. 5 (October-November 2011): 69–88.

82. Author's conversation with senior Indian officials in New Delhi during November 2011.

83. Indrani Bagchi, "PM Manmohan Singh to China's Wen Jiabao: Back Off on South China Sea," *Times of India*, November 19, 2011, 11.

84. See India Ministry of External Affairs, "Joint Statement on the Occasion of the Visit of the President of Vietnam," New Delhi, October 12, 2011, available at www.mea.gov.in/mystart.php?id=530518387; see also Press Trust of India, "India, Vietnam Sign Pact for Oil Exploration in South China Sea," *Hindu*, October 13, 2011, 1; Utpal Bhaskar, "OVL to Resume Drilling in South China Sea," *Mint*, January 9, 2012, 6.

85. See Ananth Krishnan, "South China Sea Project 'a Serious Political Provocation,' Chinese Paper Warns India," *Hindu*, September 17, 2011; see also Li Hongmei, "'Bundling Strategy' over South China Sea Will Be Disillusioned," Xinhuanet, September 26, 2011.

86. Harsh V. Pant, "India in the Asia-Pacific: Rising Ambitions with an Eye on China," *Asia-Pacific Review*, vol. 14, no. 1 (May 2007): 54–71; Anindya Batabyal, "Balancing China in Asia: A Realist Assessment of India's Look East Strategy," *China Report*, vol. 42, no. 6 (February 2006): 179–97.

87. Iskander Rehman, "Keeping the Dragon at Bay: India's Counter-Containment of China in Asia," *Asian Security*, vol. 5, no. 2 (June 2009): 140.

88. For a discussion, see S. D. Muni, "The Turbulent South China Sea Waters: India, Vietnam and China," *ISAS Insights*, no. 140 (Singapore: Institute of South Asian Studies, October 2011).

89. Hillary Clinton, "Remarks on India and the United States: A Vision for the 21st Century," speech in Chennai, India, July 20, 2011, available at www.state.gov/secretary/rm/2011/07/168840.htm; for an Indian appreciation of the geopolitical dimensions of the speech, see "Hillary Curzon," editorial in *Business Standard*, July 26, 2011, 9.

90. K. M. Panikkar, *The Strategic Problems of the Indian Ocean* (Allahabad: Kitabistan, 1944), 10–11.

91. Integrated Headquarters, Ministry of Defense, Government of India, *Freedom to Use the Seas: India's Maritime Military Strategy* (New Delhi, 2007), 60.

92. K. M. Panikkar, *The Strategic Problems of the Indian Ocean* (Allahabad: Kitabistan, 1944), 14.

93. Amitav Ranjan, "China Objects to Indian Navy's Presence in South China Sea," *Indian Express* (New Delhi), October 14, 2000, 1.

94. Integrated Headquarters, Ministry of Defense (Navy), Government of India, *Freedom to Use the Seas: India's Maritime Military Strategy* (New Delhi: Ministry of Defense, 2007), 61–65.

95. Ibid., 77.

96. Arun Prakash, "Where Are Our Ships Bound?" *Indian Express*, October 1, 2011, www.indianexpress.com/news/where-are-our-ships-bound/854100/3.

97. Author's conversation with senior Indian officials, October 2011.

98. Piyush Pandey, "ONGC Videsh Ltd Pulls Out of Block in South China Sea," *Times of India*, May 16, 2012, http://timesofindia.indiatimes.com/business/india-business/ONGC-Videsh-Limited-pulls-out-of-block-in-South-China-Sea/articleshow/13159451.cms; see also "C. Raja Mohan, "Oil Hunt Continues," *Indian Express*, May 16, 2012, www.indianexpress.com/news/oil-hunt-continues/949768/0.

99. Zhao Gancheng, "India: Look East Policy and Role in Asian Security Architecture," *Indian Ocean Digest*, vol. 21, no. 2 (July-December 2006): 38.

100. Walter C. Ladwig III, "Delhi's Pacific Ambition: Naval Power, 'Look East,' and India's Emerging Influence in the Asia-Pacific," *Asian Security*, vol. 5, no. 2 (2009): 106.

CHAPTER TEN

1. John Garver, "The Security Dilemma in Sino-Indian Relations," *India Review*, vol. 1, no. 4 (October 2002): 33–34.

2. "Security dilemma" was first defined in John H. Herz, "Idealist Internationalism and the Security Dilemma," *World Politics*, vol. 2, no. 2 (January 1950): 157–80; see also

NOTES

his later work, John H. Herz, "The Security Dilemma in International Relations: Background and Present Problems," *International Relations*, vol. 17, no. 4 (2003): 411–16.

3. Robert Jervis, *Perception and Misperception in International Politics* (Princeton, N.J.: Princeton University Press, 1976); see also Robert Jervis, "Cooperation Under the Security Dilemma," *World Politics*, vol. 30, no. 2 (January 1978): 167–214.

4. For a recent comprehensive treatment of the issues involved, see Ken Booth and Nicholas J. Wheeler, *The Security Dilemma: Fear, Cooperation and Trust in World Politics* (New York: Palgrave Macmillan, 2008).

5. Ibid., 34.

6. John H. Herz, "Foreword," in Ken Booth and Nicholas J. Wheeler, *The Security Dilemma: Fear, Cooperation and Trust in World Politics* (New York: Palgrave Macmillan, 2008), viii.

7. India Press Information Bureau, "Joint Declaration by the Republic of India and the People's Republic of China," New Delhi, November 21, 2006.

8. "India's Foreign Policy and the Andaman and Nicobar Islands," address by Shyam Saran, special envoy of the prime minister, Port Blair, September 5, 2009, available at www.maritimeindia.org/pdfs/Shyam_Saran_Address.pdf.

9. Shivshankar Menon, "Maritime Imperatives of Indian Foreign Policy," lecture at the National Maritime Foundation, New Delhi, September 11, 2009, available at www.maritimeindia.org/pdfs/SMenon.pdf.

10. Kenneth W. Allen, "China's Approach to Confidence-Building Measures," in Michael Krepon, et al., eds., *Global Confidence Building: New Tools for Troubled Regions* (New York: St. Martin's Press, 1999), 43–59; Moonis Ahmar, *The Challenge of Confidence-Building in South Asia* (New Delhi: Har-Anand, 2001); Waheguru Pal Singh Sidhu and Jing-dong Yuan, "Resolving the Sino-Indian Border Dispute: Building Confidence Through Cooperative Monitoring," *Asian Survey*, vol. 41, no. 2 (March-April 2001): 351–76.

11. See Swaran Singh, "Building Confidence with China," in Tan Chung, ed., *Across the Himalayan Gap: An Indian Quest for Understanding China* (New Delhi: Gyan Publishers, 1998), www.ignca.nic.in/ks_41064.htm.

12. For the text of the two agreements and a sharp analysis, see Sony Devabhaktuni, Matthew C. J. Rudolph, and Amit Sevak, "Key Developments in the Sino-Indian CBM Process," in *Global Confidence Building: New Tools for Troubled Regions*, edited by Michael Krepon et al. (New York: St. Martin's Press, 1999), 209–24; see also Waheguru Pal Singh Sidhu and Jing-dong Yuan, *China and India: Cooperation or Conflict?* (Boulder, Colo.: Lynne Rienner, 2003), 113–40.

13. "Agreement between the Government of the Republic of India and the Government of the People's Republic of China on the Political Parameters and Guiding Principles for the Settlement of the India-China Boundary Question," New Delhi, April 11, 2005, www.mea.gov.in/treatiesagreement/2005/11ta1104200501.htm.

14. "Memorandum of Understanding between the Ministry of Defense of the Republic of India and the Ministry of National Defense of the People's Republic of China for Exchanges and Cooperation in the Field of Defense," Beijing, May 28, 2006, www.mea.gov.in/treatiesagreement/2006/28ta2805200601.htm.

15. Jonathan Holslag, "The Persistent Military Security Dilemma between China and India," *Journal of Strategic Studies*, vol. 32, no. 6 (December 2009): 811–40.

16. See, for example, Dan Twining, "Could China and India Go to War over Tibet?" *Foreign Policy*, March 10, 2009, http://shadow.foreignpolicy.com/posts/2009/03/10/could_china_and_india_go_to_war_over_tibet; see also Edward Wong, "Uneasy Engagement: China and India Dispute Enclave on Edge of Tibet," *New York Times*, September 3, 2009, www.nytimes.com/2009/09/04/world/asia/04chinaindia.html.

17. Pranab Dhal Samanta, "Generals in Charge of China Border Head for Beijing—and Lhasa," *Indian Express*, August 31, 2009, 1; "Tibet Military Region Commander on Goodwill Visit," *Hindu*, December 10, 2009, 9.

18. Ananth Krishnan, "New Delhi, Beijing Hold Defense Dialogue," *Hindu*, January 8, 2010, 12.

19. Indrani Bagchi, "China Denies Visa to Top General in Charge of J&K," *Times of India*, August 27, 2010, 1.

20. Indian Ministry of External Affairs, "Important Travel Advisory on Chinese Visas," November 12, 2009, www.mea.gov.in/mystart.php?id=530215307.

21. For a review of China's approach to the Jammu and Kashmir dispute between India and Pakistan, see John W. Garver, "China's Kashmir Policies," *India Review*, vol. 3, no. 1 (January 2004): 1–24; for an appreciation of recent Indian concerns, see Sujit Dutta, "China's High Risk India Gamble," *Diplomat*, September 10, 2010, http://the-diplomat.com/2010/09/10/china%E2%80%99s-high-risk-india-gamble; Nikhil Lakshman, "China Wants to Be Part of Kashmir Dispute," Rediff News Online, October 14, 2010, www.news.rediff.com/special/2010/oct/13/special-china-wants-to-be-part-of-kashmir-dispute.htm; Pranab Dhal Samanta, "India Equates Jammu & Kashmir with Tibet?" *Indian Express*, November 15, 2010, 1.

22. Briefing the press in Delhi on the talks between Singh and Wen, Foreign Secretary Nirupama Rao said, "On the stapled visas issues, in fact Premier Wen Jiabao brought it up himself and he said that China takes our concerns on this issue very seriously. And he suggested that the officials of the two sides should have in-depth consultations with each other so that this issue can be resolved satisfactorily." See Ministry of External Affairs, "Briefing by Foreign Secretary on Ongoing Visit of Chinese Premier," December 16, 2010, www.mea.gov.in/mystart.php?id=530316895.

23. Pranab Dhal Samanta, "India, China Work on Resuming Defense Exchanges," *Indian Express*, April 12, 2011, 1.

24. India Ministry of External Affairs, "Briefing by NSA on PM's meetings with Chinese and Russian Presidents," Sanya, Hainan, April 13, 2011, www.mea.gov.in/mystart.php?id=530317539.

25. India Ministry of External Affairs, "India-China agreement on the Establishment of a Working Mechanism for Consultation and Coordination on India-China Border Affairs," New Delhi, January 17, 2012, www.mea.gov.in/mystart.php?id=530518925.

26. For a comprehensive review see J. R. Hill, *Arms Control at Sea* (London: Routledge, 1989); for a critique of naval arms control, see Thomas H. Buckley, "The Icarus Factor: American Pursuit of Myth in Naval Arms Control 1921–36," *Diplomacy and Statecraft*, vol. 4, no. 3 (November 1993): 124–46; see also Robin Ranger, "Learning from the Naval Arms Control Experience," *Washington Quarterly*, vol. 10, no. 3 (Summer 1987): 47–58.

27. Josy Joseph, "Indian, Chinese Naval Ships Engage in Joint Exercise off Shanghai," Rediff News Online, November 15, 2003, www.rediff.com/news/2003/nov/15navy.htm.

28. Sean M. Lynn-Jones, "A Quiet Success for Arms Control: Preventing Incidents at Sea," *International Security*, vol. 9, no. 4 (Spring 1985): 154–84.

29. Robert Hilton, "A CBM at Work: The 1972 United States-USSR Incidents-at-Sea Agreement," in *Naval Confidence-Building Measures* (New York: United Nations Department for Disarmament Affairs, 1990).

30. See Julian Schofield, "The Prospects for a Sino-American Incidents at Sea Agreement," *Korean Journal of Defense Analysis*, vol. 11, no. 1 (Summer 1999): 87–100; Micah Springut, "Managing China's Growing Assertiveness in the South China Sea," *World Politics Review*, July 27, 2009, www.worldpoliticsreview.com/article.aspx?id=4124; Richard Weitz, "Enduring Difficulties in China-U.S. Defense Diplomacy," *Korean Journal of Defense Analysis*, vol. 21. no. 4 (December 2009): 381–400.

31. Chow Chung-yan, "Chinese Navy Sees Off Indian Sub," *South China Morning Post*, February 4, 2009, 1.

32. Ibid.

33. Rajat Pandit, "Indian Sub Stalked China Warships?" *Times of India*, February 5, 2009, 1.

34. C. Raja Mohan, "Sino-Indian Naval 'Encounter' in the Gulf of Aden," *ISAS Brief* no. 97 (Singapore: Institute of South Asian Studies, February 6, 2009).

35. Ben Bland and Girija Shivakumar, "China Confronts Indian Navy Vessel," *Financial Times*, August 31, 2011.

36. India Ministry of External Affairs, "Incident involving INS Airavat in South China Sea," Press Briefing, New Delhi, September 1, 2011, www.mea.gov.in/mystart.php?id=530318137.

37. C. Raja Mohan, "Future Tense: India and the South China Sea," *Indian Express*, September 2, 2011.

38. Ashok Tuteja, "India, China to Kickstart Maritime Dialogue," *Tribune*, April 14, 2012, www.tribuneindia.com/2012/20120414/nation.htm#1.

39. The Monroe Doctrine refers to the U.S. policy of affirming its primacy in the Western Hemisphere and keeping the European powers out. The policy was declared by President James Monroe in 1823. For a substantive account of the origins of the policy, see

Ernest R. May, *The Making of the Monroe Doctrine* (Cambridge, Mass.: Harvard University Press, 1975); see also Gretchen Murphy, *Hemispheric Imaginings: The Monroe Doctrine and Narratives of U.S. Empire* (Durham, N.C.: Duke University Press, 2005).

40. For a comprehensive parsing of the notion of an Indian Monroe Doctrine for the Indian Ocean, see James R. Holmes and Toshi Yoshihara, "India's 'Monroe' Doctrine and Asia's Maritime Future," *Strategic Analysis*, vol. 32, no. 6 (November 2008): 997–1011; see also Holmes and Yoshihara, "Strongman, Constable, or Free-Rider? India's 'Monroe Doctrine' and Indian Naval Strategy," *Comparative Strategy*, vol. 28, no. 4 (September 2009): 332–49.

41. John J. Mearsheimer, "China's Unpeaceful Rise," *Current History*, vol. 105, no. 690 (April 2006): 162.

42. James R. Holmes, "Monroe Doctrines in Asia?" *Diplomat*, June 15, 2011, http://the-diplomat.com/2011/06/15/monroe-doctrines-in-asia.

43. K. M. Panikkar, *The Future of South-East Asia: An Indian View* (London: George Allen and Unwin, 1943), 104.

44. Ibid., 107.

45. Menon retired as India's foreign secretary in July 2009 and took charge as India's national security adviser in January 2010. The speech on China came in September 2009.

46. Shivshankar Menon, "Maritime Imperatives of Indian Foreign Policy," lecture at National Maritime Foundation, New Delhi, September 11, 2009, 6.

47. See M. Taylor Fravel and Alexander Liebman, "Beyond the Moat: The PLAN's Evolving Interests and Potential Influence," in *The Chinese Navy: Expanding Capabilities, Evolving Roles*, edited by Phillip C. Saunders, Christopher D. Yung, Michael Swaine, and Andrew Niern-Dzu Yang (Washington, D.C.: National Defense University Press, 2011), 67–71.

48. Andrew Erickson and Lyle J. Goldstein, "Gunboats for China's New 'Grand Canals'? Probing the Intersection of Beijing's Naval and Oil Security Policies," *Naval War College Review*, vol. 62, no. 2 (Spring 2009): 55.

49. Gabriel B. Collins and William S. Murray, "No Oil for the Lamps of China?" *Naval War College Review*, vol. 61, no. 2 (Spring 2008): 92.

50. Erickson and Goldstein, "Gunboats for China's New 'Grand Canals'?" 64.

51. Ibid.

52. Indian Ministry of External Affairs, "Joint Communiqué of the Republic of India and the People's Republic of China," New Delhi, December 16, 2010, www.mea.gov.in/mystart.php?id=530516879.

53. See Raoul Heinrichs, Justin Jones, and Rory Medcalf, *Crisis and Confidence: Major Powers and Maritime Security in the Indo-Pacific Asia* (Sydney: Lowy Institute, 2011).

54. Ibid.

CHAPTER ELEVEN

1. Alfred Thayer Mahan, *The Problem of Asia and its Effect upon International Policies* (Boston: Little Brown, 1900); for a recent reissue with an introduction by Francis P. Sempa, Alfred Thayer Mahan, *The Problem of Asia: Its Effect on International Politics* (London: Transaction Publishers, 2003).

2. Alfred Thayer Mahan, *The Problem of Asia: Its Effect Upon International Politics* (Revised Edition) (London: Transaction Publishers, 2003), 66.

3. See Halford Mackinder, "The Geographical Pivot of History," *Geographical Journal*, vol. 23, no. 4 (April 1904): 421–37.

4. Nicholas J. Spykman, *The Geography of the Peace* (New York: Harcourt, Brace and Company, 1944).

5. For a recent discussion, see Greg Russell, "Alfred Thayer Mahan and American Geopolitics: The Conservatism and Realism of an Imperialist," *Geopolitics*, vol. 11, no. 1 (Spring 2006): 119–40; see also David H. Burton, "Theodore Roosevelt: Confident Imperialist," *Review of Politics*, vol. 23, no. 3 (July 1961): 356–77; Serge Ricard, "Theodore Roosevelt: Imperialist or Global Strategist in the New Expansionist Age?" *Diplomacy and Statecraft*, vol. 19, no. 4 (December 2008): 639–57.

6. Brian W. Blouet, "The Imperial Vision of Halford Mackinder," *Geographical Journal*, vol. 170, no. 4 (December 2004): 322–29.

7. Nicholas J. Spykman, "Geography and Foreign Policy I," *American Political Science Review*, vol. 32, no. 1 (February 1938): 28–50.

8. See, for example, Kent E. Calder, *Asia's Deadly Triangle: How Arms, Energy and Growth Threaten to Destabilize Asia Pacific* (London: Nicholas Brealey, 1996).

9. Robert Kaplan, "The Revenge of Geography," *Foreign Policy*, May-June 2009, available at www.cnas.org/node/884.

10. Anthony Bubalo and Malcolm Cook, "Horizontal Asia," *American Interest*, vol. 5, no. 5 (May–June 2010).

11. James Rogers, "From Suez to Shanghai: The European Union and Eurasian Maritime Security," Occasional Paper no. 77 (Paris: European Union Institute for Security Studies, March 2009).

12. For a review, see Anushree Bhattacharya, "Linking South East Asia and India: More Connectivity, Better Ties," IPCS Special Report no. 50 (New Delhi: Institute of Peace and Conflict Studies, 2008).

13. The George W. Bush administration carved out Central Asia from its European division in the State Department and combined it with the South Asia bureau. The Obama administration has viewed the restoration of Afghanistan and Pakistan as a bridge between Central Asia and India as part of its larger regional strategy to stabilize both countries. This strategy has been described as the construction of a "New Silk Road."

14. See the speech by U.S. Defense Secretary Leon Panetta at the Eleventh IISS Asia Security Summit, Singapore, June 2, 2012, www.iiss.org/conferences/the-shangri-la-dialogue/shangri-la-dialogue-2012/speeches/first-plenary-session/leon-panetta.

15. "Remarks of the President to the United Nations General Assembly," White House, September 23, 2009, www.whitehouse.gov/the_press_office/remarks-by-the-president-to-the-united-nations-general-assembly.

16. Obama's views on use of force were expressed most clearly and comprehensively in the speech the president gave on U.S. policy toward the Libyan crisis on March 28, 2011; the full text is available at www.politico.com/news/stories/0311/52093.html. For a discussion of the "Obama Doctrine," see Council on Foreign Relations, "Democracy Promotion and the Obama Doctrine," interview with Larry Diamond, April 8, 2011, available at www.cfr.org/us-strategy-and-politics/democracy-promotion-obama-doctrine/p24621; Fareed Zakaria, "Stop Searching for an Obama Doctrine," *Washington Post*, July 7, 2011. For an earlier academic discussion, see Christian Henderson, "The 2010 United States National Security Strategy and the 'Obama Doctrine' of Necessary Force," *Journal of Conflict and Security Law*, vol. 15, no. 3 (2010): 403–34.

17. George F. Will, "Republicans Need More Than Rhetoric on Defense," *Washington Post*, February 9, 2012; for background on the issue, see Jonathan Masters, "Defense Spending and the Deficit Debate," Council on Foreign Relations, November 8, 2011, www.cfr.org/united-states/defense-spending-deficit-debate/p26442.

18. U.S. Department of the Navy, United States Marine Corps, and United States Coast Guard, *A Cooperative Strategy for 21st Century Seapower* (Washington, D.C.: Department of the Navy, October 2007).

19. Michael J. Green, "Asia in the Debate on American Grand Strategy," *Naval War College Review*, vol. 62, no. 1 (Winter 2009): 27.

20. For a discussion, see François Godement, "The United States and Asia in 2010," *Asian Survey*, vol. 51, no.1 (January–February 2011): 5–17; S. R. Joey Long, "The United States, Southeast Asia, and Asia-Pacific Security," *Asia Policy*, vol. 12, no. 1 (July 2011): 2–7; Simon Tay, "The U.S.-Asia Relationship: Questions Going Forward," *Asia Policy*, vol. 12, no. 1 (July 2011): 8–12.

21. See Arnold L. Horelick, "The Soviet Union's Asian Collective Security Proposal: A Club in Search of Members," *Pacific Affairs*, vol. 47, no. 3 (Autumn 1974): 269–85.

22. For an evolution of multilateralism and Asian regionalism in India, see C. Raja Mohan, "India and the Asian Security Architecture," in *Asia's New Multilateralism: Cooperation, Competition, and the Search for Community*, edited by Michael J. Green and Bates Gill (New York: Columbia University Press, 2009), 128–53; Guoguang Wu and Helen Lansdowne, eds., *China Turns to Multilateralism: Foreign Policy and Regional Security* (New York: Routledge, 2008).

23. Banning Garrett and Bonnie Glaser, "Beijing's Views on Multilateral Security in the Asia-Pacific Region," *Contemporary Southeast Asia*, vol. 15, no. 1 (June 1993); Susan L. Shirk, "Chinese Views on Asia-Pacific Regional Security Cooperation," *National Bureau of Asian Research Analysis,* vol. 5, vo. 5 (December 1994); Jing-dong Yuan, *Asia-Pacific Security: China's Conditional Multilateralism and Great Power Entente* (Carlisle,

Pa.: Strategic Studies Institute, 2000); Kent L. Biringer, "Security Agreements and Confidence-Building for India: Past, Present and Future," *India Review*, vol. 1, no. 4 (October 2002): 57–90.

24. Kabilan Krishnasamy, "The Paradox of India's Peacekeeping," *Contemporary South Asia*, vol. 12, no. 2 (June 2003): 263–80.

25. Ashley Jackson, "The Royal Navy and the Indian Ocean Region since 1945," *RUSI Journal*, vol. 151, no. 6 (December 2006): 78–82.

26. See Mrityunjoy Mazumdar "Exercise Milan 08," Bharat Rakshak Online, January 2008, www.bharat-rakshak.com/NAVY/Articles/Article11.pdf.

27. Vijay Sakhuja, "The Indian Navy's Agenda for Maritime Security in the Indian Ocean," *Terrorism Monitor*, vol. 8, no. 8 (February 26, 2010), available at www.jamestown.org/single/?no_cache=1&tx_ttnews[tt_news]=36086.

28. For details, see the official Indian navy website on Milan 12 at indiannavy.nic.in/Milan12/index.php.

29. For a comprehensive discussion on the evolution and implications of China's attitude to international peacekeeping, see Courtney J. Richardson, "A Responsible Power? China and the UN Peacekeeping Regime," *International Peacekeeping*, vol. 18, no. 3 (June 2011): 286–97.

30. Embassy of the People's Republic of China in Australia, "China's Military Diplomacy Scores New Success," December 30, 2003, http://au.china-embassy.org/eng/wgc/t57247.htm.

31. Section XIII of China's defense white paper, 2009, available at www.china.org.cn/government/whitepaper/2009–01/21/content_17162792.htm.

32. Ibid.

33. Ibid.

34. See Richard Weitz, "Priorities and Challenges in China's Naval Deployment in the Horn of Africa," *China Brief*, vol. 9, no. 24 (December 3, 2009); see also Gaye Christoffersen, *China and Maritime Cooperation: Piracy in the Gulf of Aden* (Berlin: Institute for Strategic, Political, Security, and Economic Consultancy, January 2010), available at www.humansecuritygateway.com/documents/ISPSW_ChinaMaritimeCooperation_PiracyGulfOfAden.pdf.

35. Vijay Sakhuja, "Maritime Multilateralism: China's Strategy for the Indian Ocean," *China Brief*, vol. 9, no. 22 (November 4, 2009).

36. For an official Pakistani account, see "Together for Peace: Aman 11," www.paknavy.gov.pk/AMAN/Intro.htm; see also Xinhua, "Pakistan's Aman09 Multinational Exercise Enters Sea Phase," March 10, 2009, available at http://eng.mod.gov.cn/MilitaryExercises/2009–03/10/content_3100804.htm.

37. B. K. Verma, "Cooperative Maritime Engagement-Exercise Aman 2009: Facilitating U.S.-Chinese Interaction" (New Delhi: National Maritime Foundation, May 1, 2009), www.maritimeindia.org/pdfs/Commentry01May09.pdf.

38. Christopher Griffin, "Containment with Chinese Characteristics: Beijing Hedges Against the Rise of India," *Asian Outlook,* no. 3 (Washington, D.C.: American Enterprise Institute, September 2006).

39. For an early assessment of the Chinese opposition, see J. Mohan Malik, "Security Council Reform: China Signals its Veto," *World Policy Journal,* vol. 22, no. 1 (Spring 2005): 19–29.

40. G. V. C. Naidu, "India and the East Asian Summit," *Strategic Analysis,* vol. 29, no. 4 (October-December 2005): 711–16; see also J. Mohan Malik, "The East Asia Summit," *Australian Journal of International Affairs,* vol. 60, no. 2 (June 2006): 207–11.

41. See Gulshan Sachdeva, "India's Attitude toward China's Growing Role in Central Asia," *China and Eurasia Forum Quarterly,* vol. 4, no. 3 (2006): 23–34.

42. Bhaskar Roy, "China Unmasked: What Next?" South Asia Analysis Group, Paper no. 2840, September 12, 2008.

43. Author's conversations with senior Indian officials from the Foreign Office, New Delhi, December 2005.

44. Gurpreet S. Khurana, "Indian Ocean Naval Symposium (IONS): Where from . . . Whither-Bound?" *IDSA Comment,* February 22, 2008, www.idsa.in/idsastrategiccomments/IndianOceanNavalSymposium%28IONS%29_GSKhurana_220208.

45. K. M. Panikkar, "Regional Organization for the Indian Ocean Area," *Pacific Affairs,* vol. 18, no. 3 (September 1945): 251.

46. K. Subrahmanyam, "Arms Limitation in the Indian Ocean: Retrospect and Prospect," in *Superpower Rivalry in the Indian Ocean: Indian and American Perspectives,* edited by Selig Harrison and K. Subrahmanyam (New York: Oxford University Press, 1989), 224–30.

47. Sanjeev Kumar Tiwari, *Indian Ocean Rim-Association for Regional Cooperation (IOR-ARC): Problems and Prospects* (New Delhi: Abhijeet Publications, 2004).

48. Dennis Rumley and Sanjay Chaturvedi, eds., *Geopolitical Orientations, Regionalism and Security in the Indian Ocean* (New Delhi: South Asian Publishers, 2004).

49. Indian Ministry of External Affairs, "Opening Media Statement by EAM upon Conclusion of the Council of Ministers Meeting of IOR-ARC," November 15, 2011, Bangalore, www.mea.gov.in/mystart.php?id=530118532.

50. See P. K. Ghosh, "Indian Ocean Naval Symposium: Uniting the Maritime Indian Ocean Region," *Strategic Analysis,* vol. 36, no. 3 (May-June 2012): 354.

51. The countries invited were Australia, Bahrain, Bangladesh, Burma, Comoros, Djibouti, Egypt, Eritrea, France, Indonesia, Iran, Kenya, Kuwait, Madagascar, Malaysia, Maldives, Mauritius, Mozambique, Oman, Pakistan, Qatar, Saudi Arabia, Seychelles, Singapore, South Africa, Sri Lanka, Sudan, Tanzania, Thailand, UAE, and Yemen; see Press Information Bureau, Government of India, "Indian Ocean Naval Symposium (IONS)-2008: Unique Maiden Initiative to Address IOR Maritime Issues," New Delhi, February 7, 2008, http://pib.nic.in/release/rel_print_page1.asp?relid=35213.

52. Khurana, "Indian Ocean Naval Symposium (IONS): Where from … Whither-Bound?"

53. Sam Bateman, "The Indian Ocean Naval Symposium-Will the Navies of the Indian Ocean Region Unite?" *RSIS Commentaries*, no. 35/2008 (Singapore: RSIS, NTU, March 17, 2008).

54. Ajai Shukla, "China's Ghost Hovers over the Naval Symposium," *Business Standard*, February 18, 2008, www.business-standard.com/india/news/china%60s-ghost-hovers-over-naval-symposium/314122.

55. Pranab Dhal Samanta, "China Wants to Join Navy Initiative on Indian Ocean, MEA Says No Need," *Indian Express*, April 21, 2009, 1.

56. Sam Bateman, "Solving the 'Wicked Problems' of Maritime Security: Are Regional Forums Up to the Task?" *Contemporary Southeast Asia*, vol. 33, no. 1 (2011): 2.

57. Ibid., 21.

58. Malcolm Cook, Raoul Heinrichs, Rory Medcalf, and Andrew Shearer, *Power and Choice: Asian Security Futures* (Sydney: Lowy Institute, 2010), 44.

59. Amitav Acharya, "Reordering Asia: 'Cooperative Security' or Concert of Powers?" Working Paper no. 4 (Singapore: S. Rajaratnam School of International Studies, July 1999): 3–7.

60. Robert Ayson, "The Six-Party Talks Process: Towards an Asian Concert?" http://epress.anu.edu.au/sdsc/architecture/pdf/whole_book.pdf, in *The Architecture of Security in the Asia-Pacific*, edited by Ron Huisken (Canberra: Australian National University E Press, 2009), 64.

61. Jonathan Holslag, "Embracing Chinese Global Security Ambitions," *Washington Quarterly*, vol. 32, no. 3 (July 2009): 114–15.

62. Robert Kaplan, "Power Plays in the Indian Ocean: The Maritime Commons in the 21st Century," in *Contested Commons: The Future of American Power in a Multipolar World*, edited by Abraham Denmark and James Mulvenon (Washington, D.C.: Center for a New American Security, 2010), 185.

63. Shivshankar Menon, "Evolving Balance of Power in Asia," speech at the International Institute for Strategic Studies Global Strategic Review, Geneva, September 2009, www.iiss.org/conferences/global-strategic-review/global-strategic-review-2009/plenary-sessions-and-speeches-2009/fifth-plenary-session-shiv-shankar-menon.

64. See Xinhua, "Full Text of Outcomes from Strategic Track of 2011 U.S.-China Strategic and Economic Dialogue," May 10, 2011, http://news.xinhuanet.com/english2010/china/2011–05/11/c_13868779.htm.

65. For a contemporary discussion of the traditional concept of balance of power, see T.V. Paul, James J. Wirtz, and Michel Fortmann, eds., *Balance of Power: Theory and Practice in the 21st Century* (Stanford, Calif.: Stanford University Press, 2004); see also Daniel H. Nexon, "The Balance of Power in the Balance," *World Politics*, vol. 61, no. 2 (April 2009): 330–59.

66. For a discussion, see Malcolm Cook, Raoul Heinrichs, Rory Medcalf, and Andrew Shearer, *Power and Choice: Asian Security Futures* (Sydney: Lowy Institute, 2010).

67. White House, *Sustaining U.S. Global Leadership: Priorities for 21st Century Defense* (Washington, D.C.: January 2012), 2.

68. For a review of the Chinese response to the U.S. initiatives in Asia during 2011, see Bonnie Glaser and Brittany Billingsley, "U.S. Pivot to Asia Leaves China off Balance," *Comparative Connections*, January 2012, http://csis.org/files/publication/1103qus_china.pdf.

69. For an assessment of the idea by two former U.S. officials involved in developing and implementing the idea, see Michael J. Green and Daniel Twining, "Democracy and American Grand Strategy in Asia: The Realist Principles Behind an Enduring Idealism," *Contemporary Southeast Asia*, vol. 30, no. 1 (2008): 1–28.

70. Indian Ministry of External Affairs, "Foreign Secretary Holds Wide-Ranging Consultations in Japan," New Delhi, April 8, 2011, www.mea.gov.in/mystart.php?id=530217528; for reported reservations in the Indian political establishment, see Indrani Bagchi, "India Develops Cold Feet on Talks with Japan, U.S.," *Times of India*, August 25, 2011, 17; Josh Rogin, "Inside the first ever U.S.-Japan-India trilateral meeting," *Cable/Foreign Policy*, December 23, 2011, http://thecable.foreignpolicy.com/posts/2011/12/23/inside_the_first_ever_us_japan_india_trilateral_meeting.

71. Brian W. Blouet, "The Imperial Vision of Halford Mackinder," *Geographical Journal*, vol. 170, no. 4 (December 2004): 328.

72. Walter Russell Mead, *God and Gold: Britain, America, and the Making of the Modern World* (New York: Alfred Knopf, 2008).

73. Ibid., 355.

CHAPTER TWELVE

1. George Modelski and William R. Thompson, *Seapower in Global Politics, 1494–1993* (London: Macmillan, 1988), 18.

2. For an early exploration, see Francine Frankel and Harry Harding, eds., *The India-China Relationship: What the United States Needs to Know* (Washington, D.C.: Woodrow Wilson Center Press, 2004).

3. For a debate, see Alyssa Ayres and C. Raja Mohan, eds., *Power Realignments in Asia: China, India and the United States* (New Delhi: Sage, 2009).

4. For a comprehensive discussion, see Ashley J. Tellis, "The United States and Asia's Rising Giants," in *Strategic Asia 2011–12: Asia Responds to its Rising Powers: China and India*, edited by Ashley J. Tellis, Travis Tanner, and Jessica Keough (Seattle: National Bureau of Asian Research, 2011), 1–32.

5. Mark Thirlwell, *Second Thoughts on Globalization* (Sydney: Lowy Institute, 2007).

6. Ashley J. Tellis, "The United States and Asia's Rising Giants," in Ashley J. Tellis, Travis Tanner, and Jessica Keough, eds., *Strategic Asia 2011–12: Asia Responds to its Rising Powers: China and India* (Seattle: National Bureau of Asian Research, 2011), 1–32.

7. Ibid.

8. For a succinct review of the U.S. policy debates, see Aaron L. Friedberg, *A Contest for Supremacy: China, America, and the Struggle for Mastery in Asia* (New York: W.W. Norton, 2011), 245–63.

9. "Transcript: Senior Ex-Diplomat on India-U.S. Relations," Financial Times Online, May 6, 2009, www.ft.com/cms/s/0/1ec735fe-3a12–11de-8a2d-00144feabdc0.html.

10. "India Bristles at Closer Sino-U.S. Ties," People's Daily Online, November 20, 2009, http://english.peopledaily.com.cn/90001/90776/90883/6818479.html.

11. For a discussion, see C. Raja Mohan, "President Barack Obama, the United States and the Sino-Indian Balance," *ISAS Insights*, no. 46, (Singapore: Institute of South Asian Studies, January 29, 2009).

12. "The two sides are ready to strengthen communication, dialogue and cooperation on issues related to South Asia and work together to promote peace, stability and development in that region." White House, "U.S.-China Joint Statement," Beijing, November 17, 2009, http://beijing.usembassy-china.org.cn/111709.html.

13. "[The] Government of India is committed to resolving all outstanding issues with Pakistan through a peaceful bilateral dialogue in accordance with the Simla Agreement. A third country role cannot be envisaged nor is it necessary." The text of the official Indian reaction to the Beijing communiqué is at www.mea.gov.in/mystart. php?id==530315323.

14. "India today is a rising and responsible global power. In Asia, Indian leadership is expanding prosperity and [...] security across the region. And the United States welcomes and encourages India's leadership role in helping shape the rise of a stable, peaceful and prosperous Asia." Obama's opening remarks at the joint press appearance with Prime Minister Manmohan Singh, Washington, D.C., November 24, 2009, www.whitehouse.gov/the-press-office/remarks-president-obama-and-prime-minister-singh-india-joint-press-conference.

15. Ashley J. Tellis, "The United States and India 3.0: Cave! Hic Dragones [Beware! Here Be Dragons]," Policy Brief no. 81 (Washington, D.C.: Carnegie Endowment for International Peace, October 2009).

16. Leon Panetta, "Partners in the Twenty-First Century," speech at the Institute of Defense Studies and Analyses, New Delhi, June 6, 2012, www.idsa.in/keyspeeches/LeonEPanettaonPartnersinthe21stcentury#.T9RoxOIthCM.

17. Manu Pubby, "China Proposed Division of Pacific and Indian Ocean Regions, We Declined: U.S. Admiral," *Indian Express*, May 15, 2009, 1.

18. Christopher Layne, "China's Challenge to U.S. Hegemony," *Current History*, vol. 107, no. 705 (January 2008): 17–18.

19. Aziz Hanifa, "U.S.-India Relationship Has Indeed Been Oversold." interview with George Perkovich, Rediff News, April 19, 2012, www.rediff.com/news/report/us-india-relationship-has-indeed-been-oversold/20120419.htm; for another view contesting this claim see, Daniel Twining, "Was the U.S.-India Relationship Oversold?" *Foreign Policy*, April 26, 2012, http://shadow.foreignpolicy.com/posts/2012/04/26/was_the_us_india_relationship_oversold_part_1.

20. Shyam Saran, "Geopolitical Consequences of [the] Current Financial and Economic Crisis: Implications for India," speech at the India Habitat Center, New Delhi, February 28, 2009, www.mea.gov.in/mystart.php?id=530114803.

21. Shyam Saran, "Geopolitical Consequences of the Global Financial and Economic Crisis: A Reassessment After One Year," speech at the India Habitat Center, New Delhi, April 26, 2010.

22. Ibid.

23. For a report on the briefing by the Indian ministry of defense after defense minister A. K. Antony's talks with Leon Panetta in Delhi during June 2012, see "India Expresses Unease over US Plans to Counter China in Asia-Pac," *Indian Express*, June 6, 2012, www.indianexpress.com/news/india-expresses-uneasiness-over-us-plans-to-counter-china-in-asiapac/958658/0.

24. For a brief review of the different schools, see Henry R. Nau and Richard Fontaine, *India as a Global Power: Contending Worldviews from India* (Washington D.C.: Sigur Center for Asian Studies, George Washington University, March 2012).

25. For the different nuances from the Indian defense ministry and the foreign office on responding to the U.S.-China dynamic, see "MoD, MEA Differ on India's Asia-Pacific Role?" *Asian Age*, June 9, 2012, 4.

26. David Shambaugh, "Coping with a Conflicted China," *Washington Quarterly*, vol. 34, no. 1 (Winter 2011): 7–27.

27. "India's Unwise Military Moves," editorial in *Global Times*, June 11, 2009, http://english.people.com.cn/90001/90777/90851/6676088.html.

28. See "Who Wins the Dragon-Elephant Contention," editorial in the *Global Times*, December 16, 2010, available at http://opinion.globaltimes.cn/editorial/2010–12/602061.html.

29. Li Hongmei, "Obama Greets India with More Than Lip Service?" People's Daily Online, November 9, 2010, http://english.peopledaily.com.cn/90002/96417/7193497.html.

30. For a discussion, see C. Raja Mohan, "India, China and the United States: Asia's Emerging Strategic Triangle," *Snapshot 8* (Sydney: Lowy Institute, February 2011).

31. China Ministry of Foreign Affairs, "Dai Bingguo: Promote China-US Sound Interactions in Asia-Pacific," www.fmprc.gov.cn/eng/zxxx/t929482.htm.

32. Dai Bingguo, "A Brighter Future When China and India Work Hand in Hand," *Hindu*, January 12, 2012, 1.

33. Paul Kennedy, "To Rule the Waves: The Rise and Fall of Navies," *New York Times*, April 5, 2007.

34. Robert Kaplan, "China's Two-Ocean Strategy," in *China's Arrival: A Strategic Framework for a Global Relationship*, edited by Abraham Denmark and Nirav Patel (Washington, D.C.: Center for a New American Security, September 2009), 57.

35. James R. Holmes, "A Founding Era for Combined Maritime Security?" *Strategic Analysis*, vol. 35, no. 3 (May 2011): 417–26.

36. For a discussion, see Barry R. Posen, "Command of the Commons: The Military Foundation of U.S. Hegemony," *International Security*, vol. 28, no. 1 (Summer 2003): 5–46; See also Abraham Denmark and James Mulvenon, eds., *Contested Commons: The Future of American Power in a Multipolar World* (Washington, D.C.: Center for a New American Security, January 2010).

37. Hillary Clinton, "Remarks on India and the United States: A Vision for the 21st Century," speech at Chennai, July 20, 2011, www.state.gov/secretary/rm/2011/07/168840. htm.

38. "Building on Convergences: Deepening India-U.S. Strategic Partnership," speech by Indian Foreign Secretary Ranjan Mathai at the Center for Strategic and International Studies, Washington, D.C., February 6, 2012, www.mea.gov.in/mystart. php?id=530118985.

39. Author's conversation with U.S. and Indian officials in New Delhi in November 2011.

40. For a review of the Chinese actions and justifications, see Michael D. Swaine and M. Taylor Fravel, "China's Assertive Behavior, Part Two: The Maritime Periphery," *China Leadership Monitor*, no. 35 (Summer 2011), http://web.mit.edu/ssp/people/fravel/ Swaine_Fravel_CLM_35_0624111.pdf.

41. Gurpreet S. Khurana, "China's Maritime Strategy and India: Consonance and Discord," *Maritime Affairs*, vol. 7, no. 2 (Winter 2011): 61.

42. David Brewster, *India as an Asia Pacific Power* (New York: Routledge, 2012), 164. For another pessimistic view see Sandy Gordon, "India's Rise as an Asia-Pacific Power: Rhetoric and Reality," *Strategic Insights* no. 58 (Canberra: Australian Strategic Policy Institute, May 7, 2012).

43. "India's Desire for Strategic Autonomy Constrains in Defense Ties: U.S.," *Indian Express*, April 7, 2011.

44. K. M. Panikkar, *The Basis of an Indo-British Treaty* (Bombay: Oxford University Press, 1946), 26.

45. Ibid, 26.

46. Ibid., 12.

47. Ibid., 13.

48. Ibid., 50.

49. Shivshankar Menon, "Maritime Imperatives of Indian Foreign Policy," lecture at the National Maritime Foundation, New Delhi, September 11, 2009, 6, www.maritimeindia.org/sites/all/files/pdf/SMenon.pdf.

50. Remarks by Senator John McCain at the Carnegie Endowment for International Peace, Washington, D.C., November 5, 2010, http://carnegieendowment.org/files/ McCainPreparedRemarks.pdf.

51. Minxin Pei, "China's Golden Decade," *Indian Express*, September 7, 2011.

52. Zbigniew Brzezinski, "The Group of Two That Could Change the World," *Financial Times*, January 13, 2009; Henry A. Kissinger, *On China* (New York: Penguin, 2011).

Index

About the Author

C. Raja Mohan heads the strategic studies program at the Observer Research Foundation in Delhi. He is a columnist on foreign affairs for one of India's leading English dailies, *Indian Express*. Mohan is also a nonresident senior associate at the Carnegie Endowment for International Peace in Washington D.C. and a visiting research professor at the Institute of South Asian Studies, National University of Singapore.

Mohan is a member of India's National Security Advisory Board. He has published widely and his books include *Crossing the Rubicon: The Shaping of India's New Foreign Policy* (2004) and *Impossible Allies: Nuclear India, United States and the Global Order* (2006).